CHICAGO PUBLIC LIBRARY
BEVERLY BRANCH
1962 W. 95th STREET
CHICAGO, IL   60643

W9-CUW-962

THE CHICAGO PUBLIC LIBRARY

CHICAGO PUBLIC LIBRARY
BEVERLY BRANCH
1962 W. 95th STREET
CHICAGO, IL   60643

FORM 19

A HISTORY OF THE DUBLIN UNIVERSITY PRESS
1734–1976

The Printing House as it is today.

RO7125 95408

A History of the Dublin University Press 1734–1976

Vincent Kinane

Gill & Macmillan

Published in Ireland by
Gill & Macmillan Ltd
Goldenbridge
Dublin 8

with associated companies throughout the world

© Vincent Kinane 1994

0 7171 2114 1

Set in Palatino 10/12 from a disk
supplied by the author and
printed on Creamatt 112 g/m² paper
by the Brunswick Press, Dublin.

All rights reserved. No part of this publication may be copied,
reproduced or transmitted in any form or by any means, without
the permission of the publishers.

A catalogue record for this book is available from the British Library.

R01011 13302

Dedicated to my father

Joseph

(1912–1992)

CHICAGO PUBLIC LIBRARY
BEVERLY BRANCH
1962 W. 95th STREET
CHICAGO, IL   60643

Contents

List of Illustrations

Preface

The Dublin University Press is the oldest printing house in Ireland. It was founded in 1734 and issued its first book in 1738. It remained in the Printing House built for it on the campus of Trinity College Dublin until 1976, when it moved to Sandymount, a suburb of Dublin. There it continues to prosper, but alas it retains no official connection with the University which spawned it.

My interest in the history of the DUP goes back to the late 1970s when I prepared a thesis 'The Dublin University Press in the eighteenth century' for Fellowship of the Library Association of Ireland (submitted 1981). Dr Don Cruickshank was my supervisor and I gratefully acknowledge all his help. I am also deeply indebted to Mary Pollard, then as now; it was she who initially suggested the topic and since then has provided encouragement and information from her unrivalled knowledge of the eighteenth-century Dublin book trade.

In the mid-1980s, with the 250th anniversary of the DUP's first printing in mind, I commenced an exploration of the College muniments looking for references to the Press in the nineteenth and twentieth centuries. The intention was to print a small history of the DUP in conjunction with an exhibition of its printings in the Long Room of the College's library. Early in 1988 I approached Michael Gill of the Dublin publishing company of Gill & Macmillan to see if he had any papers relating to his great-great-grandfather, Michael Henry Gill, who was University printer from 1842 to 1875. He turned up a fascinating collection of correspondence and later unearthed several account books, all of which he generously donated to the library. These discoveries demanded a more extensive history than I had originally planned, so the publication date had to be put back. Michael Gill was very encouraging about the project and undertook to publish the results. Subsequently in 1991 a chance remark led me to identify another account book of the Press in the possession of Eithne McManus, and she too kindly donated it to the library.

I had also started to interview retired members of the Press's staff, starting with Jimmy Stewart who has crystal clear memories from the 1930s onwards and on whose recollections I am gratefully reliant. I was granted sabbatical leave from my post in the Department of Early Printed Books of the College's library for Trinity term 1991 and took the opportunity to interview many more who had worked at the Press — Liala, Peter and Brian Allman, Ned Behan, Des Ryan, John Breslin, Jim Lawler, Seán Galavan and Fred Maybury — all of whose assistance I am pleased to acknowledge. The Allmans, owners of the DUP, offered great help, not least in undertaking to subsidise the printing of the history.

My colleague in TCD's library, Charles Benson, provided many valuable references and much encouragement, all of which was thankfully received. He also read the nineteenth-century section of the work, as did George Hetherington the twentieth-century part, and I am grateful for their helpful comments. I would also like to acknowledge the interest and assistance of my other colleagues in the Old Library — Lydia Ferguson, Aine Keegan and Rosarii Dunne in my own department, and Bernard Meehan, Stuart Ó Seanóir, Felicity O'Mahony and Jane Maxwell in the Department of Manuscripts.

I was given a welcome grant of £500 by the TCD Association and Trust which allowed me to do research in some English libraries and also to pay for the photographs used in this history. For many of those photographs I am indebted to the expertise of Brendan Dempsey. My thanks go to my brother Niall for drawing the plans of the buildings. I am further indebted to many more people for their help and have acknowledged their assistance at the appropriate places. I am grateful to several institutions for permission to quote or illustrate from material in their care: the Board of TCD, the Trustees of the National Library of Ireland, the Irish Print Union, and the DUP itself.

I have based this study by and large on the resources of the College's archives. For the eighteenth century this has meant a rather one-sided picture because what has survived are the bills the printers presented to the bursar; their own account books have not survived. For the nineteenth century the picture is more rounded (although still fragmentary) because of the information afforded by the material mentioned above. Strange to relate annual account books for all but the first twenty or so years of this century have vanished without trace. However there remains a whole host of other interesting documents from which a profile of the workings of the Press can be reconstructed. And of course there are the recollections of continuing and retired members of the staff. It is one of the fascinations of printing history that although the products of the trade survive in plenty it is tantalisingly difficult to discover in any detail how they were produced, let alone something of the printers themselves. I have therefore taken the opportunity to provide a comprehensive picture of the operations of the Printing House, based on the interviews I conducted, during its last thirty years in the College. To many much of this description will seem very elementary, but I considered it important to record the workings of a twentieth-century

Dublin printing house, especially as a hot-metal, letterpress works is almost a thing of the past in Ireland.

In the relevant parts of the history I have used the archives of the Irish Print Union (formerly the Dublin Typographical Provident Society) to put flesh on the bones of the DUP printers and on the practices in the Printing House. Likewise I have used them and the few other sources available to set the University Press in the context of the general printing trade in Dublin. It is to be regretted that there is no comprehensive history of that trade which would have given a more accurate context for the endeavours of the DUP.

Throughout the history I have taken Dublin University and Trinity College Dublin to be synonymous, which seems to be confusing given the models of the Oxbridge universities and their relationships to their constituent colleges. However from its foundation in 1592 TCD was vested with the powers of a university. It may have been intended to found other colleges as part of the University, but none was established. So Trinity has retained collegiate and university aspects.

A word on the title 'Dublin University Press': in its full form it did not become current until the last quarter of the nineteenth century when the 'Dublin University Press Series' was launched. Prior to that its imprints merely referred to the 'University Press'. In fact the full name was not registered until 1948. However for consistency's sake I have used the title throughout this work. Likewise for consistency I have transcribed pounds, shillings and pence in the form '£5-13-6', shillings and pence '13-6', and pence '6d.'.

Abbreviations

APCK   Association for Promoting Christian Knowledge
AUP   Aberdeen University Press
BCP   Book of Common Prayer
BP   Brunswick Press
CUP   Cambridge University Press
DMPA   Dublin Master Printers' Association
DSPC   Dublin Steam Printing Company
DTPS   Dublin Typographical Provident Society
DUM   Dublin University Magazine
DUP   Dublin University Press
FOC   Father of the Chapel
HBS   Hibernian Bible Society
IPU   Irish Print Union
ITGWU   Irish Transport and General Workers' Union
NT   New Testament
OUP   Oxford University Press
RDS   Royal Dublin Society
RIA   Royal Irish Academy
RUI   Royal University of Ireland
TCD   Trinity College Dublin

Introduction

The evolution of the university press, dedicated to the printing of scholarly books, was a slow process. This is not to say that printing and scholarship were not intimately interlinked from the beginning. The growth of printing in the fifteenth and early sixteenth centuries acted as a catalyst for the growth of scholarship. The inconsistencies in the manuscripts of scriptural and classical texts, discovered during copy-editing in preparation for printing, had to be resolved. The resultant books provided definitive texts from which scholars could authoritatively quote. In Stanley Morison's phrase, 'the printing press may be said to have changed learning into "scholarship"'.[1] The printing shops of Nicholas Jenson and Aldus Manutius in Venice, of the Estienne family in France and of Christopher Plantin in Antwerp, are examples of early learned presses. But they were privately owned businesses and their dedication to scholarship was dependent on the enthusiasm and competence of whichever member of the family inherited it. And of course these printers needed to make a profit. Elaborate scholarly works, which often necessitated investment in expensive exotic types and then tended to be slow sellers, did not fit easily into this commercial environment. So from the start it can be seen that the printing of learned works created a special tension.

The establishment of an institutional learned press, which could provide the continuity of scholarship, collect and preserve the special founts of type needed, foster the printing skills to allow for the necessary accuracy of production, and, most importantly, provide financial subsidies for non-commercial books, was what was required. A tall order, and one that was not fulfilled until the foundation of the Typographia Apostolica Vaticana in 1587. This was established by order of Pope Sixtus V to fulfil an order of the Council of Trent in 1546 that a correct text of the Vulgate Bible be printed (it was issued in 1590).[2] The Typographia Apostolica Vaticana combined propaganda with learned printing, just as the Imprimerie Royale, founded by Cardinal Richelieu in

1. Stanley Morison, 'The learned press as an institution' in his *Selected essays on the history of letterforms in MS and print*, vol. 2, Cambridge 1981, 361–2.

2. Morison, 'Learned press', 370–1.

1640, combined legislative with scholarly output. Learned presses owned and managed by a university did not come into being in the fullest sense until the late seventeenth century. Up until then universities were served by local printers who combined scholarly commissions with their own commercial undertakings. Although Oxford and Cambridge Universities had been granted privileges to print books in the sixteenth century it was not until 1690 and 1698 respectively that the presses which printed for them were brought under their direct control. It was Stanley Morison's opinion that these dates mark the foundation of the true university press.[3] Morison is one of the few who have written on the whole concept of a university press. This is his definition: 'An Institutional Learned Press must be directed by an uninterrupted succession of printers, whose purpose of producing works of learning . . . is guaranteed by the objects of its owners and controllers whose productions require, by the constitution of the Press, the sanction of academic standards.'[4] This definition is rooted in the hand-press period before the distinction between printer and publisher had emerged, so it would be as well to have a standard for the modern era against which to judge the success of the DUP. For that we can turn to America where there has been an extraordinary flowering of university presses in this century so that there are currently over one hundred members in the Association of American University Presses. In 1914 George Parmly Day, President of Yale University Press, offered this definition, which may sound rather lofty today but holds good in its essentials: 'To render distinct service to the world in general, through the medium of printing or publishing or both, and in such ways to supplement the work of education which commands the devotion of the university whose name the press bears.'[5]

The Oxbridge presses provided the models for other university presses in the English-speaking world, including the Dublin University Press. With regard to the latter there is direct evidence for this in the nineteenth century, as will be seen, but there can be little doubt that the same applied in the eighteenth century. Unfortunately the Oxbridge presses provided poor role models as they floundered through the eighteenth century. Both universities suffered somewhat from academic torpor throughout the century and both leased out their privileges to print bibles (something that the DUP had not got) which, had they retained them, might have been more usefully exploited to subsidise scholarly works. Thus it was that in 1780 when Oxford University could find nobody to lease its privilege it was forced to take in a partner; it did not regain full control of its Press for another hundred years.[6] However

3. Morison, 'Learned press', 380.
4. Morison, 'Learned press', 381.
5. Quoted in Chester Kerr, *A report on American university presses*, [New York] 1956, 12.
6. Peter Sutcliffe, *The Oxford University Press: an informal history*, Oxford 1978, xxv–vi; M.H. Black, *Cambridge University Press 1584–1984*, Cambridge 1984, ch. 8 *passim*.

the latter half of the nineteenth century was a period of expansion for the OUP. The 1860s saw the start of its schoolbook business and the *Oxford English Dictionary* was launched in 1884. In 1875 the Press took on its own distribution through the Bible Warehouse it had established in London, thus ending the publication agreement it had with Alexander Macmillan.[7]

The question of distribution is crucial to the success of any publisher, and even more so for a university press with its very specialist market. There is little point in going to the trouble of finding a scholarly book worthy of production, and then having it set and printed, if it is to languish in the printer's warehouse. Unfortunately for the success of the DUP the authorities of Trinity College never came to terms with the need for this final link in the book production chain. At the time of the foundation of the DUP in the 1730s, and throughout the eighteenth century, a book in Dublin was produced by a printer to the order of a retail bookseller, who then sold it in his shop. (Indeed the Dublin bookseller, unlike his counterpart in London, often had his own printing shop.) The idea of a wholesale publisher is a nineteenth-century phenomenon. This mode of distribution immediately created problems for the TCD authorities. They had nearly all the ingredients for a successful university press: scholars to write the books and a very large Printing House, expensive plant and a pool of skilled labour in the city to print them. What was missing was a regular retail outlet to sell them. This was because there was never enough work at the Press in the eighteenth century to employ full-time printers. The Printing House therefore was manned by labour sent in from a succession of master printers whenever a book was to be printed. The Press's output was then distributed through whatever retail outlet that master printer used — a wholly unsatisfactory arrangement even for local publication, let alone distribution in England, where there should have been a market for Dublin University's learned works.

This arrangement persisted into the nineteenth century, and even though the College achieved some consistency on the appointment in 1844 of the long-running firm of Hodges and Smith as distributor, it still meant the function was in the hands of one bookseller and the College had not itself taken on the task of publication. This was a pitfall identified as early as 1828 by Michael Henry Gill, probably the most influential figure in the history of the Press, when he advocated the appointment of an agent to distribute the DUP's output to the booksellers (see p. 108). Nothing came of his suggestion and as a consequence the growth of the DUP was stunted. The College was loath to get involved in what was perceived to be the vulgarity of commerce. The

---

Press therefore remained essentially a printing house and its potential as a publishing house was never plumbed. The reply in 1931 of J.T. Gibbs, DUP printer, to the Rev. A.A. Luce's query about issuing two sermons by George Berkeley, sums it all up: 'I could not undertake the publication, which would be better done through some well known publishing firm.' He went on to suggest the OUP.[8]

The growth of the DUP was also hampered by the fact that the College never employed its own printers: for most of the eighteenth century it brought in printers on commission, and thereafter it rented out the Printing House and its equipment to printers who conducted their own business there parallel with Trinity's work. (Thus by Morison's very narrow definition the DUP never was a real university press.) This state of affairs meant there was no body of the academics closely involved on a regular basis in the encouragement and supervision of the Press, as there would have been had the College taken direct control of its affairs, with the result that there has always been a curious indifference on the part of Trinity to the DUP. This was exemplified in 1948 when the College allowed the tenant printer to register the DUP as a private limited company. Trinity did have the right to appoint a director to the board of the company, but this was altered by mutual agreement a few years after the DUP left the Printing House in 1976. Thus today there is no official connection between Trinity College Dublin and the Dublin University Press. As a consequence when a series of publications was being planned for the College's quatercentenary in 1992, Trinity could not use the DUP imprint. Although it was felt the occasion would be the stimulus for the re-establishment of a College imprint, it had to use the rather unwieldy name, 'Trinity College Dublin Press'. One would hope that this choice was made somewhat to its embarrassment because it was through its own neglect that it cut itself off from the 250 years of printing tradition the DUP represents.

8. MUN/DUP/9/2/369, letter dated 25 July 1931. (All MS references are to TCD library unless otherwise stated.)

1
The Eighteenth Century:
Background

In a late sixteenth-century address to its chancellor, Lord Leicester, Oxford University stressed the need for a university press to counter-balance the influx of non-learned vernacular works printed in London. Emphasising that it was the norm for French and German universities to have access to scholarly printers, it went on to state that such a press was the best way to use the talents of the academics and to realise the potential latent in the library manuscripts. The address also underlined the propaganda value of the medium: 'Furthermore, if a printer were settled in Oxford, the western parts of England, Wales, and the hitherto barbarous realm of Ireland would in course of time be watered with happier effect and more abundantly, with pure streams of improved literature.'[1] It was the power of the press in the fight against heresy that Cambridge emphasised in its application to Chancellor Wolsey for the right to appoint three bookseller-printers in 1529,[2] and it was this propaganda potential that led to the first printing in Trinity College Dublin.

On 3 March 1591/2 'the College of the Holy and Undivided Trinity near Dublin' was founded under a charter from Queen Elizabeth with the intention of planting 'religion, civilitie and true obedience in the hearts of this people'.[3] Learning then was to be allied with military force for the political ends of sweeping away the Gaelic and Catholic traditions in Ireland and of consolidating English power and Anglican Protestantism in their stead.[4] As part of this movement the English Privy Council decided to have the New Testament translated and printed in

---

1. Quoted in Harry Carter, *A history of the Oxford University Press; vol. 1 to the year 1780*, Oxford 1975, 19–20.
2. D.F. McKenzie, *The Cambridge University Press 1697–1712: a bibliographical study*, vol. 1, Cambridge 1966, 1–2.
3. Constantia Maxwell, *A history of Trinity College Dublin 1591–1892*, Dublin 1946, 4–5.
4. R.B. McDowell and D.A. Webb, *Trinity College Dublin, 1592–1952: an academic history*, Cambridge 1982, 2.

Irish, and to this purpose a warrant was issued in 1591 to William Kearney, a native Irish speaker and a trained printer, to travel from London to Dublin with his printing equipment, a journey he apparently made in 1592.[5] About this time a state letter was circulated to the bishops of Ireland setting out Kearney's authorisation to print the New Testament 'in the Irish tongue and proper character . . . and all such other books as shall be required and necessary for the good service of the Church and commonwealth of this realm'. Furthermore the bishops were urged to exhort their clergy to contribute one-twentieth of their incomes to pay for printing the Testament.[6]

Consistent with its charter TCD offered Kearney accommodation for himself and his equipment and so the press was installed in the College and printing underway there in 1595. The Gospels as far as Luke, Chapter 6, had been printed off by late 1596 or early 1597 when Kearney secretly left, breaking his bonds and taking his equipment with him, as well as the printed sheets and some College property. There is a detailed contemporary description of the affair in the College muniments entitled, 'The heads of agreement mentioned between us and Mr Kerney 1596[–7] Marche 18' which is worth quoting in full for the insight it gives of the College's anxiety to retain its own press:[7]

> Fforgeivinge & forgettinge all the former iniuries offered by you to the Colledge & severall fellows thereof, as
>
> 1/ The close conveyance out of the house without their knowledge & consent of the press pountions [punches] & characters.
>
> 2/ The taking away of the stoles, shelves, bords etc which were in the chamber & study. The stuff of which at lest was the Colledges.
>
> 3/ The kepinge from & utter deprivinge of them of the printed sheets which by promise & bond you were bound to deliver to them after the printinge of every sheet.
>
> 4/ The disapoyntinge of your bond to finishe the worke by the time apoynted. by which also their promise was caused to be broken to the country concerning the delivery of the said books. You assuringe that nothinge should hinder you but death from the finishing.
>
> 5/ Your not issewinge the 30£ st.[erling] you had before hand according to your promise & bond to the furtherance of the work by which your bond is forfeyted by you under our arrest.

5. E.R. McC. Dix, 'William Kearney, the second earliest known printer in Dublin' in *Royal Irish Academy Proceedings*, 28/C/18 (1910) 157–61.
6. MUN/P/1/14, copy of letter undated (1593?) with nineteenth-century transcript.
7. MUN/P/1/25; a late 19th century transcript by J.P. Mahaffy is also included which has some variant readings.

6/ And laste[?] your disapoyntment of bringinge in the bonds of the primat & the rest. which you promised both to the Society & Sr. Rob. Gardner & Sr. Ant. Zelinger [St. Leger?] omittinge the very sinister delinge in complayninge to the Ld. Chancellor when they had the juste cause to complayne of you & also mought by lawe & arrest compell you to you[r] covenants. All this I say being omitted & forgeuen. The question which I would propound unto you (if either you regard the endinge of soe necessary a work for the glory of God or your own estate tò be bettered) is whether you would agre to these conditions as the society may be drawen to consent to them

1/ That they allowinge you in the Colledge the use & quiet possession duringe your lyf of a fayre chamber for your printing & another by it for your self.

2/ They allowing you frely during you[r] lif & following your trad, a fellows commons in the colledge at the fellows table.

3/ They allowinge you a boy his lodginge & his diet among the lower scolars you paying for it when you are able.

4/ They issewinge the rest of the mony of the 200 marks to you as you shal nead it yee & 20 L beside to the finishinge of the work.

5/ They also allowing you & laboring to help you to make the benefite of all the books that shal be printed whether they 500 or a 1000. that you may receive the mony of them to make up a stock for your trad.

6/ They helping you for your benefite to the printing of any other fitt things.

Whether you will enter into bonds to settell yourself in the said Colledge

1/, & follow your art & the finishinge of this work as conveniently & spedily as you may in such way as is below spoken of & that in regard of the assurance thereof & the former favors offered to you, you will bringe in your owne English press with all the fitt furniture thereof & sett it up possessinge the Colledge thereof as of a pawne bothe for your work & faythfull delinge. & also bring in all the former things taken out of the colledge which they will obtyne of the state to whom they belonge.

2/ That you will follow your callinge & trad thein in the best & fittest maner for this church & country during your life & trayne up in your art som other boy before spoken of. Who being your prentice shal be bound to serve under you & after you in the said colledge to maytayne that trad for this country.

3/ That God calling you that when the former furniture of printinge be left for the continuance of that trad in the Colledge. the nerest of your kinred having the benefite that commeth thereof without colledge loss if he be a printer therein & otherwise the party that shal leave to succed you always the furniture being possessed of the Colledge for the countrys good.

These things as from myself (not knowinge the mind of the rest) I propound you & promise to labor them as I may to agree to them.

Agreement was not reached. Kearney vanished without trace and the College was deprived of its own printing press, the lack of which would not be remedied until the eighteenth century. The printing of the New Testament was eventually finished by John Franckton and issued under his imprint in 1603 although dated 1602.

Cambridge had been successful in its early sixteenth-century petition for the right to appoint printers, and the letters patent granted to it in 1534 allowed them 'to print all manner of books' which challenged the hitherto absolute control of the London Stationers' Company. Oxford however had to wait until the appointment of Archbishop Laud as its chancellor in 1629 for any moves to be made to establish such privileges there. One of Laud's tasks in life, as set out in his diary, was 'to procure a large charter for Oxford, to confirm their ancient priviledges, and to obtain new for them, as large as those of Cambridge, which they had gotten since Hen. 8 which Oxford had not . . . '.[8] Laud was concerned to foster Oxford's printing privileges — another of his tasks was 'to set up a Greek Press in London and Oxford . . . and to get letters and matrices' — and in 1632 he secured letters patent for the University allowing it to appoint and control three 'typographi'. This was further expanded in 1633 and the whole consolidated in the Great Charter of the University in 1636. As regards printing privileges Oxford was now on the same footing as Cambridge.

Laud's influence was also felt in Dublin University where he was appointed Chancellor in 1633. Yet another of his life's tasks was to procure 'a new charter of the College near Dublin . . . and a body of new Statutes made, to rectify that government'.[9] The resulting Caroline Charter and Statutes, which took effect in 1637, superseded the original Elizabethan code and brought the College under firmer state control, as had happened at Oxford. Unfortunately there had been no consideration of granting printing privileges to the College, and there was no equivalent in the Dublin Statutes to the 'De Typographis Universitatis' section included in Oxford's. Given the turmoil of the country in the seventeenth century, it is unlikely that the College would have had

8. Quoted in Carter, *History of OUP*, 26–7.
9. William Laud, *The history of the troubles and tryal of ... Laud*, Oxford 1695, 68–9.

sufficient resources or peace to have taken advantage of such privileges had they been granted. Financial straits in the revolutionary 1640s and 1680s necessitated the sale or pawning of large amounts of the College plate, while at the latter date the fellows were forced to flee to England, following the library manuscripts and university patents, which had earlier been sent there for safe-keeping, leaving the College to be used as a billet for Jacobite troops and as a prison for the city's Protestants. The intervening period was equally bleak: the poverty of the College necessitated the postponement of fellowship elections in 1664–66, and those of scholars in the latter year; while in 1660 the vice-chancellor, Jeremy Taylor, wrote of 'all thing in perfect disorder', of there being 'scarce any ensigns academical'.[10]

The printed output of the academics in the seventeenth century was, not surprisingly, largely theological and in this James Ussher — fellow in 1600–1605, professor of Divinity 1607–21, and later Archbishop of Armagh 1625–56 — stood head and shoulders above the rest. In the 'Life' prefacing an edition of his *A body of divinity* (London 1677) the editor pleaded for the publication of the author's three volumes of divinity lectures delivered in TCD, 'the printing of which would be no small honour to that university'. Alas it was not until Ussher's *Works* were printed at the DUP in 1829–64 that the College could claim that honour. Henry Dodwell was another seventeenth-century figure of international importance who taught in Trinity. He spent the years 1662–66 as a fellow in the College, not long enough for the flowering of his gifts; he resigned his fellowship because he declined to take holy orders as required by the statutes. The paucity of publications can be explained not alone by the unsettled times, but also by the fact that the College remained in essence a seminary for training Anglican clergymen, which stunted growth in other areas of study. An anonymous author of an early eighteenth-century pamphlet on the state of learning in Ireland gave this colourful description of Trinity's achievements: 'Their first institution was wholly designed to propagate the reformed religion . . . which end they have sufficiently answered with their lives and arguments; but this limitation which was so necessary then, deprives us still of two great branches of learning so much cultivated by all the world . . . I mean civil-law and physick . . . It is not the barren brain but want of due culture; we are rather upon the other extreme, we have some luxuriant shoots that want pruning rather than manure. . . .'[11]

It is unfortunate that TCD was not in a position to undertake scholarly printing under the provostship of Narcissus Marsh (1679–1683) as he was

10. J.W. Stubbs, *The history of the University of Dublin*, Dublin 1887, 85–7, 127–33, 107–108.

11. *Some proposals humbly offered to the consideration of the Parliament for the advancement of learning*, Dublin 1707, 5–6.

a deeply learned man, with wide-ranging interests and a background in academic printing and publishing. His copy of Moxon's *Mechanick exercises* survives in the library he founded in Dublin and which bears his name; it is the only copy available in Ireland.[12] Marsh was a product of Oxford and while there Bishop John Fell had induced him to revise and supervise the printing of the translations of Balsamon and Zonaras's *Comments on the canons of the Greek councils* which was issued from the OUP in 1672.[13] This was not Marsh's first experience with scholarly editing and printing. He prepared a revision, for production at the Oxford press in 1662, of P. Du Trieu's *Manuductio ad logicam*, a text which he later re-edited as *Institutio logicae* and had it printed in Dublin (1679) for the use of Trinity students.[14] While provost he also helped to revise Bishop William Bedell's Irish translation of the Old Testament, which was eventually printed in London in 1685. It is likely however that his official duties would have limited any interest he could have taken in a university press. In his diary he complained of 'the multitude of business and impertinent visits the Provost is obliged to' and he became 'quickly weary of 340 young men and boys in this lewd debauch'd town . . . the more so because I had no time to follow my always dearly beloved studies'.[15]

During the seventeenth century there was only a handful of official printings connected with the College:

1630 *Musarum lachrymae: sive elegia Collegii . . . in obitum Catharinae Comitissae Coragiae* (Dublin: Stationers' Company).

1667 Peter Butler, *Oratio in inauguratione . . . pro admissione ad eundem gradum in Academia Dubliniensi* (Dublin: J. Windsor).

1679 [Narcissus Marsh], *Institutio logicae in usum juventutis Academicae Dubliniensis* (Dublin: S. Helsham; sheets reissued in 1681 and 1697).

1684 *Comitia philologica, in . . . Collegio, Dublinij, publicè . . . celebranda, die Lunae, 14 Julii* (Dublin: J. Ray).[16]

1685 *Comitia philologica, in . . . Collegio, Dublinij, publicè . . . celebranda, die Lunae, 13 Julii* (Dublin: J. Ray).

1687 *Comitia philologica, in . . . Collegio, Dublinij, publicè . . . celebranda, die Lunae, 11 Julii* (Dublin: J. Ray).

12. Mary Pollard, 'A Dublin copy of *Mechanick exercises*' in *The Irish Book*, 1/3 (Autumn 1960) 82.

13. Muriel McCarthy, *All graduates and gentlemen: Marsh's Library*, Dublin 1980, 13–14; refers to Madan 2916, Wing B2115.

14. Mary Pollard, 'The Provost's logic: an unrecorded first issue' in *Long Room* 1 (Spring 1970) 38–40; now recorded as Wing (2nd ed.) M735B.

15. McCarthy, *All graduates*, 13–14.

16. For these graduation ceremonies see S. Ó Seanóir and M. Pollard, '"A great deal of good verse": commencement entertainments in the 1680s' in *Hermathena*, 130–31 (1981) 7–36.

1688 *Comitia philologica, in . . . Collegio, Dublinij, publicè . . . celebranda die Lunae, 9 Julii* (Dublin: J. Ray).

1694 St. George Ashe, *A sermon preached in Trinity-College Chapell, before the University of Dublin, January the 9th, 1693–4* (Dublin: J. Ray).

From the foundation of printing in Ireland in 1551 to 1680 no more than one printer was at work in Dublin at any one time. And in fact the King's Printer was nominally given monopoly on all printing and book-selling right down to 1732, although this was challenged by 1680.[17] The monopoly however did not ensure high standards of printing especially where the classical languages were concerned. Edward Wetenhall, in the postscript to his *Of the gifts and offices in the publick worship of God*, printed by the patentee Benjamin Tooke in 1678, was forced to apologise for the typography in the following terms: 'And first, every mans eye will inform him, that the character which the printer had to use, being somewhat old and worn, there are several letters and syllables very blind, or scarce appearing, some not at all . . . Again as to our Greek character, it is very small, blind and old, and therefore many times bad accents, acutes for graves, aspirates for lenes, some false, some abounding letters have slipped in. Had the press here more incouragement, it would be better furnished.' Perhaps it was just as well that the University had so few scholarly publications to be mangled in the press.

The relative peace and stability of the early 1700s were in stark contrast to the upheavals of the preceding century. This calm was reflected in the rise in output and quality of the Dublin printers, not least being the production of editions of the classics. M.J. Ryan, in his *List of Greek and Latin classics printed in Dublin down to 1800* (Wexford 1926), notes only three editions printed prior to 1700, while for the period 1701 down to the first production of the University Press in 1738, he records at least twenty-three. Admittedly these were mostly reprints of established texts, not new critical editions, but some effort was being made to print them well. James Arbuckle, in a letter to the *Dublin Weekly Journal* on 20 August 1726, while bemoaning the neglect of printing in the city until recent years and the general lack of encouragement, yet had this to say: 'We have fallen into the way of reprinting several valuable books, which we formerly used to pay great rates for from abroad; and have given editions of some of the classicks, which deserve great commendation. I have just now in my hands a pocket edition of . . . [Horace], done here about five years ago [1721, edited by Constantia Grierson and printed by her husband George], which, in my opinion is preferable to any of the kind we have had since the days of Elzevir, either as to beauty or correctness.'[18]

---

17. Mary Pollard, *Dublin's trade in books 1550–1800*, Oxford 1989, 2–7.

18. Reprinted in his *A collection of letters and essays on several subjects*, vol. 2, London 1729, 161.

Only one of the works listed by Ryan up to 1738 was a Greek classic, an edition of Longinus with Greek and Latin parallel texts, published under the imprint 'J. Smith & G. Bruce bibliopolas, 1733'. However this was a separate issue with variant imprint of the Dutch-printed sheets issued in Amsterdam 'apud R. & J. Wetstenius, & G. Smith, 1733'. Yet there were some editions with substantial amounts of Greek text printed in Dublin in the early eighteenth century. Bishop Edward Wetenhall was better served than he had been in 1678, when a fifth edition of his *Graecae grammaticae institutio compendaria* was printed in 1718. A polyglot word-list was printed by Andrew Crooke in the following year: *Onomasticon bsachy; sive, Nomenclatura brevis, Anglo-Latino-Graeca*. Only after the establishment of the DUP were works printed wholly in Greek, and the production there of an edition of Plato's *Dialogues* in 1738 must have given courage to the Ewings to print the first Dublin edition of the Greek New Testament in 1746.

In Trinity during the first half of the eighteenth century the antipathy felt between the academics, who largely supported the Hanoverian succession, and the students, who had Jacobite sympathies, led to some unfortunate indiscipline, the most notorious being the shooting dead of a fellow, Edward Ford, in 1734 and the students' theatre riots of 1747.[19] However these were microcosmic pranks in comparison to the strife of the preceding century. An illuminating contrast between the centuries in TCD is to be seen in the numbers of provosts appointed. Whereas in the seventeenth century there were sixteen, in the eighteenth the number was six, and of these only three in the period 1717–1795.

The stability afforded by the period took time to manifest itself in scholarly publications. George Berkeley did some of his most productive work while a fellow of the College, but he was the exception. The academic body under the provostship of Richard Baldwin (1717–1758) was singularly non-productive and Trinity deservedly earned the nickname of the 'silent sister'.[20] None the less there was a growing list of official or semi-official College printings. I have noted the following up to the first production of the University Press in 1738:

1711 *To the Queen's Most Excellent Majesty; the humble address of . . . the University of Dublin . . . April 19, 1711* [Dublin: no printer].

1712 Henry Nicholson, *Methodus plantarum in horto medico, Collegii Dubliniensis* (Dublin: A. Rhames).

[c.1715] *Catalogus librorum in Bibliotheca Collegii . . . Trinitatis* (Dublin: J. Hyde).

1727 William Stephens, *Botanical elements; published for the use of the Botany School in the University of Dublin* (Dublin: S. Powell).

19. Maxwell, *History of TCD*, 111–12, 133–4.
20. McDowell and Webb, *TCD*, 39–40.

1735 *Charta; sive, Literae patentes, a* . . . *Rege Carolo Primo Collegio* . . . *Trinitatis* . . . *concessa; una cum statutis* (Dublin: S. Powell).

1735 *Novae bibliothecae S.S. Trin. Coll. Dub. descripto poema* (Dublin: S. Powell).

1736 Henry Cope ed. *Demonstratio medico-practica prognosticorum Hippocratis* [Dublin]: Typis Academiae Dubliniensis [i.e. the types belonged to the College].

1738 *Supplementum statutorum Collegii* . . . *Trinitatis* . . . *sive statutum de bibliotheca* (Dublin: [no printer]).

This expanding list and the scholarly output of the academics hardly necessitated the establishment of a College press. There was however a solid confidence about Baldwin's provostship — manifest most patently in an ambitious building programme — so that when the College was offered a gift to build a printing house it readily accepted.

2

Building and Equipment

THE BUILDING

With the completion of Thomas Burgh's monumental library in view by the early 1730s the College turned its attention to a project of a more modest scale — the building of a printing house. It was financed by a gift of £1,000 from John Stearne, Bishop of Clogher and vice-chancellor of the University. There has been considerable confusion as to the date of this gift. I have found no reference to it in the College muniments, and 1726, 1733 and even 1741 are given in other sources. Walter Harris gives the date as 1733 in a publication of 1739, and reports in the newspapers of January 1734 of the provost and fellows waiting on Stearne 'to return him thanks for this generous gift' narrow the date down to late 1733. It is likely that these contemporary reports are the most accurate.[1]

The site chosen for the building was the north-east corner of College Park at the end of 'the Mall', a tree-lined avenue running behind the residential buildings now called the Rubrics (see cover and plate 1). At the south end of this avenue was Burgh's Anatomy House of 1710 (now the site of the Berkeley Library), with which the Printing House was to provide a pleasing architectural balance. The rear of the Printing House site backed on to Carter's Alley which in turn led to Lazer's Hill (now Townsend Street — the old form of the name is preserved in the Irish version assigned to it, Sráid Cnoc Lobhar — the Street of the Hill of the Lepers). Presumably this access was a factor in the choice of the site, providing as it did a passage for bringing materials in and out without disturbing the academic tranquillity of the College.

The architect chosen to design the building was Richard Castle (some-times spelt Castles or Cassels, c.1695–1751), a native of Hesse Kassel in Germany, who had been brought over from London in 1728 by Sir Gustavus Hume on a commission to rebuild Castle Hume, Co. Fermanagh. He rapidly established a glowing reputation and by 1734 had already built several private houses (including Powerscourt, Co.

---

1. James Ware, *The whole works* ed. by Walter Harris, vol. 1, Dublin 1739, 192; *Pue's Occurrences*, 12–15 Jan. 1734; *Dublin Evening Post*, 15–19 January 1734.

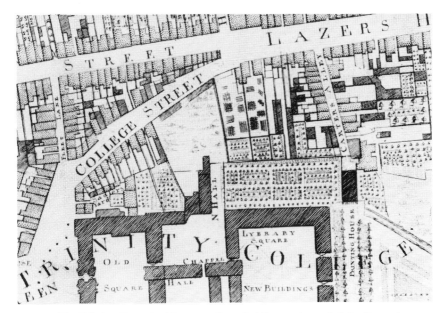

1. The Printing House backing on to Carter's Alley, as shown in John Rocque's
Exact survey of . . . Dublin (London 1757).

Wicklow, and Westport House, Co. Mayo), besides being employed as a
draughtsman for the new Parliament House in College Green by the
architect, Edward Lovett Pearce, who was warm in his praise for him.[2]
Castle's reputation as a draughtsman was still alive in 1793 when a
correspondent to the October issue of *Anthologia Hibernica* could write:
'Mr. Castles was remarkably ready at drawing, and so clear in his
directions to workmen, that the most ignorant could not err.' His plans
for the Printing House, which unfortunately do not survive, must have
been of this clarity, for the basic fabric of the building was completed
and roofed within a year of the digging of the foundations.

Given its park setting it is appropriate that Castle chose to design the
portico in the form of a garden temple of the Doric order (see plate 2).
There is a surviving plan by Pearce for a similar temple, but this does not
mean there was any plagiary on Castle's part.[3] Both designs are likely to
have derived from the current architectural pattern books, as for
example V. Scamozzi's *The mirrour of architecture* (London 1669), where
plate 8 shows a similar Doric portico, complete with recesses on either
side of the central doorway (see plate 3). Illustrations of the Printing
House portico were to be used, intermittently, as a device for the DUP

2. Desmond Fitzgerald, 'Richard Castle: architect; his biography and works' in *Irish
   Georgian Society Quarterly Bulletin*, VII (1964) 31–8.
3. H. Colvin and M. Craig eds, *Architectural drawings in the library of Elton Hall*, Oxford
   1964, liii, 31, plate 52.

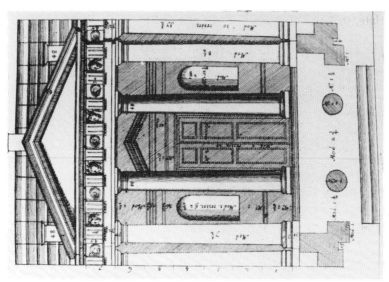

3. A Doric portico from V. Scamozzi's *The mirrour of architecture* (London 1669); this and similar pattern books would have provided the inspiration for Castle's design.

2. The portico of the Printing House in the late 1970s after the DUP's tenancy had ended.

over the centuries. Appropriately its last use was on the Georgian Society's *Records of eighteenth-century domestic architecture and decoration in Dublin*, printed at the Press between 1905 and 1915. It was even used on a bookplate, that of B.F. Haythornthwaite, designed by G. Atkinson in 1919.[4]

In May 1734, with a flush of publicity in the newspapers, work began on the building. The *Dublin Evening Post* for 11–14 May reported that 'Last week they began to lay the foundation of the College Printing House . . . The subject of the Batchellor's exercises for next Shrovetide, (who intend to write for Praemiums for Dr Madden's scheme for the encouragement of learning) will be on the Art of Printing.' The 'Batchellor's exercises' referred to were compositions in English or Latin submitted by newly graduated Bachelors in Arts in competition for prizes of £40 offered annually as part of a scheme proposed by Dr Samuel Madden in the early 1730s for the general encouragement of learning in the College. There is a list of the subjects set for these exercises in the College muniments where the title for 1735 is given as 'On the Printing House'.[5] Unfortunately the winning entry has not survived and neither is there any indication as to its author.

All was not smooth at the start of building. The bursar's quarterly accounts to June 1734 included a payment of £1-10-0 'To a labourer hurt at ye printing house.'[6] Despite this seemingly bad omen work proceeded rapidly. Of the fifty-three tradesmen's bills for the building that survive twenty-nine were presented in 1734, fifteen in 1735, six in 1736, one in 1737 and two in 1738.[7] The stone was supplied by Moses Darley, one of a dynastic family who supplied Trinity's needs throughout the century. Portland stone was used for the portico and uncut calp for the flanks, and this unusual division was underlined by two walls sweeping forward from either side of the portico.[8] The walls were erected before the end of 1734 and a stone plaque with the following carved inscription was placed over the main door:

R.R. Johannes Stearne
Episcopus Clogherensis
Vicecancellarius hujus Academiae
Pro benevolentia quam habuit
in Academiam et rem literariam
Posuit A.D. 1734

4. Copy in the E.C. Yeats collection of bookplates in the Cuala Press archive in TCD library.
5. MUN/V/27/1/6, 91.
6. MUN/V/57/2.
7. MUN/P/2/68/1–51, dated between 14 June 1734 and 28 Nov. 1738.
8. E. McParland, 'Trinity College, Dublin — II' in *Country Life*, 159 (1976) 1242–5.

Translated, it reads: 'The Right Reverend John Stearne, Bishop of Clogher, Vice-Chancellor of this University, on account of the benevolence he had for the University and for literature, erected A.D. 1734'.

Daniel Bewley was paid for roof tiles in the first quarter of 1735 and the slater Betts presented his bill on 11 March, so the building must have been roofed in less than a year from the start of the foundations.[9] John Rowlett, the glazier, presented his bill on 6 February 1736 and was paid in full in that financial quarter.[10] The plasterer, appropriately named Patrick Wall, presented the first of his two bills on 24 September 1735; the second followed over a year later on 24 November 1736, when presumably the building was substantially finished.[11] Given the protracted time it took to complete the library — twenty years from 1712 — it must have been the cause of some satisfaction in the College that the Printing House was near completion in two and a half years. Provost Baldwin evidently thought of it as one of the important achievements of his tenure. A surviving portrait of him in the College's collection shows the portico prominently in the background (illustrated in Maxwell's *History of TCD*, opposite p. 112).

One of the last bills to be settled was Castle's own. £38 of the £50 he charged for 'making a plan of the Printing House and executing the same' had been paid early in 1736, but he had to wait until 4 June 1738 for the balance.[12] This was quite a generous fee when compared to the £63-15-0 paid to Nicholas Hawksmoor in 1712–13 for Oxford's Clarendon Printing House, a much larger building.[13]

Various estimates for proposed work on the Printing House submitted by individual tradesmen survive in the College muniments,[14] but the most comprehensive is an undated one headed 'An estimate of the expence of the Printing House intended to be built in Dublin College'. This estimate sets out in detail the quantity and unit cost of each aspect of the proposed project — digging the foundations, masonry work, carpentry (including doors), roofing, plastering, glazing. The total amounts to £845-16-10, leaving a modest surplus of over £150 to cover unforeseen contingencies, when deducted from Stearne's gift.[15] However the completion of the building found this estimate overspent by nearly 50 per cent. The bursar's quarterly accounts in the period between March

9. MUN/V/57/2, bursar's quarterly account to Mar. 1735; MUN/P/2/68/1.

10. MUN/P/2/68/44.

11. MUN/P/2/68/50–1.

12. MUN/V/57/2, bursar's quarterly account to Mar. 1736; MUN/P/2/68/4.

13. H.A. Tipping, 'The universities of Oxford and Cambridge: the old Clarendon Buildings, Oxford' in *Country Life*, 63/1637 (June 1928) 800–807.

14. MUN/P/2/65/1–4, 8.

15. MUN/P/2/65/5, undated.

1734 and March 1739 record a total of £1,250 dispensed on the Printing House, an overrun of 47 per cent on the estimate.[16]

There were very few precedents in these islands at this period for a purpose-built printing house. William Bladen built one in Dublin in the 1660s, as did Samuel Powell a century later. Those in England included that built by the Cambridge University printer in 1655 and demolished in 1850; that of the King's Printer rebuilt in 1671 after the Great Fire of London, which again burnt down in 1738; and at Oxford in 1670–71, when the space allotted to the printers in the Sheldonian Theatre proved inadequate, the University built 'the new Print House of the Theater under the east wall', which in turn was demolished when the Clarendon Building was erected in 1712–13.[17]

Castle designed the Trinity Printing House on three levels: basement, ground level and first-floor attic. In this it seems possible that he had the three-fold division of the printing trade in mind: composing, presswork and paper storage. Mention is made in a list of *c.*1744–5 for materials necessary for the Printing House — which will be dealt with below — to the 'Composing Room', the 'Press Room' and the 'Ware Room'. It is likely that the basement was the pressroom, the ground floor was the composing room, and the first floor was the wareroom. This was the division of the extension that was erected *c.*1840, as will be seen.

The basement with its flagged floor and low ceiling of 8ft 6in. fulfilled the criteria set out by Moxon for a pressroom in having 'a solid and firm foundation . . . And as the foundation ought to be very firm, so ought the roof and sides of the Press Room to be, that the Press might be fastned with braces.' Although there are six windows on either side of the main area of the basement the light is not good because of the level below ground. However intensity of light, again according to Moxon, was to be avoided in the pressroom 'that the press-men, when at their hard labour in summer time, may be less uncommoded with the heat of the sun'. He went on to stress the need for 'constancy of that light, to keep the whole heap [of printed sheets] of an equal colour'.[18] In the event 'Iron candlesticks for the use of the Presses' were on another list of necessities, probably drawn up by Samuel Powell in preparation for printing in the 1740s.

The basement level of the pressroom has always left it subject to damp and even to periodic flooding when heavy rains couple with a high tide in the River Liffey near by. Today any deep hole dug on the campus will reveal water-rolled stones and shells, confirming that Trinity is built on the delta of the river. A canal — shown in Rocque's 1756 map of Dublin — was dug in College Park in 1743, perhaps with the intention of

16. MUN/V/57/2.

17. McKenzie, *CUP*, vol. 1, 25, 35; J. Moxon, *Mechanick exercises* (1683) H. Davis and H. Carter eds, Oxford 1962, 15 note; Carter, *History of OUP*, 196–7.

18. Moxon, *Mechanick exercises* (1962 ed.), 16–17.

alleviating the problem of flooding, but to no avail. It remained a problem right up until 1980–81 when the building was refurbished; the basement was damp-proofed but at the expense of six inches of concrete over the original flags. Dampness was also a problem at the OUP's Clarendon Building, where printers in the eighteenth century complained of cold and damp which was so severe that one compositor is said to have died of a sickness caused by it.[19]

At the south end of the pressroom was a room, with a cellar built under the portico branching off (see plate 4). Perhaps this was the area where the type would have been cleaned after printing, as recommended by Moxon: 'The Lye-trough and Rincing-trough . . . [the printer] will rather set them out of the room to avoid the slabbering they cause in.'[20] When the 1840s extension was built access from the basement to the ground level was incorporated in it and the eighteenth-century means of ascent removed, but it may well be that the main staircase descended to this area. The estimate of the early 1730s already referred to allowed for thirty-nine steps, while the number in the flight from ground level to the attic is only twenty-seven. This leaves twelve steps for a seven-foot drop to the basement — a not unreasonable seven inches per step. That being the case this was probably the stairs referred to in Powell's list of necessities: 'A strong door at the foot of the stairs to prevent rogues from breaking into the printing room'.

The composing room on the ground level is a bright, airy room fifty feet long, nearly twenty wide and about fifteen high (see plate 5). Six tall windows facing east, mirrored by six more facing west, would have provided adequate light for the intricate work of the compositors. A measure of over four feet between windows left plenty of room for the composing frames, allowing the comps to stand full in the light. There was a fireplace at the north end of this room which would have provided some measure of heat in winter to enable the compositors to set type efficiently. Leading off the north end of this room were two small offices, the one on the west having had a fireplace (now blocked up). This latter was probably the proof-reader's closet. Among Powell's list of necessities already referred to are 'Two grates and fire irons . . . , one for the Corrector's Office, and one for the Printing Office'. This latter may well have been the room on the south-west side of this level, on the opposite side of the main entrance hallway to that of the staircase. Any evidence of a fireplace in this room is long gone, but there is a chimney stack just behind the apex of the portico. It can be conjectured that the manager directed the operations of the Printing House from this office.

Directly above this on the first-floor level was another office which may have been designed as the warehouse-keeper's office (see plate 6).

19. Carter, *History of OUP*, 200.
20. Moxon, *Mechanick exercises* (1962 ed.), 18.

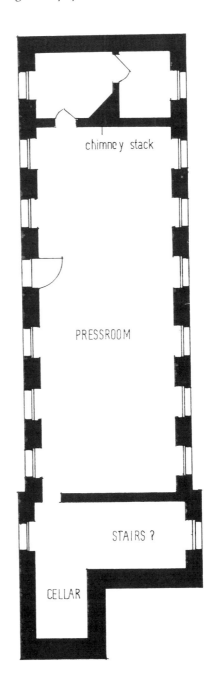

N

BASEMENT LEVEL

4. The basement level of the 1730s building.

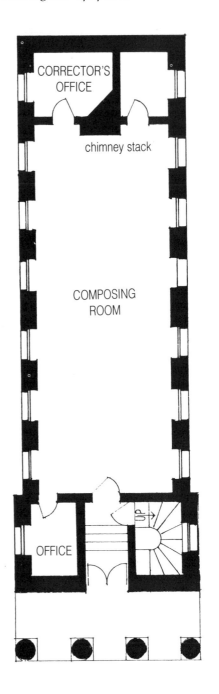

5. The ground floor of the 1730s building.

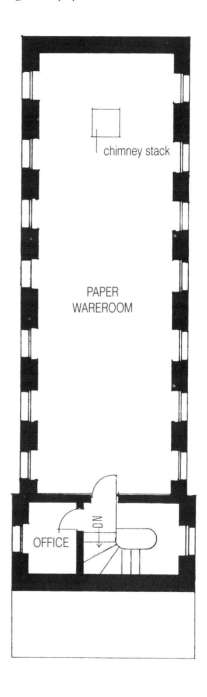

N

FIRST FLOOR PLAN

chimney stack

PAPER
WAREROOM

OFFICE

UP

6. The first floor of the 1730s building.

The wareroom itself runs from the top of the stairs right to the back of the building. Although at 7ft 9in. the wall height is low, the rafters are open and would have provided space for the poles upon which the newly printed sheets would have been hung to dry. (Dr Edward McParland has expressed doubts to me as to whether the rafters were exposed in the original structure, so this interpretation may not hold.) Here the dry sheets would have been gathered and collated ready for the binder. The room is provided with natural light from seven small sash windows on either side, in the same vertical alignment with the windows on the other floors below. In the centre of the floor at the north end of the room was the chimney stack servicing the fireplaces in the rooms below; it was removed in the 1980–81 rebuilding. It is not clear if there was a fireplace at this attic level, but some form of heat may have been necessary in winter to dry the damp sheets. Then again the output of the Printing House was so small that there may well have been little pressure to clear the poles quickly.

Each of the three floors measures approximately 19 by 73 feet giving a total area of 4,161 square feet. Allowing 300 sq. ft for the staircase, chimney stacks and internal walls, there was in round figures 3,860 sq. ft of usable floor space. This compares favourably with 2,570 sq. ft which McKenzie estimates the CUP had in the Stage House in Queen's Lane, reconstructed for its use in 1698. Prior to the building of the Clarendon Building the OUP had the use of the Sheldonian Theatre (from which they had to remove their equipment when it was needed for official functions), together with the 'new Print House' which Carter estimates to have provided 750 sq. ft. The Clarendon Building itself was a much larger structure, providing what must be five times the space, and at over £6,000 costing about five times that of the DUP building.[21]

Towards the end of the century there is evidence that the building had to be reroofed. A slater called Elliott was paid over £110 for the work in the second half of 1798.[22] There is little evidence of any subsequent major structural work on the building, beyond the change in the staircase. In fact the Printing House has remained, in the words of Dr McParland, 'unique among Richard Castle's College buildings in having survived substantially intact'. Great pains were taken during the recent refurbishment to retain as much of the original fabric as possible, even down to preserving the few 'bottle-bottom' crown glass window-panes on the attic level.

THE EQUIPMENT

Richard Castle's brief as architect apparently also included the supervision of the fitting out of the Printing House. On 18 June 1737 he endorsed

21. McKenzie, *CUP*, vol. 1, 18–19; Carter, *History of OUP*, 198–200; Tipping, 'Univs. of Oxford and Cambridge'.
22. MUN/V/57/7/16, 17.

the carpenter, John Connell's, bill for the provision of a long list of requisites:[23]

7 May 1737 Work done in ye College Printing house by John Connell

	£ s. d.
To 6 payr of Greek cases att 8/6 pr. pair	2-11- 0
To a rack yt will contain 9 pair of do cases	3-10- 0
To a table for ye composing stone with 6 drawers	1-19- 0
To a table for ye Printers bank	13- 6
To 2 gallys for do at 2/0	4- 0
To 3 dozen and a half of fornature at $3\frac{1}{2}d$. pr foot	7- 6
To 2 desks of deal wth. drawer for ye correcttor and printer	1-12- 0
To one press for ye printer wth. ten yards of work in do to house letters	1-13- 8
To a table for ye printers about 7 ft long to hould wet paper on	12- 2
To 6 oak-kean chairs wth. boorded bottoms at 9/6 each	2-17- 0
To one boord for weting paper	1- 6
To 5 boords in pantiles for drying racks for the paper	5-10
To 2 men one day making and fixing do	2- 0
To [?] nails for do	0- 5
To a machine for lifting ye wet paper [the peel]	1- 6
	£16-13- 1

Examined June ye 18, 1737 Richd. Castle.

The charges for the greek typecases were remarkably cheap. Comparable costs at the CUP at the turn of the century were 18-0 to 30-0 per pair; ordinary cases cost 6 to 7 shillings per pair. The rack to hold them was very dear. Eleven shillings was charged in Cambridge for racks and even a combination frame and rack cost only £1-4-6.[24] There must have been something exceptional about the DUP rack.

When the printer Ebenezer Rider started printing at the Press in 1737 he had to provide further fittings and materials which he set out in a bill headed 'Money laid out for the use of the College Printing House', which included:[25]

23. MUN/P/2/68/12.

24. McKenzie, *CUP*, vol. 1, 40–41.

25. MUN/P/4/41/49, paid 27 June 1737; the items have been regrouped for convenience; charges for ornaments, composing, presswork and cleaning were also included; the total came to £10-10-4$\frac{1}{2}$

To a large pair of chases	12- 0
To a Lee [lye] Brush	5- 5
To a large Jar of Lee	7- 6
To 12 Pounds of Ashes for Lee	4- 0
To Girths for the Press	4- 4
To Bran, Brown Paper, Packthread and	
oyl for the Press	3- 0
To a handle for the Bar and a Brayer	1- 7 $\frac{1}{2}$
To two Blankets	2- 2
To two Friskets for the Press	5- 0
To two skins of Parchment	2- 2
To a Rounse	1- 0
To a pair of Ball Stocks	2- 8
To two skins for Balls and Hair	4- 0
To printing Ink	1-10- 0
To Scabbord	3- 0
To a Sheep's Foot	1- 1
To papering two pair of Greek Cases and	
four pair of English	6- 6

It is worth noting that a CUP compositor was paid five shillings for papering two pairs of greek cases about 1700.[26]

Although no reference has been found to the supply of the printing press itself it is likely that it was manufactured locally. An advertisement in *Faulkner's Dublin Journal* for 19–23 May 1730 confirms that the expertise had been present in Dublin for some time: 'James Robinson, at the King's Head in Skinner's Alley, on the Upper Comb, Press and Screw-Maker, who served his time to Mr Robert Goodman, late of New-street, deceased, Makes all sort of Presses viz. for Tobacconists, Chandlers, Printers . . . &c at reasonable rates. NB. He makes all the iron, as well as Wood-work.' The press in Trinity was dismantled for some reason, probably in the early 1740s, and in 1744 when Samuel Powell set about the preparations for printing John Hawkey's series of classics it had to be reassembled:[27]

Novemr. 5th. 1744 . . .	
To putting up the Press	3-3
To putting on the Crampirons and the longbars	1-8
To squaring the hose and letting in the garter	1-1
To planning the platting	8
	6-8

26. McKenzie, *CUP*, vol. 1, 76.
27. MUN/P/4/49/14, paid through John Hawkey, 19 Feb. 1745.

The mention of 'squaring the hose' would suggest that this was of wood and not the metal of the 'improved' Dutch model.

This press must have been in poor shape. Between April 1745 and the following January the ironmonger Tim Turner provided two new friskets (6-0), a new spindle (£1-6-0), and 'a new brass box' for it. This latter, which cost £1-1-7 and weighed 9 lb 4 oz, may have been the metal stud on the back of the platen in the cup of which the toe of the spindle rested. Turner also supplied two new chases, a six-foot marble stone and some other items to a total cost of £5-12-0. At the same time he was allowed 9-4 for the old metal.[28]

By early 1746 this single press was proving inadequate, or unsuitable, and on 10 January Samuel Powell was paid 'the sum of Forty Shillings in full for working down a new Press in the College Printing House'. At the OUP in 1762 the charge was the same for this while at the CUP in 1697 the charge was £1-2-0.[29] This new press at the DUP was mentioned in an undated list, already alluded to, of 'Materials necessary in the [Printing] House':

Two grates and fire irons . . .
A lock and key to a closet door. Another to a desk in the said closet.
A hair sweeping brush to keep the House clean.
One curved do for cleaning the polls whereon the books are hung to dry.
Some rows of pins to hang cloaths &c on.
A table for laying the books on when printed off, in order to hang them up, as also in taking them down.
A step lader to clean the polls.
A key to the outward door of the Printing Office for Mr Powell.

Necessary utensils proper to Printing.
A vice, hand-vice, files, rasps, chisels, saw, hammer, a jack, slain, mallet, hammers, a pair of sheers, gimblets, and a pair of compasses. All these are frequently used in the imposing of form as in cutting and dressing furniture, rules and other uses which often occur in printing.
Shelves to the windows, for laying letter on . . .
Iron candlesticks for the use of the Presses.
A bank, sheep's foot, and wooden stand for drying letter.
Four high stands, some letter bords and some paper boards.
Chairs.

The new press to be put in order, some necessaries being wanting thereto, as also the attendance of the smith and joiner.

---

28. MUN/P/4/50/43.

29. MUN/P/4/50/36; Carter, *History of OUP*, 193; McKenzie, *CUP*, vol. 1, 43.

A strong door at the foot of the stairs to prevent rogues from breaking into the printing room.[30]

Powell appears to have drawn up this list and the one below, again undated, during 1744–45. Though showing a thoroughness that made Powell one of the foremost master printers in eighteenth-century Dublin, they also point to the unfinished state and abject neglect of the Printing House in its first decade:

Poles in the composing room and press room.
A large table for the ware room.
A small one for the composing room.
Window boards to the case and press rooms.
A large door and door case to the passage below . . .
A gathering bench for the Ware Room.
Letter boards no. six.
Paper boards no. six.
Stands of letter boards no. four.
Galleys, four 4to ones two folio ones.
A step ladder.
Chairs or stools no. 4 or 6.
A bank for the new press.
A horse to dry letter after distribution.
Covers for the ink-blocks.
Horses for the two banks.

Most of the items on this list were supplied by the carpenter John Connell, as can be seen from a paper signed by Powell and headed, 'Conveniences had in the College Printing House since the [Hawkey] Classics were begun'. Added to it were 'a small wetting trough, two hundred of coins . . . and a pair of chaces', the latter supplied by Tim Turner and which may well be those he provided on 12 April 1745.[31]

Surviving muniment records for the Printing House are few between 1750 and 1790 so it is not possible to say if there was any increase on the two printing presses already noted as having been acquired. By 1791 however a third had been purchased. On 30 August William McKenzie, the College printer, paid Ambrose Binns £6 for 'a sett of Iron work for Printing Press' followed on 29 October by £12 for '2 sett of Iron work for Printing Presses'.[32] On 21 December six friskets were also supplied by Binns. As we have seen Ebenezer Rider bought only two friskets for the original press in 1737. The titlepages of the first two books from the Press

30. MUN/P/2/65/6.
31. MUN/P/2/65/7; MUN/P/1/691, undated.
32. MUN/P/4/62/2; Binns also supplied five 'composing irons' to McKenzie in August 1791 at 5-5 each.

were printed in red and black, for which two friskets were needed. In buying six friskets McKenzie may have been allowing for the same practice, although such two-colour printing was a rarity at the end of the century. However the likely explanation for the proliferation of friskets is that it was common for printers to supply each press with several, each cut to a standard format of folio, quarto, octavo etc. which were rapidly interchanged when several works in different formats were being concurrently printed. As there is evidence of only three formats being used at the DUP in this century — quarto, octavo and duodecimo — it is possible that the six friskets were to provide sets for two presses. The third press may therefore have been a proofing press, for which no frisket was needed. By the end of the century evidence in the College muniments would seem to suggest that there was only one press. The bursar's quarterly accounts to March 1799 record a payment of £5 to the College printer, R.E. Mercier, 'for stamp licence for College press'.[33] In the troubled atmosphere in Ireland in 1798 the administration introduced a Stamp Act (38 Geo. III c. 18) which among other things required that all printing presses be licensed. However the wording of Schedule A, setting out the charges on the various items, makes it clear that the £5 covered a 'licence to any person to keep one or more printing presses'.

In having only two presses for most of the century the Trinity Press was small in comparison to those of Oxbridge. The OUP had seven by the early eighteenth century while the CUP had acquired four by 1705. The DUP was more on the scale of that at Glasgow University, where one of the conditions of appointment of the university printer in 1715 was that he provide two presses.[34] In comparison with commercial printers the DUP was small. Whereas in the sixteenth and seventeenth centuries the majority of printers had one, two or three presses, the indications are that in the eighteenth century such businesses were in the minority.[35] In Dublin even small printers such as James Finn had two presses. After his death in 1793 his property was advertised for sale in the *Dublin Evening Post* of 10 August and included 'two new presses, with mahogany cheeks'.

Although there must have been a considerable demand for engraved examination and degree certificates, and book premium labels, and although a third of the noted output of the Press in this century included engraved plates, there is no evidence that a rolling press was ever acquired in the eighteenth century. The scanty references that survive would suggest that such work was sent out to one of the commercial

33. 38 Geo. III, c. 18, clause 89, Ireland; MUN/V/57/7, bursar's quarterly account to Mar. 1799.

34. Carter, *History of OUP*, 204; McKenzie, *CUP*, vol. 1, 43–4; J. Maclehose, *The Glasgow University Press 1638–1931*, Glasgow 1931, 114–16.

35. Philip Gaskell, *A new introduction to bibliography*, Oxford 1979, 175–6.

Dublin engravers. For example John Brooks was paid £2-5-6 for engraving the second vignette of the Printing House portico, used in Hawkey's Terence of 1745; he charged a further £3-13-1½ 'for printing 2700 at 2/8 pr. hund.'[36] The work with most engravings undertaken by the Press in the century was John Barrett's edition of St Matthew's Gospel, issued in 1801, and for which sixty-four plates were cut by James Kennedy. These were finished by 27 March 1797 when Barrett reported to the bursar that he had 'examined them over & had the error in them corrected . . . [Kennedy] has not worked off more than one impression of each plate'.[37] This situation can be contrasted with the differing conditions at Cambridge and Oxford. The CUP had acquired a rolling press by 1699, but it was operated by men hired only as the occasion demanded. This proved unsatisfactory and by 1705 the work was being sent to London to be worked off. The OUP on the other hand operated on a much grander scale. It had two rolling presses as early as 1693 and the engravers were official university appointments, their names appearing in the OUP's *Specimens* of 1693, 1695 and 1706.[38]

All the fixtures and fittings bought for the Press in the late 1730s and early 1740s had been furnished by local suppliers. The supply of type was another matter. Although typefounding as a separate trade was practised in Dublin since the early 1700s, it was not until the middle of the century that a foundry of any substance was established.[39] The College had therefore to turn to England for supplies. In anticipation of the building of the Printing House George Berkeley, Bishop of Cloyne, had already presented nearly 220 lb of greek type in November 1733, which had been supplied by the typefoundry of Thomas James in London.[40] It was this fount that the College board lent to Dr Henry Cope for his edition of *Demonstratio medico-practica prognosticorum Hippocratis*, as recorded in the register on 20 August 1735: ' . . . agreed to lend Dr Cope a set of Greek types at the instance and request of the Bishop of Cloyne who gave the said types to the College, provided security be given to the Bursar for returning the same, and the Bursar is ordered to take care to see them weighed when they are delivered and that the same weight is returned.' The loan was acknowledged in the imprint when the work

---

36. MUN/P/4/50/12, dated 19 Feb. 1745/6.

37. MUN/P/4/73/33.

38. McKenzie, *CUP*, vol. 1, 50–1, 93; Carter, *History of OUP*, 200–201.

39. W. Strickland, *Type-founding in Dublin*, Dublin 1922, 24–6; see also Pollard, *Dublin's trade*, 120–23.

40. Details given in MUN/P/4/40/39/[3]; this gift was only noted in the newspapers in early June 1734, for example *Faulkner's Dublin Journal* and the *Dublin Evening Post*, 28 May – 1 June 1734.

appeared in January 1736: 'typis Academiae Dubliniensis, sumptibus J. Smith & G. Bruce'.[41]

It was to the James's foundry that the College also went for further supplies. The report of Stearne's gift in the *Dublin Evening Post* of 15-19 January 1734 included a reference to the fact that 'the Fellows will subscribe £500 for printing types, in order to print books in Hebrew, Greek and Latin, as well as in English and other languages'. According to Walter Harris's report of the gift, Stearne himself provided a further £200 in 1735 for the purpose. Using these funds the College commissioned Thomas Moore, a Dublin printer and stationer, to purchase 250 lb more of greek type and 462 lb of roman and italic from James.

In a letter to Moore dated 22 November 1735 from John James, son of Thomas, it was reported that the type had been shipped on the *Success*, and included was a description of the purchase: 'There is accents cast to the Roman & Italick & Small Capitals & Two Line Letters that I believe you will find it very perfect. Inclos'd in one of the boxes is a Couple of Specimens set up as far as he [Thomas, his father] has cast of them . . . ' An invoice included with the letter shows that 241 lb 8 oz of english greek was charged for at 2-6 per pound (£30-3-9), and 462 lb 8 oz of english roman and italic cost 11*d*. per pound (£21-3-11). A further £1-2-3 was added for carriage and duty, bringing the total to £52-11-11.[42] Moore had to pay further duty of £3-9-1 and haulage of £1-7-3[43] which, when added to the amounts charged by James for these, made the type about 11 per cent more expensive than it would have been for a London printer prepared to collect it himself from the foundry. According to Philip Gaskell type accounted for as much as two-thirds of a printer's investment in plant.[44] The total cost of the type bought by Berkeley and by the College was just £85, while the other equipment supplied by John Connell and Ebenezer Rider came to about £25. Even allowing for the cost of a printing press these figures confirm that Gaskell's observation holds true for Ireland as well. And as type was substantially dearer in Ireland it was therefore significantly more expensive to establish a printing office in Dublin than in London at this date.

The type was finally delivered to the College on 3 January 1736, having first been weighed by Moore at his own premises and

41. The *Dublin Evening Post* for 3–6 Jan. 1736 reported Cope's presentation of a copy to the dedicatee, the Duke of Dorset. The wording of the imprint has led more than one commentator to believe that this was the first work issued from the Printing House; see for example Philip White, 'The printing trade in Dublin: the first book printed at the University Press, TCD' in *Irish Printer* (June 1912) 4–8.

42. MUN/P/4/40/37.

43. MUN/P/4/40/36.

44. Gaskell, *New introduction*, 163.

deficiencies of $17\frac{3}{4}$lb noted.[45] A draft of £40 sterling towards the cost had been paid by 24 December 1735,[46] but the remainder was still outstanding on 26 October 1736 when John James wrote to Moore telling him of his father's death on 22 August:

> My mother who as the Administratrix is inconsolable for ye loss of so good & tender a Husband, hopes you'l be so kind to continue your favours in letting her have an order for some work which he was in hopes to have had sometime ago . . . The following is an Acct. on which there is £12-12-0 due on the Ballance Sterl. My Mother having a pretty pressing occassion at this time for money would be oblig'd to you if you'd remitt her a Bill for twelve Pounds & as to the remaining 12s. it is at your service if you please to accept of it to drink her health. I have likewise sent an Account of what English Greek was delivered for the use of Bishop Berkley & should take it as a favour if you'd let us know who & where to apply for the Ballance . . .

£20 of the total of £27-10-0$\frac{1}{4}$ for Berkeley's type had been paid on its receipt on 29 November 1733; there is no indication when the debt was cleared. The balance on the College's purchase was not paid until 8 June 1737.[47]

The english greek fount was Dutch in origin, the matrices for which were probably acquired by Thomas James during his visit to Holland in 1710. The face was the english greek no. 2 illustrated on page 11 of the sale catalogue of John James's typefoundry, sold in 1782 (see plate 7c); the english roman was not illustrated. Harry Carter considered that the matrices for the greek had probably made their way to the London foundries by 1709.[48] Stanley Morison was scathing about Thomas James's purchases of 1710, stating that 'the specimens in the James' Sale Catalogue prove that he was sold a miserable collection by the "sly" Dutch founders.' However he acknowledged that because of the paucity of the English typefoundries at this date, these founts had to be used by the English printers until superseded by Caslon's from the 1720s onwards.[49]

Several sources state that the greek fount was still in existence in the early part of this century, the most knowledgeable being Philip White who was a senior compositor at the Press. In his 1908 article on the DUP he reset and reprinted the first two lines from p. 10 of the Plato using

45. MUN/P/4/40/38.

46. MUN/P/4/39/9.

47. MUN/P/4/40/39, 44.

48. E.R. Mores, *A dissertation upon English typographical founders and founderies* (1778) H. Carter and C. Ricks eds, Oxford 1961, 54, 79, 110, 207 ff.; a facsimile of the James's catalogue of 1782 is appended to this edition.

49. S. Morison, 'Appendix' in Charles Enschede, *Typefoundries in the Netherlands*, ed. H. Carter *et al*, Haarlem 1978, 426–8.

ΑΡΡΩΣΤΟΣ ΤΕΤΑΡΤΟΣ.

27. ΕΝ Θάσῳ Φιλίνε γυναῖκα, θυγατέρα
τεκᾶσαν, καὶ κατὰ φύσιν καθάρσιος
γινομένης, καὶ ἄλλα κόφως διάγεσαν, τεσσα-
ρεσκαιδεκάτῃ ἐᾶσαν μ̄ τ̄ τόκον, πῦρ ἔλαβε 5
μ̄ ρίγεος. Ἤλγεε δὲ ἀρχομένη καρδίην, καὶ

(a) Cope 1736

10 ΠΛΑΤΩΝΟΣ ΕΥΘΥΦΡΩΝ.

ΕΥ. Πάνυ μ̃ ὀῦν.

ΣΩ. Φέρε δὴ, ἐπισκεψώμεθα τί λέγομεν. Τὸ
μ̃ θεοφιλές τε κὴ ὁ θεοφιλὴς ἄνθρωπος, ὁσιος·
τὸ δ θεομισὲς κὴ ὁ θεομισής, ἀνόσιος. Οὐ ταυ-
τὸν δ' ἔτιν, ἀλλὰ τὸ ἐναντιώτατον τὸ ὅσιον τῷ
ἀνοσίῳ. Οὐκ ὕτως;

(b) Plato 1738

Engliſh. No. 2.

ΕΝηκεν ο Θεος τη του ανθρωπου φυσει τα σπεξ-
ματα της αρετης· διο ο εν ημιν λογος ω των α
Bynneman 7 & 8.   Matrices 502.

(c) James's *Catalogue* 1782

ςοχάζεθ τὸν γράφονlα, δεῖποιᾶν τοῖς ἐνlυγχάνεσιν.
Εῖτ' ἐπὶ πάσης τεχνολογίας δυοῖν ἀπαιlεμένων·
πρότερε μὲν, τᾶ δᾶξαι τί τὸ ὑποκείμενον, δευτέρε
ἢ τῇ τάξει, τῇ δυνάμει ἢ κυριωτέρε, πῶς ἂν ἡμῖν
αὐτὸ τᾶτο, κὴ δι' ὧν τινων μεθόδων κτητὸν γένοιτο· 5
ὅμως ὁ Κεκίλιος, ποῖον μὲν τι ὑπάρχει τὸ Ὑψηλὸν,

(d) Longinus 1797

ΕΥ. Πάνυ γε οὖν.
ΣΩ. Φέρε δὴ, ἐπισκεψώμεδα τι λέγμεν   Τὸ

Δ|α	λλ	λπ̅	ὑπ̅ο	κὴ	δ	γ̅ν̅
δια	λλ	απο	υπο	και	ευ	γεν

πε̅	τ̅	ρα	μ̅ν̅	ος	ὀπ̅	τ̅
περι	τῆς	ρα	μεν	ος	ἐπι	τοῦ

(e) White 1908

7. Greek types: Cope 1736, Plato 1738, James's *Catalogue* 1782, Longinus 1797, White 1908.

exactly the same type which 170 years ago was used in producing [it].'[50]
There were many complicated ligatures and contractions — the James's
catalogue notes 502 matrices — and White illustrated some such, noting
with relief that they 'are now completely discarded in modern printed
Greek works.' However the specimen he gives is not the fount used in
the Plato but the English greek first used in an edition of Longinus,
issued from the Press in 1797 (see plate 7d). It is difficult to understand
how White made this mistake. He had obviously examined the Plato
very closely, describing it as 'beautifully printed, the type being very
clear and the colour uniform . . . , the margins wide . . . it is printed in
the Greek character (pica on English, giving the lines a leaded appearance).' It is probable that he transcribed the lines from the volume he had
seen in the library (or had them transcribed for him, perhaps by Dr L.C.
Purser whose assistance was acknowledged at the end of the article), and
then set them up from a fount in the Printing House which he took to be
the original, but without comparing the printed result with the text in the
library. Whatever the reason, this mistake led to further confusion in his
1912 article on Cope's *Demonstratio*. On the basis of his reprinted lines he
expressed surprise that 'the Greek type was of a differently cut fount
from that used in the . . . Plato', which it was not. This then is evidence
that the James's fount did not survive the nineteenth century. And from
a list of type at the Press in 1807, which will be considered later, it may
well be that it did not survive the eighteenth, perhaps being superseded
by the fount used in the Longinus of 1797.

The greek type as weighed by Moore was 238 lb, the roman 448 lb,
which together with the 220 lb presented by Berkeley gave a total weight
of 906 lb. This was a very low stock even for an office with a single press,
Gaskell estimating that it took 2,200 lb of type to keep one press occupied
in a busy shop.[51] The stock was soon increased however as the text of the
second work issued by the Press, Samuel Helsham's *A course of lectures in
natural philosophy* (1739), was surprisingly not set in the James's english
roman but in a pica roman; the first use of an english roman as a text
type occurred in Thomas Leland's *All the orations of Demosthenes* (1756).
The stock was further expanded in 1744 when nearly 950 lb of small pica
roman was bought in preparation for printing Hawkey's series of Latin
classics.[52] Taken with the James's type and perhaps 400 lb of pica roman,
the Press had a respectable stock of nearly 2,250 lb in 1744.

Richard Reilly was the printer hired by the College to produce
Helsham's *Lectures* and in 1740 he printed an edition of Chamber's
Cyclopaedia which contains a specimen sheet of Caslon types. Although

50. P. White, 'The printing trade in Dublin: the University Press, TCD' in *Irish Printer*
    (June 1908) 8–10, (July 1908) 8–9, (August 1908) 6–8.

51. Gaskell, *New introduction*, 163.

52. MUN/P/1/707a, 10 July 1744.

Reilly's imprint is on this it is usually assumed, because of the exotic founts shown, that it was printed in England. James Phillips questioned this assumption: 'Although no evidence to this effect has been found, it would not be surprizing to learn that the exotic faces shown had been bought from Caslon for the newly founded Dublin University Press.'[53] The specimen contains two sizes of saxon and an ethiopick, but as there is no mention of these on any list of type at the Press during the eighteenth century, Phillips's interesting idea must remain speculative.

In 1755 the recently established Dublin typefoundry of Malone and Perry submitted a printed petition to parliament for assistance in which it was stated that they had already supplied 'the King's printing house, the university, and most considerable printers, both in town and country, with large fonts or quantities of type.' Further they state that they were then 'engaged in casting a large quantity of Greek type for the University Press'.[54] It is difficult to reconcile these statements with the output of the Press at the time. I have been unable to locate any work printed there between Hawkey's Sallust of 1747 and Leland's Demosthenes of 1754. The Greek text of the latter work was set in the James's type. Each oration is however prefixed by an introduction set in a long primer greek, the first appearance of this type at the Press, and it is possible that this was the type bought from Malone and Perry.

The DUP then had a local supplier who could provide type more speedily and presumably cheaper than the foundries across the water. It is strange then that the next evidence to be had of acquisition of type points to Glasgow as its origin. On 12 December 1759 Thomas Wilson, assistant to the Greek lecturer in the College, submitted to the board proposals for printing an edition of Plutarch, one of the conditions being 'that the Greek shall be printed on a new fount of the same types with those on which the Glasgow edition of Anacreon is done.'[55] The edition of Anacreon was probably that issued in 1757 by the Foulis Press, the type being a double pica letter from the Wilson foundry in Glasgow. The board accepted the proposals and £150 was granted to 'Mr Wilson for paper & types for the edition of Plutarch.'[56] In the event the type used in the three volumes issued in 1761–62 was not the double pica but the Wilson foundry's great primer.[57]

Despite Trinity's stated intention in 1734 of issuing works in Hebrew it was not until the early 1780s that there is any evidence of such printing.

53. James W. Phillips, 'A bibliographical inquiry into printing and bookselling in Dublin from 1670 to 1800', Ph.D. thesis, TCD 1952, 340.

54. Copy in the National Library of Ireland (shelfmark: Proclamations Volume 1755).

55. MUN/V/5/3/160, board register, 24 Jan. 1760, when the proposals were recorded.

56. MUN/V/57/4/161, bursar's quarterly account to Mar. 1760.

57. For illustrations of the Wilson typefaces see P. Gaskell, *A bibliography of the Foulis Press*, London 1964.

On 15 December 1781 the board agreed 'that an edition of Buxtorf's *Hebrew Grammar* be printed at the College Printing House and that 500 copies be taken by ye College.' The bursar's quarterly account to September 1782 records the payment of £31-5-0 for printing it. However this work has proved totally elusive and so it is not possible even to say what size of type was used. Stephen Parker, who inherited the Malone and Perry foundry in 1765, included a pica hebrew in his *Specimen* of 1781 and this may have been the type used. However another Hebrew grammar, this time prepared by Gerald Fitzgerald, professor of Hebrew, was printed by the DUP in 1799 using a pica hebrew with nonpareil points, but it was not Parker's. This was likely to have been the type used in the Buxtorf.

Ornaments — both relief and engraved — occur in about 50 per cent of the eighteenth-century output of the Press, largely in the period prior to 1770 (see plates 8–11). Most of the relief ornaments in evidence were part of the printer's own personal stock, verified by their appearance in works issued under his own imprint. In establishing their use I consulted the ornament files in the Department of Early Printed Books in TCD's library. Only eighteen of the relief blocks used in the Press's output did not occur in other printers' work. As can be seen from the plates only three occurred more than once in DUP printings and these may safely be taken as part of its stock. To these may be added the three headpieces showing the College arms. There is a bill in the muniments, to be considered presently, which includes the five initial letters that occur in the 1738 Plato, and so these may safely be included in the Press's stock. Doubt hangs over the remaining seven, which have been marked with an asterisk.

Among the items included in Ebenezer Rider's bill of 27 June 1737 for 'Money laid out for the use of the College Printing House' was £3-5-3 'To the Engraver for four Headpieces, four tailpieces, three flourish'd Letters, and 17 Greek Capitals.'[58] By taking loose averages for the areas of the ornaments used in the Plato and known to be part of the DUP's stock it is possible to suggest that the greek capitals cost 11*d.* each, the headpieces 5-3 and the tailpieces 6-6. All the ornaments used in the Plato were very competently executed, unlike many used in Dublin printings of the time. One may speculate as to who the engraver was. Just as the initials 'FH' (Francis Hoffman) and 'EK' (Elisha Kirkall) occur on many ornaments in English printings of this date, so too will the initials 'EL' be found on some of the most competent ornaments in Dublin printings of the 1720s to 1750s. James Phillips suggested 'with fair accuracy' that this was Edward Lyons, a Dublin seal engraver, and gave 1726–1790 as his period of activity.[59] However Strickland's *Dictionary of Irish artists* says

58. MUN/P/4/41/49.
59. Phillips, 'Bibliographical inquiry', 427.

I 21 x 20 I 20 x 21 I 20 x 20 I 20 x 20 I 20 x 21

*T 22 x 40 T 34 x 51

*T 40 x 57 T 45 x 52

*T 57 x 65 T 61 x 72

8. Relief initials and tailpieces (reduced to 65%); those marked with an asterisk cannot firmly be identified as part of the DUP's stock. References give dimension in millimetres (height x width).

*H 32 x 84A

*H 32 x 84B

H 32 x 86

H 32 x 87

H 33 x 73

H 33 x 85

*H 33 x 86

9. Relief headpieces (reduced to 65%); those marked with an asterisk cannot firmly be identified as part of the DUP's stock. References give dimensions in millimetres (height x width).

E 52 x 68

E 57 x 54

E 57 x 56

E 57 x 59

E 57 x 60

E 58 x 75

10. Engraved ornaments (reduced to 65%). References give dimensions in
millimetres (height x width).

E 60 x 141

E 65 x 82

E 82 x 11?

E 67 x 137

11. Engraved
ornaments
(reduced to 65%
References give
dimensions
in millimetres
(height x width

E 82 x 172

that Lyons was born in 1726 and died in 1801. Perhaps as so often happened in trade a father and son business was involved.

Although Rider had four headpieces cut, in actual fact he used seven in the Plato. We can be sure that only two of these were in the Press's stock — the College arms H32 x 87 and H33 x 85. Some of the ornaments turn up in printings by Samuel Powell in the period 1745–47. There is the possibility that Powell printed these works at the Printing House — he was printing the Hawkey classics there at the time — and that these ornaments were DUP stock which he used, but there is no way of being sure. One of the tailpieces (T34 x 51) bought by Rider appeared in printings that bore the Press's imprint over a period of two decades. It also made an appearance in 1758 in a curious edition of the British Army's *Exercise for the dragoons and foot* that has no imprint, but has advertisements of the Limerick bookseller, John Cherry, at the end. The evidence of the ornament might well suggest this was printed in the Printing House of TCD.

It was to be sixteen years after the Plato before any of the ornaments reappeared in printings of the Press. They were revived by William Sleater, the first printer employed in 1754, who had a penchant for ornament, and all his College commissions were decorated to varying degrees. He obviously felt restricted by the limitations of the Press's stock and for Richard Murray's *Artis logicae* (1759) relied wholly on his own supply, using eighteen different head and tailpieces, some several times over, putting them upside-down for variety — all this in a small octavo volume of eighty pages! No other printer at the Press matched Sleater's extravagance with ornament and indeed after his last use in 1758 of these ornaments, identified as the College's, no subsequent printer drew on that stock, preferring to use one or two examples of their own, if at all. The flamboyance of some of the Press's ornaments, especially the tailpieces, obviously did not appeal to the growing taste for neo-classical austerity and a marked dropping off in the use of any ornament is discernible in the output of the Press after 1770.

Engraved ornaments, both titlepage vignettes and headpieces, occur in about 30 per cent of the eighteenth-century output of the Press (see plates 10–11). The dominant subject for the titlepage vignettes was the Printing House portico, which appeared in five different plates used in eleven different works during the century. The first plate (E57 x 56) was used in some of the Hawkey classics during 1745–47, and was drawn by John Esdall who presented his bill of £1-2-9 for it in July 1745.[60] This Esdall may have been related to the Dublin printer, James Esdall, who had a son William who became an engraver. It was the best of the portico plates: the perspective was correct and it manages to convey the tallness of the building better than the others. A second plate (E57 x 59) was also

60. MUN/P/4/49/22.

commissioned in 1745 and it was likely to have been cut by John Brooks, who charged £5-18-7$\frac{1}{2}$ about this date 'for engravien a plate . . . and for printing 2700 at 2/8 per hund.'.[61] This vignette by contrast is heavy and the perspective is seriously wrong: the most apparent mistake was the continuation of the five triglyphs on the left-hand side of the entablature at six points on the underside of the pediment. This plate must have been used as the model for the fourth portico vignette to appear (E57 x 54), as the same mistake also occurred in it, but transferred to the right-hand side of the pediment. The fifth portico vignette (E58 x 75), used in Barrett's edition of St Matthew (1801), is of special interest because it shows the Printing House from an oblique angle to the west, exposing the flank and showing the two walls sweeping out from the portico. It was never used again.

The only other College building to feature in a vignette was the West Front facing on to College Green, used on the titlepage of the 1768 quarto issue of the College statutes (E82 x 172). It was drawn by S. Sproule and is signed in the lower left-hand corner. This was not the first occurrence of a signed engraved ornament. The headpiece used in *Gratulationes juventutis Academiae Dubliniensis in . . . regis et reginae nuptias* (1761 — E60 x 141), showing Juno Cinxia, was signed 'Dixon sculp' in the lower right-hand corner. This was probably done by the Dublin engraver John Dixon. The only other signed vignette occurs in the 1784 printing of Boiardo's *Orlando innamorato* (E52 x 58); 'Esdall del & scul' — no doubt the William Esdall mentioned above — can be discerned at the foot. A harp in front of the anchor entwined by a dolphin was perhaps meant to suggest a Hibernian Aldus.

The remaining three engraved vignettes occur in two mathematical works printed in 1783, neither of which was financed by the College, so the plates were unlikely to have become part of the DUP's stock. The same applies to the Boiardo ornament, but the rest were likely to have been paid for by the College.

61. MUN/P/4/50/12; paid on 19 Feb. 1746.

3

Policy and Personnel

POLICY

A university's close monitoring of its printer's output has a twofold purpose: firstly to ensure that the quality of the printing work accurately reflects the scholarly standards of the institution; and secondly to ensure that nothing is published which would prove an embarrassment to the university either academically or politically. Archbishop Laud was acutely aware of these aspects of form and content at the OUP. He stressed the need for statutory control over the printers allowed by the letters patent of 1632–33, lest they 'do somethings prejudicial to the honour or profit of the University.' The first delegacy of the board of the university was appointed in 1633 to that end. Furthermore he ensured that provision was made in the 'De Typographis Universitatis' section of the 1636 statutes for the appointment of an 'Architypographus', drawn from the academic body, who would 'take unremitting care of the good appearance and fine workmanship of the product.'[1]

A similar structure was established at Cambridge, where the senate appointed a panel of curators or syndics of the Press, made up of some of its own members with others selected from the academic body. These syndics drew up the corpus of rules governing the running of the Press, and their control was mediated as at Oxford through an 'Architypographus.'[2] Tight controls were also written into Glasgow University's agreement with its printer on his appointment in 1715. He was not to assign the university's printing privileges to any other, or to print anything under the university's imprint, without getting its consent; he was to provide a range of scholarly types and to employ 'skillful correctors and workmen'; and, presumably to monitor his output, he was to deposit a copy of each work printed, both those for the university and for himself, in the library.[3]

1. W. Laud, *Remains*, vol. 2, London 1700, 58–60; Carter, *History of OUP*, xxiv, 31–2.
2. McKenzie, *CUP*, vol. 1, 15, 94–8.
3. Maclehose, *Glasgow UP*, 114–16.

There were no such rules codified at the foundation of the DUP, which was all the more strange since it was the College's policy for the greater part of the century not to have a printer as permanent tenant in the Printing House, but to hire one in as and when work needed to be done. One would think that a written set of rules would have been necessary as the basis for the contracts with the succession of at least fifteen printers or booksellers engaged to do the work. There is evidence however that such considerations were current in Trinity in the middle of the century, although not codified. On 21 August 1753 Thomas Leland and John Stokes, then assistants to the Greek lecturer, applied to the board for permission to use the Printing House — it had been idle since the completion of the Hawkey classics in 1747 — in order to issue 'some editions of the classick & other authors.' Permission was granted for a period of seven years and in the report in the board's register it is made evident that they were 'determined never to print any thing but what is proper to come from the university-press and [would] not begin any work without the approbation of the Board.' (Because of the small size of Trinity in comparison to the Oxbridge universities, the board exercised control directly during the century and there is no evidence of any delegation to committees.) Despite these undertakings the board register records no submissions for approval.

In handing over the Printing House to two junior academics the College was reneging on its institutional responsibility. Its non-use of the Press was a recurrent complaint throughout the century and was the subject of an attack by the pseudonymous 'Sir Tague O'Ragan' within about a decade of its first production:

> You have a Printing House Gentlemen, the donation of a pious divine, for the most noble purposes, yet it is silent, and serves for no other use, than a Theatre, where the V[icero]y is hail'd with a panegyrical puff, before we know whether he deserves it or not.
>
> The Gentlemen of your University would be fitter persons to reprint our Classic Authors, the Bible, &c than those who thrust them into the world with so many typographical errors, that in a century or two, may obscure the true sense and spirit of our best authors. If from your study and application, we are to have no new works, the least you should do, is, to transmit the writings of antiquity in a correct manner to your successors.[4]

The Printing House was on the itinerary during any visit by the Lord Lieutenant to the College and even an example of 'a panegyrical puff', addressed to William Cavendish, survives. The following is a sample:

4. *Sir Tague O'Ragan's Address to the Fellows of T[rinit]y Col.*, London [i.e. Dublin c.1750] 5.

> Accept, illustrious Guardian of Our State,
> The Muses' Welcome to the Muses' Seat;
> Where Learning, Wit, and every mental Grace,
> And Merit, more than Station, give thee Place.[5]

Indeed the Printing House seems to have been on the itinerary of most visitors to Trinity, even fictional characters. In H. Scott's epistolary novel, *Helena; or, The vicissitudes of a military life*, issued anonymously in Cork 1790 and one of the very few examples of indigenous Irish fiction of the eighteenth century, there is this fleeting description on p. 29 of vol. 2: 'Trinity College is a beautiful pile of building. We saw the museum, the library, and the printing-house; they were printing at the time . . .'

'Sir Tague O'Ragan's' other criticism concerning the under-use of the Printing House — the lack of literary output from the academics — was also a recurrent theme throughout the century and also surfaced in a fictional setting. This time it occurred in a satire in the genre of an imaginary voyage entitled, *Letters from an Armenian in Ireland*, issued with the imprint 'London 1757', but no doubt printed in Dublin; it has been attributed to Francis Andrews, later provost of the College, and to Edward Sexton Pery, speaker of the House of Commons. On pp. 53–4 will be found the following description: '. . . he led me to the Front of a small but fair Building call'd a Printing House, I was curious to see the Employment of the People within; but he informed me that since the House had been built, no Man of the Academy has employed the Press with any Original Work either of Genius or Industry: The younger Masters have too small Income, and therefore are engaged in the sole Pursuit of acquiring Pupils to support them; the Elder have too great Income, and, Opulence is an Enemy to the Exercise of Genius.'

The heavy duties of teaching and administration were advanced, not without justification and especially so in the case of junior fellows, throughout the century, and indeed into the nineteenth, to explain the appellation of 'the Silent Sister.' One commentator in 1734 summed the situation up in these terms: 'It is unfair therefore to object to them [the fellows] the figure that other universities make in the learned world. What equity is there in comparing them to Oxford or Cambridge, in either of which there are twenty or thirty foundations . . . and some of them consisting of forty, fifty, sixty Fellows, unencumbered with care or business of any kind?'[6] Similar reasons were advanced in an anonymous pamphlet of 1782 to explain 'that dearth of publications in the College of Dublin, which hath been unfairly resolved into want of

5. 'Verses addressed to the Lord Lieutenant at the Printing-House, T.C.D.' in S. Whyte, *The shamrock; or, Hibernian cresses*, Dublin 1772, 184.
6. *A second letter to G- W- Esq. concerning the present condition of the College of Dublin*, [Dublin] 1734, 9–12.

literary merit.'[7] Amid the evidence advanced by the author was the low level of basic remuneration; the fees paid by individual students taken on by a tutor brought the income to a respectable level, but at the expense of long teaching hours. In 1758 the salary of junior fellows was £40 per annum and £100 for senior fellows; with other fees it was estimated that the average annual income of the latter was £800 in 1777.[8] Of the thirty-five fellows elected between 1751 and 1780 McDowell and Webb found that thirteen had published 'some reasonably substantial scholarly work', but they go on to qualify this by stating that in the case of six of these, their publications date largely from after their retirement to a benefice, demonstrating 'how strong was the *cacoethes scribendi* among the Fellows once they were freed from the distractions of College duties.'[9]

Despite the paucity of output from the academics a considerable number of their works were given to outside printers, both in Dublin and London. I have noted over twenty such works between 1740 and 1798, some occurring in several editions, while their known output through the DUP was about forty.[10] The outstanding example of this 'disloyalty' was Thomas Leland, one of the few fellows with a respectable body of published work, who, despite the interest he showed in the affairs of the Printing House and despite the works he had printed there, yet had several volumes produced elsewhere:

1758   *The history of . . . Philip, King of Macedon* (London: T. Harrison).

1765   *A dissertation on the principles of human eloquence . . . being the substance of several lectures read in . . . TCD* 2nd ed. (Dublin: for A. Leathley).

1773   *The history of Ireland* (London: printed for J. Nourse, T. Longman and G. Robinson, and J. Johnson: revised ed. Dublin: R. Marchbank for R. Moncrieffe).

1777   *A fast sermon, preached before the University of Dublin . . . Published at the request of . . . Trinity College and of the Parishioners of St. Anne's* (Dublin: W. Hallhead).

The absence of a copyright law in Ireland and the much wider distribution network available from London would, of course, help account for its lure.

---

7. *Thoughts on the present state of the college of Dublin*, Dublin 1782, 20; often attributed to Arthur Browne, later to hold the chairs of laws and of Greek, and more recently to John Forseyeth, who held the chair of laws at this date.

8. Stubbs, *History of the U. of Dublin*, 209–10.

9. McDowell and Webb, *TCD*, 62.

10. Kinane, 'DUP in 18c.', 109.

Even some official College publications were printed by the general trade. *The memorial of . . . Trinity College, Dublin, to the . . . Board of Erasmus Smith, pursuant to . . . a scheme for applying part of the increase rents of the estate . . . to the use of the University of Dublin* was 'printed by George Faulkner, on the Blind-Quay, 1762.' Another surprising loss to the College Press was the printing of the annual Donnellan lectures. This series was founded under a bequest of Anne Donnellan in 1794 'for the encouragement of religion, learning and good manners.' Six sermons on a chosen subject were to be delivered by one of the fellows each year, for which he was to receive a fixed payment. One of the conditions of the appointment, as set out in the board register on 22 February, was that the fellow chosen was to publish four of the lectures. Thomas Elrington, who was the first appointee, delivered the first series throughout 1795. Late in that year he was paid £30 'as Donnellan's Lecturer; for printing his Sermons.'[11] When they were issued in 1796 they did so under the imprint 'Dublin: printed by George Bonham.' This set a bad precedent for subsequent volumes in the series.

An additional example of the Press's failure to secure the printing of works being generated by the College was that of inaugural dissertations presented by medical graduates. On 5 May 1792 the board resolved that every bachelor of medicine was to give printed copies of his dissertation to specified members of the College and of the College of Physicians. I have traced two of these, neither of which was printed at the Press:

Whitley Stokes *Disputatio inauguralis de respiratione* (Dublin: George
   Bonham, 1793).
Thomas Wright *Disputatio inauguralis physiolgico* [sic] *medica, de
   irritamento cordis dextri proprio* (Dublin: Graisberry & Campbell, 1797).

One likely reason for the Press's failure to secure these commissions was the high cost of printing there relative to those of the general trade, as was the case at all specialist learned presses.

Another criticism levelled at the College was its failure to see that textbooks for the students were printed at its Press. Indeed one critic in the 6 December 1770 issue of the *Freeman's Journal* was of the opinion that that was the most important function of the Printing House: 'A.B. presents his compliments to the Provost & Senior Fellows . . . [and] begs they may give directions, that the Printing House be put to its primitive use, viz, of printing the books read in the course, some of which cannot be had at any price from the booksellers in town.' Although around half of the identified output of the Press was in fact textbooks for the students, this criticism appears to have had some validity towards the end of the century. On 25 November 1785 the board ordered that Francis

11. MUN/V/75/13/37, bursar's account with T. Elrington.

Hutcheson's *Compendium of moral law* be put on the undergraduates' course in morality in place of J. Burlamaqui's *Principles of natural law*. However on the following 23 January they were forced to rescind this directive 'on acct. of the difficulty of procuring the book.' In 1791 copies of the Plutarch printed at the Press in 1761–62 seem to have become so scarce that the board agreed on 23 May to allow the junior sophisters to read Sophocles' *Philoctetes* instead of the *Vitae*; the following day it was further agreed that the senior sophisters might read Sophocles' *Trachinia* in preference to those portions of Plutarch on their course.

In this failure to take advantage of the demand for textbooks the College displayed a lack of business sense which permeated all its dealings with the Press, and which hindered its development potential. At the Oxford and Cambridge presses the money paid by the Stationers' Company for forbearance to print certain books scheduled under their printing privileges (e.g. bibles, almanacks etc.) was nominally available to subsidise the printing of scholarly works. When these privileges were eroded in the eighteenth century the universities were granted annual sums in lieu by the government.[12] Trinity had no such privileges in the eighteenth century, largely because it did not actively pursue them, and consequently had no such income. It could however have ensured a constant income by the steady production of a range of textbooks for which there was a predictable demand. The College failed to take full advantage of this potential. For example having had Richard Murray's *Artis logicae* printed at the Press in 1759, the printer William Sleater was allowed to reprint it in 1768, 1782 and 1785 to meet the students' demand, and all apparently for his private gain. Again the profits from the sale of the College statutes, a copy of which it was compulsory for all matriculating students to purchase, could have afforded the Press a steady income. Instead the profits from the various editions seem to have accrued to the editors. And on those textbooks the College did print the profit it took was very modest: $3\frac{1}{2}d$. was the mark-up on Gerald Fitzgerald's *Hebrew grammar* (1799) which retailed at 4–4.[13]

The College evidently did not wish to sully itself with an admission of any commercial interest or competence. This attitude was underlined by an event in 1803 when it was given the opportunity to sell over 300 books from the stock of the Press. The books were given to Zachariah Miller 'upon his accountable receipt . . . for the purpose of vending in America', but instead of being proud that the Press's imprint was going abroad it was ordered that 'as they are all of Mr McKenzie's Edition, with ex Aedibus Academicis, new titles are to be printed for them, omitting the words ex Aedib. Acads.'.[14]

12. McKenzie, *CUP*, vol. 1, 3, 147–8; Carter, *History of OUP*, 106, 354–6.

13. MUN/V/5/5/337, board register 31 Aug. 1799.

14. MUN/LIB/2/1, 25 Jan., 8 June 1803.

PERSONNEL

The College's failure to come to terms with both the potential and the responsibility engendered by the ownership of a printing house led it into deep political trouble in the 1780s. We have already seen how two junior academics, Leland and Stokes, were granted the use of the Press in 1753 for a period of seven years, a period during which a modest range of competent scholarly works was issued. Given the success of that tenancy the board on 12 March 1774 again agreed to sign over the use of the Printing House to another academic, this time Dr Edward Hill, professor of Physic. The entry in the register records that he was granted the use for five years but makes no mention as to what purpose. T.P.C. Kirkpatrick, in his *History of the medical teaching in TCD* (Dublin 1912), suggested that it was 'to relieve the overcrowding in the old Anatomy House'. It is unlikely to have been as simple as that. Hill, as will be seen, was engaged on a critical edition of Milton's *Paradise lost*, a task he began in 1769, and it may be that he intended printing it there. (In the event the MS was not finished until 1813 and it was never published.)

Assuming the grant of use was for printing it did not make mention of any undertaking to uphold standards or to submit works for approval prior to the commencement of printing. Although the period 1774–79 does not appear to have been particularly productive at the Press — only two works have been identified as its output in these years — Hill evidently did nothing to displease the College and, although there is no entry in the board's register to the effect, his tenancy was extended beyond 1779. The next reference to the Printing House in the register is to be found on 27 August 1784, nearly ten and a half years after the initial grant to Hill: 'Dr. Hill having this day at ye Board resigned the use of the Printing House & deliver'd up the key, the head porter was order'd to take possession of the Printing House.' Behind this bald entry were events which greatly embarrassed the College and which seriously called into question its competence to control the University Press.

The saga began in 1779, probably at the time of the extended grant of use. Prior to this Hill had used William Hallhead to do the printing at the Press, but in 1779 Joseph Hill took over the duties. Joseph may well have been Edward's brother. Among the recently acquired papers of Edward Hill in the TCD library are some genealogical charts of the family which show that Edward was the eldest son of Thomas Hill and Abigail Vize, and that their fourth of five sons was called Joseph.[15] In 1779 Joseph printed Anthony Vieyra's *Animadversiones philologicae* at the Press, the first of a succession of scholarly works which he was to undertake there in the next five years. There is no evidence that he had printing premises elsewhere in the city, unlike all but one of the other printers throughout

15. MS 10395 f.4^V.

the century, and may well have been wholly employed at the Press from this year. He was definitely established there by 1782 when his name appeared in the *Dublin Directory* with the trade address, Trinity College.

In his five-year tenure Joseph Hill undertook a range of scholarly and typographically complex works unrivalled at any other period in the eighteenth-century history of the Press. The list was dominated by books on mathematics and science, but included one of the earliest works wholly in Italian to be printed in Ireland (Boiardo's *Orlando Innamorato* 1784) and probably the first book from the Press to make extensive use of hebrew type (Buxtorf's *Hebrew grammar* 1782). Unfortunately parallel with this scholarly output he also printed a range of political tracts espousing the claims of the disaffected Volunteer Movement. The tone of these works became increasingly strident. C.H. Wilson's *Compleat collection of the resolutions of the Volunteers* (1782) was followed in 1783 by W.W. Seward's *The rights of the people asserted*. The climax came in August of the following year with a reprint of John Milton's *The tenure of kings and magistrates*, written in 1649 after the execution of Charles I to prove 'that it is lawfull . . . to call to account a tyrant' and republished with additional notes by W.W. Seward 'particularly recommended at this time to the perusal of the men of Ireland' (see plate 12). The work was issued under the anonymous imprint 'Dublin: printed in the year 1784', but according to a report in the *Dublin Evening Post* of 4 September a student, the son of a government hack, while 'sneaking about the printing-office', discovered a page of the copy which he took to Dublin Castle.

This proved too much for an already alarmed administration and Provost Hely-Hutchinson was interviewed by the Chief Secretary, Thomas Orde, and asked to account for the printer's activities. This is made clear in a letter from Orde to the provost dated 27 August, the day that Dr Hill returned the key of the Printing House:

Private

My Dear Sir,

I omitted to inform my self exactly of you, if you had examined Hill upon the point of his having printed the former edition of this pamphlet, I find that Mr Seward had very generally circulated it. Mr Hill says in his statement on the back of that, which you put in my hands, that 'the intire impression of this book consisted of 200 copies' shd. be given up; but this expression does not contradict what I hear positively asserted, of the first edition's having been also printed at the College Press. It wd. certainly be material to know this circumstance, as in that case the publication wd. be indisputable.

I shd. also be very glad to be informed, if any caution was given to Hill not to inform Seward of what has passed at the Board, and

THE

T E N U R E

OF

Kings and Magiftrates;

PROVING,

That it is Lawful, and hath been held fo
through all Ages, for any, who have the
Power, to call Tyrants to Account, and,
after due Conviction, to depofe and put
them to Death.

Originally Written by the celebrated

J O H N M I L T O N.

Now corrected, and re-publifhed with additional
Notes and Obfervations; and particularly
recommended, at this Time, to the
Perufal of the

M E N of I R E L A N D.

Dublin : printed in the Year 1784.

12. Reproduced with permission of the Beinecke Rare Book and Manuscript Library,
Yale University.

whether the enquiry and other proceedings were confined to the offence against the College without any mention of the information or interference of Government. I shd. certainly have much satisfaction in being informed, that no account of these transactions may yet have reached the Publisher Seward. You will observe (which I mention very confidentially) that these pamphlets have been given away gratis; that Mr Seward could not afford to do this — and in short that I am certain of dangerous machinations in very dangerous quarters.

. . . Have the goodness to inform me where Dr Hill lives . . . [16]

Orde's hope that the administration's role in the enquiries should remain secret proved in vain. The whole affair was soon reported in the newspapers with Volunteer sympathies, and given as another example of government tyranny. Witness the *Hibernian Journal* on 1 September:

Administration seems determined to pursue a vindictive and violent system of government by which, if it cannot bear down, it may at least terrify opposition in every possible instance; nor does it scruple to stoop to the lowest means to effect this purpose. Of this last kind may be classed, a direct application from Mr Secretary Orde to the principals of our University, requesting they would remove Mr Joseph Hill from the College Printing-Office, for having re-printed a tract written in the last century, by the celebrated John Skelton [*sic*] on a subject that our Government in its great wisdom finds some analogy to what is transacting at the present time. The principals have complaisantly agreed to the desires of the great man; and to crown the noble deed, a criminal prosecution is, we hear, instituted against Hill.

The *Dublin Evening Post* for 2 September reported that there was 'an eager desire . . . among the people to see this pamphlet' and that 'a vast number . . . [was] being immediately printed to gratify the public curiosity'. There is no evidence that it was ever separately reprinted, but the *Dublin Morning Post* published it in instalments between 21 and 28 September. The *Dublin Evening Post* continued to milk the propaganda value of the suppression, describing it in hyperbolic terms in its issue of 4 September as 'the most extraordinary attack upon the Liberty of the Press (that palladium of our liberties) that ever was known in a free country'.

No evidence has been found that Joseph Hill was in fact prosecuted and he was back in business early the following year, when he printed *A treatise on the origin of attachments and informations* for the Constitution Society. His affairs however must have been seriously disrupted by the

16. Donoughmore papers C/1/181.

events at the College Press and on 14 July 1785 the *Dublin Evening Post* reported his bankruptcy. He was established in business again in 1789 as a printer and music seller. In 1793 he joined with William McKenzie, then the College bookseller-stationer-printer, to issue a broadsheet entitled *An accurate account of the death of Louis XVI who was beheaded at Paris Jan. 21*, a joint publication which must have been disquieting to the College. Towards the end of his life he did printing for the Freemasons, including work on leather aprons from copper plates. The diversity of his activities would suggest he was having difficulties making a living. He died in April 1806.

No disciplinary action appears to have been taken against Edward Hill; in fact he was appointed to the chair of botany in 1785 when the existing lectureship, which he had held since 1773, was reconstituted as a professorship. It is likely that Provost Hely-Hutchinson did not receive much sympathy from the fellows of the College, who universally disliked him because of his corrupt political appointment — described by McDowell and Webb (p. 53) as 'a piece of ministerial jobbery which is difficult to parallel, even in the annals of the eighteenth century' — and because of his academic ignorance.

After these damaging events no serious effort was made to encourage printing in the College until 1791 when William McKenzie, the College bookseller and stationer since at least 1783, was appointed its printer with a first commission to produce a new edition of the statutes. This time the board was determined to exercise close control over the appointee and the register for 8 September records that the agreed 'regulations respecting the Printing House' were placed in the chamber of records. Unfortunately no details were given in the register, but an undated late eighteenth-century loose paper in the College muniments headed 'Conditions of granting the use of the College Printing House to their Bookseller' is almost certainly what was referred to:

1.   He shall print no book or edition of a book without the license of the Board & without first exhibiting ye type & paper by way of specimen.

2.   He shall print such books & editions of books as the Board shall direct either at his own expence, or otherwise, as shall be agreed on by the Board. Only if at his own expence it is understood the Board will provide he shall not lose by the impression.

3.   He shall procure such types in different languages, as shall be approved of by the Board within six months after he enter on the possession of the Printing House & from time to time afterwards as shall be found necessary.

4.   The walls & roof of the Printing House to be put into proper repair & kept so at the expence of the College. The other necessary

> repairs of the House & of the printing presses & other furniture to be
> done in the first instance at the expence of the College, but afterwards
> by the Printer.[17]

In this set of rules we are at last witnessing the College's dawning reali-
sation of the responsibility it had taken upon itself when it accepted
Stearne's gift of 1733. On the plus side was the acknowledgment of the
potential for scholarly publications. The College showed its intent by
having the plumbing repaired (including new lead 'for sink and lee
troughs') and the printing presses overhauled, as has been noted.[18]

In the next few years McKenzie produced a modest range of works,
mostly classics, for the College. He also used the printing plant, as all his
predecessors would have done, for his own private printing. This activity,
accepted by the College, led to some unwarranted criticism in a pseudonymous article in 1793: 'At the rere of the college, in the park, at one end of a
broad gravel walk, is a neat building with an elegant front (built at the
expence of the bishop of Clogher); in it were several men and boys busily
and I am told constantly employed printing parliamentary debates, novels, jest books &c &c for private emolument; classical works have not been
printed there these many years, to the great loss of the gentlemen students
and to the great perversion of the original design of the place.'[19] As only
about 40 per cent of the output of the Printing House was commissioned
by the College, other work was done to keep the men employed.[20] This
was, and is, the universal practice at all university printing plants. A printing plant only operates efficiently and economically on a steady supply of
copy, which a single institution is unlikely to generate. Concurrent production of several books, with a range of jobbing work to fill the gaps, was
the most efficient way to use the printing plant and personnel in academic
offices. The OUP achieved such continuity both by undertaking outside
commissions and by trading its workforce between the Learned Press and
Bible Press aspects of its production. The Bible Press, in the eastern half of
the Clarendon Building, with its large editions of bibles, books of common
prayer etc. had a more stable output than the mercurial output of the
learned side, in the western half, and could more readily absorb the
workforce when idle.[21] 'Tim Tickle' was evidently unaware of these 'laws'
of the printing trade.

17. MUN/P/1/1171.
18. MUN/P/2/152/12, £22-13-4$\frac{1}{2}$ paid to the plumber Pike in Dec. 1791;
    MUN/P/4/62/2, £18-18-0 paid to Ambrose Binns for ironwork done on the
    printing presses on 30 Aug., 29 Oct. and 21 Dec. 1791.
19. 'A tour through Trinity College, by Tim Tickle' in *Walker's Hibernian Magazine*, 2
    (1793) 525.
20. Kinane, 'DUP in 18c.', 109.
21. I.G. Philip, *William Blackstone and the reform of the OUP in the eighteenth century*,
    Oxford 1957, 6.

McKenzie's official career in the College came to an abrupt end on 10 October 1795 when the board register recorded that it was 'Agreed to dismiss McKenzie from the College business of Printer-Bookseller and Stationer. Same time Mercier was elected Bookseller.' The starkness of the report is reminiscent of Hill's dismissal, but there is no evidence of any similar scandal involved in McKenzie's departure. It was probably done on grounds of incompetence — the library muniments record the librarian's growing frustration with his poor service and his College printings abound in mis-signings, mis-paginations, poor typography and sloppy workmanship.

Despite this disappointing end to the 'revival' of printing at the Press, the College was determined not to be discouraged and in the following year paid out over £40 to put the printing plant in order and £12 to repair the roof in preparation for the production of George Miller's edition of Longinus and the first volume of John Walker's Livy in 1797. This tenacity was vindicated and in the next few years R.E. Mercier produced a series of competently printed works, at least two of which were of international scholarly importance (Walker's Livy, 1797–99, and Barrett's edition of St Matthew's Gospel, 1801) and nearly all of compositorial complexity. Mercier went bankrupt in 1807.

From one of Mercier's printings we are afforded an insight into the relationship between a College author and the College printer. The work was *A compendious view of the civil [and ecclesiastical] law* by Arthur Browne, professor of Civil Law. The two-volume work was printed in 1797–99 and although the imprint does not state that it was printed at the DUP the insight it gives is still valid. In the preface to the second volume (pp. ix–x) Browne gives the following amazing explanation as to why there were so many notes in small type: 'It was owing to the inexperience of the author as to the art of printing, which made him chuse a larger letter, as thinking the size of the manuscript would not be proportional to the intended size of the volume, whereas on the contrary he not only was obliged to omit much of his material, but also to crowd the rest in a great measure into notes.' Although none of Mercier's printings for the College displays such imbalance and the blame rests substantially on the author's naivety, there was a failure on Mercier's part to provide one of the fundamental services of a university printer — that of mediation between the needs of the scholar and the mysteries of printing.

Besides Hill, McKenzie and Mercier, the College used at least a dozen other printers throughout the century to man the Printing House. The following list has been compiled from imprints and other sources:

1738	Rider, Ebenezer
1739	Reilly, Richard

1740–41	Rider, Ebenezer
1745–47	Powell, Samuel
1754–56	Sleater, William
1758–59	Sleater, William
1761	Faulkner, George; Watson, William
1761–62	Ewing, George and Alexander
1765	Powell, Samuel, and Son
1767	Sleater, William
1768	No printer given
1769	Cecil, George; Powell, Samuel
1770?	Sleater, William
1773	Marchbank, Robert; Ewing, Thomas
1778	Hallhead, William
1779	Hill, Joseph
1782–84	Hill, Joseph
1787–88	Exshaw, John
1791–95	McKenzie, William
1797	Mercier, Richard Edward
1799–1801	Mercier, Richard Edward

Most of the printers merely occupied the Press during the production of the desired volume and had their own permanent printing offices elsewhere in the city. Philip White's statement that M.H. Gill, starting in the 1840s, was 'the first to carry on and confine his business as printer in the University Printing House without having another office in the city' is patently untrue, given the case of Hill.[22] There is also an earlier example in George Cecil, who occupied the Press in 1769, and in the notice of his death in the *Freeman's Journal* on 27 October of that year he was described as 'Master of the College Printing House.'

No consistent effort was made until the last quarter of the century to employ the same printer for consecutive works and they made their appearance almost at random. This discontinuity was responsible for the variable standards of the works issued from the Press and for the consequent lack of a discernible style. The College's casual attitude in this respect was in stark contrast to the elaborate forms and ceremonies performed at the election of a printer at Cambridge, rituals that were acknowledgments of the importance of the printer in the life of the university.[23]

The printers employed at the DUP ranged from Dublin's largest, George Faulkner, 'the Prince of Dublin Printers', down to one of the

22. P. White, 'Printing trade' (Aug. 1908) 6.

23. Set out in John Beverly, *An account of the different ceremonies observed in the . . . University of Cambridge*, Cambridge 1788, 149–50.

city's smallest, George Cecil. There appears to have been little reason for the choice of individual printers. For example the most substantial piece of printing in Greek done in the capital prior to 1738 was Cope's edition of Hippocrates in 1736; on the evidence of the ornaments this was printed by Samuel Powell. Yet two years later, when Trinity was planning the first work to be wholly printed in Greek in Ireland, it chose Ebenezer Rider to print it although there is no evidence he had any experience in that language. The brother of Presswick Rider, who had printed in Dublin in the earlier part of the century, Ebenezer was working in London in 1735 where he printed Smith's *Pocket companion for Free-masons*. Experience of the trade in the English capital may have had some bearing on his choice as the first printer at the DUP.

Richard Reilly was engaged late in 1738 to print the second volume from the Press, Richard Helsham's *A course of lectures in natural philosophy*, which was issued in the following year. Rider was back at the Press during 1740–41 to do some unspecified printing.[24]

Samuel Powell was engaged late in 1744 in preparation for the printing of Hawkey's series of Latin classics. As we have seen several bills of his survive in the College muniments setting out his charges for putting the Printing House in order, it having been idle for three years or so. Powell was one of the very few master printers in Dublin who survived wholly by their printing; most others needed a bookselling outlet to boost their incomes. And of these master printers he was probably the largest. He had a large printing office built in Dame Street in 1762 which he occupied until his death in 1775, after a career which stretched back almost fifty years.

William Sleater was the printer engaged by Leland and Stokes for their five-year tenancy of the Printing House. He was one of the larger master printer/booksellers in Dublin, having a bookshop at his printing office on Cork Hill, where he published his own newspaper, the *Public Gazetteer*. He was the first to style himself 'Printer to the University' which he did only in the imprint to George Cleghorn's *Index to an annual course of lectures* (1756). The only other printer to adopt this appellation, prior to the more rigorous appointments made after the Hill scandal of 1784, was William Watson; this he did in the only work he printed for the College, the *Gratulationes juventutis* of 1761. Sleater rivals Hill for the longest continuous tenure of the office of College printer, and was employed again during the 1760s.

George Faulkner made his only appearance at the Printing House in 1761, a busy year for College publications, there being two other printers engaged in that year. He had evidently been cultivating a relationship

24. MUN/P/4/44/68, 7 Aug. 1740; MUN/P/4/45/18–19, 21, 25 July 1741.

with the University throughout the 1740s and 1750s. During those decades he presented many books he had printed to the library, including an edition of Jonathan Swift's *Works* in a presentation binding and some novels. As fiction was not thought to be worthy of a place on the library's shelves until well into the nineteenth century, and then only very selectively, these rare examples were obviously kept so as not to offend the donor.[25]

Faulkner's cultivation of the College paid off and the following announcement was issued in the 15–18 July 1758 issue of *Faulkner's Dublin Journal*: 'It is with the greatest pleasure we can inform the publick, that the printer hereof hath obtained liberty to print a very pompous and complete edition of the works of the Rev. Dr. Jonathan Swift . . . at the University Printing Office . . . which edition will be corrected under the care and inspection of some of the Fellows who have most eminently distinguished themselves for their learned writings . . .' In a further advertisement on 28–31 October Faulkner gave the subscription details: it was to be in seven quarto volumes with copperplates by Hayman of London, and was to cost three and a half guineas sewed in blue paper or seven guineas for the few royal paper copies. Unfortunately the minimum number of 300 subscriptions was not reached and 'the most grand and correct edition of any book ever yet printed in this Kingdom' was never put to press. The fact that Faulkner was embroiled in 1758 in a dispute with George and Alexander Ewing over their piracy of Swift's works may have been the reason for projecting this 'pompous' edition.

The work that Faulkner did print at the Press in 1761 was much more mundane, a textbook of Euclid edited by Theaker Wilder. At the same time in late 1763 when he was paid for that volume Faulkner also received over £33 'for printing Corvinus &c.'[26] This refers to the edition of Jan Arnold Corvinus's *Jus feudale* which was issued in 1762 with the imprint 'Dublinii: apud G. Faulkner'. It might well have been printed at the DUP, but there is no evidence to that effect.

The father and son partnership of the Ewings was also engaged at the Press in 1761 to undertake Thomas Wilson's edition of Plutarch. A conscious effort was made by the editor to ensure that the work was finely printed. In his submission to the board on 24 January 1760, seeking help towards the work, Wilson stated that a new fount of type from the Wilson foundry in Glasgow was to be used, and that the work was to be printed on a 'fine medium Dutch paper made on purpose which will cost 40 per cent more than the usual.' There is no evidence that the Ewings were printers, and they must have brought in a printer to do the actual

---

25. Examples of these novels may be found on shelf T.mm. in the Long Room of the library.
26. MUN/V/57/4/328, bursar's quarterly account to Sept. 1763.

work. However they would have dictated the typography, and for the Plutarch they were careful to avoid ostentation, paring back on inessentials, even down to the imprint which in the first volume merely reads, 'Dublinii 1761', while in volumes two and three only 'apud G. et A. Ewing' was added. After the excesses of William Sleater their austerity is a blessed relief.

In 1773 their relation Thomas Ewing was engaged to print Joseph Stock's edition of Lucian at the Printing House. He like the other Ewings had a reputation for fine typography. In the printer's dedication to his 1771 edition of Thomas Gray's *Poems* Ewing expressed his hope, having received a copy of the Foulis Press edition of the work (1768), that the Dublin edition would stand up to comparison with it and so help to quell 'those reproaches which Ireland has long laboured under for bad printing'. His attention to detail was painstaking, as is evident from his advertisement in the *Freeman's Journal* of 19 January 1771, advising purchasers of one of his printings 'not to bind their books for sometime, as the pages are too lately printed to bear pressing without blotting each other'. After he died in 1776 Arthur Grueber, a former apprentice of his, advertised in the *Hibernian Journal* of 20 January 1777 that in setting up his own business he hoped 'by his sincere endeavours to emulate that attention and elegance in which his late master remarkably excelled.' The edition of Lucian produced at the Press was competently printed, being of even colour throughout and with adequate margins. It is a pity the College did not commission him for other works, allowing scope for the fine sense of typography he showed in his other printings.

Trinity used two other printers in the 1770s prior to the tenure of Joseph Hill at the Printing House. Robert Marchbank printed an edition of Demosthenes there in 1773 and William Hallhead produced two works: Michael Kearney's *Lectures concerning history* (1776) and an edition of the College statutes (1778). Marchbank, a native of Newcastle-upon-Tyne, was printing there in 1761. In Dublin he confined himself to printing and had no retail bookselling outlet. When his business proved insufficient, he eventually went bankrupt. Hallhead was primarily a bookseller and stationer, and may well not have done the printing himself, perhaps hiring in journeymen to man the Printing House. The form of the imprint in Kearney's *Lectures* — 'printed for William Hallhead' — would seem to indicate this. He was related to and worked for the Leathleys, who had been bookbinders and stationers to the College since the early part of the century. In the imprint to the Kearney he styled himself as 'successor to A[nne]. Leathley'. He died on 15 December 1781 and two years later his widow Sarah married William McKenzie. John Exshaw was appointed in the interregnum between Hill and McKenzie to print Joseph Stock's edition of Tacitus (1787–88). He was a substantial figure in the book trade and was elected an alderman of the city.

Evidence concerning the employees of these master printers is of course almost non-existent. The TCD library minute book for 30 July 1788 recorded that Jacob Whyte, having delivered the sheets of the Tacitus, gave an undertaking on behalf of his employer John Exshaw, 'to make good in one Kallindar month . . . any imperfection.' Another reference is to be had from reports of a bizarre incident in *The Press* for 30 November and 2 December 1797. It appears that *The Press*, a republican newspaper which was suppressed the following year, was being harassed by the Dublin Castle authorities and on occasion its messenger, carrying sheets from the printing works to the publishing office, had had them stolen at gunpoint by Castle agents. It was with glee then that it reported the mistaken seizure on 28 November of 'a mathematical volume and some proof sheets of a treatise on Logarithms' from 'Mr Wise, foreman to Mr Mercier, College Printer.' Wise, who had been bringing the proofs to the editor for correction, was detained while the tables were examined to see if they were cyphers of treasonable material. Eventually Felix O'Gallagher, whose *Essay on the investigation of the first principles of nature* had been printed at the DUP in 1784 and who may have been the editor of these unidentified proofs, was summoned to examine them. He explained the contents and Wise was released having been in custody for three hours. The College Printing House was evidently still under a cloud of suspicion thirteen years after Hill's departure.

Beyond these scanty references it is possible to speculate in some measure about the journeymen. It is likely for example that the compositor for the 1738 Plato was brought in from abroad because of the lack of skill in this area in the Dublin trade. Even the OUP and CUP in the late seventeenth and early eighteenth centuries had to turn to the Continent, most notably to Holland, for skilled comps.[27] This was the norm in the English trade well into the century. In 1747 R. Campbell had this to say of the London compositor: 'It is absolutely necessary that he should read both [Latin and Greek] . . .; by barely reading them he may make a shift to compose, but not with half so much ease . . . as if he could construe them with any tolerable accuracy. This is an advantage which few foreign printers want, and enables them to publish more correct copies in those languages than is commonly done here, where very few understand any other languages than English.'[28] Getting specialist compositors was to be a perennial problem at the Press.

At the Oxford and Cambridge presses students or recent graduates were often used as proof correctors especially during busy periods and when the author or editor was not available.[29] It would seem that Trinity

27. Carter, *History of OUP*, 47–8; McKenzie, *CUP*, vol. 1, 61, 69.

28. R. Campbell, *The London tradesman*, London 1747, 123; quoted in McKenzie, *CUP*, vol. 1, 62.

29. Carter, *History of OUP*, 257; McKenzie, *CUP*, vol. 1, 68–9.

also used a recent graduate to proof-read the 1738 Plato, if the Henry Eyre who received £3 in the latter half of 1737 'for correcting the Press' can be identified as the student of the same name who entered the College in 1725.[30] It appears that fellows also undertook proof-reading at this date. In 1739 William Evelyn, who graduated M.A. that year, wrote a poem entitled, 'Verses by Mr Evelin of Dublin College', which begins:

> In the twelfth year of George the Second's Reign
> Dick Baldwin Provost, Forster Dean . . .
> When Carteret mended Helsham's Lecture
> And Whittingham was Press-Corrector'[31]

The person referred to as corrector was John Whittingham (1703–1778) who became a fellow in 1736 and was eventually elected to the chair of civil and canon law in 1749.

Unfortunately there is a long period in the eighteenth-century history of the Press when there is no indication as to who the readers were, and it is only at the end of the century that evidence reappears. At this date the burden seems to have fallen on the author, with professional correctors making an appearance in the early nineteenth century. This burdensome duty for the author led to even further confusion in Arthur Browne's ill-fated *Compendious view* for which he apologised in the preface to volume two: 'As to the various errata, and the great defects in punctuation, he can only excuse them, by the impracticability in his great hurry of affairs of attending to the supervision of the press, and the impossibility in Ireland of getting for hire a proper corrector of the press, must therefore pray the reader to look carefully at the page [actually three pages] of Errata.'

Some evidence exists of the lot of the eighteenth-century Dublin printer's apprentice. Matthias Joyce, who later became a Methodist preacher, was apprenticed to John Exshaw in 1768 and left an account of his training.[32] Although he did not serve his time during Exshaw's tenure at the College's Printing House his description no doubt held true in large measure for the apprentices who did work there. He started serving his time at the age of fourteen. He was constantly in trouble with his master, who being *in loco parentis*, tried correcting his faults with a stick — a universal practice to which Benjamin Franklin's *Autobiography* testifies. So bad did he feel his treatment to be that he ran away to England in 1771, but soon returned to Dublin because the employment situation was so bad. Exshaw accepted him back on two bails of £20 each. He returned to his old habits of sneaking from the house at night to go gambling and drinking. His reformation

30. MUN/V/57/2, bursar's quarterly account to Sept. 1737.

31. Harvard: MS Eng 218.2, vol. 3, f. 437 (microfilm Pos. 786 in the National Library of Ireland) Orrery MSS, letters and verses.

32. 'The life of Mr. Matthias Joyce. Written by himself' in Thomas Jackson ed. *The lives of early Methodist preachers*, vol. 4, London 1866, 228–73.

however started after hearing John Wesley preach during a visit to Dublin in September 1773. He mentions the practice of printing some ephemera without knowledge of the master as if it were a common habit, but now his conscience smote him when he did it. He must have come out of his time in the latter half of the 1770s, and by 1780 he was married with one child. Joyce borrowed a substantial amount of money to set up his own business, but it collapsed shortly afterwards. He became a preacher in January 1783. Joyce's life was not that of a typical printer's apprentice, but it is interesting none the less for the glimpses it affords of this hidden area

4
Output and Finances

In my original work on the eighteenth-century Press I identified sixty-one possible works printed there; subsequently I have added only a few titles to that list.[1] In that unpublished thesis I gave a full bibliographical analysis for each work, which it is not to our purpose to reproduce here. However it is worth looking in some detail at a selection of the volumes to underline certain points about production at the Printing House.

The imperfect nature of the surviving archive of the DUP means that there is only fragmentary evidence of its book production costs in this century. And of the records that do survive, costs are given more often than not for the whole, rather than broken down under the various aspects of production — authorial expenses, composition, presswork, proof-reading, paper, overheads and profit. However there are some detailed accounts of interest and happily evidence for the Plato of 1738 has survived (see plate 13).

Ebenezer Rider, in providing his bill dated 27 June 1737 for 'Money laid out for the use of the College Printing House' included: 'To the compositor for 3 sheets of Plato's dialogues and over-running the first sheet £2-1-0 To the press-men for one sheet do. 5-0.'[2] Ignoring the allowance for 'over-running' which we cannot assess — there were major problems with the setting as evidenced by three pages of errata — the compositor was thus paid 13-8 per sheet. This cost was comparable with that being charged at the CUP in the early eighteenth century; charges at the OUP in the middle of the century would seem to have been somewhat less.[3] The Dublin Plato contains $22\frac{1}{4}$ sheets so the cost of composition would have been about £15-4-1.

The edition size was 780: 750 ordinary copies and 30 fine paper. A payment of 5 shillings per sheet represents a charge by the press crew of $1-7\frac{1}{4}$ per token (250 sheets of paper), substantially more than the 1-2 per token that was paid in London and Cambridge, and about the same as the 1-6 paid at Oxford, when the 8.33 per cent difference between the

1. Kinane, 'DUP in 18c.'.
2. MUN/P/4/41/49.
3. McKenzie, *CUP*, vol. 1, 81 table; Philip, *William Blackstone*, 88.

ΠΛΑΤΩΝΟΣ

ΕΠΤΑ

ΕΚΛΕΚΤΟΙ ΔΙΑΛΟΓΟΙ.

PLATONIS

Septem Selecti DIALOGI.

Juxta Editionem SERRANI.

DUBLINII:
E Typographia ACADEMIÆ.

MDCCXXXVIII.

13. The first book printed at the Press: Plato's *Dialogues*, 1738.

English and Irish currencies that existed throughout the century is allowed for.[4] The total cost of the presswork for the Plato would have been £5-11-3.

Henry Eyre, as has been seen, was paid £3 for proof-reading. The universal payment to the reader in the general trade was one-sixth of the compositor's charge, which in the case of the Plato should have led to a charge of £2-10-8. So Eyre must have been paid a bonus as there were no cancels to read (unless whole sheets were replaced).

In April 1737 '60 reams of fine large Genoa papr. at 13s. each' were bought from Anthony Dermott and used in the first two books printed at the Press. Rider also bought two reams of royal paper at £2–4–0 each from Dermott for the fine paper state.[5] In an undated document in the College muniments labelled 'Rider's acct of the paper' it is stated that he 'Printed 780 Books, each Book containing one Quire, and 18 Quires perfect making one Rem, is 43 Rems'.[6] (As there were only $22\frac{1}{4}$ sheets in each volume perhaps the other $1\frac{3}{4}$ sheets, bringing the stated use up to a quire per book, were accounted for by cancels; this would then help to explain the extra payment to the reader.) The ordinary paper copies thus contained 41.67 reams of paper, which at 13-0 per ream, cost £27-1-9. The fine paper copies used 1.67 reams at £2-4-0 each, which is £3-13-4. The total for the paper was thus £30-15-1.

The standard practice in the trade of the time was to calculate for overheads and profit at half the cost of the labour, which in the case of the Plato would have led to the addition of £11-17-8. There were likely to have been no editorial costs as the work was a straight reprint from Jean de Serres' edition printed by Henri Estienne in 1578. The conjectural cost of printing the Plato can now be set out:

	£ s. d.
Composition	15- 4- 1
Presswork	5-11- 3
Proof-reading	3- 0- 0
	23-15- 4
Overheads/profits	11-17- 8
Paper	30-15- 1
Total	66- 8- 1

4. McKenzie, *CUP*, vol. 1, 88–9.

5. MUN/P/4/41/23; MUN/P/4/42/8, received by Rider 8 Feb. 1738.

6. MUN/P/1/1200.

The production cost before binding was thus 1–8½ for each copy. The muniments provide some evidence of the cost of presentation bindings, especially of the large paper copies:

1738 Novr. 8th

Bindding Ten Plato's Dialogues of

    the large Paper in blew Turkey Gilt over   5- 0- 0

Bindding Twenty Do. Red Lether Gilt   6-10- 0

                                      £11-10- 0

Recd ye. above Acct from the Revd Dr. Hughes

Novr. ye 8th. 1738   Joseph Leathley[7]

McDonnell and Healy in their *Gold-tooled bookbindings commissioned by TCD in the eighteenth century* describe these as 'the most prestigious contract' of Leathley's career: 'the ten blue turkey bindings . . . are among the most sophisticated examples of the Harleian style to occur in Dublin' in the first half of the century. They traced six of the blue turkey and three of the red morocco volumes. Among the recipients of the more expensive volumes were Thomas Carter, Master of the Rolls; Henry Boyle, Earl of Shannon and Speaker of the Irish House of Commons; and Claudius Gilbert, until 1735 vice-provost of the College, who was actively collecting a fine library for presentation to Trinity, and therefore in need of encouragement (see plate 14). Bishop Edward Synge had to make do with the cheaper version.[8] On 15 March 1739 Leathley charged for binding a further nine copies in turkey, this time much less elaborately as at 5-0 each they cost half that of the first batch, and thirteen in 'Gilt Calf' at 3-0 each.[9] The majority of the edition was used for humbler purposes and judging from the copies that I have seen most were bound in plain calf and used for College prizes throughout the century. Copies were still in stock in 1800 when five were put into the lending library.[10]

The Plato provides the only detailed account of production costs at the Press until 1796 when the muniments start recording the production of John Walker's edition of Livy. As the bulk of that seven-volume work was printed in the nineteenth century it will be as well to postpone

7. MUN/LIB/10/102.
8. J. McDonnell and P. Healy, *Gold-tooled bookbindings commissioned by TCD in the eighteenth century* (Leixlip 1987) 47–8, plate G (showing Leathley's bill), and catalogue 20–8, 67 (illustrating the bindings, with explanatory text).
9. MUN/LIB/10/107.
10. MUN/LIB/2/1, 2 Dec. 1800.

14. The blue turkey binding done by Joseph Leathley's binder for the Plato, 1738, for presentation to Claudius Gilbert.

detailed consideration of it until the next section. However it can be stated that printing prices were stable in London throughout the first three-quarters of the century, and journeymen's wages only began to rise at the time of the American War of Independence; this series of increases is documented from 1785 onwards.[11] No doubt London's experience held for the rest of the British Isles. I can only assume that the same stability obtained at the DUP until well into the century and that books printed there were charged *pro rata* with the scale paid for the Plato.

John Hawkey's series of Latin classics printed in the years 1745–47 was the most ambitious project undertaken at the Press in the eighteenth century. Hawkey, a Dublin schoolmaster and an alumnus of the College, published his subscription proposals in *Faulkner's Dublin Journal* on 10–14 July 1744:

> I. A compleat Set of the Latin Classics shall be printed in neat Pocket Volumes; the Best Editions of each Author shall be examined and collated, and the most approved reading used.
>
> II. They shall be printed with a new Type, and on a Paper greatly superior in Fineness to any hitherto used in the kingdom; and, to render this Edition the more beautiful, large Margins shall be preserved.
>
> III. As all the modern Editions are monstrously faulty in the Punctuation, Whereby the Sense is in numberless Places rendered obscure, in many unintelligible to the Generality of Readers; all possible care shall be observed in pointing this Edition, in the most correct and accurate Manner.
>
> IV. The Price to Subscribers shall be a British Half-Crown for each Volume; one to be paid for at subscribing, and the same at the Delivery of each Volume in half binding.
>
> V. They shall be carried on with all the Expedition a Work of this Kind will admit of; and no more shall be printed than are subscribed for. Subscriptions are taken in by the Editor at the College, and Mr. George Faulkner Bookseller in Essex-street.

Hawkey acknowledged 'having received great encouragement from the . . . College', which subscribed for 300 copies of each of the first two volumes — no doubt the board was delighted that someone was making such prestigious use of what could have become a white elephant. Samuel Powell was the printer appointed by Hawkey and late in 1744 he arranged for the Printing House to be put in order, it having been idle for a few years. Printing proceeded rapidly and the first

---

11. P. Hernlund, 'William Strahan's ledgers: standard charges for printing 1738–1785' in *Studies in bibliography*, 20 (1967) 106; E. Howe, *The London compositor*, London 1947, 72 ff.

volume in the series, Virgil's *Opera*, was issued early in 1745. J.P. Droz in the January-March issue of his *Literary Journal* reported its publication and that it 'fully answeres the expectation of the public.' There were several cancels printed and the number of variant states with combinations of these would suggest that its passage through the press had been traumatic.

Some copies of the Virgil were issued without the engraved vignette of the Printing House portico which was to become a hallmark of the series and later a device for the Press. It seems likely that it was not originally intended to have such an ornament. John Esdall presented his bill for drawing this vignette in July 1745 and described it as 'for a frontispiece to Horace', the second volume issued (see E57 x 56 plate 10). This must have proved so pleasing that it was decided to print a cancel titleleaf for the remaining stock of the Virgil. Droz, in the issue of his *Literary Journal* for the second quarter of 1745, reported the imminent publication of the Horace and Hawkey was paid for Trinity's subscription on 10 July.[12] John Brooks engraved the frontispiece that appears in some copies of this work and there were also a few large paper copies printed 'for the curious', as Droz put it.

Droz continued to chart the progress of the series and in the last quarter of the year reported that the *Comoediae* of Terence had 'lately' come out. For this edition a new engraving of the Printing House portico was cut (see E57 x 59 plate 10). As has been noted, it was probably done by John Brooks who got the details of the entablature seriously wrong. Copies of the Terence and of the fifth volume in the series, the Sallust, are to be found with this vignette in either state. The fourth volume in the series, the *Satyrae* of Juvenal and Persius, was issued in the first quarter of 1746. The College reduced its subscription for this to 150 copies which may indicate a souring of relationships.[13] Interestingly there are two variants of the large paper state, with and without the titlepage vignette. Droz appears to have lost interest in the series and no report of the Sallust was printed in the *Literary Journal*. Hawkey was paid for the College's subscription for 150 copies in the last quarter of 1746 which indicates that it was ready by the end of that year although dated '1747'.[14] The editor's relationship with the College was now at a low ebb and the board's decision on 4 February 1747 that the subscription to the Sallust had been their last effectively killed off the series. Hawkey tried to soldier on, but his choice for the next volumes in the series was fatal. The 15–19 December 1747 issue of *Faulkner's Dublin Journal* carried 'Prosposals for printing by subscription a new edition of the works of M. Tullius Cicero in 20 pocket volumes, by John Hawkey . . . [uniform

12. MUN/P/4/49/33, 10 July 1745.
13. MUN/P/4/50/13, 3 Sept. 1746.
14. MUN/V/57/3, bursar's quarterly account to Dec. 1746.

with] the Latin Classics already published'. His confidence in the Dublin book-buyer was misplaced and the series ceased.

Edward Hill seems to have been of the opinion that Hawkey's 1747 edition of Milton's *Paradise lost* was printed at Trinity's Printing House. In the manuscript notebooks he prepared for his critical edition of the poem, compiled between 1769 and 1813, he recommends two Irish editions: 'The first was published in the year 1747, in an octavo size, by John Hawkey, the editor of some Latin classics, which issued in much purity from the press of the University of Dublin.'[15] This is an ambiguous statement as it is not clear if it is the Milton or the classics to which he is referring. J.B. Lyons, in his recent study of Hill's passion for Milton, opts for the former interpretation.[16] There is however no evidence from the book itself that it was printed at the DUP; Samuel Powell is given as printer in the imprint and none of the ornaments used was the property of the Press.

As with the Plato, Leathley was given commissions to bind many volumes of the Hawkey series of classics. McDonnell and Healy have identified a dozen volumes or parts of sets bound by his workshop, including the dedicatee, Lord Chesterfield's, copy of the Terence and a set of four bound uniformly in TCD prize bindings for Edward Wingfield, later Lord Powerscourt, awarded in Trinity term 1746. More usually the volumes turn up in modest calf stamped with the College arms. I have noted a copy of Horace given as one such prize as late as 1773.

Samuel Madden was impressed by the College's encouragement of printing and on 14 March 1748 submitted a memorial to the board suggesting an award of £50 which he was to underwrite for 'the author of the best book wch. shall every year be writ & printed in Ireland'. He proposed that the board would adjudicate, but it was diffident about its abilities in this area and apparently declined the offer. However the Dublin Society undertook to administer the premium and in 1750 it was awarded to Samuel Pullein for his translation of Marcos Vida's poems *The silk worm* and *The game of chess*, printed in Dublin by Samuel Powell. This was the first and only time the award was made, but it served as the model for the silver medals awarded for printing by the Edinburgh Society, starting in 1755.

The Printing House apparently went silent in the period from the end of the Hawkey classics to August 1753 when Leland and Stokes were granted permission to use it. The intriguing possibility that it was used for printing the eight-volume set of the first edition of the *Journals of the House of Commons of Ireland* has been suggested to me by Mary Pollard. The 778,800 sheets in this edition were printed in the period

---

15. MS 629/1 f.12.

16. J.B. Lyons, 'Milton's Dublin editor: Edward Hill MD' in his *'What did I die of?'*, Dublin 1991, pp. 40–63, at p. 46.

between March 1752 and November 1753 and issued under the imprint of Abraham Bradley, printer to the House. In fact Bradley was 'printer' in name only as there is no evidence that he had his own printing office, and he would therefore have farmed out the contract. Few Dublin printers would have had the capacity to undertake such a large commission at short notice — Samuel Powell, George Faulkner and George Grierson were the most likely candidates. Powell and Faulkner were later to give evidence before a committee of the House on the printing of the *Journals*, so they can be ruled out. Grierson was a more likely candidate and as King's printer had experience of official printing. However William Sleater was also a substantial printer and was later engaged by Leland and Stokes at the Printing House. He acted in partnership with Bradley on other occasions, and was later to print the Lords' *Journals* using the same type as used in the Commons' *Journals*. This type was from Malone and Perry's foundry and as has been seen the DUP was supplied with these. Without documentary evidence however the suggestion must remain in the realm of speculation.[17]

The first fruits of Leland and Stokes's tenure at the Press was an edition of Demosthenes' Phillipic orations with Latin translation issued in 1754. It was based on the edition of Hieronymus Wolf, the sixteenth-century classicist, and was in turn used by Joseph Stock for his edition printed at the Press in 1773. The late W.B. Stanford has pointed out that it was one of the few classical editions to come from the College during the eighteenth century that was of international importance. Demosthenes was on the undergraduate course throughout the century and Stanford felt that the orator's emphasis on liberty from a neighbouring monarch must have had an effect on those Trinity students who were themselves to become orators in the cause of liberty — Flood, Grattan, Curran.[18]

The two-volume work displays a new engraved vignette of the Printing House, again unsatisfactory in that the perspective is faulty, especially that of the columns (see E57 x 60, plate 12). The Greek text was printed in the James's fount used in the Plato. The board of the College underwrote the enterprise by agreeing on 11 February 1754 to take 250 copies 'to be distributed in praemiums'. The bursar in the third quarter of the year paid £87-10-0 for these which was 7-0 per set. Sleater advertised them for sale at 'eight shillings English, neatly bound in calf'.[19]

---

17. V. Kinane, 'A fine set of the Irish Commons' *Journals*: a study of its production history' in *Long Room*, 30 (1985) 11–28.

18. W.B. Stanford, *Ireland and the classical tradition*, Dublin 1977, 166, 207 ff.

19. Advertisement in S. Clarke's *A paraphrase of the four evangelists* (DUP 1756) at end of vol. 2.

An edition of Livy was planned in the following year. *Faulkner's Dublin Journal* for 14–18 January 1755 contains the following proposals:

> This day are published, Proposals for printing by subscription, at the University Press, T. Livii Patavini Historiarum ab Urbe Condita . . .

> I. The Undertakers of this edition propose to have the text printed with the exactest care, and with all due attention to the editions of greatest eminence . . .

> II. The whole work will be comprized in six volumes, quarto, printed with Irish types, and on a fine Irish medium paper, with maps, plans, and other pieces of engraving, both for illustration and ornament, all executed in the neatest manner.

> III. The price to subscribers will be three guineas . . . N.B. The Paris edition of Crevier is sold for six pounds, though not printed in that expensive and elegant manner in which this is proposed to be executed . . .

> Gentlemen who chuse to encourage this undertaking, are requested to send in their names and first subscription to Mr. W. Sleater on Cork-hill, or the University Printing-Office, Dublin; Mr. Cronin, in Cork; Mr. Haye, in Belfast; Mr. Ferrar, in Limerick; Mr. Ramsay, in Waterford; and Mr. Hamilton, in Kilkenny. Subscriptions are taken in at London by Messieurs Hitch and Hawes . . .; at Oxford, by Mr. Fletcher; and at Cambridge, by Mr. Bentham.

The network of booksellers taking subscriptions would seem to indicate a confidence on the part of the Printing House tenants in the scholarly worth of the DUP-printed classics. Unfortunately as with Hawkey's plans for Cicero they were proved to be too ambitious and not enough copies were subscribed for. The Press had to wait until the turn of the century to print an edition of Livy.

In 1756 Leland's English translation of *All the orations of Demosthenes, pronounced to excite the Athenians against Philip King of Macedon* was printed by Sleater at the Printing House. It was the first quarto volume that I have noted from the Press. Leland undertook the translation with the encouragement of Lord Charlemont, to whom it was dedicated. The book was issued by subscription and the subscribers' list would indicate a minimum edition of 250 copies. In fact the edition size was substantially larger as it was separately issued in London at the same time without the subscribers' list: a cancel titleleaf was printed for it with the imprint 'London: printed for W. Johnston'. There is no indication that this was the first volume of a set, but in 1760 another quarto volume was issued in London under Johnston's imprint with the title, *The orations of Demosthenes . . . volume the second.* On the evidence of the type this was printed at the University Press, but I have found no Dublin issue and there is no evidence that the titleleaf is a cancel. A third volume with the title, *The orations of Aeschines and Demosthenes on the crown,* was issued in London in 1771. Despite the fact that this work was enthusiastically received in the critical reviews and that several further editions were printed both in Dublin and London, none was issued from the University Press.

Sleater entered into a similar arrangement with Johnston for a London issue of the next work to be printed at the Press, Hugh Hamilton's *De sectionibus conicis,* published in 1758. There was another example later in the century of a DUP printing being separately issued in London with a cancel titleleaf. Matthew Young's *Enquiry into the principal phaenomena of sounds and musical strings* was printed by Joseph Hill in 1784, who also printed a cancel titleleaf with the imprint 'London: printed for G. Robinson.' Interestingly gatherings B and C in the only copy of this issue that I have seen — in Trinity's library — have been reset, suggesting that the decision to have a London issue was made only after these two gatherings had been worked off and the type distributed.

In the last quarter of 1762 the bursar's accounts record the payment of £50 to Gabriel Stokes, formerly a fellow of the College and brother of John Stokes, 'towards his editn. of the Greek tragedies'. He was paid a further £30 in the second quarter of 1765, presumably at the time the *Tragoediae selectae* by Euripides and Sophocles was issued. Although Sophocles was mentioned on the general titlepage the intended second volume containing his 'Electra' and 'Oedipus tyrannus' was never issued. A second edition was printed by McKenzie at the Press in 1794 while Stokes was still alive, and again the part-title describes the volume as 'Tomus primus'. Stokes died in 1806 and the third edition of 1820 finally dropped the pretence that there was to be a second volume. The work was a textbook for the students and the plays were on the undergraduate course from 1759 onwards and remained so into the next century. The Dublin book trade catered for the demand by printing several translated editions, including one in 1790 by Martin Tuomy, 'scholar of Trinity College Dublin', done 'from a sense of the great difficulty that usually occurs to most Junior Sophisters in reading the original'.

On 20 September 1760 the board resolved 'That the Matriculation fee of every student shall be increased 2s. 8½d. viz. the price of the duodecimo copy of the statutes'. The only edition of the College's *Chartae et statuta* that I have found prior to this date is that printed by Samuel Powell in 1735. With every student taking a copy from 1760 onwards a new edition was needed towards the end of the decade. Responsibility for its preparation devolved on the registrar, Theaker Wilder, who was paid £63-4-4½ in the third quarter of 1768 for the printing. There were two separate issues: one in quarto and the other in duodecimo, but printed from the same setting of type which had been reimposed for the smaller format. This is the only occurrence of this practice at the Press that I have discovered. There were problems in setting a correct text, and liberal cancels had to be printed. This had unfortunate consequences for the duodecimo issue — the five cancels in the larger format became a dozen in the smaller.

At the same time as the bursar paid Wilder he also paid the College binder, at this date Anne Leathley, Joseph's widow, £9-0-3$\frac{1}{2}$ for binding six sumptuous quarto copies. McDonnell and Healy have identified one of these. It is bound in red morocco with gold-tooled paper lozenge onlays on each cover. A much more elaborate binding was done for the Duke of Bedford on his formal installation as chancellor of the University on 9 September 1768, as a description of the whole ceremony in the College register records: 'And the Vice-Chancellor having taken his place on the right, when the Mace and the University Rules were laid at his feet, the Provost, assisted by the Seniors, delivered into his Grace's hand a printed copy of the College Statutes elegantly bound, promising for himself and the University all due and statutable obedience.' This binding represents a radical change in the style of the College binders. It was bound in green vellum with a panel design of red, blue and cream leather and paper onlays, all gold-tooled. The Duke's arms are painted on the upper cover, and the College's arms on the lower. Its overall effect is fussy and not a little vulgar. Leathley's binder was given another opportunity three years later when Bedford died and the Duke of Gloucester was installed in his stead. The volume bound for him, although to the same overall pattern, is a much more satisfactory artifact. It was bound in cream vellum and this time the panel design was achieved by gold fillets. The gold tooling within the panels is much freer. And as with the Bedford binding, appropriate arms were painted on the covers. Leathley was paid the enormous sum of £4-3-6 for binding this in the last quarter of 1771.[20]

Copies of the quarto statutes remained in stock for over twenty years and on 23 April 1791 the librarian could supply 'two 4° copies . . . to Provost and 2 dozen to Dr. Kearney'.[21] As the duodecimo issue sold out much more quickly it had to be reprinted in 1778. On 20 November 1777 the board accepted Thomas Leland's offer to supervise the printing of an edition of 2,000; the bursar paid him £270-16-8 for these in the first quarter of the following year. In this Leland was given the full 2-8$\frac{1}{2}$ retail price for each copy, the College not wanting to take any profit for itself.

20. McDonnell and Healy, *Gold-tooled bookbindings*, catalogue 73; for the Bedford binding see Appendix X, plates J and CV; and pp. 49–50, catalogue 74, dust jacket and frontispiece for the Gloucester binding.
21. MUN/LIB/2/1.

The same position obtained when the next edition of 2,000 ordinary and 250 fine paper copies were printed by William McKenzie in 1791. He was paid for these on 3 May at the rate of 1-1 and 1-7$\frac{1}{2}$ per copy respectively. The profit of 1-7$\frac{1}{2}$ on each copy accrued to John Waller, the senior lecturer.[22] It was not a competent piece of printing on McKenzie's part and is full of mis-signings and inserted gatherings.

Antonio Vieyra's *Animadversiones philologicae* (1779) was the first work printed by Joseph Hill at the Press. In 1776, when Provost Hely-Hutchinson persuaded the government to provide £200 annually to establish professorships in modern languages, Vieyra was appointed to the chair of Italian and Spanish. Something of a polylinguist, he compiled a grammar of Portuguese and a Portuguese–English dictionary that remained in print until the mid-nineteenth century. The board register of 9 July 1787 records his appointment as 'Teacher of the Arabic and Persic languages'. This work was a reflection of his wide philological interests. The copy presented to the dedicatee, the Duke of Leinster, in a fine green morocco binding is in the National Library.

The sheets were reissued as part of a much-expanded second edition in 1785, this time under the imprint of Luke White, but 'sumptibus Academicis'. The board had agreed to give Vieyra forty guineas on 13 November 1784 'towards defraying the charge of printing [it]' and a further £22–15–0 was paid by the bursar in the second quarter of 1785. White had engaged Daniel Graisberry to print the additional matter at his office in Back Lane. His ledger on 23 May 1785 records the following:[23]

To Printing Mr Vieyra's Dictionary	
Great Primer, & Pica 4to different Languages	
400 No. 53 Sheets & $\frac{1}{2}$ @ 15/6 per	[£]41–9–3
Alterations . . .	1–8–0
1 Cancel Leaf to former Edition of 1st. Part	3–9

There was an increasing emphasis on mathematics in the undergraduate course in Trinity towards the end of the eighteenth century, one part being Euclid's *Elements*, the first six books of which had to be read in the freshmen years. One of Joseph Hill's specialities was the printing of mathematics and in 1783 he evidently printed an edition of Euclid with some of Archimedes' theorems added. I write 'evidently' because I have found no actual copy of this printing, but have inferred its existence from the reissue of the sheets in 1785 with a cancel titleleaf with William McKenzie's imprint; the part-title to the selection from Archimedes bears the imprint: 'Ex Aedibus Academicis excudebat Josephus Hill, 1783'.

22. MUN/P/4/60/31, 1.
23. MS 10314, D. Graisberry's ledger 1777–1785, 340.

In the same year Hill undertook the most complicated piece of printing of his tenure at the Press: Joseph Fenn's *Fourth volume of the instructions given in the drawing school established by the Dublin Society*. In 1767 Fenn, a teacher of mathematics, issued proposals for printing by subscription *The instructions given in the drawing schools established in England, Scotland . . .* (Dublin: George Cecil). The response was favourable but slow. The first two volumes were printed by Alex McCulloh in 1769 and 1772; I have found no trace of the third volume and Hill printed the fourth in 1783. The latter is a small quarto of over 500 pages and is wholly mathematical in content, being substantially made up of logarithmic tables.

The highlight of Hill's Trinity career was the three-volume octavo edition of Matteo Maria Boiardo's *Orlando Innamorato* printed in 1784. As early as 30 March 1776 printed proposals for this work were issued by two TCD academics, Thomas Wilson and Matthew Young. The proposals tell us they had engaged upon the task not for 'emolument but [for] the revival and preservation of an author of . . . acknowledged merit'. The current 'taste for Italian literature', which led to the establishment of chairs of modern languages in the College in that year, was also cited. The proposals stressed that this was 'the first attempt that ever has been made in this Kingdom to publish an author in the Italian language'. (It was not; there was an *Oratione fatta 27 Sept. 1662*, addressed to James Butler, Duke of Ormonde, which was printed in Dublin in 1664.) The subscription was one guinea and the work was to be put to press when 150 had been subscribed for.

The response must have been small and when the work appeared eight years later there was no promised subscribers' list indicating that it was privately underwritten. In fact a manuscript note in one of the TCD library copies (shelfmark: OLS L–1–32) makes it clear that Edward Hill paid for it. He evidently had an appreciation of fine typography and presented copies of the Foulis Press Homer (1756–58) to Marsh's Library in 1778. Strenuous efforts were made in the Boiardo to achieve elegant typography and textual correctness. Running titles and catchwords were abandoned. *Libro* and *Canto* numbers were placed at each corner of the headline, balanced by volume number and signatures in the direction line. The work must have been very diligently proof-read as there is only one cancel in evidence, and there were no mistakes in pagination or signing — remarkable in a work approaching a thousand pages in length. It was not without reason then, if somewhat self-conscious, that the titlepage vignette depicts a harp in front of the Aldine anchor and dolphin. The edition was ill-fated however, if the near-contemporary manuscript note already referred to is to be believed. It states that 'Most of the copies of this very correct edition . . . were destroyed by fire; copies have been sold for three guineas each.' This may have been a puff to enhance the sale value because copies were reissued in 1824 with cancel titleleaves having the imprint of Harding, Triphook and Lepard, booksellers in Newcastle-upon-Tyne.

On 12 December 1776 Joseph Stock, with editions of Aeschines (1769) and Demosthenes (1773) already behind him, put forward proposals to the board for printing an edition of Tacitus, an author who figured on the undergraduate course throughout the century. The board agreed to take 500 copies of the work, to be printed in four duodecimo volumes, at 13 shillings per set. Stock resigned his fellowship in 1779 in pursuit of a clerical career — he was Bishop of Killala during the French invasion there in 1798 and wrote a first-hand account of it — and his duties must have absorbed his attention for a while because it was 1787 before the first volume appeared. However there was another reason for the delay. Warburton *et al* in their history of Dublin state that William Preston gave his poems to 'a printer' for publication, but received no money before the printer went bankrupt. They go on to relate that the printer in fact used £50 worth of paper, given him by Stock to print the Tacitus, for the poems, and that the Tacitus was not printed before his bankruptcy.[24] Preston's poems were issued under William Hallhead's imprint in 1781 and, as has been seen, Hallhead undertook the College printing in the second half of the 1770s. So it is likely that Stock gave him the paper sometime between the board's approval of the scheme in late 1776 and before Hill took up printing at the Press in 1779.

The loss of the paper must have been dispiriting for Stock and this would help account for the delay. The work was printed by John Exshaw, who finished the first three volumes in 1787 and the fourth in 1788. The College's subscription, which had been almost doubled to 950 since the original decision, was not delivered into the library until 30 July 1788, presumably shortly after the completion of the last volume. The library was by this date being used as a warehouse for the Press's output, perhaps as a means of monitoring affairs in the wake of Hill's tenure. There was an acrimonious moment next day when it was discovered that the imperfections had not been delivered with the edition, contrary to the usual practice. When these were demanded Exshaw refused to deliver them. An employee of the College bookseller, McKenzie, started to collate the sheets on 8 August. He finished on the 19th and Exshaw made good the deficiencies without dissent.[25]

Almost £550 was paid to Stock by the bursar in the third quarter of 1788 for the edition; there is no record of when the remainder of nearly £70 was paid. On the 30 August the board agreed to retail them at 16–0 per set so that McKenzie 'may receive his allowance of 12 & $\frac{1}{2}$ pr.ct. without loss to the College'. On that margin the bookseller received 2–0

24. J. Warburton, J. Whitelaw and R. Walsh, *History of the city of Dublin*, London 1818, 1211.

25. MUN/LIB/2/1.

per set, leaving a spare shilling to the College over the 13–0 per set it had paid out. Although the work was a College textbook and although on 20 November 1788 the board 'order'd that ev'ry person obtaining a Praemium for the 1st time shall take a copy of Stock's Tacitus in part of said praemium', movement of the edition was slow. Mercier in his tenure as College bookseller only bought 50 sets between 1795 and 1801,[26] while copies were advertised in the first College calendar, issued in 1833. Sufficient sheets were still in stock in the early 1860s for them to be remaindered to W.B. Kelly with other DUP editions of the classics. To these he added his own titleleaf and had them cased in cloth; he charged 6-0 for the Tacitus.

John Keill's *Introduction to the true astronomy*, first printed in Latin, London 1718, was one of the required texts on the junior sophisters' course in astronomy and natural philosophy.[27] McKenzie printed a 'seventh edition, corrected' at the Press in 1793 to meet the demand. It does not display his usual catalogue of mis-signings and mis-pagings. The only mistake he appears to have made was to forget to use signature T, which he was quick to signal in the 'Directions to the Bookbinder'. There are twenty-six folding engraved plates in the work, the second highest number in the eighteenth-century output of the Press. Twenty-five copies of this work were supplied to Zachariah Miller in 1803 'for vending in America' and for which cancel titleleaves were printed (see p. 80). I have seen a copy in private hands that was made up of the sheets of McKenzie's edition with a cancel titleleaf having the imprint, 'Dublin: printed by William Porter . . ., 1802'; this may well be one of those supplied to Miller. In 1806 what remained of the edition was collated and there were found to be '75 sets of Letter Press & only 28 sets of perfect plates'.[28]

In 1793 McKenzie also printed 'a new edition, with superb cuts' of James Thomson's *Seasons* 'at the Accademic [*sic*] Press', no doubt part of the output of which 'Tim Tickle' was so critical. This is the only work of literature in the English language I have found that was printed at the DUP in the eighteenth century. It is unique in another respect: it is the only occurrence in the output where etched plates were used for illustrations.

Although R.E. Mercier was appointed as College bookseller (and presumably printer) in October 1795 at the time of McKenzie's dismissal, it was not until 1797 that he issued anything from the Printing House. In that year he printed George Miller's edition of Longinus and the first volume of John Walker's edition of Livy; the second volume of Livy followed in 1799. Walker's work was to be one of the few DUP classics of

26. MUN/LIB/10/175a, 12 Oct. 1795 – 29 Oct. 1801.

27. R. Burrowes, *Observations on the course of science taught at present in TCD*, Dublin 1792, 41–2.

28. MUN/LIB/2/1, 26 Mar. 1806.

international importance, but as the last five volumes were to be delayed until after Mercier's bankruptcy in 1807, largely because of friction between the editor and the College, detailed consideration of it has been postponed until the next section.

On 31 October 1798, with the stock of Buxtorf's Hebrew grammar (1782) evidently nearing an end, the board 'agreed to publish at the College expence Docr. Fitzgerald's Hebrew Grammar'. Fitzgerald was professor of Hebrew and vice-provost. The printing was finished by the third quarter of 1799 when the bursar paid Mercier £104-12-7$\frac{1}{2}$ for it. The edition consisted of 500 common paper and 48 fine paper copies which gives a unit production cost of nearly 3-10, very high for an octavo volume of just over 200 pages; of course the Hebrew text was the cause of this high charge. The board had already agreed on 31 August to take the whole edition, stipulating that 'the College shall have a profit on the sale of 3$\frac{1}{2}$d. p. copy, & the Printer of 3d. & that the price of the books to the students shall be 4s. 4d. in blue paper'. By 'Printer' here the board must have meant Mercier in his role as bookseller, because as printer he would already have had a profit on the money paid for the printing. From recorded wholesale purchases by him in 1807 he was charged 3-9$\frac{1}{2}$;[29] to that he would have added his own profit as bookseller and also the College's profit to bring the retail cost up to the 4-4 agreed by the board. He evidently held on to a substantial part of the edition until 31 October 1801 when the library minute book records that 'Mr Mercier sent in, sewed in blue paper, twenty seven bundles, viz. 6 corrected & 21 not corrected . . . each bundle containing twelve setts.' An examination of the volume reveals there were four single leaf cancels in it, each marked with an asterisk. (Mercier consistently signalled cancels in this way for the works he printed at the DUP.) The volume also contains a frontispiece of the Hebrew alphabet engraved by George Gonne, a local craftsman. The edition was sold out by 1813 when another edition was printed at the Printing House.

Evangelium Secundum Matthaeum is the final work to be noted for this century. Although it was actually issued in 1801, all the records show that the bulk of the work was done before 1800. The genesis of this edition went back to 1787 when a fellow of the College, John 'Jacky' Barrett, started to decipher the faint ground text in a palimpsest in the library. On 7 March the board agreed that 'The MS . . . to be lent to Mr Barrett for the purpose of transcribing such parts of certain fragments of a very ancient MS of the new Testament discover'd by him in it, as he shall be able to make out.' As it turned out it contained 295 verses of St Matthew's Gospel in twenty-two fragments, together with some other biblical texts.

It was four years later, on 5 February 1791, that the board took the decision that the discovery warranted the publication of the text: 'Agreed

29. MUN/LIB/2/1, 9 Nov. 1807.

. . . that a correct edition of the Greek Testament shall be published (under the direction of Dr. [George] Hall and Dr. Barrett) noting the various readings of the Codex Montfortii & the fragment discovered by Dr. Barrett; an account & facsimile of each being prefixed.' It was to be one of the most important College publications of the eighteenth century and one of the most ambitious undertakings of the Press. Between March 1796 and the following March James Kennedy was engaged to engrave the plates for the facsimile. He was paid £1–2–9 for the engraving of each page and 3-6 per plate for the copper, which for sixty-four plates gave a total of £84.[30] Surprisingly information on the letterpress printing is absent from the muniments. The format chosen was royal quarto, making it the most handsome of the DUP printings during the century. It retailed at a guinea in boards.

The biblical scholar S.P. Tregelles deciphered some more of the text and published a supplement to this edition, London 1863. The copy of Barrett's edition in Trinity's library (shelfmark: T.f.43) was annotated in 1854 by Tregelles to show the text brought 'to light in the MS by chemical application'. T.K. Abbott elucidated even more and published another complete edition in the Dublin University Press Series in 1880.

From the identified eighteenth-century output the following analysis can be worked out.[31] The first point to record is that about 75 per cent of the output of the DUP was of original or newly edited works. This was in contrast to the output of the general Dublin trade of the time, where the majority were reprints. Because of the variability in information found it is difficult to be too precise, but about 40 per cent of the works printed at the DUP were paid for or subsidised by the College. In round figures 60 per cent were written or edited by the academics, and 50 per cent were textbooks for the students. As regards subject matter classics not surprisingly headed the list at 34 per cent — indeed 'Classics' was used as a generic heading in the College booksellers' accounts to denote the Press's output. However mathematical/scientific works were not far behind at 28 per cent, and surprisingly evenly distributed despite the increasing emphasis on science in the undergraduate course towards the end of the century. Works in other fields each account for less than 10 per cent of the total output.

Evidence of edition sizes range from 150 to 2,000, the most popular sizes being 500 and 1,000, with 2,000 being the next most frequent. These appear rather high for the specialised output of a learned press, but as the evidence is fragmentary the true picture might well reveal smaller edition sizes predominating. There were only three formats used: octavo (67 per cent), quarto (17 per cent) and duodecimo (16 per cent). Cancels occur in a third of the output, quite a normal proportion for eighteenth-

---

30. MUN/P/4/73/33.
31. Kinane, 'DUP in 18c.', 106–11.

century books. Greek type occurs in 35 per cent of the books, reflecting the strong classical bent of the Press. The favoured text type size was pica followed by long primer.

The middle range of paper sheet sizes naturally predominated, with crown heading the list for both quartos and octavos. As a consequence the DUP quartos tend to be small. There was one occurrence of a pot sheet used in an octavo format — an edition of Zachary Cradock's *Sermon upon the providence of God* (1784) — which gives it the look of a duodecimo. A demy sheet was the favourite size for duodecimos, although McKenzie went as low as foolscap for his pocket edition of Epictetus in 1794. Dutch paper predominated in the first-quarter century of the Press. Irish was also prominent and to a lesser extent French. The use of French paper took off dramatically during the 1760s, being used in over half the printings. This reflects the easing of French restrictions in the second half of the century.[32] The choice of Dutch and Irish declined inversely, although Dutch continued to be favoured for the fine paper states. In the last decade of the century, with the French product cut off by the Revolutionary wars, the way was open for the expanded use of the native product. Fostered for decades by the imposition of heavy duties on foreign imports and by grants from parliament, Irish manufacturers rose well to the challenge, supplying half the needs of the College Press between 1791 and 1801; the rest came from England and Scotland.

At this stage, at the close of this period, it is as well to consider how the output of the Press was marketed. The 60 per cent of printings that the College had no financial interest in need not be our concern — their underwriters provided their own distribution. Prior to the 1780s no bookseller seems to have been officially appointed as 'College Bookseller'. Various *ad hoc* arrangements were made for distribution, judging by the evidence of the imprints of the output. Helsham's *Lectures* in 1739 was printed by R. Reilly, who was solely a printer and therefore it was 'sold by G. Risk, G. Ewing, and W. Smith, booksellers in Dame-street'. William Sleater, who was engaged as printer on several occasions throughout the 1750s and 1760s, provided the outlet in his shop on Cork Hill. Thomas Ewing provided the retail outlet for the printing done by Samuel Powell in 1769 and by Robert Marchbank in 1773; neither of these printers had his own bookshop. William Hallhead could have provided the necessary outlet at his shop in Dame Street for the printing commissions he undertook in the 1770s.

It was only in the 1780s that we come across mention of an 'official' bookseller. In the August 1783 issues of the *Dublin Evening Post* William McKenzie styled himself 'Bookseller and Stationer to the University' in a

---

32. D.T. Pottinger, *The French book trade in the ancien régime*, Cambridge (Mass.) 1958, 307.

series of advertisements, and to underline this his shop in Dame Street was called the 'College Arms'. In 1788, as we have seen above in the case of Stock's Tacitus, the chain of distribution was that the printed sheets from the Press were brought to the library, where they were collated by employees of the College bookseller. The library acted as warehouse for the output and copies were released as and when needed by the bookseller. And if the Tacitus was indicative of the system, the bookseller was allowed $12\frac{1}{2}$ per cent on the retail price. Official College bookselling was not very lucrative however. For example R.E. Mercier, in the years after his appointment as bookseller in 1795, sold on average less than 140 DUP printings per year.[33]

Evidence extracted from the muniments (mostly the bursar's vouchers and quarterly accounts) show that the College expended just over £3,000 between 1737 and 1800 on the works that it sponsored from the Press. On the other hand figures extracted largely from the bursar's annual accounts indicate that the income from the sale of their publications between 1753 and 1800 was only £1,300. It is evident that the College made a substantial commercial loss on its publications. However the primary purpose of an institutional university press is not to make money, but to print scholarly books worthy of publication. Judging by the slender output of the DUP in the eighteenth century the College had still some lessons to learn.

33. MUN/LIB/10/175a (*verso*).

5

The Nineteenth Century:
R.E. Mercier: 1795–1807

The printing trade in Ireland was decimated in the wake of the Act of Union of 1800. The removal of the parliament to London meant the loss of huge contracts for official publications, political pamphleteering was curtailed and some of the wealthiest book-buyers spent long periods out of the country. The extension of the Copyright Act to Ireland in 1802 had a more far-reaching effect by doing away with the reprint business, which had sustained the Irish book trade throughout the eighteenth century. In the words of the Dublin bookseller, William Wakeman, the printing trade was 'almost annihilated'.[1] John Gilbert estimated that book production in the first half of the century decreased by 80 per cent.[2] This resulted in the widespread emigration of booksellers and printers especially to America. The printers that remained relied on jobbing for the most part in the early decades of the century, and those that were official printers to institutions were privileged indeed.

None the less Trinity was not immune from the general malaise and Richard Edward Mercier, the College's official printer and bookseller, was required to print only a handful of books at the DUP in the early years of the century: John Barrett's edition of *Evangelium Secundum Matthaeum* in 1801 (noted in the previous chapter), a third edition of Thomas Elrington's *Elementorum* of Euclid (1802); *A sermon* by George Miller (1803); a prize poem by Patrick Sharkey, *Poema heroicum* (1804); an unfinished *New translation of the Psalms, from the original Hebrew*, translated by Matthew Young, Bishop of Clonfert, and issued in 1806; and a textbook of Juvenal and Persius's *Satyrae selectae*, edited by Elrington (1807). Young's *Psalms* is of some interest because it is often found without a titleleaf and consequently catalogued as 'c.1800'. The

---

1. Evidence given in 1821 to the Commissioners of Inquiry into . . . the revenue arising in Ireland; quoted in Charles Benson, 'Printers and booksellers in Dublin 1800–1850', in R. Myers and M. Harris eds, *Spreading the word: distribution networks of print 1550–1850*, Winchester 1990, 47.
2. John Gilbert, *History of Dublin*, Dublin 1854, vol. I, 188.

TCD library copy, however, has a title with Mercier's imprint dated 1806. It was being printed by subscription in quarto and octavo formats during Young's lifetime and was worked off up to Psalm 142 and the notes to no. 149 before his premature death in 1800. A post-1830 manuscript note in the British Library copy (C.37.e.7) states that it was never published and that efforts were made by TCD to have it suppressed 'on account of its supposed heterodoxy'. How much substance there was in this allegation is not known, but when the board of the College voted on 9 May 1801 to pay £600 to Mrs Young for the bishop's manuscripts, which specifically excluded the translation of the psalms, the professor of Hebrew, Gerald Fitzgerald, dissented because it appeared to him that they were 'less perfect than he at first supposed them to be'.

The bursar's annual accounts show that sales of the output of the Press were equally sluggish. Sales of 'Classics' were put down at a nominal £10 or £20 in the early years of the century and rose to a high of £55–12–0 in 1806.[3] This state of affairs did not necessarily perturb the College as it did not consider itself involved in the 'trade' of books. A stock of over 300 works was sold to Zachariah Miller in 1803 'for the purpose of vending in America', but on condition that the 'ex Aedibus Academicis' imprints be cancelled and a general book trade name substituted.[4] The same attitude obtained at Oxford where the 'want of vent' in the early nineteenth century did not upset the delegates of the University Press because they did not want to be considered mere businessmen.[5]

The board did review the revival of the publication of John Walker's edition of Livy, of which two volumes — out of a proposed six — had already been issued in 1797 and 1799. On 10 January 1801 it debated the matter. The edition had considerably exceeded its budget, having already cost £700, and in a heated exchange a proposal was made to force Walker to finish the task 'without any further recompense'. However, perhaps realising that this work was one of the few classics of more than insular importance it had sponsored, it

> Resolved that there was a stipulation originally entered into with Mr Walker, that he should publish an edition of Crevier's Livy with such alterations as he thought right for the sum of 100 guineas.
>
> Resolved that Mr Walker having completed the first vol. . . . on a plan superior to that originally prescribed and the Board having approved of the alteration & having adjudged an additional compensation; and having acted in like manner on the publication of the second volume: the Board is now of opinion that it is desireable that the edition of Livy should be completed on this approved plan.

3. MUN/V/58/1.
4. MUN/LIB/2/1, 25 Jan., 8 June 1803.
5. Peter Sutcliffe, *The Oxford University Press: an informal history*, Oxford 1978, 3–4.

Despite this agreement the project languished, probably as a consequence of disputes over editorial payments. In the meantime Walker, ordained in the Church of Ireland, had become involved with a Calvinist sect called the 'Separatists' and found it increasingly difficult to function as a clergyman within the Established Church. Matters came to a head and on 8 October 1804 he offered to resign his fellowship, but the provost mysteriously refused to accept it and insisted on his expulsion from the College on the following day.[6] Towards the end of the month Walker was approached to see if he would continue with the Livy. His conditions for agreement, set out in a letter of 29 October to the board, included payment at 100 guineas per volume, a figure which had formerly been rejected by the College.[7] The board, mindful no doubt of the ridicule it would have been open to in the scholarly world if the edition had been abandoned at that stage, agreed on 3 November. It would be another five years, however, before the third volume appeared.

There is further evidence that efforts were made by the College to boost the output of the Printing House. In 1801 the Secretary of State for Ireland, Lord Colchester, sent a dispatch to the Duke of Portland directing that Trinity be given letters patent to print bibles, prayer books and other liturgical works, lucrative privileges that the English and Scottish university presses already enjoyed.[8] There is no trace of any separate patent having been granted to the College although the privilege was recognised in the next patent afforded to the King's printer in Ireland in 1811, as will be seen.

An Act of 1775 (15 Geo.III c.53) allowed the universities in England and Scotland perpetual copyright in certain works under special conditions, the main ones being that the work be granted to the university by the author, that it be printed on the university's own presses and that the profits be used for the advancement of learning. In 1801, by the 41 Geo.III c.107, this privilege was extended to TCD.[9] Although this provision remained in force until the middle of the present century there is no evidence that the College ever exercised the privilege.

Because of the paucity of output of the Press little is known of its operations in these years. As and when College printing needed to be done Mercier would have sent along men to open up the Printing House and do the work. This was troublesome and as a consequence it was sometimes easier to have jobbing work done in the general trade. Such

---

6. *Dictionary of national biography*; Walker's own account of the expulsion in his *Essays and correspondence*, London 1838, vol. I, 205–206 is not very illuminating.

7. MUN/P/1/1280a.

8. Historical Manuscripts Commission, *Fourth report*, London 1874, appendix, 345. The Bishop of Oxford, John Randolph, no doubt canvassed by a worried OUP, anxious about the effects on its own output, wrote to Colchester on 31 August seeking to have the patent confined to Ireland.

9. Carter, *History of the OUP*, vol. I, 367; TCD, *Chartae et statuta*, Dublin 1844, 346–7.

was the case with summonses for the College Corps, which were printed at Trinity's expense by D. and J. Carrick in 1803.[10] At times of pressure Mercier, like McKenzie before him, would have used the facilities of the Printing House to do work for himself. The College, mindful of past experience, reminded him in 1802 'not to print anything at [the] College Printing House without communicating it'.[11]

Something is known of the employment conditions of the workmen at this date because a printed broadsheet was issued in 1800 entitled *Prices of printing work, agreed upon by the employers and journeymen of the City of Dublin, commencing January 1, 1800*.[12] This is the earliest evidence we have of such an agreement in Ireland, and there is only one earlier in England, that for London in 1785. The Dublin agreement is obviously closely based on that of London — the rates are very similar — but differs in so far as it included rates for jobbing work and excludes any rate for weekly 'establishment' wages. It includes the following:

Compositors:

Art. I: common matter to be paid at the rate of $4\frac{1}{2}d.$ per 1,000 ens [a comp's notional hourly rate of output]; (art. XIII states that minion and nonpareil were to be paid at $5d.$ and pearl at $6d.$ per 1,000).

Art. III: notes to be paid at the rate of 1-0 per sheet.

Art. IV: languages other than English — 1-0 per sheet extra.

Art. V: Greek and other dead characters — 1-0 per sheet extra for each character.

Art. XI: mentions that all extra work at the stone to be paid at the rate of $6d.$ per hour.

Pressmen:

Art. I: octavo format, with page of 21 by 38 pica ems, considered the basic unit.

Art.II: $4d.$ per hour paid for work on the basic unit; (there is no mention of the 'token' of 250 sheets which was the notional hourly rate for presswork).

Art. III: formes with notes paid at $4\frac{1}{2}d.$

Art. XI: jobbing of 250 and under at $4\frac{1}{2}d.$; 500 at $4d.$; above 500 at $3\frac{1}{2}d.$

Arts. XVI–XVII: higher rates paid when better qualities of paper used.

Art. XIX: ruled or red work, $3\frac{1}{2}d.$ per hour extra.

10. MUN/V/57/8.

11. MS 4960, Thomas Elrington's memorandum book, 16 Oct.

12. There is a copy pasted in MS 10315. See also Ellic Howe ed., *The London compositor*, London 1947, 247, 253.

This and some earlier agreements at the end of the eighteenth century indicate the start of organised labour within the trade. An Amicable Benefit Society existed for printers at this date, having been founded in 1793, but this was disbanded in the early years of the century. It did however lay the foundations for subsequent organisations of journeymen. It is traditionally believed that the Dublin Typographical Provident Society was founded in 1809, but evidence given in 1838 to a parliamentary commission by Matthew Ryan, secretary to the DTPS, would suggest otherwise. He stated that a society of printers existed in Dublin in 1818, but that it was too small and fizzled out some years later. He went on to say that during the depression in the latter part of 1825, when there was high unemployment in the trade, the printers resolved to form themselves into a society for their mutual benefit. This may well have been the true foundation of the DTPS. The fact that the Society's earliest archive dates from 1827 would seem to substantiate the later foundation date.[13]

At this early date matters were fluid and there was little enforcement of work practices, or agreement on entry into the trade or length of apprenticeship. This can be seen from the case of William Price, who was a student in Trinity in the years 1800 to 1805. He used to frequent the Printing House, where he 'imbibed a taste for the business, and being a classical scholar was employed in setting up Greek works'.[14] The difficulty of finding specialist compositors was a recurrent problem at the DUP as it was in the trade in general. Frank Thorpe Porter, when a student in Trinity in the early 1820s, used to set Greek works in the evenings in the Grafton Street printing office of his father, William Porter.[15] Such casual employment would not have been countenanced by the trade in the latter half of the century.

Although there was little work being done in the Printing House the board took the opportunity on 8 February 1800 'to purchase a font of arabic types, which it appears is now to be had in England for £30'. There is no evidence of any further additions to the plant of the Printing House during Mercier's tenure. Mercier's business succumbed in the general slump in trade and he was declared bankrupt in the first half of 1807. On 3 May the board 'Agreed to purchase from the assignees of Mr Mercier types & other materials for the printing business now in the Printing House to the value of [£411–3–4½]'.[16] The inventory of the equipment had

---

13. *Second report from the select committee on combinations of workmen*, London 1838, 105–106; Brian Donnelly, 'Records of the Irish Graphical Society' in *Cló*, 2/3 (April 1985) 2.

14. J.D. White, *Sixty years in Cashel*, Cashel 1893, 7; Price went on to set up his own printing business in Cashel.

15. P. White, 'The printing trade in Dublin: commencement of the nineteenth century' in *Irish Printer*, IV/3 (Oct. 1908) 10.

16. Value left blank in the board's register but given in bursar's vouchers MUN/P/4/91/29, 8 June 1807.

been valued on 24 April by William Porter and Nicholas Kelly, and the type weighed by Daniel Graisberry.[17] The assignees, John Dumoulin and Robert Marchbank, kept Mercier's bookselling trade going and the College continued to do business with the firm until Mercier died on 3 April 1820.

17. MUN/P/1/1298–1299.

6
The Graisberrys: 1807–1842

On 6 June 1807 the firm of Graisberry and Campbell signed a £500 bond upon their appointment as University printers, whereby they

> agreed and proposed to execute and perform in the Printing House of the said College (of which they are to have the use and possession) all such printing work only as . . . [TCD] shall give them leave and permission to execute for the use of the said College only, and that they will faithfully and truly account . . . for all such paper, types, printing presses, manuscripts, books, materials and things now in the said Printing House (a schedule of which is hereunto annexed) and which from time to time hereafter shall be entrusted to them . . . and that they will when thereto required for that purpose surrender and deliver up the quiet and peaceable possession of the said Printing House and all the materials therein belonging to the said College . . .[1]

The important points to note here are that the College, which now owned all the equipment in the Printing House, was limiting printing there to its own requirements — Graisberry and Campbell were not to have the same flexibility to use the facilities for general trade printing as McKenzie and Mercier had — and that there was no period of tenure stipulated. Graisberry and Campbell, whose printing office was at 10 Back Lane, were one of the largest printers in Dublin. The business was founded by Daniel Graisberry, Senior (1740?–1785). His widow Mary carried on the business, and in 1790 entered into partnership with her son-in-law Richard Campbell. Daniel Graisberry, Junior, opened a printing, bookselling and stationery business in Capel Street in 1799 and the *Dublin Directories* indicate that he continued there until 1807. He must then have taken over the Graisberry side of the partnership, and it was he who signed the bond in 1807.

The schedule of the materials in the Printing House, mentioned in the bond, was in fact the inventory made in April by Mercier's assignees,

1. MUN/P/1/1300.

countersigned by Graisberry and Campbell on 6 June.[2] This is worth setting out in some detail as it provides a picture of how the Printing House was equipped at the start of the nineteenth century. The type, all of which had belonged to Mercier, was valued at £364-0-10 (after additions for shipping and duties and certain deductions):

		lb at	s. d. per lb
4 cases	double pica greek	255	2-2
8 cases	english greek	440	2-2
2 cases	long primer greek	82	3-3
2 cases	brevier greek	40	$5-0\frac{1}{2}$
3 cases	pica hebrew with nonpareil points	75	2-2
1 case	long primer hebrew	23	4-4
16 cases	english roman, Wilson's	1,090	1-1
14 cases	english roman, Parker's	524	$6\frac{1}{4}$
16 cases	pica roman, Caslon's	391	1-0
24 cases	small pica roman	1,322	1-3
12 cases	brevier roman	275	$2-6\frac{1}{2}$
2 cases	four line pica	52	1-0
2 cases	double pica	48	1-0
2 cases	black pica	37	1-0
	metal scabbarding	331	1-0

The total weight was 4,654 lb or just over twice the estimated weight of the stock in 1744. It is interesting that none of this type was considered to be the property of the College before being purchased from the assignees of Mercier. The original english greek bought from the James foundry in the 1730s, and which Philip White thought survived into the twentieth century, did not apparently survive into the nineteenth. And there is no mention of the arabic fount sanctioned for purchase by the College in 1800.

The rest of Mercier's equipment had been valued at £69-18-5 and consisted substantially of:

	£ - s. - d.
14 greek cases	4 - 18 - 7
68 sycamore cases	11 - 1 - 0
23 oak cases	3 - 14 - 9
4 fount cases	1 - 6 - 0
2 cripplers to support the greek cases	4 - 2
1 type case rack	1 - 19 - 3
21 chases and 5 loose crosses for do.	11 - 19 - 4
2 large standing screw presses in the Wareroom, with crow bars, 6 boards and 48 glazed press papers	14 - 1 - 0

2. MUN/P/1/1298–1299.

4 double column galleys	12 - 8
9 mahogany octavo galleys	18 - 0
2 oak galleys	4 - 8
1 large mahogany broadside galley	16 - 3
2 iron candle sticks, jointed for printing presses	6 - 6
2 composing sticks	13 - 0
1 very large composing stick	$11 - 4\frac{1}{2}$
2 pair of points	1 - 1
1 lye brush	6 - 6
2 brayers and 2 iron slices	5 - 5
1 pair of stock cards	7 - 7
1 deal nest of drawers to hold sorts	3 - 0 - 0
1 do. with doors	2 - 17 - 11
25 paper and letter boards	4 - 1 - 3
1 peel	$2 - 8\frac{1}{2}$

There is a note to say that quoins, furniture, brass rules and suchlike were not charged for.

The remainder of the equipment belonged to the College:

A pump cistern & lye trough lined with lead
Two printing presses in complete order
Two oak presses for holding type cases with two locks & one key
A large imposing stone, oak frame & six drawers
A paper stand
Two horses & banks
Four oak frames turned pillars & drawers
Six deal stands, one with a top . . .

It is likely that some of these items were survivors of the original furnishing of the Press in the 1730s and 1740s. For example the 'large imposing stone, oak frame & six drawers' was probably the 'table for ye composing stone with 6 drawers' supplied by John Connell in 1737. Of all the above equipment, however, nothing remains today except perhaps for the 'two oak presses for holding type cases' (see plate 15), which were donated by the DUP in 1975 to Trinity Closet Press, a hand-press run by the department of Early Printed Books in the library of the College.

In May 1807 both printing presses were overhauled by Michael Murphy, smith and printing-press maker of Bull Alley, in preparation for Graisberry and Campbell's takeover:

Smiths woorke dun for the Colledge printing Offis
To cloathing the spindel of 1 press with a new
    brass box for do £3 - 8 - 3
To repering 1 pair of ribes 17 - 2

15. One of two oak presses for holding typecases, now in Trinity Closet Press; perhaps the only survivors from the eighteenth-century equipment of the DUP.

To repering 1 spit	6 - 6
To 2 new friskites	1 - 2 - 9
To 1 set of bras crampes	1 - 0 - 0
To repering 1 pair of tinpans	5 - 5
To 12 pair of pointes	13 - 0
To 1 set of girths and buckels	11 - 4 $\frac{1}{2}$
	8 - 4 - 5 $\frac{1}{2}$

The bill for the second press, not quite so colourfully spelled, came to £7-11-3$\frac{1}{2}$.[3]

It is significant that the College decided to commission such expensive refurbishment rather than invest in the new iron presses, which were much more efficient than the wooden common presses and available for £63 at this date.[4] Trinity was obviously being cautious because of the depressed state of the trade. The tenor of the times is summed up in John Walker's scathing preface to his *Philosophy of arithmetic* (Dublin 1812): 'In bringing this volume through the press, I have encountered difficulties, which might not be expected to occur in a City — the metropolis of Ireland, and the seat of a learned University. Some of those difficulties have been such, as necessarily make the price of the work higher than is generally affixed to volumes of equal bulk: — though it may be remarked that, if a little more of the modern art of printing had been employed, the volume might easily have been swelled to twice its present size, without any increase of the matter.' To underline his scepticism about the printing trade the work contains a full page of errata!

Trinity's caution is reflected in the output of the Printing House during Graisberry and Campbell's tenure which ended in 1820. I have identified thirty-one such works, of which over 80 per cent were textbooks for the students — editions of the classics, Brinkley's *Astronomy*, Stack's *Optics*, and suchlike. Most of the rest related to the College and included an edition of the *Statutes* in 1813 and Whitley Stokes's *Descriptive catalogue of the minerals in the systematic collection of the museum of TCD* in 1818.

The only work of broader scholarly significance was the continuation of Walker's edition of Livy. Having been moribund for several years this project was resurrected shortly before the appointment of the new University printers. In December 1806 it was agreed to pay the editor at the rate of £150 per volume. He was paid £75 'on account' for volume three in July 1807, and by October 1808 Graisberry and Campbell had worked off twenty sheets.[5] At this stage the board had second thoughts

---

3. MUN/P/2/193/36, 41.

4. James Moran, *Printing presses*, London 1973, 52.

5. MUN/P/4, bursar's vouchers: -/89/50; -/92/39a; -/96/13.

on the project, ostensibly because of delays on Walker's part. This is evident from a letter written by him to the registrar on 17 December 1808:[6]

> . . . I do not mean to receive the £85 if the work is to be discontinued. But, in that case, I would be obliged by the Board's ordering a few perfect sets of the three volumes . . . I have only to add, that I think it very likely the printer has represented himself as delay'd by me for the index; & this is not the fact. It was only last Tuesday night that I received from him the revise of the penultimate sheet of the text; & the next morning I gave him copy for the index. I have indeed then these three weeks past been oblig'd to work double tides at forming the index, in order to prevent any delay of the press: but for this hurry I have been indebted to Mr. Graisberry's obstinate negligence, whom I could not prevail on this year past to send me a fair copy of the sheets as they were work'd off . . .

Despite the prickly nature of dealings with Walker, to its credit the board stuck with the work and volumes followed with regularity over the next few years, reaching completion with volume seven in 1813. In November of that year James Rainsford was paid £11-7-6 for 'gathering, collating and making up in setts the edition of Walker's Livy'.[7] He did this work in the library which as we have seen was used as a warehouse for the Press's output.

The various College muniments provide a detailed account for this work, the most ambitious edition printed thus far at the Press.[8] From an initial projected cost of £105 for editing, Walker was actually paid the enormous sum of £1,006. No wonder the board had grave reservations about proceeding with it. Mercier printed the first two volumes in an edition size of 1,550 copies (500 coarse, 1,000 middle, 50 fine) and charged on average £3-12-6 per sheet for composition and presswork. Graisberry and Campbell printed the remainder in a smaller edition of 1,050 copies (1,000 ordinary, 50 fine) and charged £4-2-8 per sheet. Proof-reading costs were high because of Walker's insistence in 1804 that 'the College Printer . . . employ a well-qualified press-corrector to correct the sheets before they are sent to me'.[9] The editor had evidently done all the proof-reading of volumes one and two, but for subsequent volumes separate payments for reading to named individuals are recorded. T. Phillips and Thomas Harding charged 11-4 per sheet for reading volume

6. MUN/P/1/1304.

7. MUN/LIB/11/12/9, 17 Nov. 1813.

8. See Kinane, 'DUP in the 18th century', 86–93, plate 14 for detailed breakdown of the figures.

9. MUN/P/1/1280a.

three, while Matthew Sleater charged 16-3 per sheet for subsequent volumes, the increase perhaps justified by the fact that Sleater's charges were for first and second proofs. The total proof-reading costs came to just over £100. The cost of the paper was nearly £600.

The estimated total cost of the edition was thus £2,574 for the 8,350 volumes printed, which is 6-2 per volume or £2-3-2 per seven-volume set. The retail price, given in A. Milliken's *Catalogue* of 1829, was £2-16-0 per set in boards. Allowing a retail discount of $12\frac{1}{2}$ per cent to the bookseller these figures indicate that the College would have had an $10\frac{1}{2}$ per cent profit if the edition sold out. The evidence is that in fact the work sold poorly. Volume one was reissued in 1827 'in usum scholarum', while there were enough sets in stock in 1862 for them to be remaindered to W.B. Kelly, who reissued the work under his own imprint.

According to Warburton, Whitelaw and Walsh's *History of the city of Dublin*, Walker

> proposed to superintend the University Press in the publication of . . . [other classics], for an adequate salary. We regret that this proposal was not complied with. It would be rendering an essential benefit to classical students if new editions would supply the want of books which is frequently felt and complained of even in the University, and supersede those few which issue from the Dublin press, which are as disgraceful, particularly the Greek, by the inelegance of the type and coarseness of the paper, as by the gross inaccuracy of the text. We counted 47 typographical errors in a Dublin edition of Lucian, some of which rendered the text altogether unintelligible. The classics formerly edited in Trinity College were remarkable for their beauty and correctness.[10]

From this it would appear that it was felt the DUP should have been setting the textual and typographic standards for the rest of the Dublin printing trade, while in actual fact, as the authors assert later in their *History*, 'it has, however, long since ceased to work'.[11] This latter claim, although exaggerated, was in some measure true. I have found no publications from the Press in the years 1816 and 1817, and only one for 1815. This inactivity led to two unusual claims to be allowed to use the Printing House. In 1815 James Macartney, professor of Anatomy and Chirurgery, in search for more space for his growing number of students, suggested to the board that the Printing House, 'unused, . . . locked up and falling into decay', could be saved by turning it into an

10. J. Warburton, J. Whitelaw and R. Walsh, *History of the city of Dublin*, London 1818, vol. 2, 837n.
11. ibid. 1158–9.

Anatomy House. The board, not unnaturally, declined.[12] Edward Hill, who had had the use (and abuse) of the Printing House in the 1770s and 1780s, was still alive and well in 1816 and had just completed the editorial work for his long-planned edition of Milton's *Paradise lost*. He had intended setting up a printing press in his home, so as to closely supervise its production, but could not do so as he had to move house. On 22 January he wrote to the College asking for permission to produce it in the Printing House, 'which now I am informed, lies waste and unoccupied'.[13] There is no record that the board obliged him, and given the experience of 1784, it is unlikely that Hill was granted permission.

The criticism implied in these requests must have regalvanised printing at the Press and in 1818 at least seven works were produced. The College was obviously optimistic about the future of the Press because in the same year it decided to replace its wooden presses with iron models:

Bot. of Walker & Co. 102 Dean Street Soho
Oct. 14 To 2 royal Stanhope printing presses with tympans
    and friskets platten & tympan wrenches . . . [nos.] 206 & 209 £150

With other charges for wrenches and carriage and an allowance for discount, the total cost was £160-19-3.[14]

Not all College printing was done at the Printing House. As had been the case under Mercier's tenure it was sometimes easier to have jobbing done by the general trade. Thus J. Carrick printed tender forms for meat supply in 1816.[15] Bookwork too was occasionally commissioned from outside printers. Walter Stephens's *Notes on the mineralogy . . . of Dublin* was printed in London in 1812 by direction of the board at a cost of £54-11-2 British for 350 copies.[16] And the College sometimes found it easier to take a portion of a general trade edition than to risk commissioning its own edition at the Printing House. This was the case in 1816 when the College bought 200 copies of Locke's *Essay concerning human understanding* from Brett Smith, a Dublin printer.[17]

At this stage it is worth considering the question of Trinity's privilege to print bibles and prayer books, and to claim drawbacks on duty paid for paper used in them and certain other classes of books. Interpretation of these privileges caused the College endless problems and legal opinion on the matter was sought on several occasions in the 1820s,

12. Alexander Macalister, *James Macartney . . .: a memoir*, London 1900, 105–106.
13. MS 10325/2, letter from Hill to the registrar.
14. MUN/P/4/174/49–49a.
15. MUN/P/4/158/2, 22 June 1816.
16. MUN/P/1/1353a–b.
17. MUN/P/4/158/43, 26 April 1816, at a cost of £110-16-8.

1830s and 1840s. As has been mentioned no letters patent were granted to TCD to allow it to print bibles and other liturgical works, although sought for in 1801. The privilege was however recognised in the King's printer patent granted to George Grierson on 5 August 1811:

> Reserving nevertheless unto . . . [TCD] a concurrent right of imprinting in Ireland, Bibles, and . . . books of Common Prayer and singing psalms . . . Psalters, books of the New Testament . . . primers having catechism therein, and all other books which are, or may be, commanded by lawful authority to be used in divine service . . .[18]

Interestingly the patent also recognises the right of the Oxford and Cambridge University Presses to publish and sell similar works in Ireland.

In 1818, by the 58 Geo.III c.41, which was enacted on 5 July, Trinity was afforded a drawback of 3*d.* per lb on best paper used in printing these privileged books 'or in the printing of any books in the Latin, Greek, oriental, or northern languages . . .' ('northern languages' refer to Anglo-Saxon, Old Norse etc.). This brought Trinity into line with the other privileged presses in Great Britain and Ireland. The King's printer in Ireland had this right to drawbacks since 1816 (56 Geo.III c.78), but only on the religious works. The King's printers in England and Scotland as well as the Oxbridge university presses had had the right on both categories under 34 Geo.III c.20 (1794). All the English and Scottish university presses had had the right on the secular works since 1711 (10 Anne c.19). Trinity was quick to claim its entitlement. On 27 January 1819 it was refunded £23-5-6$\frac{3}{4}$ on 1,719 lb of paper, and also £33-5-0 on 2,457 lb at an unspecified date about this time. There is no indication for which works the claims were made.[19]

Philip White gave an account of the process of claiming the drawback in his article on the Press in the *Irish Printer* for August 1908 which, although remote in time from the events, was obviously based on first-hand knowledge and worth recording here:

> When ready to print a book, the manager of the Press notified the officers of excise, who attended and weighed the paper before the stamped wrappers were removed; the scales and weights to be provided by the manager. When the edition was printed off, the officers again attended and weighed the edition unbound and in sheets, and gave a certificate specifying the name of the book, the size, number of copies, and weight for which the drawback was

---

18. Quoted in appendix to John Lee, *Additional memorial on printing and importing bibles,* Edinburgh 1826; Grierson's patent was granted for 40 years from 7 Mar. 1806.
19. MUN/P/4/176/37, 27 Jan. 1819; MUN/P/4/179/11, undated.

allowed. The manager of the Press made a declaration on the back of the certificate, stating that the book was printed for the University, and that no bookseller or other person had any share or interest therein.

The author of an article in the *Dublin Penny Journal* of 10 October 1835 stated that Trinity's privilege to print bibles etc. had never been exercised. In fact it had; and in a way that was to bring the College into conflict with the King's printer. In November 1813 £250 was paid to Andrew Wilson, 'Stereotype Office, London', for plates of the New Testament. Wilson wrote: 'the testament is undergoing another revision; and as I have a set of plates here, those that are erroneous shall be corrected here, and sent over with a competent person to rectify the bad letters . . .' Further corrections had to be made to these plates in 1815 and these were carried out locally by Timothy Bates, who was employed at the King's printing office in Rathfarnham. He had to wait until January 1817 for payment of his fee of £15 of this.[20] Whoever set the text is not indicated, but it is unlikely to have been done at the DUP.

On 6 February 1821 Grierson and Keene, the King's printers, wrote to the Commissioners of Excise stating that 'within a very short period [after the enactment in 1818] the College has exercised its privileges respecting the printing of the New Testament, and transferred their right of drawback on paper in a manner which we conceive is contrary to the intention of the legislature, and directly opposed to the practices of the universities in England, and in its operation calculated to effect our rights and privileges . . .' They went on to say that Trinity had given the 'profit of the drawback' to Mrs Watson of Capel Street with whom they had contracted to print the testaments. They asked that the drawback be withheld. (Grierson and Keene had only issued an edition of the New Testament the previous year, coincidentally printed from plates supplied by Andrew Wilson in London.) The commissioners wrote to the provost shortly afterwards seeking an explanation, but none was forthcoming. Grierson and Keene kept up the pressure and in another letter of 9 March they set out further reasons for objecting. If Trinity's action over the testaments was correct then it could also have printed editions of the classics for booksellers, and claimed the drawback even though the publisher had bought the paper. The King's printers were well informed because they could write that Trinity 'did not even pay for the press work of these Testaments but received from their overseer a consideration for the use of their stereo type plates, for each edition he puts to press'. They had made representations to the provost whose aloof reply was 'that the College did not intend to become traders'. Grierson and Keene stated that

20. MUN/P/4/137/27, 22 Nov. 1813; MUN/LIB/13/14a, letter from T. Bates to Provost Elrington, 17 June 1816; MUN/P/4/160/1, 13 Jan. 1817.

it was only as bona fide traders that Trinity could claim the drawback. The College eventually replied to the charges on 12 December and in a blanket defence stated that the manager of the Press had 'performed all the requisites of the Act' and that the drawback should therefore be paid. Unfortunately no outcome of the matter has been traced, but perhaps the fact that the wording of the next Act on paper excise (5 Geo.IV c.55 (1825)) as it related to TCD is not substantially altered would indicate that the College successfully saw off the challenge.[21] None the less the privilege to print bibles was not a right that Trinity asserted very often. There are no DUP editions listed in Henry Cotton's *Editions of the Bible . . . in English* (Oxford 1852) or in T.H. Darlow and H.F. Moule's *Historical catalogue of printed editions of the English Bible 1525–1961* (London 1968). And there is only one New Testament printed at the Press at this period in the College library, a small 24mo with the royal arms on the titlepage done by R. Graisberry in 1838 (see plate 16). It must have been a later issue, however, because some sheets are watermarked '1844'.

The bursar's vouchers for this period provide some indication as to who the suppliers to the Press were. Richard Freeman, a paper merchant of 25 Cook Street, provided substantial quantities of printing medium paper in 1807 at a cost of £1-2-9 per ream. For 150 reams purchased in 1810 the cost had risen to £1-9-0. This must have proved too much because in 1812 the account was switched to James C. Hospital, again another local paper merchant, who provided a similar paper for £1-7-0 per ream.[22] Much of this paper was for Walker's Livy. The fine paper copies were printed on a super writing medium paper that cost £4-10-0 per ream.[23] The watermark 'CMD' in this state indicates that it was manufactured at the paper mill of Christopher McDonnell at Killeen, Co. Dublin.

Type came from predictable sources and followed the named suppliers on the 1807 inventory. The Dublin typefoundry run by Stephen Parker supplied small quantities of brevier and small pica at 2-6 and 1-4 per lb respectively in 1807.[24] Caslon and Catherwood in London shipped much larger quantities during 1808 and 1809: 627 lb long primer at 3-4 per lb and 858 lb pica at 2-10 per lb. At the same time 1-3 per lb was allowed on 658 lb of old metal returned.[25] In 1808 the Wilson foundry in Glasgow sent small quantities of greek type in english, small pica and brevier sizes, at 4-0, 4-8 and 7-4 per lb respectively.[26]

21. MUN/P/1/1690/3–8.
22. MUN/P/4/92/8, 28 July 1807, 100 reams; MUN/P/4/102/13–13a, 19 Jan. 1810, 150 reams; MUN/P/4/127/9–9a, 27 June 1812, 54 reams.
23. MUN/P/4/112/9a, Dec. 1810 etc.
24. MUN/P/4/92/31, July – Aug. 1807.
25. MUN/P/4/98/2a, b, c, 31 Mar. 1808; MUN/P/4/97/3–3a, Jan. 1809.
26. MUN/P/4/104/13a, Feb., July 1808.

THE

NEW TESTAMENT

OF OUR

LORD AND SAVIOUR

JESUS CHRIST:

TRANSLATED OUT OF

The Original Greek;

AND

WITH THE FORMER TRANSLATIONS DILIGENTLY
COMPARED AND REVISED,

BY HIS MAJESTY'S SPECIAL COMMAND.

DUBLIN:
PRINTED AT THE UNIVERSITY PRESS,

BY R. GRAISBERRY.

1838.

16. Despite the date some sheets are watermarked '1844'.

Although there was considerable demand generated by the College for engraved work at this period — illustrations for books, diplomas, testimoniums, prize plates — the Printing House had no rolling press and all this work was farmed out among the many engravers in the city. The Henecys, George Shea, Brocas, George Gonne and George Waller were all used.[27] There are very few references to binding and George Mullen is the sole binder mentioned.[28]

Next to nothing is known of the workers in the Printing House in this period. As always there were difficulties finding compositors with the necessary skills to tackle the specialist output of the Press. T.R. Robinson apologised for the errors in his *System of mechanics*, printed at the DUP in 1820, by stating that 'the printing of the formulae requires a certain familiarity with symbols, which is not commonly possessed by compositors'. John Walker's insistence in 1804 that a well-qualified proof corrector be employed may have been responsible for the succession of independent readers engaged subsequently and who were not employees of Graisberry and Campbell. As they were paid independently by the bursar we know their names. I have already mentioned Thomas Phillips, Thomas Harding and Matthew Sleater in relation to the Livy. The latter is the only one we know anything about. He was the son of William Sleater, one-time College printer, who graduated from Trinity in 1778 and took an M.A. in 1781. He did a considerable amount of reading for the Press during Graisberry and Campbell's tenure and from payments to him a representative table of charges for proof-reading can be built up, starting at the cheapest for English language texts, rising through the complexities of mathematics to the dizzy heights of works in Hebrew and Greek. All are octavo works printed in small pica or long primer types and the charges were per sheet:[29]

Stack's *Optics* (1811)	1-7$\frac{1}{2}$
Hamilton's *Lectures* (1807)	2-2
[McLaurin's?] *Algebra* (1814)	5-0
Brinkley's *Astronomy* (1812)	6-6
Plutarch's *Vitae* (1814)	11-4$\frac{1}{2}$
Xenophon *Anabasis* [Latin trans.] (1810)	16-3
Hebrew grammar (1814)	16-3
Xenophon *Anabasis* [Greek text] (1809)	£1- 2-9

27. MUN/P/4/97/10, 11 Feb. 1809, Henecy & Co.; MUN/P/4/100/30a, b, 11 Feb. 1809, G. Shea; MUN/P/4/118/17, mid–1811, Brocas; MUN/P/4/136/14–14a, 7 Oct. 1813, Anne Henecy; MUN/P/4/148/7–7a, 11 Mar. 1815, G. Gonne; MUN/P/4/171/71, 5 May 1817, G. Waller.

28. MUN/P/4/172/12, 2 Apr. 1818, 100 Demosthenes; MUN/LIB/11/16/12, 16 Dec. 1819, 200 Stock's Lucian.

29. MUN/P/4, bursar's vouchers: -/115/13; -/95/8; -/143/31; -/128/15; -/111/26; -/137/10; -/99/12.

Some of the fellows of the College were also paid for proof-reading the output of the Press, as for example Henry Griffin for the 1818 edition of Stock's Aeschines/Demosthenes, and Samuel Kyle for the 1819 edition of Stock's Lucian.[30]

Something is known of the wages of the journeymen in the general Dublin trade at this time. Advances on the scale of 1800 in the piece rates to journeymen were negotiated in 1808, to take effect from 1 July, and promulgated in a printed broadsheet.[31] Richard Campbell was one of the signatories, so it can be presumed the rates were paid by Graisberry and Campbell. For the comps some of the more important clauses were as follows: an increase of $\frac{1}{2}d$. per 1,000 ens was allowed for ordinary matter bringing it to 5d.; other languages in roman type to be paid at $5\frac{1}{2}d$.; extra was to be charged for greek and 'other dead character'; MS copy (as opposed to a reprint from printed copy) was to attract a $\frac{1}{2}d$. extra. For the pressmen the rates were to be: $4\frac{1}{2}d$. per token for octavo or larger formats in long primer or larger type; smaller formats and smaller type were to be paid proportionately more, down to 18mos in nonpareil which were to be paid at the rate of $6\frac{1}{2}d$. per token; short run jobs below 750 copies were to attract more money, presumably to compensate for the time lost in make-ready; ruled or red work added an additional $3\frac{1}{2}d$. per token.

These agreements are indicative of a shift in the structure of the Dublin trade at this time. Formerly the trade was regulated, albeit in a loose and often toothless fashion, by the stationers' guild, the Guild of St Luke, which included both masters and journeymen. The guild went into a rapid decline in the early years of the nineteenth century. Only a minority of those eligible became members thus ensuring its demise, which happened in 1841. The organisation of the masters and journeymen into two distinct bodies, as indicated in the 1800 and 1808 agreements, set the course for the trade henceforth. As we have seen, the journeymen founded various societies for their mutual support and protection, culminating in the DTPS, which through an unbroken chain of succession is now the Irish Print Union. The DTPS was a somewhat shadowy body to begin with because of the illegality of any 'combinations' which acted in concert to set conditions of employment and to protect them. But in the 1830s it evolved into a powerful body within the trade which forced the master printers into 'combination' to resist it.

The 1800 and 1808 agreements are complicated documents because there are so many variables involved — language of text, size of type, format, edition size etc. For these same reasons it is difficult to get a

30. MUN/P/173/16, 7 Nov. 1818; MUN/P/4/178/18, 5 Nov. 1819.
31. *Prices of printing work agreed upon by the employers and journeymen of . . . Dublin commencing July the first 1808* [Dublin 1808]; text reproduced in *Irish Book Lover*, 20 (1932) 35–8, from copy in the Dublin Typographical Provident Society (now the Irish Print Union).

perspective on the scale of prices Graisberry and Campbell charged Trinity for printing. However the following table, compiled from the bursar's vouchers, gives some indication of the inclusive costs for composition and presswork per sheet:[32]

Type	Format	Number	Cost	Work
english with long				
primer notes	8vo	250	£1-7-8	Elrington's *Sermon* (1807)
small pica	8vo	500	£1-12-0	Hamilton's *Lectures* (1807)
pica	8vo	750	£2-6-0	Leland's *Chr. rev.* (1818)
english & long primer	8vo	750	£2-9-0	Stack's *Optics* (1811)
long primer	12mo	500	£2-10-8	Burlamaqui's *Principles* (1811)
small pica	8vo	1,000	£2-16-0	Brinkley's *Astronomy* (1813)
(Latin language)		1,000	£3-1-8	Miller's Longinus (1820)
small pica, side &				
bottom notes	8vo	1,050	£4-2-8	Walker's Livy (1808 ff.)
(Greek language)		750	£4-4-0	Xenophon *Anabasis* (1811)
(mathematical)		250	£4-4-8	McLaurin's *Algebra* (1810)
(Greek language)	8vo	1,500	£4-6-0	Stock's Aeschines (1818)
(Greek language)		2,000	£4-12-0	Stock's Lucian (1819)
(Hebrew language)		1,000	£6-12-0	*Hebrew grammar* (1814)

Occasionally the vouchers give a breakdown of the composition and presswork costs. For example for the Livy composition was £3-8-0 (82 per cent) and presswork 14-8 (18 per cent). The comparable figures for the Xenophon were composition £3-10-0 (83 per cent) and presswork 14-0 (17 per cent).

Although Mercier was declared bankrupt in 1807 his assignees continued the bookselling side of his business and 'Mercier and Co.' continued to be the official College bookseller. When Mercier died in 1820 Richard Milliken was appointed in his place. He was obliged to enter into a bond of £500 'as such a bookseller is intrusted with the custody of large quantities of books'; he was 'also intrusted with the care of the stamps and dies of the said College used for the purpose of marking the books belonging thereto'.[33] These latter probably refer to the stamps used to put the College arms on the books that were given as prizes to the students, rather than to library books. Because there were recurrent complaints about the difficulty of purchasing the Press's publications other booksellers were also used to distribute them. For example in 1808 William Porter was given 250 copies out of an edition of 700 of Elrington's Euclid, while Mercier took 220.[34] In Cork about the

32. MUN/P/4, bursar's vouchers: -/91/12, Elrington; -/95/8, Hamilton; -/172/13, Leland; -/115/13, Stack; -/115/13, Burlamaqui; -/135/7, Brinkley; -/182/10, Longinus; -/96/13, Livy; -/117/10, Xenophon; -/101/7a, McLaurin; -/173/15, Aeschines; -/179/10, Lucian; -/142/10, Hebrew.

33. MUN/P/1/1486, 6 May 1820.

34. MUN/LIB/2/1, 8 Aug. 1808.

year 1820 John Bolster, of 7 Patrick Street, described himself on his tickets as 'bookseller to His Majesty and to the University Press of Dublin'. This distribution network was abandoned on 11 November 1820 when the board agreed 'to rescind the resolution heretofore entered into by which classics were issued to booksellers other than the College Bookseller; the cause for which it was thus adopted not existing [now] . . .'. What the cause was is not revealed, but perhaps Milliken was proving to be more efficient than Mercier. The booksellers at this date were allowed $12\frac{1}{2}$ per cent on the retail price.[35]

Because the library acted as warehouse for the output of the Press the librarian was warehouse-keeper, in the sense that he kept an account of the stock. Thus in the library muniments will be found lists of the Press books supplied to the bookseller. One such list shows that between January 1807 and February 1812 Mercier received £811 worth of books.[36] The bursar's annual accounts show that the business thereafter was growing, rising to £221 in 1813 and £307 in the following year.[37] There was also a steady business in copies of the College *Statutes*, a copy of which each matriculating student had to buy, but these were provided direct to the undergraduates and did not go through the official bookseller. There is also evidence of the sale of remainders in 1815: 'The board agree to sell for ready money to booksellers the books which they have in quires, not however selling less than a bundle as now made up.'[38]

Interestingly Graisberry and Campbell are given as College printers in the *Dublin almanacks* only up to 1814. For 1815 Daniel Graisberry's name alone is given. However the name 'Graisberry and Campbell' continued to appear in University Press imprints and the partnership is listed in the *Dublin Directories* at Back Lane up to 1820. Perhaps it signifies that from 1815 Campbell managed the Back Lane business and Graisberry the College Printing House. This interpretation would appear to be borne out by a memorial presented on behalf of Ruth Graisberry, Daniel's widow, in 1822, as will be seen. Campbell's name disappears from the imprints sometime in 1820. Thus for example the imprint to the third edition of Stack's *Optics* reads: 'printed at the University Press by D. Graisberry, 1820'. He did not have time to accomplish much more — Homer's *Iliad* (vol. 1, 1820), T.R. Robinson's *A system of mechanics* (1820), another edition of Helsham's *Lectures* (1822), and an edition of the College's *Statutes* (1822) — before he too was carried off early in 1822. His widow Ruth, left with five daughters and an aged mother who was also deaf and blind, all unprovided for, determined to try and retain the office of University printer. She submitted a memorial to the board to that end:

35. MUN/LIB/2/1, 29 June 1811, 27 Jan. 1813.

36. MUN/LIB/2/1, at back of volume.

37. MUN/V/58/1.

38. MS 2374, 31 Jan. 1815, note by T. Elrington.

. . . being possessed of the presses, types, and materials for printing and having proper and respectable work people in her employ, she feels herself fully capable with the aid and assistance of several of the most respectable master printers in Dublin, who have kindly and voluntarily come forward and signed a paper undertaking to aid and assist your memorialist if necessary to carry on the business . . . [She] humbly submits her forlorn and destitute situation to the commiseration of this board . . . and entreats they will be pleased to continue her as their Printer, so long as their business shall be properly attended to and executed.[39]

The accompanying paper was indeed signed by twenty of the leading figures in the Dublin book trade — A.B. King, R. Milliken, J. Porter, Hodges & McArthur, N. Kelly & Son, Chambers & Halligan, W. Wakeman, B. Dugdale, B. Smith, W. Folds & Son, J. Cumming, M.N. Mahon, R.M. Tims, W. Porter, C. LaGrange, W.H. Tyrrell, G. & J. Grierson, A. Watson, C.W.P. Archer and another (illegible):

. . . knowing the anxiety the deceased always evinced to place the business committed to his care on the most respectable footing — to enable himself to do so, and remove everything like a suspicion of dividing his attention from its concerns, he broke up his private establishment in Back Lane thus hazarding much of his business, yet willingly risking the consequences to discharge conscientiously his duty towards you and allow himself more effectually to furnish the office in a manner worthy of so great an establishment.

This would seem to confirm that Daniel Graisberry moved his business from Back Lane to work full-time from the College Printing House, probably in 1814 or 1815, although he would have had to divide his attention between the two when Campbell disappeared in 1820. (Of course the small size of College printing would not have necessitated full-time manning of the Printing House, so Graisberry must have been doing his own printing there as well (contrary to the 1807 agreement) — it was not all virtuous service to the College.)

The petitions were successful. The bursar, James Wilson, made an inventory of the College's equipment in the Printing House on 7 March at the time of the transition:[40]

1. A press for holding letters and some type called Eng. Greek.
2. A smaller do. and some types double pica Greek.
3. A desk for writing.
4. Stereotype testament.
   The above in Mr Gibson's office.

39. MUN/P/1/900–901, undated.

40. MUN/P/1/1529.

5. 4 letter frames.
6. A small press for sorts.
   in the compositors room.
7. A press rack for holding cases.
8. 105 cases with letter in them.
9. A case rack (4 in one).
   in the small closet.
10. A large imposing stone.
11. 2 case racks (2 in one).
12. A [illegible] case rack.
13. 2 iron printing presses (Stanhope)
    in the press room.
14. A sink, trough & ley trough.
15. A paper stand.
    in the cellar.
16. A wash hole.
17. A squeezing press.
18. A long shelf [illegible].
    in the ware room.
19. 7 letter boards with pye on them
    in the paper closet.

. . . The above inventory taken with the assistance of Mr Gibson, March 7, 1822.

The 'Mr Gibson' referred to was Ruth Graisberry's manager, Robert Gibson. He sent a note to the bursar on 11 March to say that the College owned both the 'standing book presses' (Wilson's 'squeezing press') in the wareroom.[41] The only major discrepancies in Wilson's inventory, when compared with that of 1807, are that there is no mention of chases or galleys. From the listing of the various rooms there is no evidence to suggest that the layout of the building was any different from that conjectured for the 1730s.

Ruth Graisberry ran both the Back Lane and College businesses for only a year or so because the 1824 *Dublin Directory* shows that she had moved out of 10 Back Lane and P. Cummins, a brass founder, is listed in her stead. She continues to be shown in the *Dublin Almanacks* as College printer until 1842 and the address given is the Printing House in the College. In 1842 the partnership of Graisberry and Gill is listed, and in the following year M. Gill alone is listed as College printer. This introduces us to a man who was to become the pivotal figure in the history of the Press and one of the leaders in the mid-nineteenth-century resurgence of the Irish book trade.

41. MUN/P/1/1530.

Michael Henry Gill was born in 1794, son of Henry, a woollen draper of Skinner Row and a United Irishman. It is thought that the family name was originally McGill and that they came over to settle in King's County (today County Offaly) during the plantations of Queen Mary's reign. Originally Presbyterian, it seems that Henry Gill converted to Catholicism and that branch of the family has remained so since. In 1813 M.H. Gill was apprenticed to Graisberry and Campbell at the late age of nineteen, 'presumably indoor', Philip White says, 'as it is stated that a fee of £100 was paid with him'. When he became a journeyman after his seven-year term he continued to work for Daniel and later Ruth Graisberry. It was his responsibility to open the Printing House whenever the College needed work done.[42] He must have shown his potential early because within a few years he was in a position to become a partner in the business. He bought a half-share in the business on 1 March 1827, paying Ruth Graisberry £219-19-1$\frac{1}{2}$ for his share of the printing equipment, and a further £138 on account for his portion of the value of the printing stock. This partnership lasted until 8 May 1837 when Gill paid her £362-0-10$\frac{1}{2}$ for her share of the printing equipment, and also undertook to pay her £100 per year for her goodwill (see plate 17).[43] There are no sources to show what further interest Ruth Graisberry took in the affairs of the University Press, but the available evidence would seem to indicate that from May 1837, although she was still nominally University printer and the Press's output continued to appear with her name in the imprint, M.H. Gill was wholly responsible for the business.

The Irish book trade was still in deep recession in the 1820s and what output there was was typographically poor. In 1820 Henry Grattan suggested to Longman and Co. in London that a new edition of his father's speeches should be printed in Dublin. On 16 November the firm wrote in desperation to Richard Milliken, asking him to try and reason with Grattan: 'We need not tell you that it is almost impossible to have a handsome book printed in Dublin, either as to paper or printing: at least

---

42. This account of Gill and his background is based on P. White in the *Irish Printer* (Aug. 1908) 6; J.J. O'Kelly, 'The house of Gill', unpublished typescript, early 1950s, MS 10310, 3–4; Thomas Wall, *The sign of Doctor Hay's head*, Dublin 1958, 122–3; information from Michael Gill, great–great–grandson of M.H. Gill and managing director of Gill and Macmillan. Much of the material which O'Kelly and Wall used in their works was destroyed in a fire in September 1979. The bulk of the remainder was presented by Michael Gill to the TCD library in 1988 (MSS 10308–17) and in 1990 (MUN/DUP/22/1–3).

43. MUN/DUP/22/1/1–3, 21, 174. O'Kelly, 'House of Gill', 3–4, apparently not having seen this account book, misinterprets an insurance policy of 1837, since destroyed, by which Gill paid for the half-share in the printing equipment and undertook to pay the annuity for the goodwill, and takes it to mean that this was the start of the partnership. Wall, *Sign of Dr. Hay's head*, 123, fudges the issue by saying, 'In 1837 he acquired by purchase half of the type and printing materials then in joint ownership.'

we have never seen such.'[44] The state of the publishing trade was equally bleak. The success of Selina Bunbury's *A visit to my birthplace*, published by Curry in Dublin in 1821, later led the author to claim that 'Its immediate success was admitted to have been the first cause of reviving the publishing business from the decline consequent on the change in the copyright law by the Act of Union'; ' . . . its publication at the period was considered an enterprise for a Dublin publisher'.[45] (In fact her bestseller was an isolated incident and the true revival did not happen for another two decades, as will be seen.) When the general business slump hit in 1826 the book trade was thrown into further despondency. A committee had to be set up to provide relief for unemployed printers and some even ended up breaking stones on government outdoor relief schemes.[46]

Gill was frustrated by these conditions, as is evident from a letter he wrote on 5 February 1828 to C.R. Elrington, accompanying an estimate for printing an edition of 10,000 copies of the *Book of common prayer*. The letter is worth quoting in full because it sets out Gill's philosophy on university press printing, publishing, and distribution, and indeed on the Irish book trade in general:[47]

University Press Office
Feb. 5th, 1828

Sir,
I enclose you an estimate of the expense of printing 10000 copies of the 32mo edition of "The Book of Common Prayer," which I shewed you, and also take the liberty of adding a scale of terms on which they might be supplied to the booksellers.

It is, Sir, time that the press of this country should begin to exert itself, for during many years those of the Universities of Oxford, Cambridge, Glasgow, the King's Printers of England and Scotland, have teemed with various and beautiful editions of the Book of Common Prayer, the Psalms, Bibles and Testaments in different languages, &c. — the press of this country alone has remained inactive, and suffered the kingdom to be supplied with <u>millions</u> of copies that should have issued from our own printing offices. It has long been my opinion, that this superiority is chiefly owing to a want of sufficient energy and perseverance on our parts to enter into a competition with our more enterprising and successful neighbours. But if the art of printing is destined again to revive in this country, where so

44. Reading University, Longman Archive I, 101, no. 89.
45. Quoted in the *Irish Book Lover*, VII (1916) 105–106.
46. Benson, 'Printers and booksellers in Dublin', 51.
47. MUN/P/1/1581–1582.

proper — so natural — for the 1st. effort to be made, as at the <u>Press of the University of Dublin</u>. For this purpose, (at least I am not aware of any other) the Government, in an act passed in the 58th. of Geo. 3 (and re-enacted in the 5th. of his present Majesty) granted a drawback of the duty paid on paper that would be used in the printing of the above-mentioned works, and others, at the Press of this University. That its Printing Office could be fully employed, with advantage and credit to the College, in this line of printing I have not the smallest doubt, provided that proper means for accomplishing the object were resorted to. For my part I would be most happy to be permitted to add my humble efforts in promoting so laudable an undertaking, and feel sufficient confidence that editions could be produced at this Press fully equal in every respect to any published in England or Scotland. In order to insure success the following arrangements should be made. I wd. select the best and most durable types that can be procured in Scotland, where the art of type founding has arrived to a degree of excellence that can hardly be surpassed — the paper should be equal in every respect to that of the English and Scotch editions; — and the best compositors and pressmen employed. And as correctness should be considered a primary object, I would use the following necessary means for obtaining it, (subject of course to any alterations that you wd. be so kind as to suggest.) The <u>first proof</u> wd. be read in the Office, and the errors marked carefully corrected. This reading cannot in general be expected to have any greater effect, than to enable the conductor of a printing office to place the proofsheet in the hand of a corrector in a manner that he need not be ashamed of, for the mechanical details of a printing establishment occupy his mind so much, as to unfit him for bestowing on it the <u>undivided attention,</u> so absolutely necessary to enable one to detect the errors which lurk in a proof-sheet. The <u>second proof</u> should be sent to a person employed to read for the Press — likewise a <u>third</u> and both carefully corrected — at this stage <u>the drudgery</u> of the correcting department wd. terminate. I wd. then suggest the propriety of a proofsheet being placed in the hands of a member of the College, who wd. not only be competent to detect any fundamental errors that might have passed thro' previous editions, or originated in this, but would act as a censor of the College Press during the progress of each edition, and the printer should not be permitted to put the sheet to press until his signature be attached to it. Previous to its going to press care should be taken that the typographical arrangements remained undisturbed during the various corrections, that the spacing is even and that the lines, letters, and pages are perfectly straight and regular, &c. &c. Then it is "ready for press." The pressroom and warehouse departments, should then be attended to with the utmost vigilance.

The manner of bringing the work to market should next be considered, with attention, as the success or defeat of the whole undertaking rests mainly on the way which this is done. As I but join my opinion with that of men, who, as experienced traders, I hold in respect, I hope I may not be deemed too officious in making some observations arising from an anxiety that if the project under consideration be commenced, that nothing should be opposed to it that might prove fatal to its success. I would therefore take the liberty of suggesting that the College should not suffer any monopoly to exist with respect to this branch, at least, of the works which may issue from its Press, but permit the trade to be open to all who are willing to purchase on the conditions contained in the scale marked no. 2 (or any other on a similar plan that the College may think proper to adopt) if this be done, the demand will be general, and the sales great, but if there be any ground for supporting that one bookseller is favoured more than another it will excite among the rest a jealousy so strong as to be the means of stifling the undertaking at its birth. A short time ago I was induced to sound the leading booksellers on the probable exertions they might be induced to make if this line of printing was commenced (with a view of soliciting the College to give permission to its Printer to proceed with a Prayer Book, in case it was not itself inclined to do so). I received every assurance of a zealous cooperation on their parts (particularly from the house of Curry & Co. Sackville St., who bespoke at once 2000 copies) and obtained orders to the amount of one-third of the edition even previous to the type being bespoke on which it is to be printed; — but on conditions, that they should be dealt with in a fair and liberal manner, — or in other words, that no bookseller should have any advantage over another, further than what might be obtained by the quantity purchased; and as an inducement to proceed quickly, some said that they wd. regulate their orders from the other side in such a manner, as to have none of their stock on hands when the College edition comes into the market.

Therefore, in order that nothing should arise to interrupt this good understanding, I would take the liberty of suggesting, that the works should be issued to the booksellers thro' the medium of an agent, specially employed for that purpose, and paid by a commission on the sales.

In the infancy of the undertaking (that is, during the printing of one or two editions) there wd. not be a necessity to employ a regular agent, for the following reasons: — 1st. Every unnecessary expense should be avoided in this stage; — 2ndly. A large portion of the edition is already bespoke; — 3rdly. There are none who would watch over and assist in its advancement to maturity with such anxiety, as those who feel the most interest in its success. Therefore the books, when printed, might remain in the warerooms of the Printing Office, or those attached to the Library, and we would deliver them out to the solvent members of the trade, and hand over the payments to the bursar immediately on receiving them.

As the number of editions wd. increase, a regular agent should be appointed by the College, who, on giving security to the amount of £- for a faithful and zealous discharge of his duty, should open a warehouse in a central part of the city. This person should be of industrious and active habits, and possess a perfect knowledge not only of the trade of this country, but also that of England and Scotland. He should not be connected with any bookselling establishment whatsoever, but be solely occupied in the sale of the College works to the trade, and also be completely under the control of the University, and act under the denomination of "Agent for the sale of Bibles, Testaments, Prayer Books, &c. printed at the Press of the Dublin University."

This establishment might be used hereafter as an effectual and economical channel for issuing to the trade generally the works of individual members of the College, who might wish to retain a property in them. And it would also in some time gain a certain influence over "The Press" thro' the medium of its advertisements (the usual patronage of the newspaper department) that would be advantageous to persons connected with the College Press whose works have suffered, and may hereafter suffer, by their not being placed in a conspicuous manner before the public. In fact it is incalculable the advantages that would flow from apparently so small a source, not only in a pecuniary point of view, but as regards the welfare of the country. — Your printer wd. be fully and respectably employed, and thousands of hands at present idle, will thro' this means, gain employment in the various departments of printers, readers, paper makers, bookbinders, &c. &c.

I shall not, Sir, attempt to occupy your time further than to express a wish, that, if the trouble and inconvenience attending the Office would not exceed the interest which I have reason to feel convinced you take in the success of the undertaking, you might yourself be induced to patronize this first edition, as "Censor of the University Press," and "Editor".

I am, Sir,
with much respect
Your very humble and obt. servant,
M. Gill

Rev. Doctor Elrington

N.B. This day, since writing the above, I received an order for two thousand copies from Westley & Tyrrell, Sackville Street.

The accompanying estimate set out the projected costs (here paraphrased):

10,000 copies of 32mo *Book of common prayer*

Composition: $9\frac{1}{4}$ sheets, nonpareil
and pearl at £12-10-0 each	£115-12- 6
Presswork about £8-15-0 each sheet	83- 2- 6
Extra for ruled calendar	5- 0- 0
Pressing each sheet between glazed	
boards at 2-11 per ream	10- 0- 0
Corrector	10- 0- 0
	£223-15- 0
200 reams medium paper at 18-11 each	180- 0- 0
Wear on type 10% of cost	25- 0- 0
	£428-15- 0
Deduct drawback on paper at about 4-6 per ream	45- 0- 0
	£383-15- 0

(It is strange that for all Gill's attention to detail some of his calculations are wrong, as for example the presswork and the pressing of the sheets.) Gill included the terms that would be afforded to the booksellers:

2,000 copies	1-0 each
1,500	1-1
1,000	1-2
500	1-3
250	$1-3\frac{1}{2}$
100	1-4

Therefore 10,000 copies sold wholesale at on average 1-2 each would raise £583-6-8. This represents a profit of just over 50 per cent.

Gill was not the only one to identify the failure to provide a proper distribution network for the Press's output as a major weakness. A reviewer in an 1828 issue of *The Christian Examiner* mentioned the fact that English reviewers ignore Irish publications and referred to Walker's DUP edition of Livy in particular. This elicited a response from 'Observer' in the following issue which provides a damning description of the College's publication practices. He stated there was no copy of the work available in England:

> On mentioning this to a bookseller . . . I was informed, that so far from being surprised by this he had no hesitation in saying that, with the exception of the College publisher, there was not a copy in the possession of *any bookseller in Ireland* . . . The sale of the publications issued by the University of Dublin, has, for some

reason I am unacquainted with, been confined to one person, and
when other booksellers wish for any of the University publications
they must send cash to the full amount of the selling price of the
book, of which they may not receive payment for many months . . .
[;] . . . were all books offered to the trade on the same terms as the
publications of our University, I may venture to say, there would not
be many booksellers' shops in the United Kingdom.

He went on to say that, since the College does not advertise its publications, it would be a miracle if the English reviewers came to hear of
them: 'he will see advertisements [in the magazines] of books printed in
London, Oxford, or Cambridge, in Edinburgh or Glasgow, but he will
remain in ignorance that the University of Dublin has a press, and if he
think of the existence of such an institution, he will probably smile as he
remembers the ill-natured epithet, "the silent sister"'.[48] The terms offered
to the general booksellers were the subject of consideration by the Dublin
Booksellers' Society on 23 January 1834, when it was resolved to send a
letter to the provost on the matter. Even the College porters could offer
better service than the bookshops, as was recorded in the brief given to a
delegation of the Society on 25 July 1835 which was to wait on the
provost to 'lay before him the course then being pursued by certain
College porters in promising a remission of fines to those students who
purchased books from them'.[49]

Gill's manifesto and such adverse publicity may well have spurred on
the College to consider in detail the utility and responsibility of having a
university press because in 1829 Edward Willson was evidently asked to
visit and make a report on the workings of the Oxford and Cambridge
university presses, and to make recommendations for the Dublin
University Press. (Willson was a Dublin tea and sugar merchant and had
no obvious book trade connections, so he was an unusual choice for the
task.) His report is contained in a letter of 1 January 1830. He found that
at Cambridge the printing privileges were exercised by the University;
the profits went into general funds and the results were poor. At Oxford
the University exercised its privileges in partnership with its printer; the
profits were ploughed back into the Press, thus subsidising valuable
works that would not otherwise have been published. Not surprisingly
Willson suggested the OUP as the model for Trinity. He enclosed a sketch
and description of the new printing house at Oxford, mentioning that
there was room for 200 printing presses and for a steam engine — a rather
grandiose model for the Dublin Press with its two printing presses!
Willson also provided a description of the current practices at the DUP
and significantly he says that the facilities were 'freely used by the

48. *The Christian Examiner*, VI (1828) 211, 420–23.
49. O'Kelly, 'House of Gill', appx. B, XIII–XV.

College Printer on his own account'. This shows that Gill was considered to be the College printer and also indicates that the restrictive controls over the use of the Printing House in Graisberry and Campbell's bond of 1807 had been relaxed. The report reiterates the College's insistence that as they 'do not print for sale on their own account, they do not desire any profit or return . . . ' Willson concludes by recommending a partnership between the College, a printer and others (who presumably would supply the distribution), each sharing the costs. A committee of the board would control the Press and sanction publications.[50]

Trinity failed yet again to grasp the nettle and nothing came of this report. It may well be that the College's continued worries over its legal entitlements to claim printing privileges and drawbacks on paper duty inhibited action. In 1831 it sought legal opinion on the College's right, not only to print privileged books, but also to publish and sell them. On 3 June William Saurin sent in his opinion. He said that the rights to publish and sell these works was 'incidental' to the right to print. However he found it extraordinary that no direct patent had ever been granted for the right to print privileged books, and counselled that if the College intended to extend the use of its privileges (i.e. by publishing and selling them), further searches of the relevant archives should be made. He concluded that if there was no patent, then the University's rights might be open to challenge.[51]

The College seems to have been tantalised by the whole business because in 1836 it yet again sought legal opinion, this time as to whether it was entitled to order its printer to print a bible or testament, obtain the drawback, add a premium to the production cost and then sell the entire edition to a bookseller. Trinity sought the advice because it had 'an objection to be concerned with matters of trade, so far as to become retailers of copies of the work so printed'. M. Longfield supplied a favourable opinion on 18 July, pointing out that the oath to be taken by the King's printer when obtaining the drawback was more restrictive than that to be taken by the manager of the University Press. The former had to swear that the edition had been printed on his own account and for his sole benefit, while the latter had only to swear that the impression had been printed under the authority and permission proper for the purpose.[52]

The College did regularly claim its entitlements to drawback on paper duties, most often of course with regard to editions of the classics. The muniments record that the Press printed fifty application forms for such claims in 1838 and a further 100 in 1841.[53]

50. MUN/P/1690/9; the description of the Oxford printing house is at MUN/P/1/1593.
51. MUN/P/1/1688–1689.
52. MUN/P/1/1737.
53. MUN/P/4/217/9, 30 Aug. 1838; MUN/P/4/227/22–22a, 17 Feb. 1841; MUN/P/4/230/32, 10 Dec. 1841.

The continued preponderance of classics in the output of the Press led to the inevitable difficulty of finding specialist comps. In 1838 Thomas Burroughs Parker came over from England specifically to take on the job of Greek comp at the Press, and worked there until 1854. His daughter Mary married Joseph McDonagh, and among their children was Thomas, one of the leaders of the 1916 Rising. Parker was instrumental in setting up the Printers' Pension Society in London and when he applied to it for a pension in 1854, the secretary wrote to Gill asking for information on him. Gill replied that he never knew 'a better, more industrious or more competent compositor', but as Parker was then seventy and had bad eyesight he only earned on average less than 7-0 per week. One hopes that Gill's reference gained him his pension.[54] At this date the DTPS made no allowance for superannuation payments to members, so provision for old printers was a problem. Some members of the trade rose to the challenge and formed a Committee for Aged Printers which provided accommodation for the needy in a house on the Crumlin Road. Among the members of the committee as listed in the *Dublin Almanac* for 1835 were two from the DUP — M.H. Gill and Patrick Carroll.

The universality of the skills of printers ensured that they were a mobile body, so it was not unusual that T.B. Parker emigrated from England to Ireland. There was also much traffic in the opposite direction; one of the reasons for the foundation of the DTPS was to provide emigration allowances to members when times were bad in Dublin. Such an emigrant was George Fox, who was listed in the archives of the Strahans, printers in London, on 2 July 1822 as having been apprenticed to John Shea, College Green, Dublin, and 'last at the College Printing Office'.[55]

The surviving archives of the DTPS begin in 1827 and provide valuable references to personnel in the DUP and to happenings there, as well as providing background information about the trade in general. The earliest minute book covers the period 1827–30 and contains a mixture of the happenings at the weekly council meetings, to which all chapels were obliged to send delegates, and of the executive committee meetings which followed the council meetings and to which officers and members were elected by the trade in general.[56] (This structure survives substantially intact today in the organisation of the Irish Print Union.) The delegates to the council meetings rotated monthly and the names of the representatives were recorded. For the College chapel they were:

1827: Patrick Carroll, Henry Hutton, James Thompson, Robert Reed, John Hawkin, John Shine, Harlow, Bryan, Thomas Macklin, William McDermott.

54. E.W. and A.W. Parks, *Thomas McDonagh*, Georgia 1967, 2; O'Kelly, 'House of Gill', 173–4.
55. British Library: MS 48906B, f.26.
56. Irish Print Union: DTPS council minutes, 1827–30; microfilm copy in TCD library, OL Microfilm 700.

1828: Richard Peterson, Francis Tipper, Benjamin Payne, John Howlin, Palmer, Harlow, Skerrett, Ellis, Christopher McDermott, Chambers.

1829: Thomas Mullen, W. (or M.) Jennett, Gorman, Bedford, M. Gauran, Robert Nolan, James Wyley, J. Nixon, Young, Monks, Harlow, Thomas.

1830: Williamson, Stafford, Campbell, Tippen, Richards, John Howlin, William McDermott, W. Brenan, Peterson.

The minutes also record that Hutton and Howlin had been members of the Amicable Benefit Society, the precursor of the DTPS. The record further shows that Robert Reed had to be ordered from meetings in 1827 'for intoxication', a recurrent problem among printers and one which gives them an unenviable reputation even today.

The council minutes are unfortunately short on specifics so there is no knowing the reason why 'the father and mother of the College chapel' were summoned on 27 October 1827 to attend council. ('Father' and 'mother' refer to the chapel representatives of the caseroom and the pressroom respectively.) One of the issues considered at that meeting was the limitation in the number of apprentices allowed in any printing office. Excessive boy labour was a recurrent complaint in the trade in the first half of the century — journeymen printers brought the issue before the public in 1825 when they placed an advertisement in the 2 April issue of *Saunders's Newsletter* complaining of the problem. Was there an excess of apprentices at the College Printing House?

The minutes are also tantalisingly vague about an acrimonious dispute within the College chapel in 1828. John Ellis and George Harlow were ordered to attend council on 16 February when it was declared 'that Mr Harlow has broken faith with his chapel' and was fined the then huge sum of half a guinea, one of the heaviest fines recorded at this time and representing perhaps half a week's pay for a piece hand. Harlow must have refused to pay the fine because he was subsequently expelled from the Society. However there was some sympathy for him in the trade in general; so much so that on 12 April the College chapel had to have a resolution passed at council whereby its recommendation 'that George Harlowe . . . do be held in rigorous contempt by the members of this Society, be strictly attended to'. However he was readmitted to the membership in June having paid the fine and an admission fee of a guinea. (Harlow was to be disgraced again twenty-one years later when, as treasurer, he misappropriated nearly £50 of the Society's money. He agreed to repay it and gave promissory notes for the amount. When he failed to meet these the College chapel put forward a resolution to the committee on 4 June 1850 demanding that Harlow should be pursued for what he owed. Harlow replied that he had no money and there the matter rested.)

As with the council minutes those of the executive committee are also short on details. Thus it was that on 21 March 1829 the executive passed an 'unqualified censure' on the College chapel which had sent 'a certain requisition' round the trade, criticising some action of the committee as 'ill-advised & illegal'. Had this requisition been successful, the committee stated, it would have had the most dangerous consequences to the interests of the Society. The major controversy in the trade at the time was the 'closing' of certain newspapers to members of the Society because the proprietors were refusing to pay increases. On the same day as the College's censure the committee issued the directive that members who assisted the proscribed papers were to 'be esteemed a Rat of the worst description', and in July, with the dispute still in progress, fines of 5-0 for talking to 'rats', or 10-0 for drinking with them, were imposed. At this stage the payment of strike pay had led the Society almost to bankruptcy and the subscription rates had to be raised. It may well be that the College chapel, which the DTPS's minutes show to have consistently taken a conservative line, had criticised the committee for precipitating this debilitating strike. In the event the Society had to capitulate, and in November printers were allowed to take newspaper work at less than the increased wages sought.

In 1830 the University Press chapel asked the DTPS to arbitrate on a dispute over payment for setting an edition of Virgil, which was being done from printed copy. On 10 March the committee examined the cast off done by the Press and 'Resolved — That we consider from the specimen of Virgil submitted to us, that £1-15-0 per sheet is a fair valuation'.

Heretofore any detailed financial information on the operations of the Press was to be had from the surviving archives of its primary (but not the largest) customer — the College. For the decade of the Graisberry and Gill partnership (1827–1837), we are fortunate that an account book of the firm itself survives, detailing the annual figures.[57] A résumé of the more important totals can be extracted as follows (figures to nearest £):

Year	Wages	Value of printing done	Net profit	Profit as % of turnover
1827 (10 mths)	805	1,887	650	34
1828	1,004	1,887	650	34
1829	1,279	1,887	650	34
1830	1,602	3,380	1,745	52
1831	1,003	2,707	670	25
1832	1,203	2,707	670	25
1833	1,091	2,122	709	33
1834	1,099	2,853	1,172	41
1835	1,086	1,783	323	18
1836 (9 mths)	721	1,106	226	20

57. MUN/DUP/22/1.

(Figures for printing and profit in periods 1827–29 and 1831–32 are given as three-year and two-year totals and have been divided for convenience.)

Although this account book is an annual one it contains a wealth of detail about the running of the business. For example in 1833 credit of over £18 was allowed to 'Mr Donovan, Apothecaries Hall, for medicine for Mrs Graisberry'. This decline in her health may have been a factor in the slide in the profits in 1835 and 1836 and might well be the reason for her decision to sell her share in the partnership to Gill in 1837.

The volume also provides a picture of the Press's suppliers. Christopher McDonnell and Sons, Dickinson, Annandale and Sons, Summerville and Co., Greaves and Co., Cowan and Co., J. McDonnell, and Hilton are all listed as paper suppliers. There was no typefoundry in Ireland at this period — the lack of which one commentator in 1833 gives, implausibly, as an inhibiting factor on literary publishing in Ireland[58] — so the DUP got its supplies from England and Scotland. John Cumming acted as the local agent for the Wilson and Sinclair foundry of Glasgow, and several orders were processed through him including one for nearly £100 in 1834. Thorowgood and Co. of London was another recurrent supplier: £34 was spent in 1834 on hebrew and irish type.[59] Blake, Garnett and Co. in Sheffield, Caslon and Livermore, and Figgins in London were other sources of supply. Not all type was acquired new: on 17 October 1834, £11-18-6 was expended on founts bought at an auction of printing equipment at Walsh's in Sackville Street. The bursar's accounts provide further evidence of purchases of type after this period. For example sorts for a fount of syriac already owned by the University Press were supplied by Thorowgood in July and November 1839, while in January 1840 a fount of sanskrit was bought from R. Watts in London at a cost of £53-19-11.[60] Wright and Co. supplied £6 worth of printers' furniture in 1835.

The partnership account book records a huge purchase of printing equipment in 1827, which almost doubled the value of the plant in the Printing House. This was acquired for £407-0-11 from John Cumming, whose printing partnership with his brother James, which traded under the name 'Hibernia Press', was dissolved in that year.[61] There is evidence that a third printing press was bought in 1836. An entry under bills pay-

58. 'Printing and publishing in Ireland' in *Dublin Penny Journal*, I/39 (23 Mar. 1833) 309–11, signed 'F' which may be the proprietor J.S. Folds.

59. William Savage, *A dictionary of the art of printing*, London 1841, 427–8, would suggest that the irish was 'Fry's' face.

60. MUN/P/4/223/25–25a.

61. 'Notes on the rise and progress of printing and publishing in Ireland' in *The Dublin Builder*, XX (1 Feb. 1878) 35, which states that the partnership was dissolved 'about 1824' and that Gill bought the equipment. Wall, *Sign of Dr. Hay's head*, 21, misquotes this as 'in 1824' thus placing Gill in a position of management at the DUP three years before any other evidence that he had such a position.

able records 'Blundell's bill at 6 mos. for a printing press due 4 Aug. £30'. This would suggest that the press was acquired early in February. The person to whom the bill was payable may have been Joseph Blundell who is listed in the *Dublin Directory* of this date as of Mecklenburgh Street and as having a printing office in Nelson Lane, off Earl Street. It is not known if Blundell was acting as agent for a new press, and that the £30 was only a part payment, or if the sum was payment in full for a second-hand press.

Just as John Cumming acted as agent for type, the partnership accounts also reveal that he was agent for the supply of printing ink, although who the source was is not given. Thornley and Co. in 1827 and Shackell and Howe in 1835 were also used for supplies. Cumming seems to have had a finger in every pie because he also bought £108 worth of waste-paper from the Press in the period 1827–1830.

We have to resort to the burser's accounts for any evidence of engraving work being done for the College at this period. During 1835–1841 Charles Henecy did engraving and printed off copies from copper plates supplied. In 1840 G. Waller & Sons engraved a plate for testimoniums, while in 1842 John Kirkwood did a substantial amount of engraving for the College's Magnetic Observatory.[62] Although all this work was not strictly for the University Press it confirms that the Printing House had no rolling press.

There is only one reference to a binder who did work for the Press in the account book. On 23 June 1832 someone called 'Moore' was paid £5-4-5 for binding. The bursar's accounts are not much more forthcoming. George Mullen (Junior) was paid small sums throughout 1839–1840, including in 1839 an early example for the Press of edition casing: for binding 256 copies of John A. Malet's *Catalogue of Roman silver coins in the library of TCD* 'in full cloth boards 3-0-0 per 100 £7-10-0'.[63]

From the above table of annual wages it can be roughly calculated that the weekly wages bill hovered around £20. This is confirmed from passing references given for a few weeks in the account book: 8 December 1827, £18-18-9; 17 January 1829, £26-19-2; 10 October 1829, £24-4-0$\frac{1}{2}$; 15, 22, 29 October 1831, £18-6-8, £17-18-4$\frac{1}{2}$, £18-0-1 respectively. Because there are so many variables involved in the piece rates paid in the Dublin trade at this date it is difficult to hazard a guess of the size of chapel these figures represent, but based on a working week of six ten-hour days, I would suggest a workforce of perhaps 20 to 25. The piece rates paid are known from a 16-page pamphlet, *A scale of prices for compositors and pressmen, agreed upon by the employers and journeymen printers of the city of Dublin, February 9, 1829* (Dublin; arranged and reprinted, 1842). Among its many provisions are:

62. MUN/P/4, bursar's vouchers: -/212/26; -/215/24; -/221/48–48a; -/223/27; -/230/36, 46.
63. MUN/P/4/221/38, 28 Sept.

Art. I: Common matter in the English language in english and brevier type to be paid 5*d.* per 1,000 ens; in minion, 5½*d.*; in nonpareil, 6¼*d.*; in pearl, 7¼*d.*

Art. IV: Extra ½*d.* per 1,000 for MS copy.

Art. V: Extra ½*d.* per 1,000 for foreign language.

Art. VI: Greek without accent, 8*d.* per 1,000; with accents 9*d.* 'When Greek, or any dead of the characters, is intermixed, (as in grammars, &c.) to be paid as if the entire were Greek.'

Art. VII: Hebrew, Arabic, Saxon, Syriac &c. to be paid double that for common matter; Irish at 7½*d.* per 1,000.

Arts X–XI: Arithmetic, 2*d.* extra per 1,000; algebra, 10*d.* per 1,000.

Arts XVI–XVIII: Bottom, side and incut notes to attract at least 1–0 per sheet extra.

Art. XXVI: For corrections, 'all extra work at the stone to be paid at six-pence per hour'.

So complicated had the provisions become that an 'abstract of the scale' is given in a table. The pressmen's scale of prices is if anything even more complicated and is impossible to distil. However article IV is worth noting as it is a new provision: imposition of stereotype plates, whether laid by the comp or the pressman, was to be paid 6*d.* per forme for octavos or duodecimos and 9*d.* for smaller formats; the pressman was to get 6*d.* per forme 'for bringing up the plates'. Ruth Graisberry was one of the master printers who signed the agreement in 1829 and no doubt some of the provisions for the more exotic types were included with the University Press in mind.

The partnership account book provides a valuable insight into the range of customers of the business, the relative importance of their custom and the mode of payment. There appear to have been less than 100 customers who were afforded credit terms; there would also have been many small jobs done for cash. Of the £5,660 worth of business done in 1827–1830 the following tabulation shows the relative importance of the biggest accounts (I have added descriptions of their functions as appropriate):

	£	%
Cumming (publisher and bookseller)	1,493	26.4
Hodges & Co. (publisher and bookseller)	754	13.3
Curry & Co. (publisher and bookseller)	357	6.3
Trinity College Dublin	344	6.1
Dublin Society	319	5.6
Royal Irish Academy	306	5.4
Rev. Henry Harte (private, TCD)	239	4.2
Peter Byrne (publisher and bookseller)	194	3.4
Milliken (publisher and bookseller)	153	2.7
Dr Miller (private, TCD)	145	2.6

	£	%
Dr Elrington (private, TCD)	139	2.5
Coyne, Curry & Tims (publisher)	134	2.4
Rivington (publisher, London)	123	2.2
Stewart (private?)	121	2.1

It is quite a surprise to find that Trinity was only in fourth place and provided such a small percentage of the business. It is evident that the trade provided the major portion of the partnership's business, while institutional printing was a lucrative second stream, especially as it had the knock-on effect of introducing private customers such as Henry Harte, whose translations of Laplace were printed at the Press in this period.

The institutional business was especially welcome because they tended to pay cash, while the book trade customers tendered bills of exchange, payable after periods from three to thirty months. For the period March 1827 to November 1829 payment of £5,095 was received, £3,635 or 71 per cent in the form of bills of exchange, and £1,460 or 29 per cent in cash. Long credit terms led inevitably to bad debts. For example at the end of the partnership a 'list of doubtful & bad debt' included Peter Byrne, marked 'insolvent', who owed a balance on bills unpaid of £68, and Lord Athenry, whose debt for £48 was outstanding at the beginning of the partnership. The firm itself paid for supplies through bills of exchange, or by endorsing bills payable to it and passing them on.

The partnership account book does not provide details of what type of printing was done or of the charges for it, except for a 'List of expenses incurred for works on hands but unfinished on 1st. Oct. 1836 made out by Mr Gill':

Travels in Sicily 13 sh @ 13/-	8- 9- 0
Alterations on proofs & extras	1- 3- 6
Connellan English Stories 8 sh @ 20/-	8- 0- 0
do Irish Stories 4 sh @ £1-13-0	6-12- 0
Alterations & extras	2-11- 0
Diseases of the chest 20 sh @ 18/-	18- 0- 0
Alterations &c	1-18- 0
Walker's Pindar 8 sh @ £2	16- 0- 0
Translation of do. 2 sh @ £1-4-0	2- 8- 0
Alterations &c	1- 6- 0
Ordnance survey 20 sh @ £1	20- 0- 0
Alterations & extras	5-14- 6
Lectures on the wave theory 1 sh	1- 2- 0
Appx. to Napiers Curl Bill Acts 2 sh	2- 2- 0
Alterations &c	6- 6
Treatise on leases for lives 1 sh	13- 0

Report on Comm. relative to Dub. Soc.

(Dr Harty's) 4 sh @ 19/-	3-16- 0
Alterations &c	8- 0
	100- 9- 6
Add 12 per cent profit	12- 1- 6
	112-11- 0

These figures were only for composition (compare them with Graisberry and Campbell's charges set out on p. 99). A 12 per cent mark-up seems very modest, considering Gill was aiming at over 50 per cent in his 1828 manifesto. It is interesting to find that the business had nine books in progress at one time, and would inevitably have had a lot of jobbing on-going at the same time (no Irish printing house would have had enough business to specialise in bookwork; this is the pattern even today).

The bursar's accounts provide an indication of the range of jobbing the Printing House did for the College: accounts, certificates, resolutions of the board, anthems and services for the chapel, circular letters, even labels for the spines of library books. On 10 November 1836 we find the first entry for what was to become the staple of the Press — examination papers. These were charged at 12-6 per folio or quarto page regardless of whether it was English, Latin, Greek or algebra.[64]

Bookwork for the College included the first annual *Calendar* in 1833 (see plate 18, which provides an early example of the College arms being used as a titlepage device). An unofficial guide for students, *Discipline of Dublin University*, was printed by the general trade in the 1820s and this seems to have provided the impetus to produce the first official calendar, written in a large measure by James Henthorn Todd. From 1840 Charles H. Todd was paid £50 per year for editing it.[65] It was a complicated work to print, having many different faces and sizes of type, tabular matter and an almanack printed in red and black. Thus for the 1841 edition of 750 copies 'Graisberry & Co.' charged £3-8-6 per sheet, giving a total of £59-18-9 for $17\frac{1}{2}$ sheets.[66] The edition size was more than adequate, as on 24 April 1926 the board minutes record thanks from the New York Public Library for a set covering 1833 to 1895; the volume for 1848 alone was out of stock!

The 1833 *Calendar* includes a list of 'Books printed at the University Press; and printed for, or sold by Richard Milliken and Son, booksellers to the University'. The list includes stock going back to the 1787 edition of Tacitus, but those printed since the start of the Graisberry and Gill partnership are as follows:

64. MUN/P/4/212/24.

65. McDowell and Webb, *TCD 1592–1952*, 528 n. 70; MUN/P/4/222/83 etc.

66. MUN/P/4/227/22–22a, 30 Jan. 1841.

THE

DUBLIN

𝔘𝔫𝔦𝔳𝔢𝔯𝔰𝔦𝔱𝔶 𝔈𝔞𝔩𝔢𝔫𝔡𝔞𝔯,

M.DCCC.XXXIII.

CORRECTED TO NOVEMBER 20, 1832.

DUBLIN:

WILLIAM CURRY, JUN. AND CO.,
RICHARD MILLIKEN AND SON, BOOKSELLERS TO THE
UNIVERSITY, AND HODGES AND SMITH.
G. B. WHITTAKER AND CO., LONDON.

1833.

18. The first Calendar.

1827	Homer, *Iliad*, ed. J. Kennedy, vol. 2	23-0
	Laplace, *Treatise of celestial mechanics,*	
	translated and edited by H. Harte, 2 vols	35-0
	Helsham, *Selections from lectures*	3-0
	Luby, T. *Elementary treatise on plane and*	
	spherical trigonometry	10-0
	Kennedy, J. *Ten lectures on the philosophy of*	
	the Mosaic record of creation, 2 vols	15-0
1828	Luby, T. *Introductory treatise to physical*	
	astronomy	12-0
1829	Xenophon, *Cyropaedia*, ed. E. Geoghegan	6-0
	Aeschylus, *Agamemnon*, with German and	
	English translations, ed. J. Kennedy	no price
	Euclid, *Elements*, ed. T. Elrington, 9th ed.	7-0
1830	*A compendium of algebra*	5-0
	Laplace, *System of the world*, ed. and	
	translated by H. Harte, 2 vols	24-0
1831	Sadleir, F. *Lectures on . . . the divinity of*	
	Our Saviour	8-0

As can be seen textbooks predominated in the output of the Press. (Indeed on 1 March 1834 the board sanctioned the loan of the Press's greek type to Milliken who was 'engaged in the publishing of some books for the purposes of the students'.) However some of the Press's output was aimed at a wider audience. For example Kennedy's Aeschylus has the imprint 'Dublin: printed at the University Press for Rivington, London, sold by Wakeman, Milliken and Cumming, Dublin; Blackwood, and Bell and Bradfute, Edinburgh'. James Kennedy (later Kennedy-Bailie) and John Walker were the only two fellows to publish anything of consequence in the field of classics in the hundred years from 1760 because of the mathematical bias in the College's exam for fellowship.[67] Laplace's *System of the world*, published by Longman, Rees, Orme, Brown, and Green in London, was a reflection of this mathematical emphasis. There was a burgeoning mathematical school in Dublin in the early nineteenth century, based on the recognition of the French advances in the field.[68] Despite the importance of Harte's translations of Laplace and later of Poisson (1842), and despite the fact that he went to the trouble of procuring a London publisher, the works were not a success. There are very few copies in libraries outside of Ireland, and in June 1853 Gill could report to Harte's administrator that there were 109 copies of the *Celestial mechanics*, 396 *System of the world*, and 500 Poisson's *Mechanics* in the 'crowded' warerooms of the Printing

67. McDowell and Webb, *TCD 1592–1952*, 110.
68. ibid. 159.

House, and that he would be obliged if the administrator could remove them.[69]

The board must have been well pleased with the running of the Press because on 13 September 1839 it sanctioned the enlargement of the Printing House, no doubt at Gill's suggestion, approving of Darley's estimate of £1,200 (see plate 19). The extension was built at right angles to the east wall of the eighteenth-century building, jutting out into what had been ball and tennis courts for the students. The role of the Printing House as a classical garden temple in College Park had already been spoiled in the 1830s when the buildings of New Square were laid out, and in fact these screened what was a very utilitarian extension. Gill stated to the 1853 Commission on the University (to be considered below) that the new section was erected in 1842, while Philip White dated it 1844. In fact the records show that it was substantially finished in 1840 because on 5 August the pressmen were paid £2-15-0 'for taking down printg. presses in old pressroom, cleaning, and putting them up in the new building'.[70] Perhaps Gill meant 'finished' in 1842 because there is an extensive 'account of sundry jobbing work' done in the Printing House by the builders Baker and Cockburn during the years 1840 and 1841.[71] Among the items charged for were '36 block tin racks for copy made and fixed up for the compositors' and '2 doz hooks for pressmans composition rollers'. There was also a charge from the bricklayer for 'setting casting pot in small foundry'. This is unlikely to have been for stereotyping, as there would not have been the demand at the University Press for enough large editions to justify it, and later evidence proves that plates were produced by outside firms; perhaps it was for casting odd sorts for which there were matrices. The extension provided almost an extra 5,000 sq. ft of space on three levels (see plates 20–22). This was an optimistic move on the College's part at a time when the *Dublin University Magazine* could say that 'the name of Dublin on the titlepage was a sufficient reason for neglect' and when the printing trade was constricted by the scarcity of capital and the extreme caution of the local publishers.[72] There was however a growing 'spirit of literary nationalism', to quote John C. O'Callaghan, who, by insisting that his *Green book* be printed and published in Ireland, 'would have Irish manufacture connected with information for the mind, as well as with clothing for the body'.[73] Gill was no doubt alive to this spirit and indeed would be responsible for helping create it.

69. O'Kelly, 'House of Gill', 203.

70. MUN/P/4/226/24–25.

71. MUN/P/2/298/9, £52-12-11, paid Oct. 1841.

72. 'Past and present state of literature in Ireland' in *DUM*, (Mar. 1837) 365–76, at 372; P. White in *Irish Printer*, (Jan. 1909) 6.

73. J.C. O'Callaghan, *The green book; or, Gleanings from the writing desk of a literary agitator*, Dublin 1841, xxxi–ii.

UNIVERSITY PRINTING OFFICE.

19. The Printing House as shown in the *Dublin Penny Journal,* 10 October 1835.

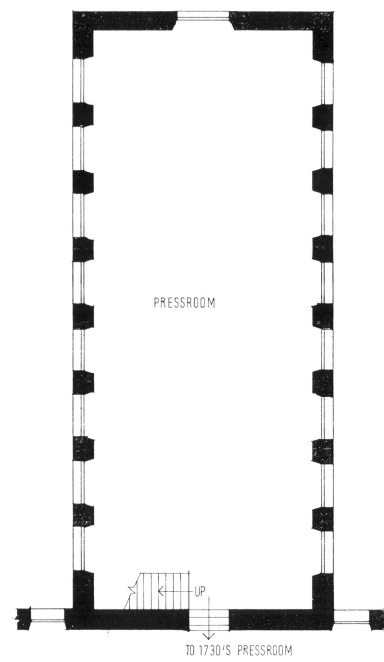

PRESSROOM

UP

N ←

1840 EXTENSION
BASEMENT LEVEL

TO 1730'S PRESSROOM

20. The basement level of the 1840 extension.

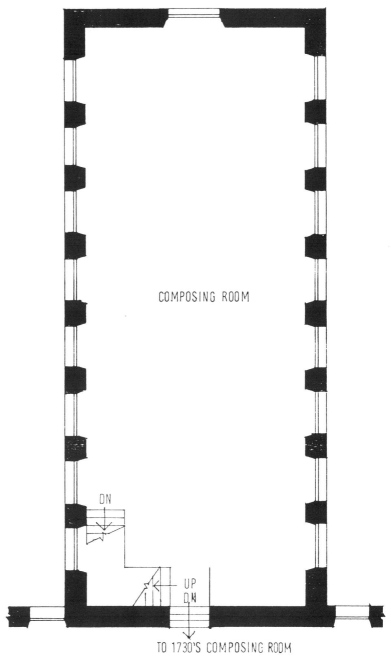

COMPOSING ROOM

DN

UP
DN

TO EXTENSION
GROUND FLOOR LEVEL

TO 1730'S COMPOSING ROOM

21. The ground floor of the 1840 extension.

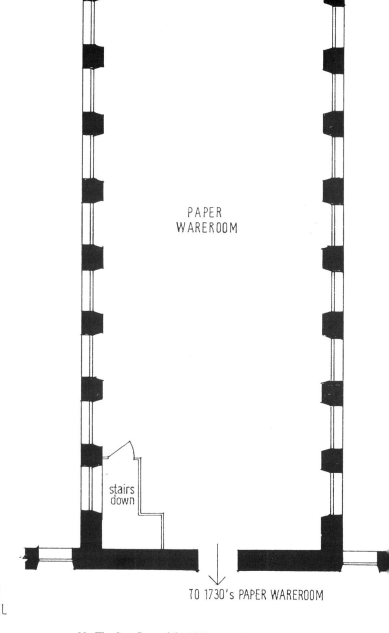

22. The first floor of the 1840 extension.

7

Michael Henry Gill:
First Phase: 1842–1855

Ruth Graisberry died sometime about mid-1842 and on 2 July the board of the College established a committee to consider the arrangements at the Printing House. On 7 September the minutes record that 'Mr Gill, printer with the late Mrs Graisberry, was elected printer to the University for five years, subject to the report of a committee . . . appointed to consider the details of his proposal.' Thus began a tenure that was to span the next thirty years, which on the available evidence ran remarkably smoothly and at last fulfilled the true potential of the University Press. The period is divided neatly by Gill's decision in 1856 to purchase the publishing and bookselling business of James McGlashan, and for the purposes of this history I will use that watershed year as a divide.

The choice of Gill, a Catholic, as printer to Trinity, a staunchly Protestant institution, was unusual. Perhaps it was the air of post–emancipation reform, but Gill's proven record of running the Printing House efficiently would have been the overriding influence. And no doubt he made 'his proposal' to take on the post — unfortunately not recorded — very attractive and may have included the undertaking to pay rent for the premises. The conditions agreed between the parties were set out in the 'Report of Printing Office committee':[1]

1. That Mr Gill's charge for all printing done for the College be at the same rate, and with the same allowances of disct. for ready money, as in his dealings with the trade.

2. That Mr Gill pay for the use of the Printing Office and all the property at present therein contained, an annual rent of £200.

3. That for any further property which the College may purchase for use of said Printing Office, Mr Gill be charged an additional 5 per ct. per ann. on their nett cost to the board, the same to be added to his rent.

1. MUN/P/1/1764.

4. That the interior of the Printing Office, glass included, be kept in full and sufficient repair by Mr Gill, and at his own charges. But that all external repairs be executed by the board, and at their expense.

5. That in case it be deemed advisable to light the Office with gas the original fittings for same be paid for by the board, but the payment for the gas itself from year to year be made by Mr Gill.

6. That Mr Gill furnish to the College an exact inventory of all the College property committed to his charge, and be held answerable for same in case the connection between him and the College should at any time be broken off.

7. That this agreement be renewable from year to year, and be capable of being discontinued by the board in case the Printer shall cease to give satisfaction or to discharge his duties efficiently.

Gill endorsed these conditions on 3 December 1842, after a note was added stipulating that by 'further property' in clause 3 was meant machinery — he shrewdly did not want to have to pay rent on type purchased by the College. A memo was also added to the agreement that the rent was to commence on 25 March 1843. That rent proved to be too high and on 15 February 1845 the board agreed a reduction to £150. When Gill sought a further reduction to £100 in 1852 the board on 15 May only agreed on condition that bookwork be done henceforth for the College at a rate 10 per cent lower than currently charged.

The decision was made in July 1843 to have gas lighting installed. The bill of the brass founder, William Mooney, for £116-2-2 for 87 fittings was paid in December and included '3 water slides with balance weights to pendants at imposing stones'.[2] In the same month the board approved the installation of a new heating system 'on Mr [William] Hunt's plan' at a cost not to exceed £65. This apparatus did not prove a success even though a second unit was installed in 1844 and the whole system had to be upgraded by Loftus Bryan in 1851.[3]

The inventory of the materials owned by the College in the Printing House that Gill was required to furnish has not survived and there is no listing of Gill's own equipment, so it is not possible to estimate the extent of the plant at the beginning of Gill's official tenure. There is evidence that new printing presses were purchased within a few years of his takeover, no doubt part of the planned expansion. Among J.J. O'Kelly's transcriptions and notes made *c.*1950 from M.H. Gill's papers is a list of Gill's suppliers in the period 1842–1872.[4] Under 'type and accessories' is Clymer

2. MUN/P/4/238/54–54a.

3. O'Kelly, 'House of Gill', 165; MUN/V/5/9, board register, 12 Oct. 1850, 11 Jan. 1851.

4. MS 10313/10–11.

& Dixon, alas with no further details. This must have been a reference to the London manufacturers who made Columbian printing presses in the period 1830 to 1845. From the above it may be inferred that Gill purchased such a press or presses between 1842 and 1845. He did not buy the larger sizes, as is evident from a letter of March 1858 to Routledge & Co., the London publishers, explaining that a work was printed as a single post ($15\frac{1}{4}$ x $19\frac{1}{2}$ inches approx.) 'as our presses do not take in d[ouble] post [$30\frac{1}{2}$ x $19\frac{1}{2}$ inches approx.] conveniently'.[5] Columbians were the presses in use in 1869 according to W.C. Trimble's recollection in 1934.[6] A royal Columbian by Clymer & Dixon survived in the Printing House into the 1960s and may well have been one of Gill's purchases.

In his reply to the 1853 Royal Commission[7] Gill stated that the College bought no presses, type or other printing materials in the period 1843–1853 'as the Printer to the University supplies himself with these articles'. This is not strictly true. In January 1844 the professor of Hebrew, Charles William Wall, ordered a small fount of bourgeois hebrew which cost nearly £30. It weighed 113 lb at 4-8 per lb, and was 'cast in a peculiar manner, to range with Hebrew capital letters'.[8] However the overwhelming majority of the equipment was purchased by Gill and we are fortunate that two of his account books survive — a journal of 1851–1857 and a ledger mainly for the 1850s and 1860s — which afford us information on his acquisitions.[9] Type came mostly from England. R. Besley & Co. was the major supplier, providing small quantities of sorts, including cuneiform, throughout the 1850s for what must have been existing founts in the Printing House. The firm also supplied a small fount of pearl music in June 1852, the first time I have noted music among the Press's type stock. It weighed 44 lb and cost 8-0 per lb. A commission to print the *The Petrie collection of the ancient music of Ireland* for the Society for the Preservation and Publication of the Melodies of Ireland, begun in 1854, was no doubt the impetus for further acquisitions of music type. In the first quarter of 1854 Gill bought a fount of ruby music from Duncan Sinclair & Sons, weighing 188 lb at 5-6 per lb. And in May of that year he supplemented it with a 145-lb fount, again Sinclair's ruby music, bought second-hand at 5-0 per lb at the auction of Holden's equipment.

Other sources of type supplies during the 1850s were Stephenson Blake & Co., Caslon, and Miller and Richard. The latter firm supplied a

5. MS 10308/100, copy of letter from M.H. Gill to Routledge & Co., 31 Mar. 1858.

6. Correspondence from W.C. Trimble in *Irish Printer*, 29 (Oct. 1934) 16.

7. *Dublin University Commission: report of Her Majesty's commissioners appointed to inquire into the state, discipline, studies and revenues of the University of Dublin and of Trinity College*, Dublin 1853, evidence 187–191 (House of Commons Papers, 1852–3, XLV).

8. MUN/P/4/253/25, 23 July 1851; Gill evidently had still not been paid for it.

9. MUN/DUP/22/2–3.

fount of brevier greek (35 lb at 7-6 per lb) on 25 August 1855, bought for an edition of J. Kennedy-Bailie's Homer, the copyright of which Gill purchased in 1852. Among the lesser suppliers were Henry W. Hewit, who provided 2 lb of small pica roman on 24 March 1853, and Robert E. Branston, who supplied cast ornaments in May of the following year.

There were only ever two or three typefoundries in Dublin throughout the 1840s and 1850s, among which was Marr, Thom & Co. Gill made use of it for type and furniture. One of the most tantalising references occurs in the journal for 17 March 1854: 'Cutting punches for pica, l[ong]. primer, & brevier Irish sorts (chiefly accented letters) & justifying matrices from May 17th to Dec. 6th 1853 £25-19-0'. There is a later reference in the ledger on 24 January 1859 to the charge for '1 matrix & punch 12-6', so it can be calculated that about 40 sorts were involved. This can only be for sorts for the founts of Petrie irish types (formerly called the 'Irish Archaeological Society' types). This provides positive evidence that an Irish typefoundry was involved in the cutting and casting of at least some of this family of types. As the types were exclusively used at the DUP, and as their history has been recently disentangled by Dr Dermot McGuinne, it is appropriate to consider them at this point.[10]

They were designed by George Petrie, who modelled them on the lettering in the Book of Kells, and had been prepared for the *Annals of the Four Masters*, printed at the Press in 1848–1851, but planned as early as 1833. McGuinne has identified two categories that were in use at the DUP:

Petrie 'A' of 1835, produced in two sizes — pica and long primer; and
Petrie 'B' of 1850, produced in long primer and brevier.

The 'B' long primer ousted that of the 'A' category about 1852, and the remaining three sizes — 'A' pica, and 'B' long primer and brevier — remained in use at the Press right down to the 1970s.

The long primer 'A' type was first used in *The ordnance survey of County Londonderry*, part of which was issued to mark the meeting of the British Association in Dublin in 1835. It was printed at the University Press 'by Ruth Graisberry' for the publishers Hodges and Smith. It is worth recording that the Graisberrys had a long-standing reputation for printing in Irish, going back to the 1810s, so much so that a fount of irish type which they used extensively was named the 'Graisberry' type, until identified by McGuinne as actually Moxon's fount with extensive revisions by Fry and renamed the 'Fry/Moxon' type.[11] Both the 'A' sizes were copyrighted by Hodges and Smith in 1844 by having a specimen sheet printed, entitled *Irish hibernian, cut and cast from original drawings*

10. Dermot McGuinne, *Irish type design: a history of printing types in the Irish character*, Dublin 1992.

11. ibid. 58–63.

executed for Messrs. Hodges and Smith, and having it entered at Stationers' Hall on 11 April. It is evident then that Hodges and Smith were responsible for commissioning the Petrie 'A' founts. It has been suggested that the engraver George DuNoyer, who worked with Petrie on other projects, may have been the punchcutter. Who the typefounders were for this 'A' type is not known, and James Christie is sometimes suggested. However given the above evidence it is likely to have been Alexander and Patrick Wilson, whose headquarters was in London; they also had a branch in Dublin in the early 1840s. The firm went bankrupt in 1845 and Dr James Marr bought out the Dublin and Edinburgh branches. The Dublin arm described itself as the 'Irish Letter Foundry' which may mean more than that it was just a typefoundry in Ireland. It probably indicates that it cast irish type. The Dublin branch ceased about 1864, but the others survived and when the firm became the Marr Typefounding Co. Ltd in 1874 it continued, according to T.B. Reed, to style itself 'Irish Letter Founders'.[12]

The Petrie 'B' types were financed by Gill himself. Writing to the Rev. John Evans on 20 April 1853 about a proposed printing of the *Book of common prayer* in English and Irish, he stated:

I have gone to considerable expense for the drawings, cutting of punches and matrices for three founts of Irish of different sizes, being the form of Irish character approved by a committee of the first Irish scholars in the country, who were aware of the many imperfections of the founts in use. I applied also to some respectable type founders to undertake the work and sell me and others the type, but they declined on the grounds that the mere casting of the founts that would be required by the printers of the United Kingdom would not repay them for the outlay, which I believe to be the fact. I therefore had to go to all the expense myself or it would not have been done.[13]

Since there were only long primer and brevier sizes identified by McGuinne in the 'B' category it may be that the pica referred to in Marr, Thom & Co.'s account of 1854 was for accented sorts for the 'A' pica fount registered by Hodges and Smith. All published accounts say that George Smith was wholly responsible for commissioning the Petrie founts. On the above evidence it is clear that Gill had at least an interest in them. That would explain why all the faces were in the exclusive use of the DUP. Had Hodges and Smith owned them they would no doubt have supplied the types to at least some of the several printers they used to do their printing.

12. Strickland, 'Typefounding in Ireland', 32; T.B. Reed, *A history of old English letter foundries*, London 1952, 264.
13. Quoted in O'Kelly, 'House of Gill', 61–2.

The punches and matrices remained in the possession of the University Press until recent times. In 1944 Colm Ó Lochlainn recorded that the Dublin firm of William Miller and Sons used to occasionally cast replenishment founts from the matrices supplied by the DUP.[14] Several members or past members of the firm remember seeing a small wooden box with the punches in it in the 1950s, stored in the wareroom in the attic of the 1734 building; it had a printed sheet of the characters inside the lid. There are even hazy recollections of the box with a few punches in it going into the early 1960s. Thereafter the fortunes of the punches and matrices remain a mystery. Some suggest that they were discarded in a clear-out; others that they were destroyed in a fire that occurred in 1965; and even some hints that they may have been stolen. Several cases of Petrie type were among the equipment removed from the Printing House early in 1976 when the DUP moved off campus. Unfortunately even these disappeared in the upheavals of the next decade as the Press changed over to computer setting and offset-litho. All that remains today of this important episode in Irish typographic history is a case of the long primer 'B' type in the possession of Trinity Closet Press.

Gill was also involved in the production of another set of irish types in 1853. Two-line initials were needed to make the Irish text match the English in the parallel text *Book of common prayer* then being planned. Gill warned the Rev. Evans that it would be very expensive to have them cut and cast, and he agreed. However Gill was able to provide the necessary letters by having them cut in wood in the style of the Petrie founts, and having these stereotyped. The local firm of T. Coldwell undertook the stereotyping stage, charging 4*d.* for each of '47 blocks Irish alphabet' on 25 June 1853. Gill's journal on 24 December records that Hodges and Smith were charged for the production of '138 two-line primer Irish capitals, for the initial letters in [the] Irish prayer-book'. Gill wrote to Rev. Evans on 15 November 1854 to say that he had gone to the trouble of having the initials made so as 'to correspond in size with those used at the commencement of the English prayers, as I felt that want of uniformity in this matter would not be creditable to the book or to the Press'.[15]

As has been seen Gill also bought type second-hand. For example he bought 750 lb of small pica roman from Coldwell on 18 April 1849 at 5*d.* per lb. And he was not averse to engaging in some brokerage. He bought some equipment from Nicholas Walsh on 9 October 1852, among which was a 797-lb fount of brevier roman costing £58-2-3½ (1-5½ per lb). He sold this on to a Mr Power on 6 November for £63-1-11 or 1-7 per lb, a seemingly modest profit of 8.6 per cent. However when it is understood that this profit was made in a month, the annualised figure can be

14. Paul Walsh and Colm Ó Lochlainn, *The Four Masters and their work*, Dublin 1944, 37.

15. Quoted in O'Kelly, 'House of Gill', 64–5.

calculated at just over 100 per cent. Such incidents afford an insight into Gill's success as a businessman.

A certain amount of type and printing equipment was bought on behalf of the College in this period, especially in 1855 when the decision was taken to keep the type of the annual College *Calendar* standing. Gill's journal for 31 December 1855 records the purchase of £34-15-6 worth of material, including a small fount of long primer syriac from Figgins & Co. (34 lb at 6-0 per lb £10-4-0) and 30 medium 12mo chases for £8-0-6 from Courtney & Stephens. Gill charged 10 per cent commission on these.

One of the questions asked of Gill by the 1853 Commission was, 'In how many languages can books be printed at the University Press?' Gill's reply provides an indication of the range of types and composing skills available in the Printing House at that date:

> Works wholly or in part in the following languages and characters have been printed at the University Press, viz.: In English, Irish, French, Italian, Spanish, Latin, Greek, Inscription Greek, Hebrew, Arabic, Syriac, Ethiopic, Sanscrit, German, Coptic, Saxon, Phonetic, Old English, Doomsday, and Cuneiform characters.

T. Coldwell undertook all the stereotyping needs of the Press in this period. Because of the nature of the output these needs were small, but they included Petrie's *Ancient music of Ireland* charged at £1-10-0 per sheet and McKay's translation of Cicero at £1-15-0 per sheet. The firm also did corrections and repairs to the plates of Wheeler's edition of Horace in 1855, the copyright and plates of which Gill acquired in 1852. Among the small amount of commercial jobbing that Gill undertook was that for Miss Hart (perhaps a relative of his wife Mary Catherine Hart), who was in the provisions trade and had thousands of labels for Guinness XX porter, Drogheda Ale, tea wrappers and suchlike printed throughout the 1850s. Because of the quantities involved Gill used to have these stereotyped by Coldwell and would then print them off at 2 or 3 shillings per 1,000. There is a handful of references to electrotyping illustrations in the journal, but no indication as to the supplier of this service.

A combination of the bursar's accounts and Gill's account books provides the names of the businesses the DUP turned to for its illustrations in the period under consideration. For example during 1848 and 1849 George McCoy and H. White charged for engraving and printing plates for Robert V. Dixon's *Treatise on heat* (1849); in 1850 Charles Healy charged for unspecified engraving.[16] Increasingly the Press turned to wood-engravings for its illustrations which had the advantage that they could be printed with the type, thus avoiding the trouble and expense of

16. MUN/P/4, bursar's vouchers: -/243/51–51a, -/246/45–45a, -/250/23.

having to have engravings printed by outside firms. Good impressions from the blocks were, however, difficult to achieve, and Gill charged extra 'for bringing them up at press'. William Oldham seems to have been the wood-engraver Gill relied upon most heavily, and he provided blocks throughout the 1850s. Such was the reputation of the Press in this area that it merited a mention in John Sproule's *The Irish Industrial Exhibition of 1853* (Dublin 1854, p. 323): 'London is the great emporium of this kind of work . . . A high degree of excellence in this department has, however, been attained in the College office, in this city, the style of some of the work executed in it leaving little to be desired . . . Machine printing is not well adapted for working off the finer kinds of engravings.' Sproule's work was printed at the DUP and as if to prove his point it is liberally illustrated with wood-engravings. The Press's collection of blocks was the envy of the trade and in 1855 Robert M. Chamney of the *Dublin Advertising Gazette* entered into negotiations with Gill for the purchase of it; no outcome is recorded.[17]

Gill's journal records that ink came from three major suppliers: Shackell and Edwards, who provided ordinary black ink in 1851 at 6 shillings per lb; John Gilton & Co. in Liverpool, who throughout 1852 and 1853 provided the coloured and specialist inks needed for woodcuts at 7-6 per lb; and A.B. Fleming & Co. who provided supplies in 1854 and 1855 at 3 and 6 shillings per lb.

Trade customers generally supplied their own paper, but for institutions and individuals Gill bought in large quantities, mostly imported. Cowan & Co. was the biggest supplier in the first half of the 1850s, and indeed seems to have had a virtual monopoly on the custom in 1853. Grosvenor, Chater & Co. was another major source, providing the middle to fine qualities. They also provided the occasional parchment, charging 3-6 per skin measuring about 19 x 16 inches. Thomas Seery supplied the mid-range qualities, while M. Ryan & Son provided the top-range plate papers. J. McDonnell & Sons was the only local source and then only for small quantities of the cheaper qualities.

George Mullen was favoured with the binding of the books printed at the expense of the College in the first half of the 1840s, as was his successor, Frederick Pilkington, in the second half. Gill himself seems to have preferred John Galwey. Gill bought two arming presses in the 1850s — one for £7-15-0 from Nicholas Walsh on 9 October 1852 and another for £8 from a stationer, Jane Neaton, on 8 August of the following year — so he may have been contemplating setting up his own bindery, but no evidence remains that he ever did.

Something of the workforce at the University Press can be gleaned from various sources. The DTPS committee minutes reveal that the numbers employed were very volatile, as it was in the rest of the trade, because the

17. O'Kelly, 'House of Gill', 91.

majority of the men were employed on piece rate and could be let go at a few hours' notice. From votes of the various chapels returned to the DTPS on different occasions it is known that there were 35 in the College chapel in November 1847, making it the biggest in the trade at that date, and in September 1855 there were 19, putting the College in fourth place. To these figures should be added 'management', which meant from overseers up, i.e. 4 or 5, and labourers and apprentices. These latter categories are difficult to quantify, but going on later proportions the ratio of chapel members to labourers was about 4 or 5 to 1, indicating perhaps 8 labourers in 1847 and 5 in 1855. There was an agreed ratio of apprentices to men, but as the number of journeymen fluctuated so much it is difficult to know what benchmark was used. Five or six boys at the DUP would seem reasonable. The total workforces can then be posited: in 1847 about 54; in 1855 about 34.

The men were still paid at the scale agreed in 1829, and this was to hold until 1870, but an appendix was added to the 1853 reprinting of the rates to embody 'the usage of the trade' for matters not covered in the agreed articles. This indicated that the working day for those paid on the 'stab was to be of ten hours, with one-hour breaks for breakfast and dinner to be taken in the men's own time. Thus if work began at 7 a.m. it ended at 7 p.m. Anything after that was considered overtime and paid accordingly. The men worked the first two hours of overtime at the usual 6*d*. per hour; they were paid 9*d*. per hour for the next two; and double time for anything up to 6 a.m. the following morning. Those paid on piece rates only worked overtime 'on account of extraordinary hurry'. The usual rates applied for the first two hours; the following two were charged at 3*d*. extra above what he managed to earn; and for all after that up to 6 a.m. at 6*d*. extra per hour. The Society found it necessary to make this explicit because it had been the practice not to pay a premium for extra hours. The working week was a full six days and holidays were a far-off concept.

The complexity of the piece rates led to some disputes at the University Press. On 21 September 1846 a deputation attended the DTPS committee to ascertain the correct charge for some presswork which the men had assessed as a royal broadside, but which Gill was insisting was pot. The committee came down in favour of the men, but Gill refused to accept the decision and the matter was put to arbitration on 30 September. The outcome unfortunately was not recorded.

There was another case before the DTPS in the following year when yet again the outcome, tantalisingly, was not recorded. On 2 March 1847 P. Read and Hall, two pressmen at the DUP, asked the committee to investigate a charge of 14 shillings for spoiled work that Gill was imposing on them. The minutes for 9 March record that a half-sheet of a law work had been turned wrongly and consequently spoiled. The matter was complicated by the fact that there were no signatures on the sheets, so it was unclear which of the two pressmen, who had both been working on the job, was responsible. Even though a sample of the spoiled sheet was produced and its press pin holes compared with those of sheets printed on both presses, no conclusion could be drawn and the committee referred it back to the chapel to investigate further and to submit the results to Gill. In insisting on compensation Gill was not being malicious. What was in dispute was which pressman was culpable. It was standard practice in the trade right down to the 1930s for the man responsible to pay for spoilage and it was written into the working conditions agreed with the Dublin Master Printers' Association on 17 June 1930. Thereafter the DTPS resisted it, the increasing speed of presses no doubt being a major factor, so that by 20 May 1935 the committee could instruct the father of Hely's chapel 'that spoiled work must not be paid for'.

The mobility of journeymen within the trade led to frequent cases of men leaving 'horse' behind them, that is filling out bills on Saturday for more than they had actually done, with the intention of compensating for it in the following week's bill. The DTPS had to constantly invoke its powers to enforce the men to pay, and in extreme cases would compensate the employer itself. The University Press was not immune from this practice. On 21 December 1846 Gill applied to the Society for 1-3 'horse' left by J. Armstrong. Armstrong had a poor reputation in this area and when he joined the DUP in June of that year he had left 'horse' at his previous employer, McDonnells.

The DUP chapel occasionally figured in internal Society disciplinary matters in the period in question. No member of the DTPS could refuse work if offered it, and if they did so they were disbarred from claiming benefit from the Society. This was the case with a journeyman called Bowles who was offered work at the Printing House in 1846, as reported in the committee minutes on 1 and 8 July. A similar case was reported on 31 May 1853 when Edward Clarke was found guilty of claiming against the Society when he could have had work at the DUP; he was ordered to repay 6-0 and was disbarred from benefit for two months.

As we have seen, there was an agreed ratio of apprentices to journeymen allowed in the trade, but when Gill applied to the DTPS on 2 September 1851 to be permitted to take on his son Henry Joseph as a supernumerary apprentice, 'compliance, under the circumstances, [was] deemed prudent'. On 14 October of the same year the son enrolled in the University and, while still apparently serving his apprenticeship, went on to graduate B.A. in 1857. Apprentices at this date were specialising either as comps or pressmen, where formerly they were trained in both branches. This is evident from a letter from C. Ross, secretary of the DTPS, to the *Freeman's Journal*, recorded in the committee's minutes on 17 April 1860. In it he stated that when machine presses were introduced in Dublin about thirty years since, one of the normal hand-press crew of two was left in charge and the other transferred to the caseroom, 'printers formerly having been reared to both branches'. This was the case with a Mr Farley who came to Gill sometime about 1856 looking for work and who bore a letter from another Dublin printer, F. Chambers, which pointed out that Farley could work at case and press. It is not clear if apprentices at the University Press still were afforded that comprehensive training, but it seems unlikely that such a large establishment would have been out of step with the practices in the rest of the trade. Most of the apprentices passed through their time without any problems, no doubt considering themselves lucky to have a position in depressed times, but occasionally one turned out to be a failure. Such was the case with Matthew Cavanagh. In 1853 Gill wrote to his sponsor, the Rev. Joseph Keatinge of Athy, Co. Kildare, expressing dissatisfaction with the boy because of his neglect of business and stating that he was cancelling his indentures.[18]

The names of many of the other workers in the Printing House occur in various sources, especially the DTPS minutes, but seldom is there any flesh on the bones. An exception was William McMullen whose obituary appeared in the *Irish Printer* for November 1909 (see plate 33a). He was born in Dublin in 1819 and was apprenticed to his father, a printer and stationer. He joined the DTPS in 1843 and was a trustee for many years. He was employed by Griersons for a short while, but 'for upwards of fifty years he worked as a compositor in the Dublin University Press, being one of the first hands engaged by . . . Gill, after the erection of the extension of the Printing House . . . and was principally employed on classical work for the College authorities'. In 1869, with John Weldrick, a relation of George Weldrick who was to become Gill's manager at the Press, he founded the Typographical and Benevolent Fund. He retired in 1901 and died on 31 October 1909. O'Kelly (p.178) adds the information that about 1856 Provost MacDonnell recommended his half-brother Joseph McMullen to Gill for employment in the Printing House.

And so to the output of the Press in the 1840s and the first half of the 1850s. The Great Famine of 1845–1847 had a devastating effect on the book trades, with 25 per cent of the 284 insolvencies in the Dublin trade in the first half of the century occurring in the period 1844–1848, including the College bookseller Andrew Milliken in 1844.[19] For the journeymen printers the situation was equally bleak. On 1 July 1847 the DTPS, at that date forming part of the western district of the National Typographical Association, had to refuse to give relief to members from outside Dublin 'in consequence of the unparalleled depression of trade'. It had over a hundred claimants and its members were paying a levy of seven times the original weekly subscription of 6*d*. Even so there were several instances where there was not enough money to pay the Dublin

18. O'Kelly, 'House of Gill', 177; 172.
19. Benson, 'Printers and booksellers', 57.

claimants. This situation was the occasion for the secession of the DTPS from the NTA, a decision taken on 26 October 1847, the motion put by Mr Parker of the College office. And the negative aura of former decades still hung around Irish printed and published books. Writing to Alexander Spencer on 10 May 1847 Charles Lever had this to say: '. . . because I was an Irish author, printed and published and mostly sold in Ireland, [I was] branded with the nationality of blunder in type as well as errors in thought, and the same professional reputation hangs to me still'.[20]

Because the DUP relied on wealthy institutions for much of its business — Trinity itself, the Royal Irish Academy, the Royal Dublin Society, etc. — it was cushioned from the worst of the depression and it turned out the best bookwork being done in Dublin at this date. Gill informed the 1853 Commission of the amount of business the College had provided directly to the Press for printing the *Calendar*, exam papers and other works in recent years: 1849 £489; 1850 £485; 1851 £359. The College *Calendar* was the largest piece of recurrent bookwork. Gill's journal reveals that 750 copies of part 1 and 250 copies of part 2 for the 1852 issue cost nearly £120.[21] Amazingly it was still reset every year. On 12 March 1853 the board register records that J.H. Todd was paid £200 for the copyright he had in it 'on the understanding that he will present to the College the MSS of a history of the University which he is at present engaged in preparing'; at the same time Joseph Carson was appointed editor at an annual salary of £25. It was Carson who persuaded the board a month later, on 9 April, to invest in enough type and printing materials to allow the work to remain standing. No immediate savings were effected, even when the cost of new materials was discounted, and it was to be some years before it settled down, as will be seen.

Other administrative bookwork done for the College in this period included an edition of the College *Statutes* in 1844, together with a supplementary volume and a digested form in 1855, all edited by Hercules McDonnell; issues of the *University Intelligence,* printed each term from at least 1845 onwards; Robert Ball's *Reports on the progress of the Dublin University museum,* 1846–1848; James Apjohn's *Descriptive catalogue of the simple minerals in the systematic collection of TCD,* 1850; and a supplementary catalogue of the library, printed in 1854 in a futile attempt to keep the folio catalogue then in progress up to date. The 1844 edition of the Statutes was one of the earliest printings to use the College arms on the titlepage as a device. The previous edition of 1839 carried on the eighteenth-century tradition of showing the Printing House portico.

20. Quoted in Edmund Downey, *Charles Lever: his life in his letters*, Edinburgh 1906, vol. 1, 235.

21. MUN/DUP/22/2, 1, 28 Feb. 1852.

Foremost among the jobbing done for the College were the exam papers. Again Gill revealed the figures involved to the 1853 Commission:

Year	Number	Copies	Average
1849	152	9,569	63
1850	133	9,902	74
1851	136	7,219	53

Gill's journal reveals that he charged on average 11-6 per folio page for composing and printing these, regardless whether it was English, Latin, Greek or algebra; paper was extra. The cost for the Michaelmas 1851 papers for example was £44-8-3. There must have been some pressure to reduce the charges because for 1853–1854 they cost 10-6 per page. In 1855 this dropped to 8-6 for the Trinity term exams and to 6-10 for those of Michaelmas. The bursar's accounts reveal the reason for the dramatic drop — they were now being printed in octavo format. The overall cost had actually risen, to £73-5-4 for Michaelmas 1855.[22]

The size of jobbing runs ranged from '6 copies of inscription on trowel, to be presented . . . to the Lord Primate on laying the first stone of the Belfry' in 1852[23] to recurrent orders for 10,000 copies of dockets for the library. The usual size however was from 25 to 250. One wonders if it was economic to set up and print 25 copies of some short notice; surely it would have been easier to have it written out? The likely explanation is that printed official notices have more authoritative weight than those hastily written out.

In his reply to the 1853 Commission Gill listed 34 works that he had been able to discover which had been printed at the Printing House entirely at the expense of the College prior to the year 1830, starting with the Plato of 1738. For the period after 1830 he was able to list 32 such works and a further 13 that had been partly paid for by the College. It was common for Trinity at this period, when it did not itself publish a work by a member of the College, to pay half the cost of printing it at the DUP. Examples were Andrew Searle Hart's *Elementary treatise on mechanics,* Dublin: William Curry, 1844, a half-share of which, for 1,000 copies including binding, came to £44-12-7;[24] and an edition of 750 of George Salmon's *Treatise on the higher plane curves,* Dublin: Hodges and Smith, 1852, towards which the College contributed £72.[25] Trinity also made a contribution towards the odd worthy book which had no direct connection with the College. Such was the case with John O'Donovan's *Grammar of the Irish language published for the use*

22. MUN/P/4/260/24, 18 Dec. 1855.

23. MUN/DUP/22/2, 25 Nov. 1852.

24. MUN/P/4/239/21, 28 Feb. 1844.

25. MUN/P/4/256/30, 28 Feb. 1852.

of . . . *the College of St. Columba,* Dublin: Hodges and Smith, 1845; the work was printed by Gill using the Petrie irish type and the College provided a subsidy of £25.[26]

Most of the books on Gill's list of works paid for entirely by Trinity were either administrative, as documented above, or textbooks. There were however a few of major scholarly importance. One such was Archbishop James Ussher's *Whole works,* an astonishing work in seventeen large octavo volumes, which took nearly forty years to complete and was the most ambitious piece of printing undertaken thus far by the Press. Printing was begun under Ruth Graisberry's tenancy in 1829 and was finished in the second period of Gill's career at the Press in 1864. I have therefore deemed it appropriate to consider the full edition while documenting the era straddled by both these periods.

There had been pleas to Trinity as far back as the seventeenth century to print its distinguished one-time member's works. In the biography prefacing the London 1677 edition of Ussher's *Body of divinity* the editor pleads for the publication of the three volumes of divinity lectures which he delivered in the College, 'the printing of which would be no small honour to that University'. It took the College 150 years to initiate the project. On 10 October 1825 the board resolved 'that Archbishop Ussher's works be collected and printed at the expence of the College'. Charles Richard Elrington, professor of Divinity, was appointed editor. The delay in publishing anything elicited the following scathing comment in the same review by 'Observer' which criticised the distribution of the DUP's output, printed in the *Christian Examiner* in 1828:[27] 'Some three years ago we heard it was taken in hands, and that the whole works of this admirable scholar and divine would speedily come forth, properly edited and uniformly printed from our University press. Say Sir, is the mountain in labour, and when will parturition take place?' The next we hear of it is in the 10 October 1835 issue of the *Dublin Penny Journal* where it is stated that 'a large portion of this great work, which will occupy fifteen or sixteen volumes, is already finished'. It is evident that criticisms such as those of 'Observer' spurred the College on, and printing was started in earnest in 1829.

Most of the volumes were issued without titleleaves (volume 1 being an exception), but were published as they were printed off; titleleaves were provided for the full set when it was completed in 1864. This is evident from the preface to volume 17 written by James H. Todd, who took over the editorship in 1850 after Elrington's death, where he gives a list of 'the exact dates at which the several volumes were at first issued' (here recast from numerical to chronological order):

26. MUN/P/4/241/32, 15 July 1844.
27. *Christian Examiner,* VI (1828) 423.

Volume

2	7 November 1829
4	9 June 1830
5	16 October 1830
3	1 September 1831
6	30 October 1831
8	3 April 1832
7, 9	14 June 1832
11	1 August 1832
10	13 October 1832
12	12 December 1833
15	18 May 1834
13	29 June 1844
16	6 November 1846
1	5 January 1848
14	17 May 1862
17	25 April 1864

Todd regretted, as Elrington before him had, that the volumes were issued at different intervals: 'it is attended with this inconvenience, that it must necessarily cause many broken sets, and there will no doubt ultimately be left unsold a large number of odd volumes'. Todd's prediction proved to be true. Among the residue of the Press's stock, which had been warehoused in the library and which today is given a reluctant home in an outlying repository and in the basement of building no. 6 in the College, will be found hundreds of volumes of Ussher, but very few complete sets.

For whatever reason the volumes only begin to be bound in quantity in 1842. The bursar's accounts on 25 February record George Mullen's charges for 'boarding in cloth' 400 ordinary copies of volume 2 at one shilling each and 29 large paper copies at 1-3 each.[28] Gill submitted a bill for printing part of this volume on 1 June, indicating that the edition was of 500 ordinary copies.[29] There followed in rapid succession bills from Mullen for casing succeeding volumes, so that by July 1844 volumes 2 to 10 had been bound.

Volume 1, containing Elrington's life of Ussher, at last appeared early in 1848 (although dated 1847), with the editor's apology for the long delay, pleading other duties and repeated illness: 'He fears, too, that in some places errors of the press have occurred. For this his apology must be, that he was at a considerable distance from the printing office when most of the work was printed, and that the printers had to struggle against the difficulties of very bad writing, more particularly in the

---

28. MUN/P/4/231/56–56a, account presented 23 Apr. 1842.

29. MUN/P/4/231/30.

Eastern languages.' The volume had indeed proved difficult for the printers. On 5 January 1848 Gill submitted a three-page account for printing it to the bursar, which is littered with such extras as 'heavy bottom notes and Greek interspersed' and a genealogical appendix 'of a very difficult and complicated nature'. Gill's charge for setting and printing this volume was £241-9-6 and must have drawn criticisms of overcharging. This would account for the unusual level of detail in this bill and for the uncharacteristic irate comments he added: 'To these items are to be added a proportion of the various expenses of the Printing Office, such as the wear and tear of type, overseers, warehouse department — rent, coal, gas, interest of money &c. What remains, (after giving the work all the personal attention in my power) is the profit. . . . An inspection of my books will shew that the above statement is correct.' The College apparently was not convinced because it delayed paying the account until 21 December.[30] This volume was also issued as a separate publication in the same year in an edition of 750 copies and there were also queries over the charge of £114-5-0; payment was delayed until 14 March of the following year.[31]

Elrington died unexpectedly on 18 January 1850 and the momentum of the work was lost. Todd agreed to complete volume 14 and to edit the next volume, and William Reeves undertook the task of compiling the indexes for the final volume. Gill recorded that the printing of the fourteenth volume had begun in 1843.[32] It had been delayed, Todd informs us at the start of the last volume, because Elrington had had problems deciphering the manuscript and because he had discovered a mistake in his chronological arrangement of the lectures therein. Todd ends his introduction by stating that 'the total cost of this great work to the University, that is to say, of the printing and paper, exclusive of the payments made to transcribers, advertising, and other incidental expenses, amounts to the large sum of £3800'. Constantia Maxwell in her history of the College says the work cost more than £6,000, so editorial charges of over £2,000 must have been involved.[33] Gill's final bill included a charge of £5-10-0 for printing 500 copies of titlepages for the first sixteen volumes, thus bringing them up to date.[34] This explains why some sets have all the volumes dated 1864 and why other sets range from 1847 to 1864.

Among the books listed by Gill for the 1853 Commission as having been paid for 'entirely by the College' were two 24mo editions of 25,000 copies each of the *Book of common prayer*. Gill had at last persuaded the

30. MUN/P/4/243/24–24a.

31. MUN/P/4/244/30–30a.

32. MUN/V/62/5/43, Gill's bill for printing it, 12 Sept. 1862.

33. Constantia Maxwell, *A history of TCD 1591–1892*, Dublin 1946, 202, n. 29, unfortunately not quoting a source.

34. MUN/V/62/6/54, 9 May 1864.

College to take advantage of its printing privileges, which he had so ably argued for in 1828. Paper was laid in for the first edition on 13 January 1844: 430 reams of royal paper at 16-4$\frac{1}{2}$ each, and 25 of fine royal for the fine paper issue at 20-5 per ream. After discount the bill was £358-14-1.[35] The work was issued in the following year with the lengthy imprint: 'Dublin: Printed at the University Press by M.H. Gill, Printer to the University, for the Association for Discountenancing Vice, and Promoting the Knowledge and Practice of the Christian Religion. Sold at the Association's Depository, 133, St. Stephen's-green, West, 1845. Nonpareil 24's. Cum privilegio'. The Association paid for these as and when it took the stock from the Printing House — payments were recorded as late as January 1849[36] — so the College did actually pay for the printing and it was keeping to the letter of its privileges. The work contains 300 unnumbered pages in half-sheet gatherings, and was issued with Tate and Brady's *Psalms*, which has the same imprint.

Trinity must however have been having doubts about its position because in 1846, in anticipation of the renewal of the Queen's printer's patent, upon which the College's privileges depended, it sought legal opinion yet again on the whole question. And this time it got a reply to match its fears. Mountiford Longfield, the Regius professor of Feudal and English Law, reported on 10 February 1846 that he did not think that Trinity had an exclusive right to print bibles and *Books of common prayer*. He argued that the first grant restricting the printing of the bible, 31 Henry VIII, rested upon the absolute power of the crown. He did not think that the crown now possessed the power to prevent anybody printing bibles or prayer books. For precedence in Ireland he quoted the case of *Grierson* v *Jackson* in 1794, of which none of the lawyers consulted earlier seems to have been aware. The King's printer, George Grierson, had challenged Zachariah Jackson for printing the *Universal family bible*, with annotations by Benjamin Kennicott, in the Court of Chancery on 28 July 1794. The Lord Chancellor, Lord Clare, refused to give a ruling until the patent privileges had been established at law. 'I cannot conceive that the King has any prerogative to grant a monopoly as to bibles for the instruction of mankind in revealed religion', he observed.[37] Such a put-down must have shaken Grierson because he appears not to have taken it further. Longfield counselled that rather than seek a separate patent, Trinity should submit a petition, 'praying the Crown to preserve the ancient and usual privilege of the university in any grant to be made to the Queen's Printers'.[38]

35. MUN/P/4/239/19–19a, paid 13 Mar. 1844.
36. MUN/P/1/1795–1796, record payments from 11 Dec. 1848 to 11 Jan. 1849.
37. W. Ridgeway, W. Lapp and J. Schoales, *Irish term reports*, vol. 1, Dublin 1796, 304–11.
38. MUN/P/1/1773–1774.

Accordingly a petition was drafted and submitted to the board on 21 February for approval. It pointed out that because of the destruction of records in Ireland no separate patent for Trinity had been discovered, but that its privileges had been recognised in other charters and acts. Further the College had never abused the privilege and that 'no pecuniary profit can be obtained' from it, a statement based on Longfield's opinion that no bible then being printed in Ireland could compete 'with the English & Scotch editions and therefore . . . the privilege is not of any real pecuniary value'. The fact that the Griersons continued to print bibles and that Trinity was energetically pursuing its own privileges would point to the contrary. The petition ended by asking that the privilege be granted in perpetuity. The board must have had second thoughts on this sweeping request because the minutes for 28 February record that the petition was not forwarded to the government as it was felt the privilege would be granted without having to make the admissions contained in the document.

And such was the case. The first edition of the 24mo *BCP* was exhausted by the end of 1849 and with so much invested in composing the text and keeping it standing, the College did not delay on the second edition (or strictly speaking the second issue of the first edition). Gill's ledger and the bursar's accounts reveal that, after some necessary alterations made by the editor William Reeves, the first 2,000 copies were printed off on 23 March 1850, Gill charging £6-8-0 per 1,000 copies for presswork. Further batches of 5,000 were printed off on 7 December, and on 22 February and 2 August of 1851, and the final 8,000 of the 'edition' on 18 October. (What a nightmare such staggered printing could create for any bibliographer who has to identify and describe them!) The total charge came to £171-5-2.[39]

Unfortunately the cost of composing and printing the 'first' edition is not known as it would have been revealing for comparative purposes. The 'second' edition sold out quickly because a 'third' was printed and charged for by 23 December 1854.[40] Again it consisted of 25,000 copies charged for as before, but the account gives the added information that it contained $7\frac{3}{4}$ sheets and 8 pages, that is 380 pages, thus revealing that the Tate and Brady *Psalms* found bound with it was considered integral to the *BCP* which contained 300 pages. The cost was £160.

Some idea of the modest profit accruing to the College from these editions can be had from an estimate prepared by Gill on 28 July 1855 at the behest of the bursar, William Digby Sadleir, for an edition of a 48mo *BCP*.[41] The cost in rounded figures of the type, printing materials and composition would have been £510; that was the capital expenditure. Presswork for each edition of 25,000 would have been £140, and 380

39. MUN/DUP/22/2, 18 Oct. 1851; MUN/P/4/256/31–31a, 1 May 1852.

40. MUN/DUP/22/2.

41. MUN/P/1/1869.

reams of paper, £270 — total recurrent costs £410. Sold at 4*d.* each the edition would realise £417, to which would be added £37 drawback on the paper, giving a total income of £454. When the recurrent costs were subtracted from this the 'profit' was £44. Gill somehow calculated this to represent an 8 per cent return on investment if the edition sold out in a year, 4 per cent per annum if sold in two years. He added the observation that it took on average three years to sell each edition of the 24mo *BCP*, so he implied that a return of less than 3 per cent could be expected. This of course was the profit to the *publisher*. Gill as printer would already have had his mark-up. He was optimistic that the 48mo edition would sell better: 'It is probable that the University of Oxford sells at least 50,000 copies in the year of their edition of the 48mo Prayer Book, which gives them 16 per cent per annum on their outlay. If we could find a sale in the English market for these books it would be attended with great advantage, but to obtain this some influence would have to be used with the Societies and others there who purchase them.' Gill was ever willing to extend the frontiers of the trade and to take on the British market as he was to prove in the following year when he bought out McGlashan. Nothing however seems to have come of this proposed edition.

Although it leads us beyond the watershed year in Gill's career, it is worth pursuing at this point the other editions of the *BCP* printed by him. On 22 October 1858 the Rev. D.A. Browne of the Association for Discountenancing Vice wrote to the registrar, J.H. Todd, proposing conditions for a fourth edition of 25,000 of the nonpareil 24mo and 10,000 of a long primer edition in the same format.[42] The Association was to pay 4½*d.* each for the nonpareil and 1-0 each for the long primer, amounts that apparently previously applied. The Press was to store them and to provide yearly accounts for the copies drawn on by the Association. The society undertook to purchase not less than 6,000 of the smaller size, and 3,000 of the larger per annum. This was agreed to by the College and accordingly paper was laid in for both editions in the first quarter of 1859. Nearly 2,000 lb of long primer type was also bought from Besley & Co. at a cost of £186, while Marr & Co. provided £32 worth of leads, rules and furniture.[43] The printing of the long primer edition was charged for on 11 August. The presswork worked out at £8 per sheet and the account notes that some of the prayers (and the *Psalms*) were remade up from the nonpareil standing matter; why this patchwork was resorted to is not stated. The total cost was £155 and Gill had to wait until August 1861 to be paid.[44] The nonpareil edition was also printed in 1859, with the innovation that each page was framed by rules. Gill presented his bill for this edition on 2 November 1860, charging £6-8-0 per 1,000 copies for presswork — is

---

42. O'Kelly, 'House of Gill', 72–3.
43. MUN/V/62/3/40, 31 Aug. 1859.
44. MUN/V/62/3/43.

there any significance as to why the long primer edition was charged for by the sheet and the nonpareil by the 1,000? — at a total cost of £171 including alterations.[45] Despite the undertaking of the Association to take a substantial portion of each edition every year we know that three years later there were still 18,000 of the nonpareil and 8,000 of the long primer in stock. This is known from Gill's charge in 1862 for printing cancels for each to replace those prayers which had 'Prince Consort', changing it to 'Albert' after the death of Queen Victoria's husband.[46]

Among the works of extra-mural scholarly significance paid for by the College was William Rowan Hamilton's *Lectures on quaternions* published in 1853. Hamilton, a mathematical prodigy who was offered and accepted the chair of Astronomy while still an undergraduate, has left several letters documenting the passage of this work through the press and which, taken with references in the bursar's and Gill's accounts, provide an interesting picture of the process of printing a complicated book at the DUP. In a letter to the bursar on 31 January 1851 he recorded that the printing began about October of 1848.[47] On 19 June Gill submitted a bill which indicated that he had expended £100 on the work thus far, the extensive wood-engraved diagrams making it expensive. In an accompanying letter Hamilton recorded the view, admirably objective for an author, that these expenses were such that 'it would be too sanguine to hope for much return in the way of sale'.[48] Not alone were the wood-engravings expensive, but they were also the cause of considerable delay. In a letter to the bursar on 20 September he wrote of 'long delays occasioned chiefly by the engraver'.[49] William Oldham was the engraver responsible and Gill's ledger provides evidence of the prices he charged. Amounts varying from 6-6 to 25-0 per diagram were entered on 29 September and 17 December.[50]

The same accounts show that by December signature 2G had been worked off, Gill charging £2-18-0 per sheet for composition and presswork for the edition of 500 copies. March 1852 saw the finish of gathering 2L and also the start of the lengthy preliminaries, up to signature d having been worked off. The bursar's accounts on 26 June record the completion of gatherings 2U and i. Hamilton noted on this bill that this was 'probably the completion of the work' and that the 'whole estimated expense so far [was] £288-14-5'.[51] There was however some distance to go yet. Gill was evidently despairing at the growth in the

45. MUN/V/62/4/53.
46. MUN/V/62/4/37, 3 Mar. 1862.
47. MUN/P/4/251/29–29a.
48. MUN/P/4/253/26–26a.
49. MUN/P/4/254/19.
50. MUN/DUP/22/2.
51. MUN/P/4/257/5a.

work. In a letter to Humphrey Lloyd at this time, seeking further finance from the board, Hamilton wrote that 'the printers tell me that I have "grown almost as bad as Mr Salmon or Mr Jellett!" which of course I take as a compliment'. In return for further finance he set aside 100 copies for the College's disposal.[52]

Hamilton estimated that the work would retail at £1 and Gill's ledger records *contra* entries for several subscriptions of 10-0 from students during 1852. The ledger also records the completion of the work on 20 July 1853. He charged an extra 12-6 on each of $49\frac{1}{2}$ sheets 'for additional algebra . . . being much more difficult than the commencement of the work, from the MS of the first sheet of which the original estimate was formed, which was only interspersed with occasional astronomical signs, bearing no resemblance to the work as it progressed.' Although Gill had been paid varying amounts on account as the work progressed, he had to wait until late 1854 for his bill to be settled. On 22 April Hamilton wrote to him to say that he thought the board would clear the account: 'I was not to be allowed to be a pecuniary loser by the publication of a work which cost me so much labour, & which has been considered so creditable to the University.' It was another five months before the board agreed to pay the bill, as Hamilton informed Gill on 11 September. The letter also reveals that the total cost of the work was £335-1-2.[53]

It was just as well for Gill's business that such long credit was matched by almost no inflation in the economy. And although a five-year gestation for an academic book was unusual it was by no means exceptional. By contrast the Press could turn out work with extraordinary speed when required. In 1849 Sir William R. Wilde wrote to his publisher, James McGlashan, about his *Beauties of the Boyne and Blackwater*, then being printed at the DUP:

> Unless there is some great effort made to-morrow or that the printers worked on Sunday, which I suppose they won't, there will not be a chance of the book being out at all next week, and I intend to go away about the end of it . . . But unless some great effort be made at the press work there will not be perfect books for at least seven or eight days. If they put two presses at work to-morrow (Saturday) and keep them at it until we are finished it is just possible that there might be perfect books upon this day week . . .
>
> Will you like a good man poke up the printers and don't leave all the abuse to me for I have enough to do without it. Indeed I cannot complain of them. They are doing for Gill's people [i.e. customers] wonders, but I want them to do more. I want them to do miracles, which I am doing at present. If I don't live to see the book finished

52. MUN/P/4/257/5b.

53. MS 10312/30, O'Kelly's transcripts.

write my elegy — Killed by a book — Slain by a book-seller —
Squeezed to death in a printing press — Made a pye of, or anything
literary of that description.[54]

When the 272-page work appeared the preface contained congratulations
to Gill 'upon the admirable manner in which the work has been printed,
— printed, moreover, within the short space of one month'. So the Press
presumably had met Wilde's gruelling deadline.

Publication of the books paid for by Trinity was effected through the
University bookseller. Up to 1844 this had been Andrew Milliken but, as
we have seen, this family business which went back to the 1770s failed in
the depression of the Famine years. Milliken used to style himself
'Bookseller & Publisher to the University' on his billhead. The same
criticisms levelled against preceding University booksellers also applied
to Milliken. Writing to Gill at an uncertain date but probably about 1840
C.R. Elrington asked about the possibility of having no publisher's name
in the imprint of a work he was having printed, but merely 'printed at the
University Press'; 'and then I would give as many copies as I pleased to
each bookseller. I know the booksellers wish to have their names on the
title-page — but to give the book to Milliken is the same as prohibiting its
sale — and it is awkward to omit the name of the College bookseller from
a College book.'[55] Milliken's business was taken over by Hodges & Smith
— Gill was one of the signatories on the deed of assignment of the
premises in Grafton Street.[56]

The post of University bookseller was prestigious but not lucrative.
Gill informed the 1853 Commission that £122 worth of College books
were sold in 1849, £96 in the following year and only £87 in 1851. In 1852
Hodges & Smith sold books to the retail value of £113, on which they
took 10 per cent commission as well as being provided with 25 copies for
every 24 charged for. They also took 5 per cent on sales of £27 by the
College's London publisher, Whittaker & Co., so the firm must have
been acting as the channel of supply to London as well.[57] With such a
paltry amount of business being done in London it is understandable
that TCD's business was not high on Whittakers' list of priorities. This
led to a switch, the board minutes on 24 November 1855 recording that
'the editor of the University Calendar was authorized to engage Messrs
Longman as London publishers of the work, in place of Messrs
Whittaker by whom its interests appear to have been neglected'. This
was the start of a long relationship.

54. Quoted in T.G. Wilson, *Victorian doctor: being the life of Sir William Wilde*, London 1942, 163 without giving source.
55. MS 10312/180, O'Kelly's transcripts, misdating it after 1856.
56. O'Kelly, 'House of Gill', appx. B, XVIII.
57. MUN/P/4/259/3, Nov. 1852.

A perspective on the prices that Gill was charging both the College and other customers for printing can be had from an 'Abstract of prices of some works printed by M.H. Gill at the College Printing Office' which he submitted in May 1852 when seeking a reduction in rent; the figures exclude extras and paper:[58]

G. Salmon *Analytic geometry*	500 demy 8vo @ £4-9-0 per sheet
J.H. Jellett *Treatise on calculus*	250 8vo @ £4-1-6
W. Fitzgerald *Selections from Nichomachean ethics of Aristotle*	750 8vo @ £2-19-0
J. Henry *Commentary on Virgil*	250 8vo @ £1-17-6
Kennedy-Bailie *Inscriptiones Graecae*	500 4to @ £3-4-0
R. Dixon *Treatise on heat*	750 @ £3-14-0
Physicians *Pharmacopoeia*	500 8vo @ £1-17-6
P. Burrowes *Memoir & speeches*	500 8vo @ £2-3-6
Whitley *Life everlasting*	500 royal 8vo @ £2-5-0

The Dublin booksellers were very anxious that the trade be given better terms by the printers than those afforded to institutions or the public. On 12 September 1832 the Dublin Booksellers' Society resolved that no printer was to be employed who did not provide at least a 25 per cent differential.[59] As will be recalled it was part of the agreement upon Gill's appointment in 1842 that he did College printing at the same rate as he charged the trade. In 1852 Trinity evidently felt that this was not being honoured and may have been the reason why it demanded an extra 10 per cent discount in return for the reduction of £50 in the rent. Gill may well have been under pressure from the trade to maintain the differential. When asked by the 1853 Commission whether there was any inducement to members of the College to print their works at the Press he was very careful in his choice of words in his reply: 'Works printed for the Fellows of the College, at their own expense, are done at a cheaper rate than those printed for the public.' He skirted any mention of trade charges.

Because of the complexity of much of the work printed at the University Press it was in its interest, if it was to remain competitive, that the elaborate scales for such matter, set out in the DTPS rates of pay, be adhered to in the trade. Even the journeymen were aware of this, as is evident from a complaint by the College chapel to the DTPS on 23 May 1848. This stated that Goodwins were printing Kane's *Chemistry* but were paying their comps 'less than what the cast off of the work came to'. The comps in question were called before the committee and, when they admitted they had made a mistake, were requested to amend the situation. They reported back on 13 June that the proprietor Mr Nethercote had afforded an extra shilling per sheet.

58. MUN/P/1/1782.
59. O'Kelly, 'House of Gill', appx. B, XII.

A perusal of Gill's account books will indicate the range of work undertaken at the University Press — largely scholarly, legal or medical bookwork with very little of the commercial jobbing that would have featured in the normal Dublin printing house at this time. It will also indicate the importance of corporate customers — the various learned bodies including Trinity itself — both for the printing they provided and for the private customers they introduced. Printing for the booksellers/publishers was the other staple of the Press.

Printing the proceedings and transactions of such bodies as the Royal Irish Academy, the Royal Dublin Society or the Kilkenny and South East of Ireland Archaeological Society brought in valuable recurrent income, especially the RIA whose *Transactions* tended to be complicated and expensive. The Press was not automatically given this type of work. In March 1855 the RDS informed Gill that it had been suggested that Thoms could print its *Proceedings* for less than the DUP was charging. Gill had to write and defend his price, pointing out that it would be impossible for Thoms to do it for less and also underlining a resolution of the Society that printing contracts were to be given on the basis of competition and not favour — Gill obviously knew that some backdoor undercutting was afoot.[60] There were also commissions to print books for these societies, as for example William Petty's *History of the survey of Ireland* (1851) and the *Leabhar imuinn* edited by J.H. Todd (1855) for the Irish Archaeological and Celtic Society. And as has been seen the DUP printed *The Petrie collection of the ancient music of Ireland* (1855) for the grandly named Society for the Preservation and Publication of the Melodies of Ireland, using the recently acquired founts of music type. This folio work of 500 copies was composed, stereotyped and printed off in parts throughout 1854–1855. Gill charged £6 per sheet for setting the music and £1-17-0 for the text; stereotyping was £2 per sheet and presswork a further £1. Interestingly the Irish text is set in Fry's type up to p. 40 and in Petrie's thereafter. Coldwell did the stereotyping work, not always very carefully, as the ledger for 17 August 1855 reveals a charge against him for composing p. xix and another third of a page which had been 'battered'.[61] The work proved too expensive for the Society and only volume I and the first part of the second volume were published before the money ran out. Gill was forced to write to the Society in October 1856 seeking payment for the last three parts.[62] The Press also did work for lesser known institutions, as for example a *Catalogue of the exhibition of paintings and drawings by amateur artists in aid of the Ladies Relief Association for Clothing the Poor,* held in the RDS in 1850.

The University bookseller, Hodges & Smith, not unnaturally was one of the Press's best book-trade customers. It provided such works as

60. MS 10312/133, Gill to L.S. Foot, O'Kelly's transcripts.
61. MUN/DUP/22/2, 17, 25 Aug. 1855.
62. O'Kelly, 'House of Gill', appx. C, XXV.

Daniel O'Connell's *Trial for conspiracy* (1844, 891p., 8vo), George Petrie's *Ecclesiastical architecture of Ireland* (1845, 521p., 4to with 256 illustrations) and the *Dublin Quarterly Journal of Medical Science*. It also commissioned the printing of several tourist guides such as *Three days on the Shannon* (1852) throughout the 1850s, concentrating on Ulster, Killarney and Dublin, especially for the Great Exhibition of 1853. The ledger also reveals at one point that Hodges & Smith added 15 per cent to Gill's charges when it was commissioning printing on behalf of a private customer.[63]

The most prestigious work commissioned by Hodges & Smith, and one of the highlights in the entire history of the Press and of printing in Ireland, was *Annala Rioghachta Eireann: Annals of the Kingdom of Ireland by the Four Masters*, edited by John O'Donovan, issued in seven large quarto volumes in 1848–1851. Popularly known as the *Annals of the Four Masters*, they were compiled in the early part of the seventeenth century at the behest of the Irish Franciscans at Louvain, as part of their intention to preserve what they could of Gaelic culture after the collapse and routing of the native Irish in the aftermath of the Battle of Kinsale in 1601 and the Flight of the Earls in 1607. A printing press had been set up by the friars at Louvain and it was anticipated that material garnered, including the *Annals*, would be printed there. Brother Michael O'Clery was sent back to Ireland in 1626 with the daunting task of seeking out the material. He worked for several years before gathering a team of assistants to write the *Annals*, which was to document the history of Ireland up to 1616.[64]

They finished their task in 1636, having prepared two copies in the Irish language. Unfortunately any printing of the text had to wait two centuries. Charles O'Conor prepared an edition of the first portion, covering the period to 1171, and this was printed with parallel Latin translation as volume III of *Rerum Hibernicarum scriptores veteres* (Buckingham 1826). John O'Donovan, one of the leading lights in nineteenth-century Irish studies, was scathing of O'Conor's efforts. In one letter in 1836 he wrote: 'to make a rough calculation I should suppose that on average his accuracies and errors would stand in this proportion — Errors, 99 — Accuracies, 199'. In another he showed more frustration: 'Dr O'Conor was a fool or very nearly a fool — though a very learned man; but a man may be very learned and at the same time a very great Amadawn' (*amadán* is Irish for *fool*).[65]

---

63. MUN/DUP/22/2, 9 Jan. 1852, for John Mulcahy's *Principles of modern geometry.*

64. This account of the *Annals* is based largely on Hodges and Smith's announcement of the work, 1848, the text of which is given in Colm Ó Lochlainn, 'John O'Donovan and the Four Masters' in *Irish Book Lover*, XXIX (Apr. 1943) 4–8; Walsh and Ó Lochlainn, *The Four Masters*; and Patricia Boyne, *John O'Donovan (1806–1861): a biography*, Kilkenny 1987, ch. 6.

65. Letters quoted in Boyne, *John O'Donovan*, 44.

George Petrie bought a manuscript of the second part of the *Annals,* covering 1172 to 1616, at the sale of Austin Cooper's library in February 1831, and read a paper on it before the RIA shortly afterwards. Subsequently he was asked to name his price for it by an agent of the bibliomanic Sir Thomas Phillips, which he refused, instead agreeing to hand it over to the Academy for the price he had paid — £50. O'Donovan was fascinated by the *Annals* and within a short time was quoting them in a series of articles on 'The annals of Dublin' which appeared in the *Dublin Penny Journal* during 1832 and 1833. Full publication of the *Annals* was planned in 1833 and Eugene O'Curry set about transcribing the manuscript in the Academy, collating it with an imperfect copy in TCD. As yet however no definite steps towards printing were taken. In 1839 O'Donovan wrote to James Hardiman that the RIA had resolved, at the suggestion of the Lord Lieutenant, to publish the *Annals,* but when no grant was forthcoming the resolve wilted. However when George Smith, of Hodges & Smith, offered to publish the work entirely at his expense, O'Donovan readily accepted. Sir Samuel Ferguson remembered the reactions when the project was settled on: 'I was at the dinner-party at George Smith's when the publication of the "Annals" was determined on, and I remember the faces of all present, from the gentle exaltation of Petrie to the shrewd lines of speculative intelligence round the eyes of Smith . . . .'[66]

The subscription proposals make it clear that only the second part from 1172 onwards was to be printed. It was to be in two quarto volumes containing about 1,600 pages, and was to be printed in an edition of 500 copies. The cost to subscribers was six guineas and eight to others. It was to be put to press when 200 subscriptions had been received and a list of the subscribers was to be published from time to time. 'Considerable expense and trouble have been incurred in selecting models for the Irish type . . . The publishers are happy to say that their selection has met with full approbation of all persons capable of forming a judgement on the subject; and has been adopted by the Royal Irish Academy, and the Irish Archaeological Society . . .'[67] The type referred to, as we have seen above, was that designed by Petrie and modelled on the lettering in the Book of Kells.

A committee was set up by the publishers on 7 February 1845 to decide on the style of the work and they issued a set of rules for the printing. The committee consisted of James Henthorn Todd, Petrie, Aquilla Smith and Joseph Smith.[68] So printing cannot have begun until after that date. The

66. Mary Ferguson, *Sir Samuel Ferguson in the Ireland of his day,* vol. 1, Edinburgh 1896, 70, quoting a letter from Ferguson to Sir Thomas Larcom (no date given).

67. *The annals of the Four Masters, edited by O'Donovan, subscription book* [cover title, Dublin c.1840] 9; this copy in the National Library (with copies of the *Annals* shelved at IR 941 A5) must be a late issue because it contains a list of nearly 250 subscribers.

68. Michael O'Clery, *Annals of the Four Masters,* Dublin 1848–1851, vol. 1, xxxviii–ix.

delays had meant that a rival edition was being put to press at this time and was published in Dublin by Brian Geraghty in 1846. It was an English translation of the second part of the *Annals* done by Owen Connellan, with notes by Philip McDermott, and the whole polished by James Clarence Mangan. O'Donovan however did not see it as a serious rival and referred to it as 'that vulgar translation . . . by Owen Connellan, a peasant from Tireragh, who has as much brains as a hatching goose, and Philip MacDermott, an apothecary from Cavan'.[69] The printing of O'Donovan's version was finished at the University Press late in 1847 and the work, containing about 2,500 pages in three volumes, was published early in 1848.

The critical reaction to the work was such that Smith agreed to finance the publication of the first part, edited by O'Donovan, in the same style. The editor received £150 from Smith for this between early 1848 and May 1849.[70] O'Donovan did not have access to an autograph copy of this part — the copy used by O'Conor was locked away, unusable in the Stowe library — so he relied on the printed version, collating it with later manuscript copies in the RIA and Trinity. As a consequence the text published in 1851 was not as accurate as the 1848 publication. The 1851 part was issued in three volumes together with an index volume. So as to bring the full set into line new titleleaves for the three 1848 volumes were also issued with instructions to the binders on how to bind the seven volumes. The whole work consisted of nearly 4,200 pages with upwards of 11 million characters. O'Donovan rightly considered it as his *magnum opus*. Its progress led to a flurry of honours: membership of the RIA in 1847 and that body's Cunningham Gold Medal in the following year; an honorary LL.D. from Trinity in 1850; and membership of the Royal Prussian Academy in 1856.[71] It paved the way for subsequent critical editions of other Irish annals. Douglas Hyde later described it in his *Literary history of Ireland* as 'the greatest work that any modern Irish scholar ever accomplished'.

Eugene O'Curry was loud in his praise of George Smith 'at whose sole risk and expense this vast publication was undertaken and completed'. Conscious that these were the Famine years he continued:

> There is no instance that I know of, in any country, of a work so vast being undertaken, much less of any completed in a style so perfect and so beautiful, by the enterprise of a private publisher. Mr. Smith's edition of the Annals was brought out in a way worthy of a great national work, — nay, worthy of it, had it been undertaken at the public cost of a great, rich, and powerful people, as alone such

69. Letter from O'Donovan to Denis McCarthy, quoted in Boyne, *John O'Donovan*, 84.

70. Colm Ó Lochlainn, 'John O'Donovan and the *Annals*' in *Irish Book Lover*, XXVII (1940) 179.

71. Boyne, *John O'Donovan*, 86.

works have been undertaken in other countries. And the example of so much spirit in an Irish publisher — the printing of such a book in a city like Dublin, so long shorn of metropolitan wealth as well as honours — cannot fail to redound abroad to the credit of the whole country . . .'[72]

John Gilbert was one of the few contemporaries to consider the typographic achievement in any detail. In a review of 1851 he wrote:

A peculiarly exquisite Irish type, modelled from the characters in the venerable 'Book of Kells', was manufactured expressly for the work. The rules to be observed in printing the text and translation were determined upon by a Committee selected for that purpose; and that the external appearance of the volumes might be in keeping with the character of their contents, the covers have been designed from the elaborate case of the shrine of St. Maidoc, or Aidan, the first Bishop of Ferns, the age of which, in the opinion of some of the most skillful antiquaries of Great Britain, can hardly be later than the eighth century . . . The accuracy with which the whole has been produced is highly creditable to the University Press; although the work exceeds four thousand pages, we have been unable to detect any important error or misprint . . .'[73]

It was the assessment of Colm Ó Lochlainn — no mean typographer — nearly a hundred years later that 'no finer piece of printing has ever been achieved in Ireland' (see plate 23).[74]

Unfortunately Gill's surviving account books are too late to afford any details of the printing. The earliest reference we have is in his journal for September 1852 where Hodges and Smith are charged for putting names of subscribers on the backs of titlepages; on 22 March 1853 he charged 3 shillings for doing so on a large paper set.[75] On 7 January 1854 he printed six sets of titlepages for the work, presumably to make up a deficiency in the number originally printed. The journal also reveals that he printed thousands of prospectuses for the *Annals* throughout 1855 and 1856, indicating that despite its critical acclaim the work was a slow seller. The 'second edition' published in 1856 was in fact a reissue of the sheets of the first edition with new titleleaves; there is a charge in the journal on 26 October 1855 for 'Composition of title-page for Annals of Four Masters

72. Eugene O'Curry, *Lectures on the manuscript materials of ancient Irish history*, Dublin 1861, 161.

73. John Gilbert, 'The Celtic records of Ireland' in *Irish Quarterly Review*, I/4 (Dec. 1851) 697–8 n.

74. Walsh and Ó Lochlainn, *The Four Masters*, 37.

75. MUN/DUP/22/2.

178   aNNaza RIoᵹhachca eIReaNN.   [535.

Ⴑⲣι ⲣιⲥhιⳅ ⲣⲉⲁⲛóιⲣ ⲣⲣⲁlⲙⲁⲥh, ⲁ ⲉ́ᵹlⲁⲥh ⲣιⲟᵹ̇ⲃⲁ ⲣⲉⲙⲉⲁⲛⲛ,
Ꙃⲁⲛ ⲁⲣ, ᵹⲁⲛ ⲃⲩⲁιⲛ, ᵹⲁⲛ ⳅíⲟⲣⲁⲩ̇, ᵹⲁⲛ ᵹⲛιⲟⲙ̇ⲣⲁⲩ̇, ⲁⲥ́ⳅⲙⲁⲩ̇ léιᵹιⲟⲛⲛ.
Ⴑⲉⲁⲣ ⳅⲣí ⲣιⲥhιⳅ ⲣⲥ́ⲣ ⳅⲣí céⲟ, ⲁⲣⲥⲁⲣⲩιⲛ ⲁⲣ ⲣⲉⲁⲛ ⲁⲛ ⲟ́éⳅ,
Ní ⲙó cιⲛ óᵹⲁⲛ ⲣⲟ ᵹ̇ⲁιl, ιⲣ ⲁιⲉ́ⲣιⲟ̇ⲉ ⲁⲛ ⲣⳅ́ⲛⲣⲓⲁⲥⲁιl.

aⲟιⲣ Cⲣιⲟⲣⳅ,cⲩ́ιⲥⲥ céⲟ ⳅⲣιⲟⲥhⲁ ⲁ cⲩιᵹ. aⲛ ⳅⲟⲥhⳅⲙ̇ⲁⲩ̇ blιⲁⲟ̇ⲁιⲛ ⲟⲟ Ⴑⲩⲁⳅⲁl.
Ⴇⲁⲥlⲁιⲣ Ꙋⲟιⲣⲉ Cⲁlᵹⲁιᵹ ⲟⲟ ⲣⲟⳅhⲩᵹhⲁⲩ̇ lⲁ Colⲟⲙ Cιllⲉ, ιⲁⲣ ⲛⲉⲟ̇ⲃⲁιⲣⳅ ⲁⲛ bⲁιlⲉ
ⲟⲟ ⲟιⲁ ⲟⲉⲣbⲣ̇ιⲛⲉ ⲣéⲛ .ι. Cⲉⲛⲉl cCⲟⲛⲁιll Ꙃⲩlbⲁⲛ ⲙιⲥ Néll.
Cⲟⲣbⲙⲁⲥ, ⲙⲁⲥ Oιlιllⲁ, ⲣι Lⲁιᵹⲥ́ⲛ, ⲟéⲥⲥ.
Oιlιll, ⲉⲣⲣⲥⲟⲣ aⲣⲟⲁ Ⲙⲁⲥhⲁ, ⲟⲟ éⲥⲥ. Ꙋⲟ Uιⲃ bⲣⲥ́ⲣⲁl ⲟⲟιⲣιⲟ̇ⲉ bⲉⲟⲣ.
aⲟιⲣ Cⲣιⲟⲣⳅ, cⲩ́ιⲥⲥ céⲟ ⳅⲣιⲟⲥhⲁ ⲁ ⲣⲉⲁⲥhⳅ. aⲛ ⲟⲉⲁⲥhⲙ̇ⲁⲩ̇ blιⲁⲟ̇ⲁιⲛ ⲟⲟ
Ⴑⲩⲁⳅⲁl. S. Lⲩᵹhⲁιⲟ̇, ⲉⲣⲣⲩⲥⲥ Cⲟⲛⲛⲉⲣⲉ, ⲟéⲥⲥ.
Cⲁⳅh Slιᵹιᵹhⲉ ⲣιⲁ bⲢⲥ́ⲣᵹⲩⲣ Ᵹ ⲣιⲁ ⲛꙊⲟⲙ̇ⲛⲁll, ⲟⲁ ⲙⲁⲥ Ⲙⲩιⲣⲥ́ⲣⳅⲁιᵹ, ⲙιⲥ
Ⴇⲁⲣⲥⲥⲁ, ⲣιⲁ ⲛaιⲛⲙιⲣⲉ, ⲙⲁⲥ Séⲟⲛⲁ, Ᵹ ⲣιⲁ ⲛaιⲛⲟιⲟ̇, ⲙⲁⲥ Ꙋⲩⲁⲥh, ⲣⲟⲣ Ⴇⲟᵹⲁⲛ
bⲉl, ⲣι Cⲟⲛⲛⲁⲥhⳅ. Rⲟ ⲙⲉⲁⲃⲁιⲟ̇ ⲁⲛ ⲥⲁⳅh ⲣⲥ́ⲙⲣⲁ, ⲟⲟ ⲣⲟⲥhⲁιⲣ Ⴇⲟᵹⲁⲛ bél, ⲟιⲁ
ⲛⲉbⲣⲁⲩ̇ ιⲛⲟⲣⲟ.

     Ⴑιⲥhⳅⲉⲣ ⲥⲁⳅh Uⲁ Ⴑιⲁⲥhⲣⲁⲥh, lⲁ ⲣⲥ́ⲛⲥⲥ ⲣⲁⲟⲃⲁιⲣ, ⳅⲁⲣ ιⲙbⲉl,
Ꙃⲉⲣⲓⲣ bⲩⲁⲣ ⲛⲁⲙ̇ⲁⳅ ⲣⲣι ⲣlⳅ́ᵹhⲁ, ⲣⲣⲉⳅhⲁ ιⲛ ⲥⲁⲥ́ ι Cⲣιⲛⲟⲉⲣ.

" Ⴑιⲁⲥⲩιl Ⲙⲟⲥ́ⳅⲁ, bⲁ ⲙⲁιⲥ́ béⲣ! ⳅⲣí céⲟ blιⲁⲟ̇ⲁⲛ (bⲩⲁⲛ ⲁⲛ ⲥ́ⲣ)
Ꙃⲁⲛ ᵹhⲩⲥ́ ⲛιⲟⲙⲣⲩιll ⲣⲉιⲥ́ⲉ ⲣⲩⲁⲣ! ᵹⲁⲛ ⲙ̇ⲥ́ⲣ ⲛιⲟⲛⲙ̇ⲁιⲣ ⲣⲉιⲥ́ⲉ ⲣⲥ́ⲣ.
Nιⲣ bó ⲟⲟⲥ́ⳅⲁ ⲙⲩιⲛⲛⳅⲉⲣ Ⲙⲟⲥ́ⳅⲁ! Lⲩᵹⲙⲁιᵹ lⲥ́ⲣ:
Ⴑⲣí céⲟ ⲣⲁᵹⲁⲣⳅ, ⲩⲙ céⲟ ⲛⲉⲣⲣⲟⲥ! ⲙⲁιllⲉ ⲣⲣⲓⲣ,
Ⴑⲣι ⲣιⲥ́ιⲟ ⲣⲉⲁⲛóιⲣ ⲣⲁlⲙⲁⲥ́! ⲁ ⲥ́ⲉⲁᵹⲗⲁⲥ́ ⲣιⲟᵹ̇ⲟ̇ⲁ ⲣⲉⲙⲉⲛⲟ :
Ꙃⲁⲛ ⲁⲣ, ᵹⲁⲛ bⲩⲁιⲛ, ᵹⲁⲛ ⲥιⲟⲣⲁⲩ̇, ᵹⲁⲛ ᵹⲛιⲟⲙ̇ⲣⲁⲩ̇, ⲁⲥ́ⲟ ⲙⲁⲩ̇ léᵹⲉⲛⲟ."

" Dentes Moctei, qui fuit moribus integer, spa-
tio trecentorum annorum (quantus rigor!)
Nec verbum otiosum extra emisere, nec quid-
quam obsonii intra admisere.
Non fuit angusta familia Moctei, Lugmagensis
   Monasterii :
Trecenti præsbyteri, et centum Episcopi, erant
   cum ipso

Sexaginta seniores psalmicani, choristo ejus
   familia augusta et magnifica,
Qui nec arabant, nec metebant, nec tritura-
   bant, nec aliud faciebant, quam studiis in-
   cumbere."—*Acta Sanctorum*, p. 734.

Colgan then goes on to shew that ⳅⲣí céⲟ
blιⲁⲟ̇ⲁⲛ is an error for ⳅⲣí ⲣé céⲟ blιⲁⲟ̇ⲁⲛ, or
ⲣⲣⲓ ⲣé céⲟ blιⲁⲟ̇ⲁⲛ, i. e. for a period of one
hundred years; and he quotes four lines from a
poem by Cumineus of Connor, to shew that
Mochta lived only one hundred years in this
state of austerity.
    * *Doire-Chalgaigh.*—Now Derry or London-
derry. The name Doire-Chalgaigh is translated
Roboretum Calgachi by Adamnan, in his Life
of Columba, lib. i. c. 20. According to the
Annals of Ulster this monastery was founded
in 545, which is evidently the true year.
" A. D. 545. Daire Coluim Cille *fundata est*."

---

23. A page (reduced) from volume 1 of the *Annals of Ireland* (1851) showing
the three sizes of Petrie type.

4-0'. Both 'editions' have the same five-page addenda and corrigenda which confirms that they were printed from the same setting of type and at the same time. Had the type been kept standing — and ignoring that this would have been an impossible task for such a vast hand-set work — corrections would have been made in the type before any reprinting. The edition did sell out by the end of the century and copies became much sought after, so much so that at least one bookseller contemplated having portion of it reprinted at the University Press to make up defective sets. On 3 July 1914 the Press quoted John Weldrick £5-10-0 for 'Composition, printing, and paper [for] 6 copies of "Annals of the Four Masters" 16 pages 4to'.[76] A new edition was planned by Father Paul Walsh in the 1940s, but he did not live to see it through. O'Donovan's edition was photolithographically reproduced in 1990 and published by De Búrca Rare Books in Dublin, with the addition of some missing text and a short introduction by Kenneth Nicholls.

Hodges and Smith may well have been the DUP's largest trade customer at this date, but many of the other Dublin booksellers/ publishers are represented in Gill's account books: William Curry & Co., George Herbert, James McGlashan, Cumming & Ferguson, W.B. Kelly, Rooney & Co., and Fannin & Co. all feature. Examples of the type of work done were V. Bythner's *Lyre of David*, a work with much Hebrew edited by N.L. Benmohel and printed for Cumming & Ferguson in 1847; Ledwich's *Anatomy of the human body*, printed for Fannin in 1852; and Daniel Foley's *English-Irish dictionary*, done for Curry in 1855. The journal also reveals that the practice of several booksellers coming together in a partnership to publish a book was still alive in mid-nineteenth-century Dublin. Rooney & Kelly's account is debited in December 1851 with a charge of £72-5-4 for printing an edition of Euripides' *Hecuba* edited by Wheeler; the *contra* side shows that Rooney paid £24, Machen £17-10-0, Cornish the same, and Bellew £11-8-0 towards the cost.

And of course the Press had its private customers. One of these was James Kennedy-Bailie, a classicist and one-time member of the College, who resigned his fellowship to take up the clerical living at Ardtrea in Co. Tyrone in 1831. A clutch of his letters survives which gives an insight into Gill's relationships with his customers.[77] While his *Fasciculus inscriptionum Graecarum* (issued in three volumes in 1842–1849) was being printed he wrote a long series of letters to Gill. The correspondence indicates they were on very familiar terms. On 22 June 1844 Kennedy-Bailie thanked Gill for having been 'exceedingly reasonable with me — indeed I may say liberal — in the matter of charges'. At the same time he complained that Rivingtons, his London publishers, were being apathetic, and went on to discuss the failure of 'poor Milliken': 'What a tumble down it has been for

---

76. MUN/DUP/9/1/246.
77. MS 10308/1–68, 1844–53.

the family of the University Bookseller, who were in his time so eminent in the trade!' Kennedy-Bailie was aware of the technical difficulties his manuscript was presenting. 'I suppose you rubbed your eyes a little at the sight of the strange Greek capitals and contractions', he wrote on 10 February 1845, but felt that the challenge of printing them would 'augment incalculably the fame of the establishment over which you preside, and reflect great honor on Irish art'. He was not always so complimentary about the Press. In a letter of 15 October 1846 he mentions that recently there had been 'a little of a game at cross-purposes between the Gentlemen of the press and me' whereby compositors had been undoing corrections he had made on proofs; 'this never happened in the good old times'. A letter of 15 November 1847 reveals that Gill provided him with news from the capital, and had recently written of the suicide of James McCullagh, professor of Natural and Experimental Philosophy, and of the failure of Cumming & Ferguson's business. Kennedy-Bailie was full of the importance of his work: 'the publication of this series will mark an era in the typography of our poor depressed and contemned country. I am, in truth, embarked in a patriotic enterprize.' He took a more sober measure of its importance on 22 December 1848 after he had received Gill's bill. He asked for credit until July: 'You must be cautious of fixing on too high a price [for the work] . . . I hardly expect to dispose of a copy . . . in this country — perhaps in England I may, a few, and on the Continent, just sufficient to pay the expenses of advertising, but no more.'

A similar correspondence was exchanged over Kennedy-Bailie's 'Memoir on two large medallion busts which are preserved in the Manuscript Room of the Library of TCD', published in vol. XXII of the RIA *Transactions* in 1852. He constantly found mistakes that he had made in sheets that had been passed for press, and in one letter on 28 April 1852 had to tell Gill to recancel an existing cancel of pp. 187–8 after he discovered an incorrect source. Gill scrupulously attended to his corrections, as a letter of 24 June 1852 attests: 'I perceive clearly that great attention is paid to my corrections, and feel grateful to you for it.' Earlier on 8 June he wrote anxiously to ask if Gill had received his last batch of manuscript. When he had heard nothing from the University Press and knowing that Gill was 'always so correct in matters relating to your department', he began to feel uneasy that it had been lost in transit, 'more especially as I have to deal with Presbyterians here — a clan of persons who, from their indomitable self-will often do queer things — and occasionally, in consequence, subject <u>gentlemen</u> to . . . disappointment'.

On 3 July he commiserated with Gill for the trials he was giving him: 'I pity you very much for having any concern with these outlandish pages of mine and wish you speedy release.' This did not happen until November. As late as 23 October he was having cancels inserted: 'In the binding I depend implicitly on your oversight [i.e. overseeing] of the several <u>cancels</u>, that you will not count too much on the ready wittedness of the workmen, but see that my latest improvements have been duly inserted.' He went on to request that copies be sent to the heads of the Queen's Colleges and of Maynooth College, a Catholic seminary. He evidently thought that Gill was a Protestant because he felt the need to defend his request: 'I think it likely that perhaps you and the Messrs H & S felt suprized [sic] at this . . . Now, I detest and abjure, from my heart and soul the narrow bigotry which would interfere, merely on the ground of a discrepancy in religious sentiment, with the cordial fellowship which should link together all members of the literary brother-hood.' He expressed a fear that intellectual sectarianism would debar him from the recognition he felt he deserved. True to form, when the work had been published he discovered other mistakes, and wrote on 17 November that cancels for pp. 291-4 and a new corrigenda would have to be printed and sent to purchasers. At last on 6 December he was satisfied: 'So now, for the honor of the [Royal Irish] Academy and the Doric temple [i.e. the University Press], let the copies reach their respective destinations . . .' All through the correspondence Gill also had to put up with a running account of Kennedy-Bailie's obsessive belief that he was related to the Marquis of Ailsa. It is a great shame that we do not have copies of Gill's replies, but there is little doubt that he treated his tedious correspondent with scrupulous courtesy.

William R. Wilde was another demanding customer, both in his private and institutional capacities. The printed copy he provided for his *Diseases of the ear* was 'so much altered as to be as troublesome as manuscript' and extra was charged accordingly. Alterations at proof stage caused havoc and pages constantly had to be overrun. The extra charges for these often came to half the basic cost of composition and presswork.[78] Yet Wilde was not as bad as John Murray. Gill's journal for November and December 1852 records that for Murray's pamphlet, *Wellington: the place and date of his birth ascertained,* alterations and overrunning cost more than the basic charges. By contrast the Rev. J.A. Galbraith and Rev. S. Haughton provided valuable recurrent income for the straightforward printing of large editions of their perennially popular textbooks: manuals of *Plain trigonometry, Optics, Hydrostatics* and *Arithmetic.*[79]

As has been mentioned Gill printed *The Irish Industrial Exhibition of 1853* in 1854 for the editor John Sproule. This was a lucrative commission, the edition of 2,000 costing £657 including paper. Gill's journal provides some interesting figures for it. He charged £2-9-0 for composing each octavo half-sheet in bourgeois type, and £2-16-0 for brevier. Presswork cost £1-14-8 per sheet if there were no wood-engravings in it, and £2-2-8 if there were, a 23 per cent premium. On top of that he charged an extra 4-6

78. MUN/DUP/22/2, 8 Oct. 1852, and 1853 *passim.*
79. MUN/DUP/22/2, 20 Aug. 1852, 29 Dec. 1853, 20 Feb., 31 Mar. 1855.

per sheet for bringing up the illustrations at press. On the paper bought in at about £2 per ream Gill charged 5 per cent commission. The following résumé to the nearest £, with the percentages of the total cost they represent, can be worked out from the entry for 25 August 1854:

Composition	£169	26%
Presswork	138	21%
Extras	14	2%
Alterations and cancels	38	6%
Paper	298	45%

An earlier spin-off from the Exhibition for the Press was a commission from McGlashan to print a quarto edition of Shakespeare's *Midsummer night's dream*. This must have been connected with the exhibition there of W. Boyton Kirk's dessert service based on the play.[80] The University Press also had a display at the Exhibition. On p. 330 of Sproule's work will be found the following entry: 'Gill, M.H., University Press, Dublin. Various volumes of books in 4to and 8vo, printed in the English, Latin, Greek, Hebrew, Oriental and Irish languages. Specimens of illustrated and scientific printing.' It was not the first time that Gill had exhibited his printings. He partook regularly in the RDS's exhibitions, which started in 1834 and continued at first annually and then triennially after that, before ceasing with that of 1864. The RDS's *Report . . . on the exhibition of Irish manufacture . . .* (Dublin 1847) records that he was awarded a large silver medal for specimens of printing shown. The list of 34 works given includes Ussher's *Works*, Hart's *Mechanics*, the RDS *Proceedings*, works done for the Irish Archaeological Society, and the second edition of John MacNeill's *Tables for . . . the calculation of earth work* '(four copies printed on coloured papers)'. He also won a medal in 1844, as also a certificate in 1850.

Among the jobbing undertaken for non-trade customers were exam papers for such bodies as St Columba's College, the Academic Institute and the Excelsior Institution. This was the start of the Press's reputation for security printing beyond the walls of Trinity. Prices varied from 6-6 per page for English to 11-6 for Greek.[81] The small amount of commercial jobbing done included lists of members and books for the Fitzwilliam Book Club, notices of cocks of hay for sale by Michael Donovan at Templeogue, illustrations on coloured paper for Hutchinson's Snuff Manufactory, a circular with illustration about the erection of the Church of Our Saviour for Rev. Dr Russell, and the thousands of bottle labels and tea wrappers for Miss Hart already mentioned.[82]

80. MUN/DUP/22/2, 27 May 1853; for an illustration of the dessert service see Mark Bence-Jones, 'Ireland's Great Exhibition' in *Country Life* (15 Mar. 1973) 665–8.

81. MUN/DUP/22/2, 15 Dec. 1851, June 1855.

82. MUN/DUP/22/2, 15 Jan., 13 May, 7 Aug., 3 Sept., 1852, 26 Feb. 1853, 23 Jan. 1855.

The Press also did some very specialised work, as for example printing on satin or silk. A case in point was recorded in Gill's journal on 4 July 1855: a Mr Cahill was charged £1-15-0 for a broadside address to Rochefort B. Hunt, printed in gold on satin, with twelve copies on paper. The Press also did specialist setting for other printers, as for example on 13 February 1852 'Composing in pica & l. primer Irish, the Hymn of St Patrick, &c and motto for Catholic laymen in pica Irish' for Purdon Brothers; or composing 32 lines of pearl music for a musical soirée programme done for Underwoods on 4 May 1855.

There is little evidence of the mode of payments at this period, but my impression is that there was more settlement in cash and less reliance on promissory notes. Credit periods continued to be long with payments being made quarterly or even annually, as in the case of the College of Physicians. The Press's suppliers were less accommodating, and Gill for example had to pay his binder monthly and was not even afforded discount for prompt payment. Debts owed by customers were pursued vigorously. In 1835 Thaddeus Connellan had R. Whately's *Easy lessons on money matters* in English and Irish printed at the Press at a cost of £180. Gill was reluctant to release the work until payment was forthcoming — Connellan must have had a bad reputation — and it was not until 1843 that agreement was reached on annual instalments of £20 and the works handed over. When Connellan died in 1854 there was still £30 outstanding.[83]

Although Gill was essentially a printer his interest in publishing had been lifelong and his involvement in it had been growing since the mid-1840s. His 1828 'manifesto' identified distribution as the key to the success of any book. Although he always had opinions on this end link in the book chain Gill took a decisive step in 1852 when he purchased several copyrights from the assignees of Cumming and Ferguson who had been declared bankrupt on 24 July 1847.[84] He paid £62-15-0 for the rights to Kennedy-Bailie's Homer, McCaul and Wheeler's Horace (including the stereotype plates), Waring's Horace, Walker's Lucian, Hoole's *Terminations*, Jackson and Trotter's *Book-keeping*, and Murray and Trotter's *Abridgement of English grammar*; he also got a half-share in V. Bythner's *Lyre of David*.[85] Whitakers in London got the other half-share in the latter work and in this Gill felt hard done by. As has been noted the work had been printed at the Press for Cumming and Whitakers, his London partner, in 1847, but Gill had not been paid before Cumming's failure. He applied to Whitakers for payment without success, they feeling that they had already paid their share. This Gill reluctantly accepted as equitable if not legal.[86]

83. MS 10312/159/1b, Gill to Connellan, Aug. 1839, Sept. 1843, O'Kelly's transcripts.
84. *Dublin Gazette*, 3 Aug. 1847.
85. MUN/DUP/22/2, 24 Apr. 1852, paid to A. Armstong; MUN/DUP/22/3/32.
86. MS 10312, O'Kelly's transcript of draft of letter from Gill to Whitaker & Co., London, 17 July 1852.

Of these works Jackson's *Book-keeping* seems to have been the only one that sold, quantities of it being disposed of throughout 1852 and 1853, as recorded in Gill's journal. It retailed at 3-6 and Gill gave varying terms to wholesale purchasers, selling it to some at 2-0 and to others at 25 per cent discount, with a further 10 per cent for cash. He also gave the usual free extra copy for every dozen bought. Gill also acquired stocks of Owen Connellan's *English-Irish dictionary* in 1852 and of Marcus Trotter's *Commercial arithmetic* in 1855, but the journal does not show if he owned the copyright in these. One other copyright he did acquire was Cicero's *Orations* translated by McKay and the journal records the printing of an edition of 500 for 'M.H. Gill (Copyright)' on 2 October 1855. Gill acted as publisher for only a handful of customers; the University Press was not geared up for distribution. John Smith, professor of Music at the College, had his *Treatise on the theory and practice of music* printed at the Press in 1853 and his account is credited with the sale of a small number of copies. Gill's journal also records the sale on 21 December 1853 of a substantial number of song sheets and of the *Treatise* to Henry Smith in Cambridge.

Thus we arrive at the mid–1850s. The reputation of the Press was at its height. William Reeves' comments in 1855 on a work he had had printed there is indicative of the respect which the DUP had won: 'The style of the printing was beautiful & chaste — just of a piece with the University Press which can take a hint where another would require a harangue, and can then do its work offhandedly while its neighbour is bungling over a job.'[87] Gill, just turned sixty, was, in Kennedy-Bailie's phrase, 'the worthy director of the leading typographical office in Ireland'[88] and might well have been expected to ease back on his workload. In fact he was planning the expansion of his publishing interests.

---

87. MS 10308/386, Reeves to Gill, 6 Aug. 1855.
88. MS 10308/60, Kennedy-Bailie to Gill, 30 Nov. 1852.

8

M.H. Gill: the man

Before turning to consider that expansion let us consider the man himself. One feels because M.H. Gill's name occurs in hundreds of imprints that the man himself is accessible; but the opposite is the case. He left no published work that we can be sure of or diaries, and must have been very retiring as no portrait or even photograph of him appears to have survived. Yet something of his character can be reconstructed from the remnants of his business papers and from a few published recollections of him.

He made friends of many of the authors and business people with whom he dealt, and these friendships ran deep. Among the people he obliged with a loan was Cotterell William Mercier, son of the former University printer and bookseller, R.E. Mercier, who seems to have led a troubled life. Cotterell wrote to him in January 1846: 'I feel so deeply obliged by your former kindness to me and that at moments when I stood so much in need of the aid of a friend.'[1] Gill became so familiar with some of his authors that they even felt they could ask him to do the most intimate errands, as the case of Joseph Kennedy-Bailie shows. Among the many letters he wrote to Gill while his *Fasciculus inscriptionum Graecarum* (1842–1849) was going through the press was one on 9 January 1847 asking him to obtain on his behalf from a Dublin medical hall 'a pessary of the much approved construction' for a complaint that he had. Kennedy-Bailie, a clergyman in Ardtrea, Co. Tyrone, felt the need to be secretive: 'N.B. Do not divulge my name.'[2] One wonders did he take any account of Gill's sensitivities.

Gill's friendship and admiration for George Petrie led him to refuse to print a work which reflected badly on the antiquarian. On 26 January 1856 Henry O'Neill wrote from London seeking proofs of a reprint of his article from the *Kilkenny Archaeological Society's Journal* on the Cross of Cong, which corrected some of Petrie's misreadings of the inscriptions. He complained that the text had been altered by James Graves, the editor

1. MS 10308/278–279, two letters, 4 Dec. 1845 and 15 Jan. 1846.
2. MS 10308/11.

of the journal, without authority. Gill was obviously shocked that the transmission of text from author to printer had been thus tampered with and replied that he had not been aware of the alteration. However he observed that it had been 'judicious . . . made probably with a view to mitigate the pain that Dr Petrie . . . might feel on reading the passage'. O'Neill replied on 31 January that he was merely setting out the facts, and that the whole affair surprised him 'not a little'. Gill stuck by Petrie out of personal respect and admiration of him for his scholarship, and refused to reprint the article with the offending paragraph. O'Neill wrote to Gill on 2 February saying that as he would not print it as the author wished he was withdrawing it.[3] The affair later led to a pamphlet 'skirmish' between John O'Donovan and O'Neill.

Gill himself was a subscriber to the Kilkenny Archaeological Society — his account books record his subscriptions as well as the odd donation — and also to other learned societies. He did printing for many of these societies so it could be inferred that it was just good business practice to take out a subscription, but there can be little doubt that he had a genuine concern for Irish studies. The mid-nineteenth century witnessed an explosion of scholarly interest in Irish culture and as printer of many of the most important texts Gill was at the centre of the movement.

O'Kelly has documented that Gill's correspondence was peppered with solicitations of favours and loans.[4] An example of his encouragement of a provincial printer occurred in 1853 when he lent some titling type to a printer in Mullingar for the titlepage of a book on grand jury laws. This transpired to be John Charles Lyons of the Ledeston Press.[5] Gill's ledger documents the odd occasion of charity, as when in April 1861 he charged £5-3-0 to the Rev. John Spratt for printing 1,500 prospectuses for *Night Refuge* and entered on the *contra* 'By my subscription to "Night Refuge" £5-3-0'.[6] Another occasion for his charity, as has been seen, was his membership on the committee of the Asylum for Aged Printers in the 1830s. And in 1851 he sent out circulars to other printers asking them to subscribe to a raffle for the stereotype plates of *The poor man's manual* in aid of Thomas Coldwell, a Dublin printer on hard times.[7]

Gill seems to have been a good employer — W.C. Trimble remembered him in 1869 as 'an elderly and nice gentleman'[8] — but he was also a stickler for detail and proper conduct. One of the most revealing occasions of this occurred in 1863. On 25 July Dr Samuel Butcher, later to be Bishop of

3. MS 10308/371–375.

4. O'Kelly, 'House of Gill', 164.

5. ibid. 172–3. For an account of John C. Lyons see Marian Keaney, *Westmeath authors*, Mullingar 1969, 92–3.

6. MUN/DUP/22/3/116, Apr., 9 Aug. 1861.

7. O'Kelly, 'House of Gill', 171.

8. Trimble, 'Dublin University Press', 16.

Meath, wrote from Ballymoney Rectory, Co. Cork, complaining at the delay in printing MacNiece's sermons delivered in the College Chapel and threatened to take it to another printer. (Butcher was a very prickly customer; he never started a letter with 'Dear Mr Gill', but would launch into the third person: 'Dr Butcher begs to remind Mr Gill . . .') Gill must have had things speeded up because a second sheet was worked off shortly afterwards. On 31 July Butcher wrote to R.C. Gerrard, Gill's manager at the University Press, to say that he had not said whether the edition was to be 750 or 500, yet the larger number had been worked off 'and he regrets for Mr Gill's sake that such a mistake has been made.' A note in Gill's hand has been added at the end of this letter: 'Recd from Mr Gerrard Tuesday Augt. 4th after a 2nd. sheet of 750 was worked.' The manager was apparently dismissed over this affair, not because the extra sheets were printed — he could and did pay compensation for these — but because he tried to cover his mistake by withholding correspondence from Gill. All was revealed in a long letter from Gerrard at his private residence at 29 Arran Quay on 5 August. He wrote that he did not want to show Gill the letter until the edition size had been clarified, 'knowing that, whether right or wrong, it would have brought me censure, of which I received more than a reasonable share during the last week of my stay in the office'. Gill had asked him to search among his private papers for other letters belonging to the office. Gerrard rejected this insinuation that he 'improperly appropriated what did not belong to [him]' and assured Gill that he had shown him all the letters he had received as manager. Gill emerges from this incident as a rather authoritarian and unbending figure.[9]

Another occasion reveals him to have been very fair. On 21 November 1864 the London publisher, George Philip, wrote to him asking for a reference for William Robertson, a bookseller in Dublin that Philip was obviously contemplating supplying. Robertson was despised in the trade for his sharp practices and had been declared bankrupt in the previous year, a failure which cost Gill dearly.[10] Yet Gill could reply that, although they were not on the best of terms because Robertson's trade practices had 'gone far beyond the bounds of propriety', his former bankruptcy was 'not from any want of exertion on his part'.[11]

Gill was scrupulous in the care he took in the output of the Press as also in his code of conduct as a printer. Witness his patent shock over Henry O'Neill's article (1856) when he realised that the text had been tampered with, unknown to the author. Another instance of his self-imposed code of ethics as a printer was given in the following year when he wrote to a Rev. Dr Moore, asking him for permission to show a text to

9. MS 10308/321–324, 346–347.
10. MS 10308/358, Gill to William Lee, 25 July 1863.
11. MS 10308/377.

Samuel Haughton who had requested it, 'as it is an invariable rule with me not to give a copy of any document intrusted to me for printing, without the permission of the author'.[12]

The same scrupulousness was evident when Gill expanded his book-selling and publishing interests after acquiring McGlashan's business in 1856. Thomas Hodgson, the London publisher, wrote to him soon afterwards that 'McGlashan always had opposition, so will you.' He goes on, however, to say that Gill's business practices were melting the opposition: 'It is an unbounded satisfaction to hear you so well spoken of by all . . . This cash and quick settlement of yours will act like a charm . . . It is a new epoch in the wholesale trade in Ireland.' Gill enhanced his reputation with Hodgson in later years by providing him with substantial loans.[13] In Ireland Gill was perceived as a liberal nationalist bookseller. On 21 April 1859 John O'Connell wrote to John O'Donovan asking him to further the sale of a work of his on Shakespeare, which was being published by Black in Edinburgh, by recommending a Dublin partner. O'Connell did not think that Hodges and Smith would be suitable because of the anti-English spirit in the work, but suggested McGlashan (i.e. Gill) 'who is I understand a man of extended custom and probably amongst the Irish proper'. O'Donovan passed on the letter to Gill with a note to his 'dear friend': 'He takes you to be among the liberal class of Irish booksellers.'[14]

Gill was well respected among his peers and from an early date was prominent in what became the Dublin Master Printers' Association. For example he was involved in the joint DTPS/master printers' attempts to wrest government contracts from Thoms in the latter half of the 1840s. Thoms was despised by the DTPS throughout the century because it was an 'unfair' house which did not pay the Society's rates and employed an inordinate number of apprentices. A report to the DTPS committee on 17 February 1845 recorded that there were 22 men and 24 boys. Many of the men were anxious to join the Society, but to do so publicly probably meant dismissal by the proprietor Alexander Thom. He had a core of loyal Scotsmen — Thom was Scottish himself — who kept things going. The employers in the 'fair' houses resented him because he got away with paying lower wages and therefore put them at a disadvantage in any tenders. To challenge Thoms the DTPS was anxious that another master printer should compete for government contracts. The Society approached several employers to see if they would take up the mantle, but they declined. However the suggestion did stimulate the master printers to consider the matter at a meeting that took place in Gill's house at 194 Great Brunswick Street on 2 March 1846, as the DTPS

12. MS 10308/365, 25 Mar. 1857.
13. O'Kelly, 'House of Gill', 310–12, 317.
14. MS 10308/369–370.

committee minutes recorded on the following day. Nothing however transpired until nearly four years later when agreement was reached on 16 January 1850 between the Society and Griersons, whereby certain articles in the agreed scale of wages were suspended to allow the firm to tender for government bookwork, which hitherto Thom had made his own. The minutes recorded that the Society 'rejoiced at the enterprising spirit which has led . . . [Griersons] to compete for that important work, and [the committee was] happy to reciprocate the warm good feeling evinced by them [Griersons] at all times towards the working man'. Griersons was successful in its tenders, but the mutual 'warm good feeling' did not last very long. After just a month Griersons invoked the concessions afforded to dismiss six men paid on the establishment, which otherwise would not have been allowed by the rules. And on 22 October the DTPS had to send a deputation to meet a committee of four of the employers, which included Gill, to explain that the concessions made to Griersons applied only to government contract work, and not to municipal work that the firm had recently won.

Given Gill's involvement at every level of the book trade it might be thought that he would have had no time for any other business interests. But in fact he had extensive dealings in the provisions trade and in property. According to O'Kelly he was involved in the tea, wine and spirits business through contacts with his in-laws, the Hart family.[15] O'Kelly also recorded that 'through a readiness to lighten the burdens of friends and share the responsibilities of relatives, M.H. Gill came to own or have heavy pecuniary interests in many premises'. He instances 1–4 Lower Merrion Street, 16–18 Lower Ormond Quay and 12 Swift's Row (17 Lower Ormond Quay and 12 Swift's Row immediately behind it had been the premises of John Cumming before his bankruptcy in 1847). Gill also owned 42 Great Brunswick Street (later renumbered 180, and later still 194), which backed on to the courtyard beside the Printing House and where he lived from 1832 to 1848. It seems strange that although he continued to own all these properties, for the next sixteen years he lived in rented houses, first in Mount Haigh at 68 Upper George's Street in Kingstown (now Dun Laoghaire), a growing town on a railway line to the south-east of the city, and later from 1852 in Horton House in Roundtown (now Terenure), a village south of the city. He returned to town in 1861 to live in the McGlashan and Gill premises at 50 Upper Sackville Street (now O'Connell Street), renting it until he purchased it in 1864.[16]

The portrait of Gill that emerges from what can be gleaned of him is of an astute and tireless businessman, scrupulous and meticulous in all his dealings which led to him being unbending on occasion when crossed. Yet in the main he was a very fair and charitable man whose qualities led

15. O'Kelly, 'House of Gill', 15.
16. ibid. appx. A, I–V

to firm friendships. He was of a scholarly bent and retiring in temperament. Any man who, as a Catholic, could bestride the sectarian divide to become printer to the conservative, Protestant dominated University, and yet be perceived as a liberal nationalist bookseller, must have been an exceptional character.

9

M.H. Gill:
Second Phase: 1856–1875

In 1855 James McGlashan ran one of Dublin's biggest bookselling and publishing houses from premises at 50 Upper Sackville Street.[1] He was one of the wave of Scots, that included the Thoms and Pattison Jolly, who moved into the Irish book trade in the first half of the nineteenth century. (For some inexplicable reason there seems to have been an influx of Scottish horticulturalists and gardeners as well.) McGlashan seems originally to have worked for Blackwoods, the Edinburgh publishers, and came to Dublin about 1830. He formed a partnership with William Curry, Junior almost immediately, which lasted for sixteen years. A shrewd businessman, McGlashan spotted the potential of the fledgling *Dublin University Magazine* which was launched in January 1833, and bought it out for the partnership within six months with the intention of making it the Irish *Blackwood's* or *Frazer's*. He even took over the editorship from Isaac Butt in December 1838, but persuaded Charles Lever to take on the mantle in April 1842. McGlashan launched out on his own in 1846 and took the *Magazine* with him, an event recorded in the *Freeman's Journal* on 8 April: 'The proprietorship has passed into hands, new to the general public [but] not unknown to the secret few who long recognized in the ability, energy, and enterprise of Mr McGlashan the qualities that formed and worked the magazine . . . To the spirit that has lately arisen to originate and support a national literature, Mr McGlashan has essentially contributed.' He continued to publish some of the novels serialised in the *Magazine* and also a broad range of general books and a whole host of periodicals.

'Jemmie' McGlashan was, in Charles Lever's terms, 'a devil of a screw . . . [who] will fight to the last for low terms', but also 'the very ablest man in his walk'. He was also a *bon vivant*, who enjoyed conversation

---

1. This account of McGlashan is based on V. Kinane and M. Gill, 'McGlashan and Gill' in *Dictionary of literary biography vol. 106: British literary publishing houses, 1820–1880*, Detroit 1991, 203–205.

over a good dinner and was especially fond of the bottle. Whether the latter had anything to do with his failing mental powers is not known, but in July 1855 he informed the Dublin Booksellers' Society that his health would oblige him to call a meeting of his creditors. There were rumours that he was insolvent and pressure was mounted to have him declared bankrupt, but this was successfully resisted. He had returned to Edinburgh by October, 'utterly ruined in health and fortune' as he wrote to Lever. He lived on in a deranged state for another few years and died on 4 March 1858.

At a meeting of McGlashan's London creditors on 24 November 1855 it was agreed to sell the *DUM* to its English distributors, Hurst and Blackett, for £750. The meeting also accepted M.H. Gill's offer of £2,966 for the copyrights and stock of the *Magazine,* and for the other copyrights, goodwill, fixtures and fittings and lease of the premises.[2] These agreements were ratified by the Dublin creditors and took effect from 1 January 1856.

To retain the goodwill associated with McGlashan's name Gill renamed the business 'McGlashan and Gill'. The move into bookselling and publishing in such a big way now made Gill one of the most powerful, if not *the* most powerful figure in the Dublin book trade. It was not the type of monopoly figure that others in the trade liked. As early as 1832 the Dublin Booksellers' Society considered a motion 'that the . . . Society . . . give no encouragement to any bookbinders who are, or may become, booksellers, or to any printer who may become a publisher'.[3] But the move opened up a whole new range of contacts for Gill, especially in England, contacts that were to rebound to the benefit of the University Press through printing commissions. We have seen how Gill's scrupulous business practices and quick payment endeared him to the London trade, among whom were Routledge, Frederick Warne, Richard Bentley, William Tegg, Smith, Elder & Co., Kent & Co., Trubner & Co., Sampson, Low Son & Co., Murray, and Longman, Brown & Co.

Not all the contacts with London were smooth. For example on 3 September 1856 William Tegg wrote to complain that Gill's estimate for printing Bishop Joseph Butler's *Analogy of religion* was 12 per cent higher than London even without carriage. This may well have been commercial posturing because the work went ahead.[4] Gill was not afraid to challenge the monolithic London trade when his rights were being infringed. In the early 1860s he wrote to Charles Skeet pointing out that their intention to publish Isaac Butt's *Romance of College life,* which had

---

2. These figures are quoted in 'Anent the Dublin University Magazine' in *Irish Builder* (1 Dec. 1877) 346. O'Kelly, 'House of Gill', appx. B, XXII–III, says Gill paid £250 for the *DUM* and £500 for the rest, but these figures are too low and O'Kelly has often proved inaccurate in his account.
3. O'Kelly, 'House of Gill', appx. B, XI.
4. ibid. 342–6.

been first printed in the *DUM*, would infringe his copyright. As the sheets had already been printed Gill suggested that he be given a third-share in the profits, and that McGlashan and Gill be given the sole rights for Ireland.[5] The work appeared in 1863, but there is no indication that Gill's conditions were met.

It was a recurrent complaint of Irish authors that their London publishers were apathetic in the promotion of their works. The Irish trade too had a constant battle to assert itself in the face of London's overbearing shadow. On 25 May 1861 McGlashan and Gill had to write to Longmans about delays in the supply of Galbraith and Haughton's *Mechanics,* a work which had been printed at the DUP: 'Knowing that a quantity . . . was forwarded to you at the beginning of the week we were disappointed at seeing on your invoice "none in town". When they do arrive, you would oblige by letting us have as soon as possible the 100 copies ordered on the 23rd inst, which includes the 50 asked for on the 4th, but not yet received.'[6] And even though there was constant rivalry between W.H. Smith & Son and McGlashan & Gill, as two of Dublin's largest booksellers, there was unanimity between the proprietors in 1862 over the threat that the spreading railway system and the improved postal service posed for wholesale booksellers in Dublin. London was now beginning to service Ireland directly, Belfast getting supplies through Fleetwood, and Cork and Waterford through Bristol.[7]

McGlashan & Gill cast its net wider than London. It became wholesale agents for many Scottish publishers, and opened up contacts in the United States, Canada and Australia. Scribner & Co. in New York acted as commission agents from the early 1860s. Not all the Dublin works were well received and at one stage Scribners wrote for permission to dispose of slow-moving stock at auction. M.A. Pitt & Co. wrote from Melbourne in September 1860 asking for McGlashan & Gill's trade catalogue. It transpired that the Pitts had formerly been Pitt Brothers in Wexford.[8]

Gill continued to build up his portfolio of copyrights, specialising in school and college textbooks. He had an agent, William Ridings, travelling Ireland and later England on his behalf. On 11 September 1856 he wrote to Gill from Clonmel: 'I have great hopes that your school-books, Horace, Homer, Lucian and the rest will be taken up in the country.'[9] It is not surprising that Gill decided to concentrate his publishing efforts on what he knew best — academic works. Thus when William Carleton

5. ibid. 140–48.

6. ibid. 367.

7. ibid. 299, quoting letters between Gill and Charles Eason, Jan. 1862.

8. ibid., 406–409.

9. O'Kelly, 'House of Gill', 259. Ridings had worked for McGlashan and later became chief clerk for Gill in Sackville St. In the 1870s he set up his own bookselling business in Grafton Street and for a period in 1876–77 published the *DUM*.

wrote to him on 1 December 1864 offering him his new novel — 'It would be worth your while to make the experiment . . . you would not lose by it' — he declined.[10]

He was cautious about some scholarly books as well. In July 1863 the Rev. William Lee wrote to him offering the third edition of his work on the *Inspiration of the Holy Scripture*, a work that was on the divinity course in Trinity. Gill replied that he could not risk tying up capital in such a large work (the second edition ran to over 600 pages) that would be a slow seller. He mentioned that he had recently paid £400 to a London publisher for the copyrights and stock of a number of textbooks; 'This outlay, with a very heavy loss I have sustained by the failure of a book-seller in this city will compel me for some time to be cautious . . .' However, as he 'should be sorry to see any work by an Irish author go "out of print"', he suggested that if Lee paid the expenses Gill would give him favourable credit terms — half to be paid after six months and the rest another six months later. Lee declined, accepting George Smith's terms instead.[11]

The copyrights referred to by Gill as having been offered by a London publisher are set out in a document headed 'Description of copyrights & stereo-plates offered to Mr Gill May 23rd, 1862': Alvary's *Prosody* by Wheeler; ditto by Baillie; Baillie's *Psalms* in Hebrew and his *Hebrew grammar*; Wheeler's edition of Euripides' *Hecuba*; Gaskin's *Geography*; Grote's *Homeric theory*; Grove's *Geography* 18mo and 8vo; *Handbook of English grammar*; Homer's *Iliad* 2nd ed.; Byrd's Juvenal; Livy books 1–3; Edwardes's Lucian; Sheridan's Lucian; Pontet's *First French teacher*; ditto third series; Pontet's *Table of French verbs*; Rorkem's *Globes*; Faupet's Terence; Virgil's *Aeneid, Georgics* and *Eclogues*; and Young's *Spelling*.[12] The assignment of copyright from Chalmers and Ferguson to Gill was not signed until 1863.[13] Gill's ledger records the printing of many of these works throughout the 1860s under the account of 'M.H. Gill Copyrights'.

Gill's business interests were now spread across the full range of the book trade: from printer to publisher, to wholesale and retail bookseller. The division of his interests between two premises caused some confus-ion to his correspondents, with occasional letters being addressed to the 'University Press Office, Sackville St.', or 'McGlashan & Gill, University Press Office'. The pity was that Gill's business was not synonymous with the University Press, for had it been the DUP would have arrived at the status of a true university press. As it was the books commissioned by the

---

10. MS 10308/328.

11. MS 10308/356–360, Lee's letter to Gill, and copies of Gill's replies, July – Aug. 1863.

12. MS 10308/423.

13. Typescript list of Gill papers made by Bridget Lunn *c*.1975, in the possession of Michael Gill, mentions this agreement.

University took up only a minor portion of the DUP's printing capacity, and they were not published through Gill's distribution arm but through the University bookseller. It is an interesting contrast that at this period Oxford University was coming to terms with the challenge of control over the OUP and with the problem of publication. The 1860s saw the appointment of a full-time secretary to the delegates of the Press, who acted as liaison between this committee of dons and the printer, and the establishment of a partnership with Alexander Macmillan in London to distribute the OUP's secular works. The business expanded rapidly thereafter.[14]

The foundation of the Catholic University of Ireland in 1854 presented a rival to the monopoly of the DUP. The establishment of a Catholic University Press was among the objects that John Henry Newman, the first rector, conceived as part of the plan for the University at its foundation and which he set forth in a memorandum in 1854.[15] Newman was of course well acquainted with publishing and printing from his Oxford days.[16] Although the Catholic Press never was a serious threat to the DUP its foundation and progress are worth considering in some detail because of the insight they give on the contemporary attitude in Ireland to the idea of a university press. A very well developed philosophy and plan for the Press was worked out and was outlined in the Senate report of 1859.[17] The Senate committee believed 'that in no way could the University confer more benefit upon Catholic education than by means of the press'. It could achieve this end by publishing: 1 periodicals, 2 lectures, 3 'works of an abstract character', and 4 textbooks for students. *Atlantis* was given as an example of a periodical that the University was already printing, and it was recommended that the *Catholic University Gazette*, which had run for twenty-one issues in 1854, should be revived 'as a most useful means of keeping the progress and work of the University before the public'. O'Curry's *Lectures*, then in the press, was cited for the second category: 'Great attention has been bestowed upon the form in which these lectures have been printed, in order that all future lectures of this solid character may be printed uniformly with them, and thus, in time, constitute a series of University Lectures of a high class.' Works in the third category would be undertaken, even though they would not be commercial speculations, because it was 'the especial province of universities to foster [them]'. Editions of the rare classics, Irish manuscripts, oriental and scientific works, were given as examples. Textbooks were left as self-explanatory.

14. University of Oxford, *Report of the Committee on the University Press*, Oxford 1970, 19–20.
15. Catholic University of Ireland, *Report on the conditions and circumstances of the Catholic University of Ireland presented by a committee of the Senate July 1859*, Dublin 1859, 67.
16. See Lawrence N. Crumb, 'Publishing the Oxford Movement: Francis Rivington's letters to Newman' in *Publishing History*, XXVIII (1990) 5–53.
17. Catholic University, *Report*, 71–4, appx. I.

The methods of finance were elaborated in some detail. The periodicals would be printed at the expense of the University and it should hold the copyright in them. The third class should also be printed at the expense of the University, which would hold the copyright until the capital was reimbursed, if ever, by the sales. For lectures and textbooks it was suggested these could be wholly paid for by the University or it could take a part share, receiving a proportionate share in the returns. Where a commercial publisher was found to undertake a work there would be no need for the University to get involved, save 'where the University may desire to give a book the prestige of its name, in order that it may be accepted more generally and immediately by Catholic educational establishments'. The committee was of the opinion that a series of Catholic University textbooks would be a commercial success and strongly recommended that it be undertaken for the benefit of Catholic education and to enhance the credit and success of the University. A University Press Fund should be established from which allocations would be made. The £300 already set aside for O'Curry's *Lectures,* published in 1861, was in effect the nucleus of this fund. A University Press Committee should be appointed to administer the fund, and also to make recommendations on works that ought to be undertaken. The Senate committee did not make any recommendations on the actual publishing arrangements as it felt this was something which 'the University Press Committee should maturely consider'.

In 1856 when O'Curry's *Lectures* was being planned, it was found that no suitable irish type was available, 'those in common use being bad and incorrect, and those belonging to Trinity College printing-office and to Mr. Thom not being available'. It was therefore decided to have another fount designed and cast. George Petrie was responsible for this type, which the *Report* modestly described as 'the most beautiful type which has ever been designed'.[18] Lynam, not being aware of the Catholic University connection, refers to the resulting type as the 'Keating Society' face because it occurs frequently in that body's publications. McGuinne, who first unravelled its genesis, has aptly named it the 'Newman' type.

Newman had a lengthy correspondence in 1856–57 with John Edward Pigott, a friend of O'Curry's and a candidate for the post of professor of Law at the University, on the matter.[19] Pigott wrote that the Petrie founts at the DUP, which were 'the property of Mr. George Smith of Grafton Street, the publisher to the Protestant University', were 'not suffered to be used except in the College Printing Office'. Apparently even Petrie could not procure this type, 'either for money or as a friendly loan'. He was therefore forced to have his *Ancient music of Ireland* printed at the

18. ibid. 68.
19. Quoted in McGuinne, *Irish type design,* 118 ff.

DUP 'at a greatly advanced price'. Pigott informed Newman that each matrix would cost about 13–6, so that two sets of matrices of small pica and brevier sizes would cost in the region of £100 including the expense of the designs. The founts were prepared locally, probably by James Marr & Co., and were ready by early 1858. Interestingly the DUP, which so jealously guarded its monopoly of its own Petrie type, acquired founts of both sizes of the Newman type in 1874. (A case from this purchase, containing small pica caps and accented letters, survives in Trinity Closet Press.) There is one interesting difference in that the lower case 'a' of the larger size was cast at an odd angle, which McGuinne thinks may have been an error in casting.[20] Lynam refers to the supply of these two founts to the DUP and records that they were supplied by Charles Reed and Sons, who also sent over the matrices. Unfortunately he quoted no source for this information, but states that the matrices had disappeared without trace.[21] The design of the Newman type had a profound influence on modern irish types and became the prototype for the later Figgins type, which in turn was the model for the Monotype series.

The Catholic University does not seem to have considered setting up its own separate printing plant. Browne and Nolan were initially considered as University printers, but John F. Fowler was settled on. This lack of direct control led it into a dispute which it would no doubt have rather avoided. In November 1864 the DTPS challenged Fowler over his excessive use of boy labour, refusing 'fat' to piece hands, and working men long hours without being given overtime rates. The Society wrote to the rector of the University setting out the reasons for the resulting lockout. Compromise was not reached until February of the following year.[22] Although the Catholic University Press existed solely as a publishing medium, strangely enough it did not put its name in the imprints of the works it did finance. Indeed there were few of these and the ambition of publishing a series of Catholic University Press lectures and textbooks was never realised. The idea and the reality fizzled out. It was not until 1925 that another university press was established in Ireland. But the Cork University Press was wholly a publishing body and indeed commissioned the DUP to do some of its printing. That there was no rival to the 'Protestant' printing plant at the DUP was a want that still rankled in 1932, when a resolution was passed at a meeting of convocation of the National University of Ireland that a University Printing Press be set up based at University College Dublin. The proposer stated that the National University 'should be independent of the press of another University'.[23] Nothing came of the matter.

20. ibid. 124.

21. Lynam, *Irish character*, 36.

22. IPU: DTPS committee minutes, 8 Nov. 1864, 8 Feb. 1865.

23. *Irish Printer*, XXVII (Mar. 1932) 2.

To return then to the activities of the DUP in the final twenty years of Gill's tenure. The mood in the trade was one of cautious optimism after the depredations of the hungry 1840s. The 15 November 1859 issue of the *Irish Literary Advertiser,* which McGlashan and Gill published, stated that the sale of books was buoyant although the publishers were conservative. For the specialist output of a university press Gill was more circumspect. Writing to A.J. Maley on 4 February 1860 about his *Historical recollections of the reign of William IV* he noted that 'in these days of cheap literature a man will look at a pound note 20 times before he will give it almost for any book'.[24] The mood of optimism was reflected in the growth in the printing trade. The DTPS committee minutes for 28 February 1871 record that there were 57 printing offices in the city, employing nearly 700 men.

The Printing House was evidently running efficiently throughout the period because there were no major changes to the structure of the building or large purchases of machinery (not even of steam presses) or plant. On 8 February 1868 the board approved the expenditure of £58 for repairing the wall of the building. This may have been for the redashing of the exterior. There is a very interesting photograph of about this date in the College muniments which shows the crumbling state of the dashing on the extension (see plate 24).[25] This photograph is also of interest because it shows the wall with a gate continuing from the portico across Printing House Lane, a wall that has long since been removed. And the figures on the steps are also intriguing, especially the bearded figure in the frock coat and tall hat. Could this be Gill himself? Alas this is not the figure of a man in his mid-seventies, and may well be Gill's manager at the Printing House, who at this date was Peter Murphy.

Purchases of type were made from all the leading foundries throughout this period, including Marr & Co., but they were usually of small quantities to make good established founts. The occasional full fount was acquired, as for example 683 lb of long primer roman no. 9 '"Patent" (wide 2 nick)' from Besley & Co. early in 1856 at a cost of £63.[26] The expansion of Gill's commercial printing activities in the wake of his takeover of McGlashan necessitated that he equip the Press with more ornaments. Several purchases of these are recorded, as witness the acquisition of 10 lb 5 oz of 'variable festoon border' for £1-0-8 from Figgins & Co., entered in his journal on 10 January 1856. Old type was sold locally to Coldwell and Marr & Co. at 3*d.* per lb.

There were also purchases of exotics to make good the founts owned by the College. The acquisition of some hebrew and arabic sorts to the value of £8-2-10 in the latter half of 1872 was queried by the auditor, A.S. Hart: 'By whom was this ordered?', he annotated the bill. He subsequently

24. MS 10308/220.
25. MS 4251 no.12.
26. MUN/DUP/22/2, 28 Feb. 1856.

24. The Printing House in the late 1860s (MS 4251/12).

crossed this out and substituted: 'The above type was purchased for the use of the College and is duly entered in Mr Gill's book as being the property of Trinity College.'[27] This is the first reference I have seen to the existence of such a book. It was evidently compiled at the College's insistence — perhaps it was felt that Gill's business was now so diverse that its property (and its interests?) were in danger of being lost sight of. On 21 January 1874, at which time Gill may well have decided to relinquish tenure of the Printing House, he charged the College 4-6 for a 'book for entering stock of printing material the property of Trinity College' and a further 10-0 for the time spent in writing it up.[28] Unfortunately the book has not survived.

The staff numbers in the Printing House fluctuated depending on the pressure of business, as it had done in former years. Votes taken on DTPS issues reveal that there were twelve in the College chapel in February 1861, making it one of the bigger book houses; the newspapers were of course larger, *Saunders's Newsletter* for example having double the College number. At another date in 1861 the DUP had the biggest return at eighteen. The numbers fluctuated wildly from week to week, so that in two consecutive weeks in October the College chapel returned twelve and twenty-four votes. Such variations at first made me suspicious of relying on these returns, but it was compulsory to attend chapel meetings, so they are likely to reflect the number of journeymen employed. And besides the University Press relied heavily on piece hands, who were hired on a day-to-day basis. Figures given in the DTPS committee minutes for 5 November 1870 reveal that in the first week of October there were five comps on piece rate to two on the establishment at the Press; a week later there were eleven piece hands and still the same two 'stab hands.

The wage rates continued to be those agreed by the trade in general in 1829. The College chapel was in the vanguard during agitation for an increase in the pressmen's rates in 1865. It suggested to the DTPS committee on 30 May that a meeting with the employers should be arranged, which it was, and agreement on increases was subsequently arrived at. There was a problem with Gill over the payment of the increases, and three pressmen, Thomas Molloy, Arthur Griffith (father of the politician and president of Ireland, himself a trained printer) and Christopher McLoughlin appeared before the committee on 9 January 1866 to make representations on the matter. The outcome of the dispute is not recorded.

It was not long before there was agitation for other increases. A special delegate meeting of the DTPS was held on 24 March 1869 to consider the matter. In its printed report, dated 13 May and given in the committee minutes on 11 June, it was stated that Dublin printers worked longer hours for less pay than other printers in the United Kingdom or other trades in

27. MUN/V/62/16/139.
28. MUN/V/62/16/141.

the city. The working week was given as sixty hours. The maximum that line comps earned was £1 and the minimum 16-0; by comparison Dublin bookbinders earned £1-4-0 for a fifty-eight hour week. It was also noted that although comps' wages had not advanced since 1829 prices had risen 50 per cent. The report also underlined the fact that business had been good in the trade in recent years so that 'almost every printing office is now supplied with steam-printing machinery'. Armed with this information it was unanimously agreed to present a memorial to the employers.

A copy of the printed memorial is given in the DTPS minutes for 6 August. Besides setting out the above (and revealing that lithographers were paid £1-8-0 per week) it also stressed 'the high degree of mental labour' that is required of compositors, and also the poor physical conditions under which they worked, which resulted in a high rate of consumption. After interminable meetings with the master printers, of whom Gill was chairman, agreement was finally reached on 9 March 1870.[29] Among the signatories for the journeymen was George Weldrick, a comp at the DUP, and later to be manager and partner there. An extra halfpenny was conceded to the comps, bringing the book house rate for ordinary matter to $5\frac{1}{2}d$. per 1,000 ens; smaller sizes of type were paid pro rata, down to $9\frac{3}{4}d$. for diamond. Corrections at the stone were advanced from 6d. to 7d. per hour. Most of the other provisions for extras were as in the 1829 agreement. However by the 1870 document provision was made for the first time for music, perhaps at the behest of the University Press: 'Music to be paid on time, or by mutual agreement'. There was also provision in the appendix of usages of the trade for the setting of old spellings, dialects, slang, contractions etc. Where these were interspersed in a work an extra $\frac{1}{2}d$. per 1,000 was to be paid. (This was an interesting provision and would have had expensive implications for any printer setting novels with a lot of phonetic spelling of regional accents.)

The 1870 document did nothing to simplify the complexity of the scales. This complexity left the proprietors open to overcharging by his men. There is one case reported in the DTPS minutes — that of Webb's comps 'robbing' him on a catalogue which was recorded on 24 March 1857 — but human nature being what it is there were no doubt many more. I.J. Smyth, acting manager of the Dublin Steam Printing Company, tried to have a simplified scale introduced shortly after the 1870 prices were agreed. The DSPC companionship submitted a document to the DTPS on 5 November setting out the advantages — speed, accuracy and punctuality which allowed the firm to win large English and Scottish contracts. By way of demonstration that it was to the advantage of the men a comparative table of wages in three other Dublin printing houses is given for two weeks in October:

29. DTPS, *Compositors scale of prices. Revised and adopted, March 1870.* Dublin 1877 (I have not seen a copy of the 1870 edition.)

Oct. 1	No. of 'stab and piece hands	Av. wage	No. of piece hands	Av. wage
O'Tooles	12	18-6	10	15-3
Droughts	7	23-0	5	19-0
College	7	26-6	5	23-0
DSPC	16	27-0	10	26-0
Oct. 8				
O'Tooles	14	22-3	12	19-0
Droughts	4	22-0	3	18-0
College	13	26-0	11	25-0
DSPC	16	27-0	10	26-0

This illuminating perspective shows that the men at the DUP were paid comparatively well, reflecting the complexity of the setting being undertaken. Smyth's scheme did not prove so beneficial to his men — it lowered the overtime rates — so that on 29 March 1871 they were given permission by the DTPS to come out on strike. The Society was just as pleased that the experiment had not worked; what it wanted was uniformity across the trade, whereby no house could have advantage over the next and no man could be jealous of another's wage rates.

The bookhouse 'stab employees gained nothing by the 1870 agreement. Both case and press hands were paid £1-10-0 for a sixty-hour week, conditions that the DTPS committee minutes for 26 March 1872 state had stood since 1808 when records began to be kept. An extra 3-0 was sought at that time and a reduction of three hours in the working week. These were conceded by the majority of the employers, including the University Press, and took effect from 1 April. However Gill refused to give the extra penny on the 6*d.* per hour afforded to piece hands when they were doing alterations. A deputation from the College, consisting of W. Moore and R. Barnes, attended the committee meeting of the DTPS on 9 April to state the case. The committee was adamant that Gill should abide by the agreement, which must have happened because nothing further was heard of the matter.

Emboldened by its successes the Society immediately decided to press for compensation for the time jobbing, book, and newspaper piece hands were left waiting for copy. By a printed proposal of 30 April 1872 it sought compensation at the rate of 7*d.* per hour for the book and jobbing hands, and 9 to 10*d.* per hour for those in the newspapers. It was the start of the movement for the abolition of piece rates: 'the only way to get over the difficulty of the book and jobbing offices is to get a universal 'stab', the document asserted. The employers successfully resisted these demands and they had to be reiterated on 24 March 1874. The DTPS decided to try presenting the bookhouse employers with an ultimatum, recorded in its minutes of 21 July. Claiming that it had been the general trend in the past ten years for men to work on the 'stab, it stated that from 2 November no printer would work on piece. The employers rejected this in a document of 31 August, asserting that piece work was the 'only certain guide for enabling employers to estimate their work . . .' They were worried that a uniform wage would not reflect the individual's ability to earn it. Among the signatories to this document was Gill's son, Henry Joseph, then in his mid-thirties and gradually taking on his father's business. He signed the document 'for self and father'.

The employers beat the Society's bluff and piece work continued well into the next century. This was especially so at the University Press, where increasing production of exam papers, both for the College and outside bodies, led to huge seasonal fluctuations in demand for printing. It suited the Press to hire piece hands on a day-to-day basis rather than 'stab hands, who after six weeks' employment were entitled to a fortnight's notice. However the evidence is that M.H. Gill treated his piece hands fairly. This is illustrated by an incident in January 1862 when there was a delay in delivery of stereotype plates from the foundry of William Littlejohn. Gill's ledger records that he paid the pressmen 5-0 compensation 'for time lost in waiting for plates'.[30]

With his attention divided between the Printing House and Sackville Street, Gill appointed a manager at the University Press. The first person to hold this position was John Dillon who was employed in the capacity from about 1857. He took over the day-to-day running of the Printing House, dealing with authors, publishers and the DTPS. He seems to have been diplomatic enough to get on with the union. On 29 April 1862 the DTPS minutes acknowledged his 'great service' to the Society in the matter of a dispute at the *Daily Express* not alone by being sympathetic to the cause, 'but [also] by the accommodation he afforded to those members employed in the College office while they were engaged in the affairs of the Society, which contributed materially to the reclamation of the house involved in the dispute'. He died rather suddenly at the end of 1862. W.R. Hamilton wrote expressing his regrets to Gill on 3 January 1863 — he had been dealing with Dillon over the printing of his *Elements of quaternions* (1866): 'I had no notion of his being ill at all, & was somewhat surprised to see your signature to a recent memorandum.'[31]

As we have seen he was replaced by R.C. Gerrard, who lasted only a little over half a year. Gill must have been shocked by Gerrard's behaviour because there is no evidence that he placed his trust in anyone else to manage the DUP until the end of the decade. Peter Murphy's name begins to appear in the DTPS records late in 1868, complaining about the behaviour of several journeymen at the College, so he was evidently

30. MUN/DUP/22/3/260.
31. MS 10308/154.

manager there from at least that date. (Murphy made several complaints over the succeeding years, mostly about men leaving without giving due notice, so much so that there is a hint that the Society was irritated by his constant referral of these matters to it.) The College bursar's vouchers begin to be initialled on payment by Murphy in December 1869. Both he and George Weldrick performed this duty throughout the following year, indicating that they shared the management in some measure. When Murphy entered into partnership with Edward Ponsonby in 1874 to run the Press Weldrick continued to be involved in the management, and took over Murphy's place in the partnership in 1880.

The compositors in the Dublin trade of the day were, in the reminiscence of an employee of Thoms, 'a very "tony" crowd, and used to call themselves "Gentlemen Compositors"'.[32] They used to come to work in a tall hat and frock coat, carrying a rolled umbrella. It was quite acceptable for boys from respectable, middle-class families to be apprenticed to a printer. The example of Samuel Edward Busby at the University Press will serve to illustrate this. He was the son of Edward Busby, who was involved with the Dublin branch of the Young Men's Christian Association. The son served his apprenticeship at the DUP, and was later employed there, chiefly as a proof-reader. He served on the executive of the DTPS in 1858. While still engaged in the Printing House he enrolled as a student at the University, taking his B.A. in 1864. He was ordained in the following year, and served the ministry in Dublin and Belfast. He was awarded the degree of LL.D. in 1871.[33]

Despite Busby's qualifications, proof-readers at this date did not need to be trained printers. They were not usually members of the DTPS and no scales of pay for them were set out in the Society's rates. However when they were trained printers they were encouraged to join the union, as was the case with Thomas Corbett, reader at the DUP, in 1872. On 4 June the Society's minutes record that he had served his time under his father. In 1870 he joined the Dublin Steam Printing Company as a reader and had remained on there during a recent strike. At no point was he asked to join the union although he now wanted to. He was admitted on the usual fee of ten shillings and no fine was imposed. Not every proof-reader for the Press was an employee. The Rev. William Reeves was engaged to do this task for several works printed there during the 1850s and 1860s.

There were some criticisms of proof-reading at the Press from customers at this time. On 16 January 1860 William R. Wilde wrote to John Dillon about the RIA museum catalogue then being printed: 'I am well aware that from the state of the manuscript & the great haste obliged to

---

32. *Irish Printer* (May 1934) 1, noting presentation to Michael Enright after 65 years of service at Alex. Thom & Co.

33. O'Kelly, 'House of Gill', 192–3; obituary by Philip White in *Irish Printer* (Mar. 1915) 5–6.

be employed in printing [it] . . . that it was a very troublesome job & probably was very expensive to Mr Gill.' However he baulked at the cost of corrections. In his own defence Wilde wrote on 9 March: 'I do not think your reader is as careful as of old, nor are your printers quite so accurate.' He instances gathering T for which 22 hours of corrections were charged and it still had 'frequent instances of two words running into one another'. 'It ought to have been better', he concluded.[34]

An accepted mode of preparation for apprenticeship was to spend a while as reader's boy. In April 1859 the Rev. Brother J.A. Grace wrote to Gill recommending William Moore in this capacity and in the following year he wrote another letter canvassing for an apprenticeship for him. His brother Charles Moore was apprenticed there in 1861.[35] The College chapel made representations to the DTPS on 22 February 1859 on behalf of Gill for permission to take on a supernumerary apprentice, and this was granted on the understanding that it did not set a precedent. Besides being worried about the excessive numbers of apprentices in some firms, the Society was also concerned about the calibre of the boys being taken on, so much so that it felt the necessity to include a recommendation in the 1870 *Scale of prices* that only boys 'of at least an average education should be taken as apprentices'. At the same time it called for the end of the 'turn over' system whereby boys could change masters several times during their apprenticeship, a practice that Gill no doubt would not have countenanced.

Beyond the general scales of wages and working hours surviving records provide only glimpses of what the working conditions were like in the Printing House in the 1850s, 1860s and 1870s. On occasion the men worked throughout the night on a rush job. This was the case with a *Report of the proceedings at a visitation* printed for Trinity in 1858. Gill charged extra for 26 men on overtime on four nights, including 'Tuesday all night'.[36] Not everything was done with the same expedition. In the middle of 1861 Robert Cassidy wrote to Gill from Belfast criticising the delay in printing an *Appeal to the House of Lords:* 'In London I can get a long Bill in Parliament printed in one night, and laid before me in the morning without a mistake.' Perhaps because Cassidy had to wait until January 1862 for the completion of the work, Gill had still not been paid by 1865.[37]

The great movements in the staff at the Printing House are reflected in the records of the DTPS. William Smith was hauled before the committee in June 1856 for working in the College without joining the union. He agreed to join and was admitted on an exceptionally large fine of £3, it

34. MS 10308/306, 309.

35. O'Kelly, 'House of Gill', 186–7.

36. MUN/V/62/1/39 [B], 14 June 1858.

37. O'Kelly, 'House of Gill', 276–80.

having been discovered that he had worked in an unfair house in Liverpool for the previous five years. It is significant that the Society had to call the father of the College chapel to explain why Smith was working there; there was obviously no question of the men refusing to work with a non-amicable.

Several cases are recorded where men left without giving notice. Such was the case with Thomas Carey and 'the Messrs Lawrence' in February 1870. The Lawrences had apparently worked in a London house during the parliamentary session for a number of years and had been given their emigration allowance and London cards by the secretary of the Society, unaware that they had failed to give notice. Carey had been offered a job at short notice on the *Standard* newspaper and had taken it, no doubt because newspaper work paid more. In his defence Carey pleaded that he left no outstanding work at the College. And besides he was dismissed by the newspaper when it was discovered that he had not given notice to Gill. The committee imposed no fine because it considered the loss of his job sufficient punishment.

Unlike Carey not every man left having cleared his commitments. John Murphy appeared before the committee on 12 May 1874 accused of leaving 8-7$\frac{1}{2}$ 'horse' at the University Press. Murphy admitted liability, but said he had been employed on an 'unfair font' — that is one that measures less than its name implies — but did not receive the usual allowance for bastard letter. The committee rejected his assertion and gave him two weeks to clear the account or the Society would pay it and recoup it from him. Murphy must have cleared some of the debt, but the printed quarterly accounts of the Society on 30 June show that it had to pay 6-0 'horse' on his account.

It was a recurrent complaint of the pressmen in the trade that the DTPS did not take sufficient interest in their affairs. However the committee did occasionally have to consider a complaint from the College pressroom, which provides some insight into its activities. On 14 February 1871 a deputation of DUP pressmen, consisting of Cooke, Griffiths and Constable, complained that work being set up in the Printing House was being given to Pattison Jolly to machine. The men were not drawing attention to the fact that it was being printed elsewhere — such shared printing was a common feature in the trade — but as Jolly's was an unfair house members of the Society were being deprived of rightful work. The father of the chapel was instructed to speak to Gill about the matter, with the result that Gill undertook 'to remedy the situation'.

The College chapel precipitated a debate within the Society in 1871 which underlined the conservative nature of the chapel and also pointed to the fact that the executive of the union and the members were not always of one mind. On 7 March 1871 Patrick Lynch, a deaf mute who had served his time on the *Clare Journal*, was admitted to the Society. Two weeks later the DUP chapel wrote to the committee asking it to reconsider its decision as Lynch might become a burden on the DTPS. The committee rebuked the chapel stating 'that it was better to have persons so unfortunately affected inside than outside the pale of [the] Society'. (The committee's attitude was not one of disinterested compassion. There was a printing shop in one of the city's institutions for the education of the deaf and dumb and the intention was no doubt to bring it under the influence of the Society.) The College chapel was not satisfied with the committee's response and forced the issue within the trade, with the result that on 28 April it was resolved that mutes were barred from becoming members. To be fair to the men it should be pointed out that the prevailing attitude even in medical circles was that without the benefit of education the deaf and dumb were given to uncontrolled passions and were little above brute creation. This is the description given in William Wilde's *On the physical, moral and social conditions of the deaf and dumb*, printed at the DUP in 1854. (One wonders if any member of the chapel of 1871 remembered setting it!) Attitudes had changed within the union however by 1895 when on 14 May the committee raised no objection to a Typographical Society member called Park from Belfast, who was deaf and dumb, seeking employment in Dublin.

Having considered the workforce let us now turn our attention to the suppliers to the University Press at this period. Gill's account books and the College muniments reveal that paper came from much the same sources as in the earlier period: locally from John McDonnell & Co.; and abroad from Venables, Wilson & Tyler, Grosvenor, Chater & Co., Cowan & Co., Thomas Seery, M. Ryan & Co., Bowles & Gardiner, and T.H. Saunders. Venables, Wilson & Tyler were one of the bigger suppliers, especially of superior quality papers. For example in the years 1856 to 1858 they provided quantities of royal 32 lb paper at 23-3 per ream, double cap 35 lb at 25-6, and royal plate paper at 43-6.[38] By comparison McDonnell & Co. provided lesser quality papers, charging for example 7-10$\frac{1}{2}$ per ream for 22 lb letter quality paper in 1856.[39] Thomas Seery was one of the largest suppliers and Gill used to run up annual accounts of about £700 with him.[40] For paper bought on behalf of the College Gill charged 10 per cent commission.[41] Waste-paper was sold to Robinson, and D. MacDougall in Manchester and Samuel Johnson in London. Robinson paid 25-0 per cwt for waste in quires, 18-0 for old pamphlets and 15-0 for old proofs.[42]

38. MUN/DUP/22/3/41.

39. MUN/DUP/22/2, 7 Mar. 1856.

40. MUN/DUP/22/3/126, £688-12-5 worth of paper bought in 1859.

41. For example MUN/V/62/4/36, paper bought for 1863 *Calendar* from Grosvenor, Chater & Co.

42. MUN/DUP/22/2, 28 Jan. 1852; O'Kelly, 'House of Gill', 85.

Gill evidently contemplated buying stereotyping equipment in 1857 and corresponded with B. Manning in London about it.[43] He must have decided against making the heavy investment and continued to employ local firms as necessary: Coldwell in 1856, John Falconer in 1856-1860 and William Littlejohn in 1861-1862 (and probably beyond that date although no records remain to document who Gill employed after 1862). The works stereotyped were those that were expected to have large sales, so that there were few books commissioned by the College which warranted having plates made. Gill had plates cast for many of the textbooks in which he owned the copyrights. Falconer and Littlejohn provided the occasional electrotyping needed, usually casts from wood-engravings of the College seals. One account of 1866 from Gill to the bursar shows that these College arms cost £1-17-6 to engrave and 2-10 to electrotype and mount.[44]

A broader range of processes was being used for illustrative matter in the output of the Press at this period: steel-engraving, lithography and photographic plates were added to the usual copper- and wood-engravings. George Hanlon continued to be the artist favoured for wood-engravings. W. Hayes and C. Henecy were engaged to provide copper plates, while Thomas Cranfield provided steel-engravings. G. Christie & Co. did small amounts of engraving, ruling and lithographic work. For prestige work the Press turned to London. James Basire provided the lithographic and engraved plates for *Observations made at the magnetical and meteorological observatory of TCD* printed in 1865.[45] G.W. Wilson provided the photographic plates for Andrew Armstrong's *Jim Blake's tour from Clonave to London,* printed at the Press in 1867.

Blocks that had outlived their use at the University Press could occasionally be sold on to another printer, as was the case with those in A.S. Hart's *Elementary treatise on mechanics,* first printed in 1844, with a second edition in 1847. On 5 July 1856 Robert Young wrote from the Irish Presbyterian Mission Press in Bombay, stating that an edition in Gujarati was being planned and asking for blocks or stereotypes of the diagrams. Gill wrote back to say that Hart was willing to let him have the blocks of the diagrams for £4-10-0, the original cost having been £11-11-0.[46]

Throughout the 1850s A.B. Fleming & Co. supplied inks, as did Shackell & Edwards and John Gilton & Co. Ordinary inks cost from 3-0 to 6-0 per pound, while coloured inks, usually supplied by Gilton, cost 7-6. G. Herbert was the major supplier throughout the 1860s.[47]

43. O'Kelly, 'House of Gill', 79–80.
44. MUN/V/62/8/51, 13 Mar. 1866.
45. MUN/V/62/7/79, 27 Apr. – 8 Aug. 1864.
46. O'Kelly, 'House of Gill', 203–204.
47. MUN/DUP/22/2–3 *passim.*

The scale of Gill's business led at least one customer to believe that the Press had its own bindery. Writing to Gill on 11 June 1860 William Glenny Crory stated that he had made no arrangements for the binding of his *Industrial resources of Ireland*, then being printed at the DUP: 'I was under the impression that your house did that work.'[48] We have seen that Gill had acquired arming presses in the early 1850s, perhaps with the intention of setting up his own binding unit, but there was no spare room in the Printing House at this date so he evidently abandoned the idea and continued to send his binding out to the specialist firms in the Dublin trade. (The Gills did not acquire their own bindery until after M.H. Gill had ceased to be University printer. His son Henry Joseph bought the firm of Mercer & Co. in January 1884 while the workforce was on strike; he succeeded in breaking the stoppage by threatening to bring over labour from London.)[49]

Evidence from the binders' tickets in the output of the DUP would suggest that the favoured binder in the 1850s and 1860s was Francis Cavenagh, in the 1860s and 1870s John Galwey, and from 1870 John Mowat. Examination of the records however reveals a more complicated story.[50] Frederick Pilkington, the College binder, was not unnaturally engaged to do the binding of the works commissioned by Trinity. William Richardson was also employed to do a small amount of the College's work in the first half of the 1860s. However the records do not make it clear if he was an independent binder or an employee of the College binder; I suspect the latter to be the case. Pilkington was superseded by Francis Cavenagh in 1874. For non-Trinity work Gill favoured John Galwey, with a minor amount of business going to Pilkington and to Cavenagh. An unnamed binder was responsible for spoiling the twentieth number of the Kilkenny Archaeological Society's *Journal*. On 29 July 1859 an irate Rev. James Graves, honorary secretary of the Society, wrote to Gill complaining that the issue had been cropped against explicit instructions and as a consequence the plates were mutilated. He demanded that it be reprinted at Gill's expense. On 31 October Graves was more conciliatory and expressed satisfaction that Gill had changed binders, 'for there were more faults even than the cropping'.[51] Perhaps Pilkington was the culprit as he was given very little non-College work in this period and at a later stage had to be threatened with dismissal by the board because of the 'injuries' done to some of the library's books during binding.[52]

48. MS 10308/107.
49. C.J. Bundock, *The story of the National Union of Printing, Bookbinding and Paper Workers*, Oxford 1959, 39–40.
50. MUN/P/4 *passim*, MUN/V/62 *passim*, MUN/DUP/22/3 *passim*.
51. MS 10312/137–141.
52. MUN/V/5/14/79, board register 14 June 1879.

The College continued to be Gill's most important customer, not because it was the biggest — there are no absolute figures available, but it would have been one among several substantial accounts — but because Trinity was also the landlord. And because the Printing House was so accessible to the members of the College there can be little doubt that they were demanding customers. Indeed it was later written into the tenant's lease that the College was to get priority over other accounts. The bursar's ledgers reveal that Trinity provided about £100–200's worth of jobbing work per year in the 1850s. Among the more interesting jobs were printing '100 copies of note requesting witnesses to come forward in reference to the conduct of the Police' in March 1858, after the celebrated riot in College Green, and a job in 1869 with an edition size of two: '2 copies each of Quin labels for library from 1 to 200' (these were for the Bibliotheca Quiniana which were bequeathed to the library in 1805).[53] The jobbing also included exam papers, for which in 1856 Gill charged at an average of 7-0 per duodecimo page. By the early 1870s he was itemising the subject of the paper and charged from 5-0 per page for English to 21-0 for Hebrew.[54]

Even though the College *Calendar* was being printed from standing type its cost continued to be high. In 1856 when the heavy investment in standing material still had not resulted in a reduction Joseph Carson, the editor, felt obliged to defend the charges for that year's issue: part I had been overrun to increase the line measure 'to make it correspond with the Oxford and Cambridge Calendars'.[55] The editions of 500 copies soon ran out and for the 1857 issue second and third printings of 250 copies each were needed.[56] Among the charges for the subsequent edition was £10 for a 'large rack & letter boards for securing the standing forms'.[57] Gill's bill for the 1858 edition will provide an indication of the breakdown of the costs for it (given here in summary):[58]

500 copies, $19\frac{1}{2}$ sheets and 8 pages, 12mo

Composing 142p. new matter	£22-13- 3
Altering standing type	15- 9- 0
Alterations from proofs	12-12- 0
Composing advertisement of books pr. at DUP	7-10- 9
Presswork at 9-4 per sheet	9- 6- 8
Extra for red and black	3- 2- 8
Paper, printing demy 22 rm 19 qr at 22-6 per ream	25-16- 4

53. MUN/P/4/271/20, 13 Mar. 1858; MUN/V/62/11/150, 8 Apr. 1869.
54. MUN/P/4/263/19, 4 July 1856; MUN/V/62/15/131, 28 Mar. 1873.
55. MUN/P/4/261/23–23a.
56. MUN/P/4/265/12, MUN/P/4/267/12.
57. MUN/P/4/268/33, 22 Sept. 1857.
58. MUN/P/4/269/12, 1 Feb. 1858.

500 copies of supplement		36-12- 5
250 copies of 2nd ed.		19- 9-10
After some minor adjustments	Total	£149- 0- 3

There was a variety of non-recurrent administrative bookwork commissioned by the College at this period, among them reports of visitations, editions of the statutes, catalogues of the lending library and of the pictures in the Provost's House. More substantial works were Humphrey Lloyd's *Observations made at the Magnetical and Meteorological Observatory of TCD* (1865), the first volume of which cost the astonishing sum of £420. Nevertheless a second volume was sanctioned and printed off in 1869 at a similar cost.[59] Another substantial work was the first *Catalogue of graduates*, edited by J.H. Todd, which was over a decade in preparation and issued in 1869. A work that was even longer in preparation was the catalogue of Trinity's library which also had its first publication in the 1860s. The initial volume of *Catalogus librorum impressorum qui in bibliotheca Collegii . . . Trinitatis . . . adservantur*, popularly and understandably referred to as 'the Printed Catalogue', appeared in 1864. The work was not finished until 1887 and proved to be the single biggest work ever undertaken by the Press. It is therefore worth considering in detail at this stage even if it does lead us out of our period.[60]

We have to go back to 1837 to find the seed of the Catalogue. On 11 February the board 'ordered that two hundred pounds per annum be applied out of the Library fund . . . [towards] preparing a copy of the Library Catalogue for the press'. At the same time James Henthorn Todd, a fellow of the College, was appointed as editor. Even before his appointment as librarian in 1852 he worked diligently on behalf of the library, ensuring that its copyright deposit privileges were fully pursued. He was a man of amazing energy and scholarship. However his rigidly conservative nature militated against his appointment as provost in 1852 and accounted for his lack of pragmatism which hindered the progress of the Catalogue.

In the decade after his appointment as editor, and amid his other extensive commitments, Todd planned the Catalogue. He chose as his model Bulkeley Bandinel's catalogue of the Bodleian Library, published in 1843. He compiled his own set of cataloguing rules, basing them on Bandinel's and those of the British Museum, but with many local variations. A printed specimen was at last ready for submission to the board and was approved on 16 December 1848; printing began shortly

59. MUN/V/62/8/82; MUN/V/5/12/184–5, board register 27 Jan., 3 Feb. 1866; MUN/V/62/12/392.

60. For a detailed consideration of the Catalogue see V. Kinane and A. O'Brien, '"The vast difficulty of cataloguing": the Printed Catalogue of TCD (1864–1887)' in *Libraries & Culture*, vol. 23 no. 4 (Fall 1988) 427–49; I have drawn extensively on it for my account.

afterwards. The format chosen was a demy folio in two columns, set in small pica with occasional long primer notes. It was a very complicated work to set, with frequent changes between roman and italic, numerals and small caps, not to mention a full range of foreign languages which included Arabic, Syriac and Sanskrit. Todd was still unsure about the whole plan of the Catalogue and kept the first few sheets in standing type for over a year while he consulted with other libraries on the matter.[61] He was incensed when the 1853 *Dublin University Commission* criticised the unnecessary level of detail in the entries and would later answer its charges in the preface to the first volume of the Catalogue.[62]

The work was off to a bad start and it was not until the latter half of 1853 that the letter 'A' was completed. Gill charged £203-17-6 for printing the 42 sheets, which works out at £4-17-1 per sheet including paper.[63] No edition size was stated but it was probably 250, the size settled on for later volumes. It took over a decade to complete letter 'B'. Todd's insistence on a high level of cataloguing detail was no doubt the prime cause for the delay, but the library roof had to be replaced in the latter half of the 1850s, so there was good reason for the diversion of his attention. It was mid-1864 therefore before the first volume of the Catalogue, containing letters 'A' and 'B', was published. John Power greeted its appearance in his *Irish Literary Inquirer* of 16 April 1866 with this assessment: 'Whatever may have been the case formerly, it is certain at the present time, most Irish printed books will compare favourably with those of any other country; we instance the folio Catalogue of Trinity College Library, executed at the University Press, as compared with the Bodleian Catalogue.' Such praise did not however serve to keep up the momentum and no further printing was done by Todd's death in June 1869.

Indeed no further action was taken until 1872. On 29 June the board agreed that the library committee should report on the best mode of obtaining a person to continue the editorial work. T.K. Abbott, later to be one of the most industrious librarians that the College has ever had, may well have been the cause of the revitalisation of interest in the Catalogue; he had been appointed to the library committee earlier in that year. The board recognised that a thoroughly professional approach was needed if the task was to be completed, and that the full-time attention of an editor was required, not the divided attention given by Todd. An advertise-ment was placed in all the Dublin morning papers, and in the *Academy* and the *Athenaeum*, seeking someone who had previous experience of cataloguing a library as also a knowledge of Greek, Latin, French and German.[64] Out of the surprisingly high number of forty-two applicants

61. *Dublin University Commission* (1853), evidence, 175.

62. ibid. report 76–7; Printed Catalogue, vol.1, vii (note).

63. MUN/V/57/12, Sept. 1853.

64. MUN/LIB/12/26.

Henry Dix Hutton was chosen. He was a barrister by profession and had written extensively on Irish land law reform; he was also a disciple of Positivism and knew Auguste Comte. At the same time a Dutchman, Jan Hendrik Hessels, was appointed as his assistant. Hessels was a scholar of early printing and had championed Haarlem as the place of origin of the craft. They started work on 1 November 1872.

In the meantime, during June of that year, estimates were sought from five printers for completing the Catalogue — Gill, Thom, Chapman, Purdon and Webb.[65] This was a new departure for College printing, which formerly would automatically have been done by the University Press. Perhaps the board was frightened at the magnitude of the task and the cost of the work thus far produced. However there was a shift in its relationship with Gill, and this is borne out by the fact that the University Senate's *Report of the proceedings at a special meeting . . . 25th February 1873 . . . to consider Mr Gladstone's University Education Bill* was given to an outside firm, Porteous and Gibbs, to be printed in 1873. The board may also have been worried about Gill's health as he approached the end of his working life, and there was definitely something desultory in the University printer's estimate. He reported that he only had the capacity to print three sheets per week for an edition of 500. His calculation that there were only forty weeks of 'solid work' in a year left a generous allowance for sickness and holidays, not at all the profile of the over-worked printer portrayed in the minute books of the DTPS. Gill calculated that it would take ten years to complete the estimated 1,250 sheets. He quoted a cost of £3-8-0 per sheet plus alterations and extras, giving a total of £5. However when the field was narrowed down in November to himself and Thom he had altered his margins significantly and was now quoting £3-16-0 per sheet for 500 against Thom's £5.[66] On 5 April 1873 a contract with Gill for an edition of 250 at £3-2-0 per sheet was approved of by the board.

Although a single column format in foolscap folio was considered it was decided for uniformity to follow the style of the first volume. However Gill did employ a more legible small pica typeface. This legibility unfortunately was achieved by a broader set — what would be termed a 'paper hungry' type today — so it was not as economical as the earlier fount. Printing recommenced on 10 May and over the next two years the $192\frac{1}{2}$ sheets of volume two, containing the letters 'C' and 'D', were worked off. The bursar's voucher books record Gill's charges and reveal that each sheet cost nearly £4. Subsequent volumes however were less costly and ranged from £3-7-4 to £3-17-10. However alterations, charged at 1-0 per hour, continued to run at a high figure of between 20–25 per cent of the printing costs, a figure that incensed the auditor Joseph Carson. At a meeting of the board on 7 July 1875 he drew attention

65. MUN/LIB/3/1/27 ff., 19 June 1872.

66. MUN/LIB/3/1/37, 27 Nov. 1872.

to the fact that the Catalogue was costing four times the estimated price. This overrun must have been on the cataloguers' side because Gill's bills never exceeded 27 per cent of his estimate.

And indeed all was not well between the cataloguers. The library minutes for 19 December 1872 record that Hutton and Hessels were expected to produce five sheets per week ready for printing. However a clash of personalities between them meant that by 1875 the output had dropped to three sheets per week. Hutton complained to the library committee about the quality of Hessels' work, while he in turn complained about 'the incompetency of the so-called editor'.[67] The squabbles adversely affected the flow of the sheets through the Press. On 8 May 1878 Ponsonby and Murphy, who had taken over the Press from Gill in May 1875, wrote to the library committee complaining that they had seven sheets standing awaiting return of proofs from Hessels.[68] It was more than the committee could stand and it was unanimously agreed on 10 October not to renew Hessels' contract in November.

T.V. Keenan was appointed in Hessels' stead, but output was not improved and in fact slipped to two sheets per week in 1882. The relationship between Hutton and his helper was amicable; sickness was the excuse given for the slippage in the editor's annual reports. Volume 8 containing the letters 'T' to 'Z' was completed in 1885 and the final supplementary volume appeared two years later, over fifty years after the decision was taken to prepare the Catalogue and nearly forty years after printing started. The sequence of the volumes can be seen from the following table:

Volume	Year
1 (A–B)	1864
2 (C–D)	1875
3 (E–G)	1876
4 (H–K)	1877
5 (L–M)	1879
6 (N–Q)	1880
7 (R–S)	1883
8 (T–Z)	1885
9 (supplement)	1887

On 12 February 1887 the board proudly agreed that complete sets of the Catalogue should be sent to forty-eight institutions throughout Europe, America and Australia. Alexander Thom & Co. was later engaged to bind up sets and charged 11-6 per volume in half morocco or 4-6 per volume in cloth.[69]

67. MUN/LIB/3/1/84, 19 Dec. 1876.

68. MUN/LIB/15/Box II.

69. ibid. account dated 21 Mar. 1889.

Although the edition size was small the Catalogue was the single biggest work ever undertaken at the University Press, containing 1,401$\frac{1}{2}$ folio sheets or 5,606 pages. Some calculations can be done on the likely total costs of producing it and they are staggering. Printing costs were in the region of £5,250 and binding about £500. Cataloguing was about twice the printing charges, say £11,000, and to that must be added the wages of the library clerks who assisted the cataloguers. The final total must have been in the region of £20,000. To put that figure in perspective, the total budget for the library, excluding salaries, in the academic year 1886–1887 was just £1,800.

The Catalogue remains as a working tool in the library for access to most of the oldest material. Sadly the paper on which it was printed is now embrittled and does not stand up to the constant use that any library catalogue gets. The whole work was therefore microfiched in 1987, the centenary of its completion, and given a new lease of life, albeit in a less majestic format. There is also a project underway in the Department of Computer Science in the College to scan the Catalogue using optical character recognition and thus to read it into a computer. The resulting database should then be capable of being manipulated to provide much more flexible access to the records of the books, allowing for example keyword subject searches. Thus the University Press's nineteenth-century typography also lives on digitally on a computer disc.

Among the non-administrative bookwork commissioned or paid for in part by the College and printed at the University Press were several textbooks, for example Samuel Downing's *Elements of practical hydraulics* (2nd ed., 1861) and *Elements of practical construction* (1873); an edition of John Brinkley's perennially popular *Elements of astronomy*, revised by J.W. Stubbs (1872); and Benjamin Williamson's *Elementary treatise on differential calculus* (1872).[70] Trinity of course also supported more weightier tomes, as for example William Henry Harvey's *Thesaurus Capensis* (1859–1864), or Ovid's *Heriodes*, edited by A. Palmer (1874).[71]

As with W.R. Hamilton's *Lectures on quaternions* in the 1850s, his *Elements of quaternions* of 1866 was also paid for by the College, and some surviving letters allied with the bursar's accounts provide an interesting insight into the passage of a book through the Printing House at this date. March 12, 1860 marks the start of Hamilton's surviving letters to the University Press on the work. Addressing Gill he expressed anxiety that printing should begin 'without further delay' and that the wood-engravings were to be ordered from Oldham 'who gave me — & you too — all possible satisfaction before'.[72] The bursar's accounts show that gatherings B to I had been worked off by 17 May. Other letters followed

70. MUN/V/62/3/103, 5 Mar. 1861; MUN/V/62/15/328, 31 Mar. 1873; MUN/V/62/14/129, 14 Dec. 1872; MUN/V/62/14/365, 4 Jan. 1872.
71. MUN/V/62, 1859–65 *passim*; MUN/V/62/11/314, 1869; MUN/V/62/16/316, 24 Jan. 1874; MUN/V/62/17/128, 1 May 1875.
72. MS 10308/139.

from Hamilton, several with reference to typographical matters, including one of 1 April 1862 when he suggested that perhaps a second compositor could be employed for signatures 3F–3G. This would indicate that only one compositor had been assigned to the task of setting this difficult work.[73] It is also evident from the correspondence that Hamilton was writing the work while it was being printed, and that it was ever expanding.

The progress of the work can be traced from a comprehensive statement of the expense set out in the bursar's voucher books and dated 17 May 1866.[74] This reveals that for the medium octavo work in an edition of 500 copies the Press charged from about £3 up to £5 per half-sheet (including paper) depending on complexity. The chronology of the printing can be summarised as follows:

Date	Signatures
17 March 1860	B–I
December	K–N
18 March 1861	O–X
18 December	Y–2U
31 March 1862	2X–3D
May	3E–3I
August	3K–3Q
13 September	3R–3S
7 October	3T–3U
26 August 1863	3X–4N
27 November	4O–4Q
17 February 1864	4R–4U
23 November	4X, b–f
30 May 1865	4Y–5B, g
10 January 1866	5C–5E, h–i, A

Although Gill was paid sums on account throughout the printing, at the end there was still £172 outstanding. The full cost of the 52 sheets (it was printed in half-sheets) was posted in Gill's ledger on 10 January 1866.[75] The total cost including cancels in 2K and 4F, 85 woodcuts and binding 150 copies at 1-0 each was £421-12-3.

John Pentland Mahaffy, professor of Ancient History, was a recurrent recipient of support from the College. His translation of K. Fischer's *Commentary on Kant* (1866), *Prolegomena to ancient history* (1871) and *Kant's critical philosophy* (1872) were all printed at the University Press and generously supported by the College.[76] However for his *Twelve lectures on ancient*

73. MS 10308/146.

74. MUN/V/62/8/113.

75. MUN/DUP/22/3/270.

76. MUN/V/62/8/102, 28 Feb. 1866; MUN/V/62/14/362, 2 Nov. 1871; MUN/V/62/14/391, 16 July 1872; and MUN/V/62/16/309, 22 Mar. 1873.

civilization (1869), for which Trinity paid half, Porteous and Gibbs were the chosen printers.[77] And four years later T.K. Abbott's *Kant's theory of ethics* was given to the Dublin Steam Printing Company, with the College picking up half the bill.[78] Some other works subsidised by Trinity, which one might have expected to have been printed at the DUP, were in fact printed in Cambridge by William Metcalfe: Richard Townsend's *Chapters on the modern geometry* (1863–1865) and Thomas Maguire's *Essays on Platonic ethics* (1870).[79] And when *Hermathena,* a scholarly journal written by members of the College which continues to this day, was launched in 1873 it was Metcalfe who was given the printing of the first two issues.[80] *Kottabos,* a College miscellany of playful verse and prose, often in Greek and Latin, was another journal which one might have expected to have been printed at the Press. In fact its five volumes, starting in 1870, were printed by Porteous & Gibbs and later by C.W. Gibbs, further evidence of a growing coolness in Gill's relationship with the College and its members.

Such was also the case with George Salmon, later to be provost of the College. In September 1858 he wrote in complete trust to Gill about the printing of a work of his: 'Although the present Post Office regulations permit me to print as easily in London as here, I have not asked for an estimate from anyone else, for I feel sure you will do the work as economically as you can.'[81] By the time the second edition of his *Treatise on the analytic geometry of three dimensions* was being prepared in 1865 Salmon was less amenable. He wrote to Gill stating that he had had an estimate from Metcalfe and Palmer in Cambridge of £5-5-0 per sheet for an edition of 750, while the DUP was quoting £5-13-3 for an edition of 500: 'As many copies are sold in England I cannot hope to succeed if I cannot afford to bring it out as cheap as works of the same kind printed in England.'[82] The work proved to be a bestseller and when an enlarged edition was needed in 1874 it was also given to the Cambridge firm, the College agreeing to pay half the cost of £185.[83] Economics was not the only reason for choosing a printer other than the DUP for College work. During Trinity's challenge to Henry Fawcett's attempts in the late 1860s and early 1870s to have religious tests abolished in the University, the College employed Vacher & Sons in London on at least two occasions to print with expedition petitions to be distributed to members of parliament.[84]

77. MUN/V/62/11/332, 16 Oct. 1869.
78. MUN/V/62/15/339, 1 Aug. 1873.
79. MUN/V/62/7/117, 7 Mar. 1865; MUN/V/62/13/338, 19 Sept. 1870.
80. There had been other periodicals associated with the University — the *Dublin University Magazine, Dublin University Review* and the *College Magazine* — but these were more literary than scholarly and were not supported by the College.
81. O'Kelly, 'House of Gill', 133.
82. MS 10308/402.
83. MUN/V/62/16/313, 24 Mar. 1874.
84. MUN/V/62/12/524, 31 Mar. 1870; MUN/V/62/15/323, 1 Mar. 1873.

The College continued to exercise its privilege to print bibles, more for the good of religion than for the profit involved. In 1858 Riobeárd Ó Catháin's translation of the New Testament into Irish was issued from the Press 'air na chur a gcló le Hodges, Smith, & C., leabhar-dhíoltóiríghe do Cholláisde na Tríonóide'. This work is a small quarto, printed in two columns and set entirely in Petrie type. Although an article signed 'J.L. Dublin', published in *Notes and Queries* on 10 June 1865, says that 'only a few score of this uncommonly beautiful edition were printed, the expense being considerable', Gill's ledger reveals that in fact 2,000 were printed at a cost of £186.[85]

In 1859 Gill quoted the Hibernian Bible Society for printing 10,000 copies of St John's Gospel. The price of £6-5-0 per 1,000 copies in pica 24mo was endorsed by J.H. Todd as registrar of TCD and accepted by the Society in June. The work proved a success and in November Gill was asked to quote for similar quantities of other books from the Old and New Testaments.[86] The College was charged £59 for St John's Gospel by Gill and so made a very modest profit of £3-10-0 when the edition was sold to the HBS.[87] No doubt Gill had a more handsome margin than that. This account provided valuable recurrent business for the Press well into the 1870s. The bursar's voucher books record commissions for printing various books of the Bible in editions of 10,000 on eighteen occasions between 1859 and 1874.

The *Book of common prayer* in Irish and English appeared in 1861 after considerable delay and much bickering.[88] Early in 1853 the Society for Promoting Christian Knowledge approached Gill to know if he could print it in the style of the Society's Spanish edition. Because it was a privileged book Trinity had to approve the edition and there was friction between the College's nominees to oversee the work, Drs Todd and Graves, and the proposed translator, the Rev. Daniel Foley, so much so that it was decided to reprint an existing text of 1712 without alteration. In the meantime, as has been seen, Gill had arranged to have two-line initial letters cut in wood and cast for the chapter openings of the Irish text. Gill's estimate of £208-19-6 for 1,000 copies was accepted by the Rev. John Evans on behalf of the Society in October 1855. Evans had earlier warned Gill that the work would be stereotyped and that the plates would be sent to London, with no assurance that the DUP would be given the printing of subsequent editions. Gill set out his regrets at this loss to the Irish printing trade in his reply. Nobody seemed pleased with the work. The Rev. Robert King, who was proof-reading the work, wrote from Armagh to Gill on 2 October 1856 bitterly complaining that 'this prayer-book will be a

85. MUN/DUP/22/3/114, 13 Dec. 1858.

86. MS 10312, 23 June 1859; 30 June 1859; 8 Nov. 1859.

87. MUN/V/62/2/39, 13 Dec. 1859.

88. The following account is based on O'Kelly, 'House of Gill', 58–72.

most scandalous and disgraceful production, most discreditable . . . to the University Press degraded to the office of giving renewed existence to such a production — a degradation to be perpetuated . . . by the stereotyping process'. He was still bemoaning the fact that he became involved with the project two years later. Whatever about the contents, typographically it is a handsome duodecimo work of just over 600 pages of parallel English and Irish texts, with the latter set in Petrie type using the two-line initials already employed in Ó Catháin's NT in Irish.

Hodges & Smith became Hodges, Smith & Co. in 1856 and continued to be the local outlet for the College's publications. (The firm confusingly became Hodges, Smith & Foster in 1868, and Hodges, Foster & Co. in the following year.) On 30 January 1864 the board allowed the firm to 'assume the title Publishers to the University'. Hitherto the style had been the more antiquated 'Booksellers to the University' and this change of name was in keeping with the general separation in the trade of the functions of bookseller and publisher. Hodges, Smith & Co. continued to act in a very offhanded way as regards the University's publications, if Gill's letters to the firm in 1859 and 1862 were indicative of its attitude. He wrote in the name of McGlashan and Gill to James Drew, presumably an employee of Hodges, Smith & Co., to complain that they had been charged full price for College exam papers, and had previously been refused copies on any terms.[89]

As formerly, Hodges, Smith & Co. took 10 per cent commission on the sale of the College's books, besides being allowed a discount in the form of a free copy for every so many bought (the proportion varied depending on the work, but was usually 25/24). The amount of business done was small. For example in 1856 the firm sold just £107 worth of 'classics' (a catch-all name that included the *Calendar*). Business through both Longmans and Whittakers in London, on which the Dublin firm took 5 per cent commission, was miniscule at £15 and £10 respectively.[90] Ussher's *Works* then in progress was afforded its own account, but again the amount sold was pitifully small at just over £6 for 1856 after all deductions.[91] Hodges, Smith & Co. handled the College's books on a sale or return basis. The stock of 'classics' it held never went beyond £100 and the lists included many works printed in the early part of the century, such as Walker's Livy and Stock's Lucian and Demosthenes. The firm decided on a radical clear-out in 1859 and £65 worth of books were returned to the College, leaving just £33 worth in stock.[92] This in turn must have galvanised Trinity to clear out its own warehouse in the library because quantities of DUP classics appeared shortly afterwards in 1862 under the imprint of William Bernard

89. O'Kelly, 'House of Gill', 297.

90. MUN/P/4/264/38.

91. MUN/P/4/264/39.

92. MUN/P/4/253/11.

Kelly. Among them were Stock's editions of Tacitus (1787), Demosthenes (1818), and Aeschines/Demosthenes (1818), Walker's Livy (1797–1813) and Miller's Longinus (1820). These works with their original titleleaves in place were cased and a new titleleaf added stating 'University Press Edition' and giving Kelly's imprint. They were sold at 3-0 or 3-6 per volume.

Institutional customers continued to provide a substantial portion of the Press's business. The journals of the RIA, Royal Geological Society of Ireland, Natural History Society, Belfast Medical Society, and Kilkenny Archaeological Society were some of the periodicals the DUP handled. These institutions also provided bookwork, and the RIA was foremost among them in this regard. 1857 saw the start of printing of its *Descriptive catalogue of the antiquities . . . in the museum of the RIA;* part 1 in an edition of 1,250 copies cost £164-2-4.[93] The high cost of the alterations delayed the continuation until 1860. On 20 February W.R. Wilde, the compiler, wrote to state that unless these were kept below 10 per cent the work could not continue.[94] At the end of the following month a letter from him quantified this as 14-0 per sheet; Wilde himself undertook to pay anything extra after that. True to form Wilde was demanding and critical: 'The plan pursued in the College printing office of charging an hour each time a "forum" [i.e. forme] is touched and also of giving the revision into the hands of the compositor who sets up is incompatible with economy. I do not blame Mr Gill as long as it is the rule of his office, but I feel that some day it must be reformed.' In the event when printing was resumed the excess on the alterations did not cost Wilde too much — £1-14-3 on the first six sheets, and £11-3-2 on the remaining nineteen of part 2.[95] Part 2 was published in 1861 and part 3 in the following year. Another institutional bookwork commission of significance at this period was George Petrie's *Christian inscriptions in the Irish language,* printed for the Royal Historical and Archaeological Association of Ireland, and issued in VIII annual parts between 1870 and 1877; it was also issued in two volumes in 1872 and 1878. It has 140 plates, including wood-engravings, lithographs, collotypes and photographs.

With regard to printing for the trade, Gill proved to be one of his own best customers in the form of McGlashan & Gill. His ledger records constant reprintings of the textbooks the copyrights of which the firm owned: Bell's *Speaker,* Walker's Lucian, Cicero's *Select orations,* Waring's Horace, Pontet's *First French teacher,* Jackson's *Book-keeping.* Not every book McGlashan & Gill commissioned from the Press was a reprint. In 1858 it paid £153 for printing the two volumes of Selina Bunbury's novel, *Sir Guy D'Esterre.*[96] We know from Gill's correspondence that she offered this

93. MUN/DUP/22/2/48, 28 Aug. 1857.

94. This and the following letters from Wilde are from MS 10308/296–315.

95. MUN/DUP/22/3/83, July 1860, Jan. 1861.

96. MUN/DUP/22/3/75, 29 Mar. 1858.

work to McGlashan & Gill in the previous year for £50. On 19 September she wrote to suggest publication at £1-11-6 and a cheaper reprint at 5-0 or 6-0: 'I would much prefer to bring out this work with you at the cheap price at once, so as to allow it to circulate among my private friends who now chiefly get my books from libraries.'[97] McGlashan & Gill also provided other business in the form of the *Irish Literary Advertiser*, begun in December 1858 and issued monthly, various catalogues and a whole range of jobbing. The catalogues included hundreds of monthly circulars of new books sent to a network of booksellers throughout the country, among them Henderson in Navan, Edwardes in Carlow, Eccles in Coleraine, and Oldham, Herbert and Rowse & Co. in Dublin.

Among the Press's other trade customers were E. Milliken, William McGee and of course Hodges, Smith & Co. Although the latter was University publisher it felt no special loyalty to the University Press and employed it among several others in the city. The DUP did however get its more complicated and scholarly commissions, as for example James Graves's and John G.A. Prim's *History, architecture and antiquities of the cathedral church of St Canice, Kilkenny*, printed in 1857 at a cost of £178-9-6.[98] Because of its reputation for confidentiality and accuracy the University Press also attracted commissions from the legal profession to print briefs and reports on cases. These were produced in small editions of 25 or 30 and so helped keep the caseroom if not the pressroom busy. Smith & Whitestone provided such commissions from 1858 to 1861, especially in the case of *Malcolmson* v *O'Dea* which went all the way to the House of Lords.[99]

Gill also continued to secure printing commissions from the London trade, as for example Edward B. Sinclair and George Johnston's *Practical midwifery*, printed for John Churchill in 1858.[100] Churchill was reluctant to allow McGlashan & Gill to publish it in Ireland. There was some correspondence on the matter which culminated in a frosty letter from Gill: 'As our business is confined mainly to a wholesale trade, it would not suit us to lend our name to any book that we could not sell on wholesale terms, and therefore we shall not require to have our names on the imprint.'[101] Churchill capitulated. William Tegg engaged Gill to print an edition of Milton. On 14 February 1861 Gill provided an estimate of just over £235 for printing 2,000 copies.[102] Tegg reported to Gill on 4 January 1866 that 'the book sells well from its beauty and general appearance' and suggested a reprint and

97. MS 10308/79.

98. MUN/DUP/22/3/7, 30 June 1857.

99. MUN/DUP/22/3/69, 115.

100. MUN/DUP/22/3/92, 4 Dec. 1858; 750 copies cost £233-6-1.

101. O'Kelly, 'House of Gill', 372–3.

102. MS 10308/431.

stereotyping.[103] The London trade also provided the occasional periodical to print, as for example the *Natural History Review*, the first issues of which were printed at the Press for Williams & Norgate in 1861.[104]

The DUP was essentially a bookhouse, but it did a range of jobbing for its regular customers. A more unusual example of this was 300 wine labels printed in 1869 for one of the Press's largest private customers, J.A. Galbraith.[105] Another job out of the ordinary came from Willis & Sotheran in London. In March 1858 Gill reprinted pp. 467–468 from volume III of O'Conor's *Rerum Hibernicarum scriptores* for them, presumably to complete a copy. Willis & Sotheran had been unable to borrow a copy to have the work done in London, and gave the commission to Gill presumably because he had access to one, probably that in the College library. 'We must trust to you to match the paper as nearly as possible', they instructed him.[106] It is not clear whether Gill used the copy of the work in the College library or the *Annals of the Four Masters* as copy text. Gill's ledger reveals that the DUP continued to set and supply exotic types for other Dublin printers. The DTPS committee minutes for 5 June 1866 reveal that the Press set some arabic type for O'Tooles and the comp there who had to handle it wanted to know could he charge for it; the committee wisely suggested a private arrangement with the proprietor. Another customer for this service was William Underwood, to whom the Press supplied small quantities of pearl music throughout the period 1857 to 1860. Underwood in turn printed posters for an art exhibition and cattle show for the DUP, indicating that the Press had no poster type and underlining the fact that it was not geared up for commercial jobbing.[107]

The Press had a large number of private customers. These ranged from Galbraith and Haughton for thousands of copies of their mathematical textbooks, D.F. MacCarthy for his poems, J.T. Gilbert for his extensive *History of Dublin*, to William Glenny Crory for his *Treatise on the industrial resources of Ireland*. For this latter work Crory issued a subscription form and succeeded in enlisting over 1,000 subscribers, perhaps partly because it was so reasonably priced at 2-0. Two thousand were printed, the second 1,000 of which Crory determined to put out as a 'second edition'. There was a delay in publication of the work because Gill refused to accept a promissory note for the printing costs of £91 from George Louis Silo, to whom Crory later assigned the rights in the work. The matter was settled in August 1860 and the work published. 290

103. O'Kelly, 'House of Gill', 346–8.

104. MUN/DUP/22/3/238.

105. MUN/DUP/22/3/110, 9 Feb. 1860.

106. MUN/DUP/22/3/74, 15 Mar. 1858; Gill charged 10-6; O'Kelly, 'House of Gill', 372.

107. MUN/DUP/22/3/63.

copies were sent to booksellers throughout the country, although the concentration was in the northern counties (an interesting demographic pointer).[108] Gill was not averse to reissuing works with new titleleaves. In June 1859 he told John Francis Waller that a large number of his book of poems entitled *The Slingsby papers* remained unsold, and advised that it be reissued at a lower price with 'a more popular title'. Such practices make sound commercial sense even if they do confuse bibliographers today.[109] Gill's correspondence provides other insights into his dealings with private customers. By definition they were less informed in the mysteries of the trade and as a consequence could be more demanding. This was the case with Arthur B. Rowan's *Brief memorials of the case and conduct of TCD 1686–1690*, printed at the Press in 1858. He wrote to Gill in an appalling hand on 7 March enclosing the MS: 'I hope you will have no difficulty in decyphering my MSS.' Earlier he had expressed the fear that he would be surcharged for alterations 'for I never can tell how my book will be until I see it in type'.[110]

The Press's reputation for printing foreign and exotic languages was the reason for several private commissions. In 1859 it turned out the Rev. George Longfield's *Introduction to the study of the Chaldee language* and the Rev. R. Wrightson's *Introductory treatise on Sanscrit hagiographa*, while in 1863 it completed John Morisy's *Hindustani grammar*.[111] And in 1870 the Press printed G.W.F. Howard's *Lines on a withered tree in the Viceregal grounds*, with translations in Latin, Greek, French, German, Italian and Portuguese. The same reputation interestingly also attracted a commission from the Rev. Patrick Murray of Maynooth College to print his monumental *Tractatus de ecclesiae Christi* started in 1860. The first volume contained 802 pages; the second (1862) 799, and the third (1866) 902. Richard Coyne, who had been publisher and printer to Maynooth, died in the late 1850s, which would help explain why Gill printed the work and McGlashan & Gill acted as publisher. To further its sale Gill wrote to the Catholic Publishing & Bookselling Co. in London asking about a Paris distributor for it. However his ledger records that all 1,250 copies were sold to Maynooth College in the years 1860–1867. The Press also printed several Catholic pamphlets for Murray, the total value of his business being £470 in the years 1860–1863.[112] Gill also secured the contract in 1862 to print William Jennings's *Logicae seu Philosophiae rationalis compendium* — it was published by McGlashan & Gill — which was essentially a textbook for Maynooth students. Significantly Gill's

108. MUN/DUP/22/3/230, 29 June 1860; MS 10308/105–135.

109. MS 10308/418.

110. MS 10308/388–390.

111. MUN/DUP/22/3/113, 104; O'Kelly, 'House of Gill', 247–8.

112. MUN/DUP/22/3/252; MS 10308; MUN/DUP/22/3/123.

imprint was omitted from Murray's work, and appeared in Jennings's volume without any mention of the DUP, in contrast to his almost invariable style 'Printed at the University Press, by M.H. Gill'. Could it be that since Gill had branched out as McGlashan & Gill he was attracting more printing commissions for the Press from Catholic institutions and authors, and that the College was apprehensive that its Protestant ethos was being undermined by having Catholic works issued under its University Press imprint?

Another symptom of the degeneration in the relationship between the College and Gill was his charges. When it was decided to keep the annual *Calendar* in standing type Gill sought 10 per cent handling commission on the extra printing materials that had been bought. It was refused by the auditor Thomas Luby.[113] This auditor was a constant critic of the Press's charges and several times during his tenure he added adverse comments on its bills. 'This acct. is correct but extravagantly high', was his note on the bill for miscellaneous printing for the second half of 1856.[114] Such comments may have prompted Gill to allow 5 per cent cash discount to the College on certain items in its account, as for example the *Calendar*, from about 1860 onwards. Gill offered the same discount to his trade customers. Of course many in the trade preferred to take credit and offered bills at anything from two to six months. Bills were also accepted from private customers. George B. Wheeler wrote to Gill in June 1864 asking for a renewal of a small bill falling due in a few days, as money matters were pressing.[115]

Not everyone could or would meet their commitments. On 17 July 1858 Madden & Oldham of the *Irish Ecclesiastical Gazette* office wrote to Gill seeking an extension on one of their bills. By October they had been declared bankrupt but did manage to pay 15-0 in the £.[116] Gill was less successful in collecting money from H. Butler Stoney for printing his *Victoria: with a description of its principal cities*. When he was pressed for payment in November 1856 Stoney went on the defensive: 'I think there should be some less charge for the lithographs which do not appear a whit better than woodcuts. . . .' The author was aggrieved that Gill was reluctant to release the work until payment was made and hoped 'that further delay will not be shown in binding & circulating the work'. Whatever accommodation was reached £52 was still outstanding in October 1857. It transpired that Stoney had a bad reputation that extended to London, where he had left an unpaid bill with Routledge & Co.[117] Gill was tenacious in his pursuit of debts as Joseph Hawe found to

113. MUN/P/4/270/23, June 1856.

114. MUN/P/4/264/25.

115. O'Kelly, 'House of Gill', 179–80.

116. ibid. appx. C, XXVIa.

117. MSS 10308/280–295, 10312.

his regret. Hawe's *Insula sacra; or Garlands from Celtic bowers* was printed at the Press late in 1858 and he paid for it by a bill due on 20 March of the following year. He must have defaulted on it because in October 1860 Gill employed J. Mathews to collect the debt of £22. Hawe lived in Clonmel, where he was organist in one of the churches, and Mathews had attempted to find him there without success. However he did report to Gill that he was prosperous. In December Gill wrote to Hawe's employer, the Rev. M. Burke, asking him to intervene with the result that Hawe was dismissed. Gill continued to pursue the debt, but there is no evidence of the outcome.[118]

It is evident from the feebleness of Gill's endorsements in the College bursar's accounts that he suffered some illness during 1872. Although his signature had recovered its vigour by 1873 it may well be that his advancing years, coupled with the College's evident increasing lack of confidence in him, determined him to give up the post of printer to the University. The *Irish Builder* of 15 October 1870 tells us that McGlashan & Gill's premises in Sackville Street had recently been entirely rebuilt, and this may have been part of a plan to go entirely independent. Of course the College may have indicated that his contract was not to be renewed. The muniments are silent on the matter. Whichever was the case the board minutes record the appointment of a committee on 14 March 1874 'for arranging the terms on which a successor should be appointed to Mr Gill the present printer to the College'. The appointment of Gill's manager, Peter Murphy, in his stead was minuted on 10 July 1874: 'Mr Murphy's estimate for printing was accepted and he was appointed printer to the College for one year subject to the rent of £100 for the printing office as heretofore paid by Mr Gill.' Thus ended Gill's career at the College Printing House, a career which stretched back over fifty years.

The Gill family businesses were thus consolidated at 50 Upper Sackville Street, with the printing plant behind the premises in Moore Lane. The father judged it was time to hand over the reins to his son Henry Joseph. We have seen how the son represented the family interests at the meeting of the Dublin Master Printers in August 1874. In 1876 the name of the firm was changed from McGlashan & Gill to M.H. Gill & Son, thus acknowledging his interest. When the father died on 20 March 1879, at the age of 85, Henry assumed complete control. Under his guidance nationalist and Catholic (sometimes stridently Catholic) literature came to dominate the firm's lists. (This shift is reflected in the respective headstones of the father and son in Glasnevin Cemetery: whereas Michael Henry's consists of a modest Celtic cross atop a plinth of native granite, Henry Joseph's is of imported marble capped by an elaborate Celtic cross with an Italianate figure of Christ crucified.) The trend set by Henry was continued by succeeding generations of the

118. MUN/DUP/22/3/122, 2 Dec. 1858; MS 10308.

family. The firm was incorporated as M.H. Gill & Son Limited in 1903, the year Henry died. The firm continued to have its own printing plant until 1965, when it was decided to concentrate on publishing and bookselling. In 1968 a partnership was formed with the Macmillan publishing company, and the publishing interests of the firm transferred to the new company, Gill and Macmillan. Retail bookselling continued under the old name in O'Connell Street until 1979, when it was decided to close the shop and concentrate on publishing. Today Gill and Macmillan is one of the largest publishers in Ireland and its managing director, Michael Gill, is the great-great-grandson of Michael Henry Gill.

10
Ponsonby and Murphy: 1875–1880

When he took on the role of University printer, Peter Murphy entered into partnership with Edward Ponsonby, a well-known bookseller and publisher of Grafton Street who specialised in legal texts. So it would seem that Ponsonby supplied capital and Murphy the printing skills to manage the Printing House. From the records of the DTPS it will be found that Murphy had worked in the College at least as far back as 1850.[1] According to Philip White in the August 1908 issue of the *Irish Printer*, Murphy had been a partner in the printing firm of Moore & Murphy (listed in the *Dublin Directories* from 1859 to 1863) before returning to the DUP. He may then have been brought in by Gill as manager in the Printing House after Gerrard's dismissal in 1863. Although the College's board minutes for 10 July 1874 record Murphy's appointment for a period of a year at a rent of £100, there was a period of transition and Gill remained on in office until the early part of 1875. Gill's imprint appears in the 1875 *Calendar*, which would have been printed in late 1874, and in which he is also listed as University printer. During the transitional period some bills were paid to Gill and some to Ponsonby and Murphy. Gill was still presenting bills for work he had done on the College's *Printed Catalogue* as late as 18 March 1875; Ponsonby and Murphy's first bill for it was presented on 5 May. So it can be conjectured that the partnership took over formally *circa* April 1875.

One of the first things the partnership did was to introduce powered printing presses. This event was recorded by Philip White in the article referred to above: 'as a result the output of work was very considerably increased, while the concern was enabled to compete on equal terms with other offices in the city and elsewhere'. It was a comparatively late introduction of machinery although there were good reasons for the delay. The first powered presses in Ireland were installed by Philip Dixon Hardy in 1834 to print the *Dublin Penny Journal*. In the issue of 10

---

1. DTPS committee minutes 26 Feb. 1850 record that he was the College representative at a delegate meeting of the Society appointed to consider efforts to urge Dublin printers to join agitation for the abolition of stamp and paper duties.

May 1834 he described his plant and noted that a steam press was only suitable for editions of 2,000 and above, which the University Press seldom printed. Accuracy, not speed, was of the essence at the Press. The complex composition at the DUP took a disproportionate amount of time relative to presswork, so savings on the latter were not of critical importance. And although the DUP was probably the last major house in the Dublin printing trade to be mechanised, a steam press was still something of a novelty among the smaller printers. D.W. Carroll proudly recorded that he was a 'steam printer' in his imprint to P. Ryan's *School arithmetic*, Dublin 1873.

As no charge for any machinery during Ponsonby & Murphy's tenure appears in the College bursar's accounts it can be taken that the partnership paid for it. Indeed the only plant acquired by the College during this period was 180 lb of bourgeois roman and 317 lb of brevier greek purchased in October and November 1875. Shortly afterwards there was a clear-out of old founts owned by the College, which weighed 2,000 lb and realised 3*d.* per lb. The clear-out continued throughout 1877, right through to January 1880.[2]

The DTPS minutes make reference to some of the workers at the DUP in this period, most notably Frederick Harte, George Hoyle and George Wade, all of whom served on the executive of the union on various occasions in the late 1870s and early 1880s. The minutes also provide some insights into working practices at the Press. On 19 January 1875 the chapel officers, D'Alton and Wade, attended the committee's meeting, as did George Weldrick on behalf of the management, in an attempt to resolve a dispute over 'clearing away', that is removing the leads, furniture, headlines etc. from matter that had been worked off and distributing them back into their proper places; tying up the remaining text type and papering it in preparation for distribution was also part of the task. The line hands at the University Press had heretofore done this, as well as distributing the text if sorts were needed, 'to the injury & injustice of the workmen', because it was a rule of the chapel. However as there was no Society rule to compel the piece hands to do it the committee decreed that it was to cease. This principle was reiterated in the following year when on 21 March the secretary was instructed to write to the father of the chapel of the Dublin Steam Printing Co., informing him that the practice of line hands 'clearing off' was 'altogether unknown' in Dublin offices, such work being carried out by establishment hands. If a line hand ran out of sorts the practice was for him to '"turn" for them [that is, substitute another sort of equal thickness but setting it upside-down], and let the deficiency be supplied by the house'.

The DTPS committee minutes also record a dispute in 1877–1878 over 'bastard' founts in which the University Press was implicated. It was a

---

2.   MUN/V/62/18/114, Oct., Nov. 1875, May 1876; MUN/P/4/275/48, 1880, credit note from William Miller for £56-14-6.

recurrent complaint by the newspaper chapels that founts were thinner than the normal standard and thus operated against the line hands. It was a matter that was rarely raised in the bookhouses. However the chapel in Gill's printing works complained of such founts at the start of 1877. The committee upheld their complaint on 8 February and instructed that in setting from these founts the men were to be paid at the standard of 26 ens per alphabet. Michael and Henry Gill disputed this, stating that 24 ens was the standard in the London trade. As a general trade principle was involved there was a meeting between the union and the Master Printers' Association in 50 Upper Sackville Street, which was reported in the DTPS minutes on 1 March. The Gills suggested that a survey be carried out of houses that had thin founts to see if they paid at the rate of 26 ens. The answer must have been in the affirmative because the Gills paid an extra farthing on these founts. However the firm informed the DTPS a year later on 14 May that it was withdrawing the increase because it believed that the College, Dollards, Droughts, and Porteous & Gibbs had not paid the increase on bastard founts. When the various chapels were summoned to answer the accusation the University Press chapel submitted a printed document with specimens of ten founts in use in the Printing House and a resolution dated 28 February 1878 (see plate 25) which stated 'That, after examining the different founts of type at present in this office, it is the opinion of this chapel that they are of a fair average standard, and therefore do not come under the class of bastard or fraudulent founts'. The Gills were still not satisfied with the replies of the various houses and forced the union to pursue the issue. A delegation was thus sent round the offending houses, as reported on 28 May. Dollards was paying the extra money; Drought was paying it on some founts; while Porteous & Gibbs refused to pay. At the University Press Weldrick stated that the founts 'never were ordered with the intention to defraud the compositor' and in fact were 'the thickest standard in Reed & Fox's specimen book'. He suggested that, 'in these inauspicious times', the 24 en London standard be accepted. How the matter progressed was, unfortunately, left unrecorded.

The 'inauspicious times' mentioned by Weldrick referred to the disastrous printers' strike of 1878, a strike that nearly crippled the union. In decades to come old printers would refer in awe to the events of '1878' much as Irish republicans referred to '1798'. On 3 December 1877 the union submitted a memorial to the employers seeking increases for both the book and jobbing houses, and the newspapers. For the former the demands were 6*d*. per 1,000 ens (i.e. an extra $\frac{1}{2}d$.) for line hands, an extra 2-0 on the 'stab wage bringing it to £1-15-0 per week, an extra penny per token for pressmen, and a range of other pro rata increases. These were unanimously rejected by the master printers on 11 December. At a special delegate meeting of the union on 10 January 1878 the University

The following Resolution, being proposed and seconded, was unanimously adopted at a Special Meeting of the College Chapel, held on Thursday, February 28th, 1878 :—

" RESOLVED—

" That, after examining the different founts of type at present in this Office, it is the opinion of this Chapel that they are of a fair average standard, and, therefore, do not come under the class of bastard or fraudulent founts."

G. HOYLE, *Father.*

COLLEGE OFFICE, *Feb.*, 1878.

25. Part of the resolution of the College Chapel on the question of bastard founts, entered in the minutes of the DTPS on 17 May 1878; reproduced by kind permission of the Irish Print Union.

Press representative stated that he thought it was a mistake to look for an advance on the establishment rate, but that he was in favour of the increase in the piece rate. This is not surprising when most of the compositors were line hands. The mood of the meeting however was militant and the delegates voted for 'extreme measures' to be taken to further all their demands.

Some compromises were offered by the employers, but the men were in no mood to hear these at the general meeting of the trade held in the Rotundo Exhibition Room on 16 February. When Mr Moore of the College chapel suggested that they should accept the compromise the secretary recorded that 'the uproar was tremendous, it was impossible to hear the sense of what he was speaking . . . The chairman . . . wanted to know if anything but boxing was to be done.' The secretary, in a rare lapse of the convention, allowed himself to stray from the purely descriptive and noted that the meeting would 'live in memory as one of great disorder, caused solely by about six members appearing in a state of intoxication'. The meeting broke up with the resolution that two weeks' strike notice be given on 18 February.

The master printers met the challenge by advertising widely in Britain for men willing to break the strike and sent out a printed circular to its members inviting them to a meeting on 26 February to choose from a list of those who had replied. The implications of this 'caused no little excitement' to the union. Ponsonby & Murphy did not have to take advantage of this list as subsequent evidence showed they had paid the increases and so were not affected by the strike. M.H. Gill & Son were affected and at least some of their men walked out when the strike took effect. As the dispute bit, the Society imposed a three-fold levy of dues on those still in employment in an effort to keep the strike fund afloat. Nevertheless, with strike pay by the end of March already totalling £600, funds were seriously depleted and in April the union sought loans from other Irish and English typographical societies. At a special delegate meeting on 20 April the College representative Mr Burke objected violently to the proposal of a further levy of 2*d*. in every shilling over £1 earned. He suggested instead that an extra levy should only apply to 'stab hands and this was agreed. In May a six-fold levy was imposed. At this stage many members were in revolt over the continuation of the strike and when the secretary of the union was on business at the University Press in June he was openly berated by George Hoyle, father of the chapel, who said that the 'impertinent letters' which had been sent to employers by the secretary had caused the strike and that while he remained in office 'the trade would not be out of trouble'.

The finances of the union were in a perilous state. In the second quarter of the year nearly £1,100 was paid out in strike pay. With no solution in sight the union had appealed in May for a parliamentary inquiry, especially into the conduct of the Queen's printer, Alexander Thom, who had a staff of 60–70 journeymen still working, many brought over from England, and was sending work to Scotland for completion. Parnell and F.H. O'Donnell raised the matter in the House of Commons on behalf of the union and two autograph letters from the former are pasted into the minute books.

In October when the strike was in its eighth month a benefit concert was organised in the Round Room of the Rotundo. With a wry sense of humour the programme of songs included 'Nil desperandum', 'We don't know who is to blame' and 'Happy dreamland'. On 19 October a special delegate meeting was informed that there were only funds for another week. A letter was read from C.W. Gibbs of Porteous & Gibbs complaining that the length of the 'ill-advised strike' was putting fair houses at a disadvantage and that they would have to lower their rates of pay to compete. It was decided to canvass the opinions of the chapels. These were given at a meeting on 28 October. The University Press chapel was unanimously of the opinion that the men should be allowed to return to the closed houses at the old 'stab rate of £1-13-0, and that the $\frac{1}{2}d$. per 1,000 ens compromise offered to the piece hands in February should be accepted. There was little fight left in the men. A defeated yet defiant speech by R. Dunne of Powell's chapel was recorded: the strike 'should come to an end, drive the scoundrels [scabs] out of the city, give a chance to our own men, . . . did not believe that Paddy should travel from his own country to suit the convenience of the Saxon'. The committee was sanctioned to 'take some decisive measures . . . <u>at once</u>, with the view of a settlement'.

The employers smelled blood and several were unwilling to compromise. Further there was no guarantee that they would let the non-amicables go when they had served them well during the strike. On 11 November the College chapel proposed that an 'adjunct committee' be formed to negotiate with the employers based on a reversion to the 'stab rate of £1-13-0, but retaining the $\frac{1}{2}d$. extra on the piece rate. It was decided to have the chapels vote on this resolution, which they did overwhelmingly in favour.

It was agreed that the adjunct committee should call on all the employers in the city proposing a conference on the dispute. George Weldrick said he would consult Ponsonby & Murphy, but added that as 'the firm had not taken any part in the former meetings of employers . . . it was not likely they would now do so'. In the event Weldrick did turn up at the conference in Wynn's Hotel on 21 November — one of very few who did — and stated that the partnership would honour the payment of the new scale for works that had already been estimated at the higher rate; but the implication was that thereafter they would return to the old rates. The union sought a compromise $\frac{1}{4}d$. increase for the line hands, but the employers were unyielding. At a special delegate meeting of the union on the following day the reality was accepted and the meeting voted 171 to 76 for a return to work at the pre-strike rates. Even though there was not the necessary two-thirds majority there was full agreement that for the good of the union the resolution be deemed as carried. The return to work took effect on 25 November.

Thus ended a bitter lesson for the DTPS. The after-shocks of the strike were to reverberate in the union for years to come. Among the legions that were summoned before the committee on 23 October 1879 for owing more than £1 in arrears were a dozen from the College office: Robert Cruickshanks, William Dow, Senior, Joseph Doyle, W.F. O'Reilly, James Rodgers, M. McGowran, Thomas Corbett, Thomas Rooney, Thomas Swords, William McMullen, John Weldrick and even his brother George Weldrick. Most of the arrears were because of defaults on the heavy levies during the strike and a few refused to clear them, pleading that the trade had never voted on their imposition. John Weldrick and William McMullen sent letters in which they stated that as they were trustees of the DTPS they were exempt from subscriptions. Both tendered their resignations as trustees, but must have been persuaded to withdraw them as they held that office for many more years. Indeed their arrears were still on the books in January 1886 when they were at last nominally expelled. However Weldrick was still a trustee in 1892 as was McMullen at the time of his death in 1909.

Robert Cruickshanks was later to give an insight into the turmoil the imposition of the levies had created in the University Press. When he applied for American emigration allowance on 5 October 1880 he was refused because he owed £1 in arrears. In his defence he stated that during the strike he had been 'very unjustly misled by the old members of the College chapel', who resolved that they would not pay the levies after the thirteenth week and he had followed their advice. In fact he discovered that many continued to pay the dues unknown to him and thus had remained in benefit. The minutes record that he 'stigmatized the conduct of the old members . . . in marked terms'. He was refused the emigration allowance and had to wait until 26 February 1881 for his application to be approved.

The relative stability in the journeymen's wages at this period meant that printing charges would have been fairly stable at the DUP. However the College was worried about the increase in the amount of printing being done on its account. This led the board on 1 May 1875 to establish 'a syndicate . . . whose sanction shall be required for all printing to be charged to the College account'. One of the first things the syndicate did was to order more printing, in the form of '500 copies of order to print, bound in 5 books'.[3] It had some beneficial effect however as figures later supplied by bursar Carson showed:[4]

3. MUN/V/62/18/121, 6 July 1875.
4. MUN/V/5/14/98.

Printing and Stationery costs	1874	£1,269
	1875	1,376
	1876	1,333
	1877	1,133
	1878	1,140
	1879	855

Despite the evident savings in 1879 the bursar was still seeking to keep printing costs down. On his motion the board on 18 November 1879 resolved 'that in order to diminish the great expence of the Printing Office a committee of management be appointed to consist of the vice provost, Mr Jellett and Mr Galbraith, who shall have power to make such regulations as they may deem necessary for keeping the printing expences within moderate limits'. Seventy-five copies of the regulations drawn up were printed shortly afterwards.[5] Alas none appears to have survived.

The printing of several hundred exam papers each term was an expensive item in the College's account and ran to over £200 per year. Initially Murphy charged the same as Gill had, ranging from 5-0 per page for English to 21-0 for Hebrew. He reduced his prices in 1876 and made further cuts in the following year. For example Hebrew was charged at 14-6 in 1876 and 13-9 in 1877.[6] The annual *Calendar* was another high recurrent cost. Economies were effected here by printing only 750 copies from 1877 on, where formerly 1,000 had been the edition size. Paper was charged for separately. The bursar's accounts record that 32 reams of printing demy was bought on 7 June 1875 for the 1876 issue. With Murphy's 10 per cent handling commission it cost £52-9-5 and came from Venables, Tyler & Son in London, one of the few instances where we have the name of a supplier to Murphy.[7]

Other bookwork commissioned by the College from Murphy included new editions of the *Statutes, Catalogue of the lending library* and *Astronomical observations*, all of which were printed in 1879.[8] The bursar's accounts provide a detailed breakdown of the cost of the *Statutes*:

1000 copies demy 8vo	
Composition at 2-0 per page incl. small type	£29-12- 0
Presswork on 18½ sheets at 16-0 each	14-16- 0
Presswork on sign. C cancelled (8p.)	1- 5- 4
Alterations on MS from proofs	2-10- 0
Paper at £1-13-4 per sheet	30-16- 8

5. MUN/V/62/22/111d, 23 Dec. 1879.
6. MUN/V/62/17/137, 1 July 1875; MUN/V/62/18/126, Trinity term 1876; MUN/V/62/19/126, 3 Oct. 1877.
7. MUN/V/62/17/133.
8. MUN/V/62/21/121, 126, 174, 3 July, 25 Aug., 5 July 1879.

Printing and paper for cover   1- 5- 0
Stitching 250 copies   1- 6- 3
                                                81-11- 3

(I have failed to discover why composition for some works was charged for by the page, while the norm was by the sheet, and similarly why paper was sometimes charged for by each sheet of the edition, where the norm was by the ream.)

Despite the general unease at the charges for College printing and the escalating costs of the library catalogue in particular, the College did not shrink from ambitious plans. On 12 October 1878 the provost proposed to the board 'that it be referred to a committee . . . to consider the advisability of printing the records of Trinity College, other than those connected with legislative enactments'. Nothing came of this, but a plan that did take off was the Dublin University Press Series. The groundwork for this series was laid in 1855 through the reform of the fellowship examinations, which encouraged more classical scholars to enter, where formerly mathematics was rigidly dominant. The encouragement of scholarship under provost Humphrey Lloyd (1867–1881) was another factor, as were the changes made in the appointment of the senior fellows following a royal commission in 1877.[9]

There must have been extensive discussions and planning of the series throughout the first half of the 1870s, but the College muniments are surprisingly silent about it. The seed of the project was announced in the board register on 27 March 1875 in these terms:

> On the motion of the provost it was resolved that the board will aid the publication of approved works, written by the fellows or professors of Trinity College, belonging to either of the following classes, and from the nature of the subject not likely to pay their expences: viz. 1, works required for the academic curriculum; 2, works which in the opinion of the board extend the boundaries of useful knowledge. The assistance given shall be in general, one half of the cost of printing and paper of a first edition of 500 copies.

When the series was established these terms had been expanded so that Trinity usually paid the full cost of production and it was not confined to works by members of the College.

It was not an auspicious time to launch the project. Irish publishing was going through one of its periodic troughs, as was documented by a contemporary commentator:

> At present the Irish publishing trade is almost non-existent. Our publishers are nominal booksellers in fact, and mere English and

9.   McDowell and Webb, *TCD 1592–1952*, 265.

Scotch publishers' agents . . . there is a want of enterprise and energy, as well as a want of capital; and if the former requisites were more often evidenced, the latter would be forthcoming. The London mint mark is still thought indispensable to sell a book — a London publisher's name, even although a Dublin typographer turns out the work . . .[10]

With the series the DUP reached its fullest expression as a university press, so it is worth dealing with in detail although it will bring us well beyond our current period. It should be noted that the title of the series is the first use that I have encountered of the actual name 'Dublin University Press' (see plate 26). Hitherto the normal form of imprint had been 'Printed at the University Press', which was provincial in that it presupposed no other university press. With the new series it was as if the College was consciously expecting these works to circulate abroad and wanted them to be distinguished from the output of the other university presses, notably the OUP and CUP.

To begin with there follows a chronological listing of the series as far as I have identified it, noting only the first edition of each work. There is no numbering so I have given them essentially in the order they were accessioned by Trinity's library (subsequent editions have not been included):

1878   Macalister, Alexander, *Introduction to the systematic zoology and morphology of vertebrate animals.*
1879–1901 Cicero, *Correspondence,* edited by Robert Y. Tyrrell and Louis C. Purser, 7 vols.
         Leslie, T.E.C., *Essays in political economy.*
         Griffin, Robert William, *The parabola, ellipse, and hyperbola, treated geometrically.*
1880   Haughton, Samuel, *Six lectures on physical geography.*
         Par palimpsestorum Dubliniensium. The codex rescriptus Dublinensis of St Matthew's Gospel, new edition by T.K. Abbott.
         Monck, William H.S., *Introduction to logic.*
         Goethe, J.W. von, *Faust,* translated by Thomas E. Webb.
         MacCullagh, James, *Collected works,* edited by J.H. Jellett and S. Haughton.
1881   Casey, John, *A sequel to the first six books of the Elements of Euclid.*
         Burnside, William S., and Arthur W. Panton, *Theory of equations.*

10. C., C.H., 'Notes on the rise and progress of printing and publishing in Ireland part 22' in *Irish Builder* (1 June 1878) 163.

DUBLIN UNIVERSITY PRESS SERIES.

AN INTRODUCTION

TO

THE SYSTEMATIC ZOOLOGY

AND

MORPHOLOGY

OF

VERTEBRATE ANIMALS.

BY

ALEXANDER MACALISTER, M. D. D^{UBL.},

PROFESSOR OF COMPARATIVE ANATOMY AND ZOOLOGY, UNIVERSITY OF
DUBLIN.

DUBLIN: HODGES, FOSTER, & FIGGIS, GRAFTON-ST.
LONDON: LONGMANS, GREEN, & CO., PATERNOSTER-ROW.

1878.

26. The first book in the Dublin University Press Series.

	Southey, Robert, *The correspondence of Robert Southey with Caroline Bowles*, edited by Edward Dowden.
1882	Plato, *Parmenides*, edited by Thomas Maguire.
1882–5	Graves, Robert Percival, *Life of Sir William Rowan Hamilton*, 2 vols.
	Hobart, William Kirk, *Medical language of St. Luke*.
	Trinity College Dublin, *Dublin translations: translations into Greek and Latin verse by members of TCD*.
1883	Aristophanes, *The Acharnians*, translated by R.Y. Tyrrell.
1884	Purser, John Mallet, *A manual of histology and of histological methods*.
	Evangeliorum versio antehieronymiana ex codice Usseriano, edited by T.K. Abbott.
	Roberts, Ralph A., *Collection of examples on the analytic geometry of plane cones*.
1885	Webb, Thomas E., *The veil of Isis: a series of essays on idealism*.
	Aeschylus, *The Eumenides*, edited and translated by John F. Davies.
	Wilkins, George, *The growth of Homeric poems*.
	Casey, John, *Treatise on the analytic geometry of the point, line, circle, and the conic sections*.
1886	Virgil, *Aeneid*, translated by William J. Thornhill.
1889	Allman, George J., *Greek geometry from Thales to Euclid*.
	Stubbs, John William, *History of the University of Dublin*.
1892	Abbott, Thomas K., *Short notes on St. Paul's Epistles*.
1897	*The Apocalypse of St John, in a Syriac version hitherto unknown*, edited by John Gwynn.
1901	Hamilton, William Rowan, *Elements of quaternions*, 2nd ed. edited by C.J. Joly.
1902	Fitzgerald, George F., *Scientific writings*, edited by Joseph Larmor.
1905	Abbott, Thomas K., *Catalogue of fifteenth-century books in the library of TCD*.
1910	Whittaker, E.T., *History of the theories of aether and electricity*.
1912	Appollonius Rhodius, *Argonautica*.
1916	Alexander, Thomas, *Elementary applied mechanics*, 3rd ed.
1930	Suetonius, *De vita Caesarum*, edited by George W. Mooney.
1932	Van der Stel, Simon, *Journal of his expedition to Namaqualand 1685–86*, edited by Gilbert Waterhouse.
1936	Gellius, Aulus, *Noctium Atticarum liber I*, edited by Hazel M. Hornsby.
1939	Daniel, Becclesiensis, *Urbanus Magnus*, edited by J.G. Smyly.
1941	Tate, Robert William, *Orationes et epistolae Dublinenses (1914–40)*.
1943	Tate, Robert William, *Carmina Dubliniensia*.

The first work in the series, Macalister's *Introduction to the systematic zoology*, was in fact a continuation of his *Introduction to animal morphology*, printed at the Press in 1876 and for which the College paid half. The second instalment was being planned in October 1876, as evidenced by a bill from George Hanlon at that date for four wood-engravings.[11] Ponsonby & Murphy presented their bill for £108-6-6 for the printing on 4 November 1878; binding cost an extra £17-8-3 for the edition of 511 (presumably the 11 were fine paper copies), including £1-5-0 for 'cutting block for University Press Series'.[12] An Italian edition was planned in the early years of this century, as the following entry in the board register for 20 February 1904 would indicate: 'Permission was given to Ponsonby & Gibbs to have clichés made from the blocks of Professor Macalister's work on Morphology for the use of Bocca Freres Turin.'

The second work in the series, Cicero's *Correspondence*, was to be the *magnum opus* of Robert Y. Tyrrell, professor of Latin, and also a comparative bestseller for the Press. After the first volume in 1879, a further six volumes following at intervals of a few years: volume 2 in 1886, 3 in 1890, 4 in 1894, 5 in 1897, 6 in 1899, and an index volume in 1901. Second editions of all volumes were called for between 1885 and 1933, and a third edition of the first volume was printed in 1904. University Microfilms contemplated issuing the index volume in 1965, and an edition was apparently printed in Germany in the early 1970s with the College's permission.[13] Casey's *Sequel to . . . Euclid* (1881) *was* a bestseller and eight editions followed in the series by 1910. Another mathematical work enjoyed even greater longevity — Burnside and Panton's *Theory of equations* (1881). Being a textbook for the students, editions of 2,000 were regularly run off up to the 1930s. It was given a new lease of life in 1954 when it was reprinted by Chand & Co. in Delhi, and in 1964 there was a proposal from Micro Photo of Cleveland to photolithographically reproduce it.[14] Interestingly it was not initially anticipated that any of these would be 'bestsellers' and no stereotype plates were made from the first editions. Casey, and Burnside and Panton seem to have been the only works for which plates were prepared after the second editions had been set.

A DUP Series committee sat to choose works that were to be printed and to oversee the accounts. Bursar Carson also provided tight financial control. In his report on income and expenditure for the years 1874 to 1879, submitted to the board in November 1879, he recorded that £166-16-6 was expended on the series in the initial year and £443-5-7 in

---

11. MUN/V/62/19/324, submitted and paid in Jan. 1877.

12. MUN/V/62/20/339, printing; MUN/V/62/21/326, binding.

13. DUP/Brunswick Press files, copy of letter from Liala Allman to treasurer's office, TCD, 12 Feb. 1976; royalties were being pursued by the College.

14. TCD board room files, 26 June 1964. (These files have recently been incorporated into the College muniments in the College library.)

the current year: 'the favourable critical notices of some of the works . . . are a proof of the literary credit which the series has reflected upon the College, even at this early stage in its existence'. There was obviously a real fear that the series would run away with itself and become a costly burden, because when J.A. Galbraith took over as bursar in 1880 he too kept comprehensive accounts on it, entering the details in two Vere Foster copybooks.[15] In them he recorded that the first ten works published had cost a total of £1,679-1-8 to print, bind and publish, while on 5 November 1881 sales of £508-6-0 had been made, representing nearly a 30 per cent return on the College's investment. A further £508-6-0 had been expended on the next seven works then in the press. Thus Trinity's total outlay on the series in the five years since the first publication was nearly £2,240, a not inconsiderable sum.

Occasionally the College muniments provide an insight into the printing of the series beyond the bald figures given in the accounts. Such is the case through a handful of letters from Thomas Webb to members of the College about his *Veil of Isis* (1885).[16] In a letter of 17 May 1879 he revealed that there were 377 pages in standing type and that a further 40 or 50 would complete the work. If it was the norm at the Press at this date to set entire works before printing them off it would indicate that there must have been huge founts of text type available. A work of 400 pages would have needed about one and a quarter tons of type.[17] To cap it all Webb was a 'rewriter' after text had been set and although he promised to have the work finished by Christmas 1882 it was another two years before it was printed off. When Weldrick's bill for the work was submitted on 23 December 1884 it reflected Webb's practices. Among the charges were £19-5-10 for 'numerous alterations from MS on proofs' and a further £5-14-3 for 'composition of 80 pages cancelled'.[18]

Such profligacy caused alarm among the fellows and on 31 October 1885 the bursar put a motion to the board that they return to the former system of aiding authors rather than publishing them and 'that the committee of the Dublin University Press Series be directed not to undertake the publication of any fresh works in connexion with that Series'. This was too radical for some and J.K. Ingram proposed an amendment, which was accepted, whereby the committee was not to accept any new work without consulting the board.

By October 1885 twenty-six books, including reprints, had appeared in the series. A comprehensive return of the number of copies printed, sold and remaining in stock was printed at that time (see plate 27).[19] Besides

---

15. MUN/P/1/2394a.

16. MUN/P/3/1200–1203, 4 letters 17 May 1879 – 15 Nov. 1884.

17. Gaskell, *New introduction*, 116.

18. MUN/V/62/27/48.

19. MUN/P/1/2417.

DUBLIN UNIVERSITY PRESS SERIES.

RETURN showing the Number of Copies Printed. Copies sent to Authors and Publishers, and Stock in Printing Office, on October 23rd, 1885.

TITLE OF WORK		Date of Publication.	Copies Printed.	To Author or Editor.	To Reviews, &c.	Longmans.	Hodges & Co.	Bound.	Sheets.	TOTAL. Copies on hands.	OBSERVATIONS.
				COPIES.		COPIES TO PUBLISHERS.		COPIES ON HANDS.			
Introduction to Morphology,	(Dr. Macalister).	1878, Nov. 7.	500	25	9	226	62	188	—	188	
Correspondence of Cicero, Vol. I.,	(Prof. Tyrrell).	1879, May 14.	500	30	12	300	164	—	—	—	
Do. do. 2nd Ed.	(Prof. Tyrrell).	1885, Feb. 6.	1000	22	1	50	50	127	750	877	
Essays in Political and Moral Philosophy,	(Prof. Leslie).	1879, May 14.	500	25	20	385	69	—	—	—	
Parabola, Ellipse, and Hyperbola, treated geometrically,	(Dr. Gregg).	1879, Oct. 16.	500	25	10	100	56	8	300	308	
Six Lectures on Physical Geography,	(Dr. Haughton).	1880, Mar. 27.	500	59	10	325	81	24	—	24	
Codex Rescriptus Dublinensis of St. Matthew's Gospel Z.	(Dr. Abbott).	1880, May 1.	150	26	52	13	12	49	—	49	
Introduction to Logic,	(Mr. Monck).	1880, May 11.	500	25	11	150	225	90	—	90	
Faust: from the German of Goethe,	(Dr. Webb).	1880, Dec. 16.	1000	25	15	100	149	110	600	710	
Mathematical and Other Tracts of Mac Cullagh,	(The Provost).	1881, Jan. 12.	500	—	*47	125	25	2	300	309	* Presentations to both Senior and Junior Fellows.
Sequel to Euclid, 1st Edition,	(Dr. Casey).	1881, Mar. 29.	1000	51	1	530	425	—	—	—	
Do. do. 2nd. do.	(Dr. Casey).	1882, Feb. 22.	2000	50	9	851	1100	—	—	—	
Correspondence of Southey,	(Dr. Dowden).	1881, Nov. 2.	500	20	23	250	43	176	—	176	
Theory of Equations,	(Profs. Burnside and Panton).	1881, Nov. 2.	1000	54	10	600	342	—	—	—	
Parmenides of Plato,	(Dr. Maguire).	1882, Mar. 3.	250	25	8	45	25	25	125	150	
Life of Hamilton, Vol. I.,	(Rev. R. P. Graves).	1882, Sept. 30.	750	*56	14	175	141	13	350	363	* 31 paid for by Mr. Graves.
Do. do. Vol. II.,	(Rev. R. P. Graves).	1885, June 19.	750	*58	16	50	88	87	450	537	* 33 paid for by Mr. Graves.
Medical Language of St. Luke,	(Rev. Dr. Hobart).	1882, Nov. 10.	1000	312	—	50	26	12	100	112	
Dublin Translations,	(Prof. Tyrrell).	1882, Nov. 27.	750	26	*25	100	100	79	450	529	* 24 paid for by Contributors.
The Acharnians of Aristophanes,	(Prof. Tyrrell).	1883, April 23.	750	35	10	101	62	91	450	541	
Manual of Histology,	(Dr. Purser).	1884, Jan. 10.	1000	25	1	150	392	31	400	431	
Evangelia Antehieronymiana ex Codice Vetusto, Dublinensi,	(Mr. Abbott).	1884, Feb. 11.	500	25	1	48	7	68	350	418	
Examples on Plane Conics,	(Mr. Roberts).	1884, April 21.	500	25	1	100	50	74	250	324	
Veil of Isis,	(Dr. Webb).	1884, Dec. 24.	500	25	3	75	62	34	300	334	
Eumenides of Æschylus,	(Prof. Davies).	1885, June 24.	750	*82	1	50	50	117	450	567	* 57 paid for by Dr. Davies.
Homeric Question,	(Mr. Wilkins).	1885, Oct. 17.	500	25	1	100	25	99	250	349	

27. The state of the DUP Series in October 1885.

giving the edition sizes, it also pinpointed the exact publication dates, showing for example that MacCullagh's *Collected works,* although dated 1880 in its imprint, was not actually published until 12 January 1881. It revealed that 812 copies of the edition of 1,000 of Hobart's *Medical language of St Luke* (1882) were sent to the author, indicating that he paid for the printing and had had it included in the series for the status it provided. Some interesting and unexpected patterns emerge about the distribution of the works. Hodges, Figgis & Co. was used as the Irish publisher, and Longman, Green & Co. in London as the overseas publisher (they charged regular amounts for advertising in India and in America, where Lippincott in Philadelphia was the distributor). A total of 18,150 copies had been printed in the series thus far. Of these 8,880 (49 per cent) were sent to the publishers, and surprisingly London took more (5,049 or 28 per cent) than Dublin (3,831 or 21 per cent). So the series can be adjudged to have been a success beyond Ireland. There remained in stock 7,379 copies (41 per cent), the remaining 1,891 (10 per cent) being accounted for by copies for the authors or review. The terms afforded to Hodges, Figgis & Co. were similar to previous transactions with them, that is 13 copies were supplied as 12 at a trade price, and a further discount of 10 per cent was given on sales. This cumulatively represented a margin of about 40 per cent.[20]

The tight financial watch that bursars Carson and Galbraith had kept on the series in the initial years had slipped somewhat by the end of the 1880s and the accountant A.G. Bailey was set to do an audit of it, which he completed 'after spending a great deal of time, and labour' on 15 February 1889.[21] It provided debit and credit balances for each work. Armed with these figures the board decided to face economic reality and on 1 November 1890 wrote off £2,749-5-2 due from the series that hitherto had appeared as an asset in the bursar's accounts. However when the auditor was asked to look more closely at the accounts for the series in 1893 he reported to the board on 24 June that only £1,570 of the amount written off in November 1890 should be deemed irrecoverable and that the remainder be restored as an asset to the balance sheet. He must have felt that the previous decision was too pessimistic and that there were potential sales among the moribund stock. The board approved his recommendation.

This was the time of the College's tercentenary (1892) and the publication of John William Stubbs's *History of the University of Dublin* (1889) in the series may well have been planned as part of the celebrations. On 14 February 1891 he was authorised by the board to commence a second

20. MUN/P/4/275/32–33, 1 Jan. 1883.
21. MUN/DUP/1/14, 'Accounts of the Dublin University Press Series 1877'; it was kept up to date down to 1914 and was succeeded by MUN/DUP/1/15, 16, 1914–1938.

volume of the *History* covering the period 1800 to the present, but this never appeared. The series thus far was a modest intellectual success, if not an economic one, and served to heighten the profile of the University at home and abroad at the time of its 300th anniversary. The board minutes record the sending of several sets overseas as ambassadors of Trinity's scholarship. However the publication of the series was now on the downturn. When Prof. James E. Reynolds offered a work on thiocarbomide for the series the board declined at its meeting on 21 December 1895, stating that the 'issue of books in the Series was for the present discontinued'.

A book that was planned but never published was Prof. Arthur Palmer's edition of the *Odes* of Horace. The board approved its publication as part of the DUP series at its meeting of 3 December 1892. The work was set, printed off and corrected down to the third proofs, as is evident from two surviving sets discovered by L.J.D. Richardson in a bookstall on the Dublin quays in the early 1920s.[22] The work is in crown octavo format and consists of ten and a half sheets. The Press's set of proofs was read by M.N. Kane and is stamped and dated 16 September 1895. The author's set has the Press's label with instructions to the author, and was initialled 'Press. A.P. Oct. 3 1895' (see plate 28). Why it was not completed is not known. Richardson speculates that pressure of other business and the onset of Palmer's final illness — he died in 1897 — may have been the reasons, as also the fact that there had been other recent editions of the *Odes*.

The College must have been flattered to have been asked by the British and Foreign Bible Society for permission to use Gwynne's Syriac text of the Apocalypse to complete its edition of the New Testament. The board readily agreed at its meeting on 12 October 1912. Given the time and expense that had gone into establishing the reputation of the DUP series the board was strangely compliant in allowing its name to be used. Thus for example permission was granted on 22 May 1908 to Maurice A. Gerothwohl, professor of Romance Languages, to use the title 'the Dublin University Series of French Texts' for works he was editing for a London publisher. Similarly no objection was raised on 6 March 1915 to the more oblique 'Dublin Text Books of Science', a series of maths works by George W. Parker. The College itself seems only to have contemplated extending the use of the series' title once, and that at a very late stage. On 2 July 1934 the board 'authorised the institution of a new series of publications, to be known as the Dublin University Series of Irish Texts'. Nothing however came of this.

Not all the suggestions for publications originated within the College. Such was the case with George F. Fitzgerald's *Scientific writings* (1902),

---

22. L.J.D. Richardson, 'An unpublished edition of Horace's *Odes* by the late Professor Arthur Palmer' in *Hermathena*, LX (1942) 87–111. Prof. Richardson presented the proofs to the TCD library in 1975 (shelfmark OLS 198.q.46).

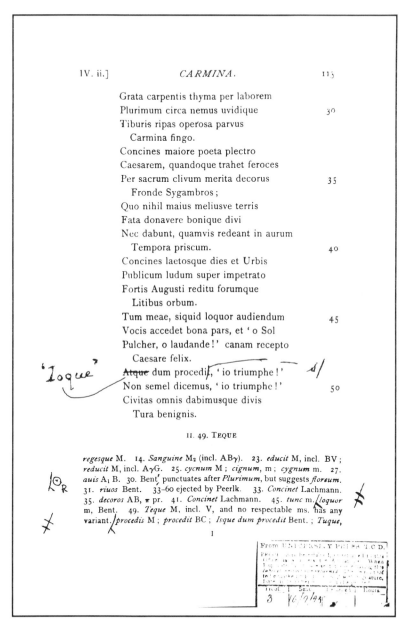

Grata carpentis thyma per laborem
Plurimum circa nemus uvidique   30
Tiburis ripas operosa parvus
    Carmina fingo.
Concines maiore poeta plectro
Caesarem, quandoque trahet feroces
Per sacrum clivum merita decorus   35
    Fronde Sygambros;
Quo nihil maius meliusve terris
Fata donavere bonique divi
Nec dabunt, quamvis redeant in aurum
    Tempora priscum.   40
Concines laetosque dies et Urbis
Publicum ludum super impetrato
Fortis Augusti reditu forumque
    Litibus orbum.
Tum meae, siquid loquor audiendum   45
Vocis accedet bona pars, et 'o Sol
Pulcher, o laudande!' canam recepto
    Caesare felix.
Atque dum procedit, 'io triumphe!'
Non semel dicemus, 'io triumphe!'   50
Civitas omnis dabimusque divis
    Tura benignis.

'*Toque*'

11. 49. TEQUE

regesque M.   14. *Sanguine* M₂ (incl. ABγ).   23. *educit* M, incl. BV;
reducit M, incl. AγG.   25. *cycnum* M; *cignum*, m; *cygnum* m.   27.
auis A₁ B.   30. Bent! punctuates after *Plurimum*, but suggests *floreum*.
31. *riuos* Bent.   33–60 ejected by Peerlk.   33. *Concinet* Lachmann.
35. *decoros* AB, π pr.   41. *Concinet* Lachmann.   45. *tunc* m./*loquor*
m, Bent.   49. *Teque* M, incl. V, and no respectable ms. has any
variant./*procedis* M; *procedit* BC; *Isque dum procedit* Bent.; *Tuque*,

1

From UNIVERSITY PRESS T.C.D.
...
3   16/9/95

28. A page from the proofs of A. Palmer's edition of Horace's *Carmina*, printed at the Press
in 1895 but never published.

the impetus for which seems to have come from Joseph Larmor in Cambridge. The board gave approval for the project on 17 April 1901 and agreed on 11 May that it could be included in the DUP series. It was not a bestseller, as emerged when a reprint was planned by the Johnson Reprint Co. of London in 1964. Upon investigation it was found that 400 copies in sheets of the original edition of 750 were still in stock in the Printing House! These were then sold to Johnson Reprint for a nominal £100 and brought back from the dead as it were.[23] (I have found no evidence that the work was in fact reissued.)

Although the board appears to have paid the full cost of producing most of the works in the series, it is evident that several other formulas were employed. The combinations sometimes became complicated, as was the case with Whittaker's *History of the theories of aether and electricity* (1910). On 7 May 1910 the board offered the author the choice of having the College pay the cost of publication; the repayment of this cost would be the first charge on sales and the profits thereafter would be split in the proportion of one-third for the College and two-thirds for Whittaker. Alternatively the College and the author would share the cost of publication and the profits would be divided one-sixth to five-sixths in favour of Whittaker. He chose the latter, which proved to be the right option as the edition appears to have sold out quickly. Interestingly Longman, Green & Co. was given first in the imprint, not Hodges, Figgis & Co. as was usual in the series.

The College was now very wary of the costs. On 27 January 1910 the board decided to restore a debt of £185 due to the College from the series, which had been written off in 1893–1895. And on 24 May 1913, when considering a letter from Alfred Perceval Graves about publishing a selection from his uncle Robert's *Life of . . . Hamilton* (1882–1885), the board only gave permission on condition that it cost the College nothing. This caution was indicative of the fact that the series had run out of steam. Nothing original appeared under its banner in the 1920s and after a few well-spaced books in the 1930s and early 1940s (which will be dealt with in the next section), the series ceased in 1943 with Robert W. Tate's *Carmina Dubliniensia*.

To return then to our chronological narrative in the 1870s. Just as the College set out to support the DUP series by paying half the cost of printing, so too were there other works which it supported. *Hermathena* continued to attract this subsidy and the College must have been satisfied with Murphy's performance because the third issue, printed in 1876, was given to the Press. Trinity's contribution for it and subsequent numbers during Murphy's tenure came to about £40 per issue. Ponsonby appears to have taken a 42 per cent stake in it.[24] Among the other DUP

23. TCD board room files, letters Feb., Apr., June 1964.
24. MUN/P/1/2297a.

printings supported by Trinity was William H. Ferrar's *Collation of four important MSS of the Gospels* (1877), completed by T.K. Abbott. An interim account in May 1875 indicates that three proofs were taken for this work, which, from earlier evidence, may have been the standard at the Press.[25] The College was also very generous in its support of the RIA's edition of the *Book of Leinster* published in 1880. The 90 pages of letterpress were printed at the University Press but the 410 pages of lithograph facsimile were done by the City Printing & Litho Company. The bursar's voucher books show that between 1875 and the publication date the College contributed £587-15-0 towards the publication.

The relative richness of archival material for Gill's period is not present for Murphy's tenure so it is not possible to indicate the range of his customers beyond the walls of Trinity. Ponsonby did provide some textbooks and meaty law books — his specialities — as for example W.H. Kisbey's *Statutes relating to bankrupts and debtors in Ireland* (1876, 476p.) and William Dillon's *Supreme Court of Judicature (Ireland) Act 1877* (1879, 469p.). But it is difficult to see how the new partnership could have attracted the range of business that Gill had through McGlashan & Gill and his extensive contacts in the Dublin, London and Edinburgh trades. No doubt the intention, given the heavy investment in machine presses, was to build up a similar business, but Murphy's death interrupted these plans. Philip White in his August 1908 article in the *Irish Printer* says that Murphy died 'after a severe illness' in 1879, but he must be mistaken in this. Murphy's name appears in 1880 imprints and his death was announced at the College's board meeting of 24 April of that year.

25. MUN/V/62/17/131.

11

Ponsonby and Weldrick: 1880–1902

At the time of the announcement of Murphy's death to the board of the College on 24 April 1880 an application was also considered 'on the part of Mr. Ponsonby . . . and Mr. Weldrick the managing superintendent of the Printing House — that Mr. Weldrick might be admitted to the same position . . . as that held by . . . Mr. Murphy . . . The application was agreed to, subject to the condition of proper security being given.' The board reiterated that the College printer was 'on no account to print any document at the College Printing House with the College arms at the head thereof — unless countersigned by the registrar'. It took time to arrange affairs formally, but it is evident from the surviving private ledger of the partnership that it took over at the start of October 1880, the start of the academic year.[1]

This is an appropriate stage to look at Weldrick's career in more detail.[2] According to Philip White he served his apprenticeship under Gill, and worked at the University Press as a journeyman and afterwards as a book-keeper; he was 'practically acting as manager during Mr. Murphy's short tenure'. W.C. Trimble tells us that he was the son of 'the senior and highly-respected pressman'. A pressman of that name is recorded in the DTPS minutes as working at the DUP at least as early as 24 January 1849. Three of George's brothers were also active in the book trade. Joseph was in his last year of apprenticeship at the DUP when he was involved in the escape of the Fenian James Stephens from Richmond Prison in December 1865 and had to flee to America. He died in New York on 29 July 1892. Another brother John, as we have seen, also worked at the University Press and was a long-standing trustee of the DTPS. Towards the end of the century he worked as manager for Henry J. Gill in Sackville Street. He was related to the Gills by marriage, having married one of the Harts, the family of M.H. Gill's wife. John left the

---

1. MUN/DUP/1/1a 'Private leger of Messrs. Ponsonby & Weldrick University Press'.

2. The following account is based on P. White in *Irish Printer* (Aug. 1908) 7 and (Aug. 1911) 8–10; W.C. Trimble in *Irish Printer* (Oct. 1934) 16; DTPS committee minutes; papers supplied by Michael Gill; *Printing World* (July 1892).

employ of Gill in some indignation, together with his brother Frank, because they were not taken into partnership — Henry had too many sons of his own. They set up a bookselling business on the opposite side of Sackville Street, but it did not survive long.

As a journeyman George Weldrick was actively involved in union affairs. He was auditor to the Irish Typographical Union in the 1860s and was secretary for winding up its affairs in 1868 when the DTPS decided to go it alone. Weldrick was interested in the welfare of his fellow printers and was one of the founding members of the DTPS Benevolent Fund in 1869, a fund set up to give sickness, unemployment and pension benefits to printers beyond what the Society could provide. He was well respected within the union and was called upon to act as treasurer in September 1875 after the previous treasurer was relieved of the office, having embezzled over £80 of the Society's money. Even after he became a master printer his high estimation within the trade remained. When there was a dispute in Fowler's office in August 1881 over payments to compositors, the DTPS referred the proprietor to Weldrick or George Drought 'for the usage and custom of the trade'. Weldrick reciprocated the union's confidence in him by insisting that all his printing staff were members. On 11 March 1890 Thomas Dolan, employed as a reader in the DUP, applied at Weldrick's insistence for membership of the DTPS, even though the Society did not require readers to be on its books.

Weldrick took over the Printing House at the same annual rent of £100 that Murphy had been paying. No major structural changes were made during his tenure although there is evidence that it was bursting at the seams. The board minutes for 11 December 1885 record that he requested space in the library 'for a large quantity of stock for wch. he has no room in the printing office'. However the librarian stated that the library was already 'choke-full' and that it was imperative that another store be found. This may well be the origin of some of the dumps of DUP material that are to be found to this day in the basements of various buildings around the College. The extent of the Printing House about this date can be seen from the plan of the campus published in *The Book of Trinity College, Dublin 1591–1891*, Belfast 1892 (see plate 29; the narrow projection from the 1839–40 extension was probably sheds rather than useful factory space). In October 1901 the College was paid compensation through Weldrick for 45 copies of vol. 1 of Tyrrell's Cicero destroyed by fire, so there may have been a minor fire in the building; yet again it may have occurred at the binders.[3] The profit and loss accounts of the partnership reveal that Weldrick had a telephone installed in 1884 – later notepaper gives the number as '163' — a very quick use of modern technology, and well before many of the other printers in the city, including Thoms who did not install one until near the turn of the century.

3. MUN/DUP/1/14/76.

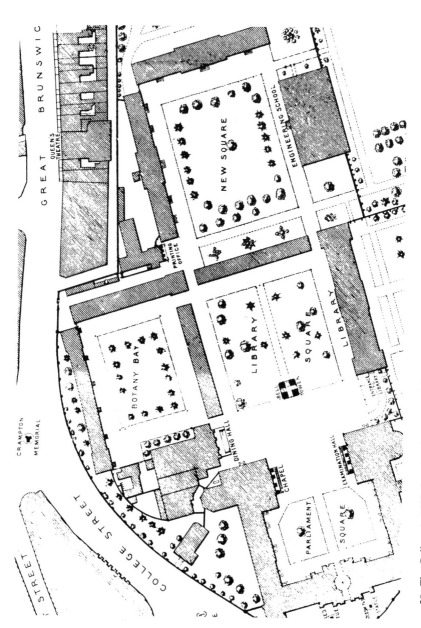

29. The College in 1892 showing the extent of the Printing House (from *The Book of Trinity College Dublin*, Belfast 1892).

Weldrick was not so quick to adapt to the introduction of the new mechanical typesetters. These made their appearance in Dublin in the 1880s and on 21 December 1886 the DTPS issued its *Rules for working type composing machines*. The *Freeman's Journal* early in 1888 was one of the first to install the Thorne 'cold metal' machines, while the Dublin Steam Printing Company was the first with 'hot metal' Linotypes, purchased in mid-1893. Yet again, as with the late introduction of machine presses to the Printing House, speed was not of the essence for the University Press and the machines' lack of flexibility in setting mathematics and exotic characters would have militated against their introduction. There was also the fact that some discriminating printers preferred the appearance of hand-set type, as Andrew J. Corrigan tells us in his account of a contemporary Dublin printing office, 'mainly because the Old Style book faces then offered on machines were undoubtedly weak in line, and compared unfavourably with foundry type'.[4] Ponsonby & Weldrick's balance sheets show that there was no major investment in plant during their tenure. On 30 September 1880 it can be calculated that the 'machinery & plant' was valued at just £310, while the 'type & composition requisites' had a book value of £2,227. The machinery was depreciated at 5 per cent per year, as was the type usually, although because it was understandably more prone to wear $7\frac{1}{2}$ per cent or 10 per cent was sometimes written off. Neither category grew at the rate of more than £100 or £200 per year so that at the dissolution of the partnership in 1903 the machinery was valued at £1,113 and the type at £3,615, a total of £4,728. The College of course owned some additional materials in the Printing House but, as will be seen, this only consisted of type to the value of £677 and no machinery.

Examination of the DTPS records reveals that there was usually about 30 members in the DUP chapel in this period. It ranged from a low of 21 on 29 October 1888 to a high of 39 on 23 April 1898. The Press was one of the largest bookhouses in the city, with a staff comparable to Falconers or Dollards; Pilkingtons and Thoms would have been among the few that were bigger (and these by a factor of two or three). The make-up of the workers at the DUP was given in a report on 11 November 1890 in the course of a dispute over the abolition of piece work: 'stab 20, piece 14, apprentices 6. What is surprising in these figures is that the establishment hands outnumbered the line hands — the University Press was usually pointed to as an example of the abuse of the piece system. But the report shows other houses far more at fault. For example the Dublin Steam Printing Company had 10 'stab, 18 piece and 35 boys. Porteous & Gibbs had 3 on 'stab but 9 on piece.

There had been rumblings in the trade against the whole system of piece work throughout the 1880s. This manifested itself at the University

---

4. Andrew J. Corrigan, *A printer and his world,* London 1944, 117; Corrigan worked in Corrigan & Wilson of Sackville Place at the turn of the century.

Press on a few occasions. On 18 August 1885 M.N. Kane and Robert Bisley made a written submission to the DTPS complaining about a fellow comp, Ross Mahon, who had told Weldrick falsely that all three were refusing to do piece work on Tyrrell's Cicero and would leave if not paid on the 'stab. Apparently E. Hayes and Joseph Pasley, both establishment hands, were also working on it. Weldrick refused to be intimidated and so Mahon left his employment, but gave the impression that the other two comps reneged on their agreement with him. Fortunately Weldrick had not believed him otherwise Kane and Bisley would have been dismissed. Mahon was constantly in the wars with his employers. He was re-employed by Weldrick late in 1886 — one can only imagine through sheer desperation at a shortage of comps at the time — but left without giving due notice. When he was called before the DTPS committee on 9 November to explain his conduct he said he had been badly treated by Weldrick and had not been given a fair run of piece work since July. And besides he said that he was ignorant of the rule that line hands had to give notice. In March of the following year he was dismissed from *The Nation* office for not having 'a fair composing stick'.

Another eruption of the piece-work problem happened in July 1886 when the Gills' chapel put forward a motion for the abolition of the system. Philip Gaynor spoke on behalf of the chapel and cited the College office as an example where the system was abused, every bit of 'fat' being taken from the line hands and given to the house. This accusation had several of the College delegates on their feet to defend Weldrick. E. Hayes said that DUP piece hands were sometimes paid even more than the rules called for. This was corroborated by M.N. Kane who said that he was being paid 50 per cent extra for the work he was then setting. Another delegate spoke of the Press as being an 'exceptionally good office'. The delegate from Gills backed down somewhat and made it clear that the chapel was not advocating a strike on the matter.

A strike, however, did take place in 1890 over piece work. The DTPS minutes record that on 20 May the Leckie chapel put forward a resolution urging the union to seek shorter hours and better wages, especially for the line hands 'whose average earnings . . . [did] not reach 20s. per week — a labourer's wage'. It was debated whether the Society should seek an extra penny per 1,000 ens or push for the abolition of the whole system. The trade voted for abolition on 12 July and a memorial to that effect was then sent to the employers. A written reply to it of 30 September from Ponsonby & Weldrick, recorded in the minutes for 24 October, stated that they could not allow it and that such a serious change would have to be coupled with the adoption of a uniform system throughout the trade as regards numbers of apprentices, union and non-union members, etc. Weldrick expanded on this written reply during a visit of a DTPS delegation to the Printing House on 14 October. He said he could not give the 'stab rate to some men 'as they were not competent to earn anything like it'. There were some old friends of his that he employed on piece as an act of charity to allow them to earn a little and they were grateful. He was reticent about helping to arrange a conference with the other employers on the matter as he did not want to appear to be a leader, and besides he claimed he hardly knew them — 'he was only an individual going along quietly'.

The College chapel came out strongly in favour of the abolition of piece work and of bringing the men affected out on strike if it was not conceded, even though it was pointed out that it would need a four-fold levy on dues to fund the strike pay of the 90–100 piece hands it was calculated were in the city. The College delegate, James Graham, at a meeting of 11 November gave a description of the system as it operated in the Printing House. He said 'both systems' applied, meaning presumably that piece hands were paid either by the 1,000 ens, where the comp was responsible for the make-up, or by the 'magazine' practice of 100 lines, where no make-up was involved. 'Fat' was done by the house. When a sheet had been worked off the comp responsible for it had to take out the furniture, unlead it and paper up the type ready for future distribution. It was, as we have seen in regard to the 1875 dispute at the DUP over the matter, contrary to the custom of the trade for line hands to do this work. Regardless it had apparently persisted at the Press. Graham reported that there was no delay due to lack of materials, as there was at other offices, but that the comps were often kept waiting a long time for a 'take' of copy. He concluded by saying that the average wage was £1-4-0 per week for line hands.

A conference with the employers was held on 20 November, at which Weldrick attended, but there was no resolution. On 2 December the employers' delegation agreed to suggest to their members that the penny per 1,000 be conceded, bringing the rate to $7\frac{1}{2}d$., but that there could be no question of the abolition of the system. Apparently the union unilaterally decided that the rate was to apply from 20 December and that the magazine system was to operate, the house being given the responsibility of doing the make-up. Not unnaturally some employers, including Ponsonby & Weldrick, refused to pay it. As a consequence the piece hands at the University Press and several other houses walked out. A ban on overtime was introduced on 6 January 1891 for the 'stab comps remaining in the houses that had not conceded the new rates. Arthur Griffith, the College's representative on the DTPS committee, was suspended on 18 January for allowing overtime to be worked at the DUP; apparently he had suppressed the letter entrusted to him which conveyed the instruction to the Press's chapel.

Weldrick had re-employed as 'stab hands four of the fourteen piece hands who had withdrawn their labour. One of these was Effingham Wilson — no doubt a relation of the proprietors of the London printing firm of that name — who on 15 January sought permission from the union to set the *Law reports* at the Press on piece. Apparently he had been an excellent line hand and made more on piece than the 'stab provided. Weldrick did not want to deprive him of the benefit and was even willing to pay him the extra penny. However the committee refused permission because Weldrick still wanted him to do the make-up. It is evident that Weldrick's resolve was wavering because he let it be known through Wilson that he was going to concede to the union's demands at the end of the week even if a meeting of the employers, planned for the following day, came to no conclusion. And indeed nothing seems to have come of this meeting as it is not recorded in the DTPS minutes, and it is not clear if Weldrick did in fact concede the demands as indicated. A meeting with the employers did take place on 7 February where they agreed to concede the extra penny, but suggested that it be left optional to the house to make up the matter or not. This was rejected by a vote of the trade 437 to 83. There was no clear cut resolution of the strike — heavy amounts of strike pay were recorded in the first quarterly accounts of the year — but one by one the employers capitulated and granted the demands.

Emboldened by its success the union decided on 24 April to try and bring uniformity into the 'stab rates being paid and proposed 'That as the wages is now 35/- per week in almost all the book and jobbing offices, we ask that the trade endorse it by a vote, and that no member of the Society accept work under that rate (35/-) per week'. The University Press was not among the defaulters and the handful that continued to pay 33-0 had dwindled to two by June — Burkes and *Freemans* jobbing office — where the men remained out on strike. Further concessions were won by the union in the succeeding decade — the DTPS minutes mention a 'new scale of prices' on 7 January 1893 and payment by a new rule on 10 December 1901 — but these must have been minor adjustments as they were not set out in the records and did not cause any strikes.

Disputes over the application of piece-work rules continued to occur at the University Press throughout the 1890s. M. O'Toole had occasion in May 1893 to leave the office because he refused to set a difficult classical work on piece — it was so complicated that he could earn little on it. His dilemma echoed that of Robert Salmon and Michael Keogh in Pilkington's office in December 1889. They were piece hands setting a catalogue whose MS was so bad that Salmon resigned and Keogh spent his time 'going from one reader to another to see if they could make out the manuscript until the readers told him he was a nuisance'. Another attempt was made in April 1896 to have piece work done away with, this time on a resolution of Cahills' chapel, which said that the system as it operated was a disgrace, with several employers not recognising the scale. Weldrick was numbered among these, but there were conflicting reports as to whether it was true or not. The resolution was passed for the abolition, but there was little will among the executive to pursue it, no doubt because the employers had so vigorously defended it only five years previously, and Cahills' chapel had to remind the committee to implement the resolution on 15 January 1898. That too was long-fingered by the union and piece work lingered on for another thirty years.

Cahills was the source of another complaint at this time and again the University Press was cited as being at fault. On 30 April 1897 the chapel called for the prohibition of the system whereby some offices required 'stab hands to write up their work for weekly bills at line scale as if they were piece hands, rather than as hours worked. R. Chapman confirmed that the system prevailed at the College. Cahills' resolution was passed, but on 1 June Weldrick sent a deputation to the DTPS's committee to ask for time to rearrange his system and this was granted. Weldrick sent a further delegation on 20 July wanting to know if the 'clicker' could cast up the value of the output of the companionship on a particular job. Weldrick made it clear that he did not want to compare the men's outputs so the union raised no objections.

The trading accounts in Ponsonby & Weldrick's private ledger show that the annual wages climbed somewhat erratically throughout the 1880s and 1890s mirroring the changes in sales but also reflecting the rises in wage rates; (the financial years ran from 1 October, and the figures are quoted to the nearest £):

Year	Wages	Sales
1881–1883	£7,194	£15,460
	(2,398 p.a.)	(5,153 p.a.)
1884	2,960	5,770
1885	3,251	6,391
1886	3,362	7,811
1887	3,264	6,098
1888	3,197	6,182
1889	3,758	7,006
1890–1899	38,756	73,203
	(3,876 p.a.)	(7,320 p.a.)
1900	3,928	6,842
1901–1903	8,363	17,621
(28 months)	(3,584 p.a.)	(7,552 p.a.)

After its success over wage rates the union decided in 1892 to seek a three-hour reduction of the working week to 54 hours. The DTPS minutes of 15 October make it clear that a memorial to that effect had been sent to the employers and that some, including Weldrick, had returned a favourable response. A letter from the master printers was also considered which stated that although favourable in essence they wanted to get comparable figures for Belfast, Edinburgh and other towns. The College chapel, usually conservative in its outlook, took an uncharacteristically militant view over this stalling tactic, and on 29 October put forward a resolution that members of the union cease work in houses that had not conceded the new hours on 4 November — 'we believe that action short and sharp on our part will prove successful'. The trade voted for the resolution and the strike was on. The union was in one of its periodic positions of strength because the houses capitulated one by one so that on 1 December its minutes could record a total victory on the matter.

The hours worked in the trade in Dublin were now 8 a.m. to 6 p.m. on Mondays, 8 a.m. to 7 p.m. on Tuesdays to Fridays, and 8 a.m. to 1 p.m. on Saturdays, with an hour for dinner on weekdays.[5] Andrew Corrigan estimated that comps worked only at about 75 per cent capacity — 'an eighty per cent worker was a very unusual one' — and that the remainder was wasted time or clearing time. It was important for the manager to take this into account when estimating.[6] Overtime would on occasion be worked in all offices, but there is evidence that it was particularly onerous at the University Press. On 10 September 1880 George Wade sent apologies for not attending a meeting of the committee on the Trade Union Congress, which was to be held in Dublin that year, because of a rush job received at the DUP whereby it was 'necessary for the whole companionship to work late every night for a few weeks'. Such a regime proved too much for some of the older employees on occasion. David Lawson applied to the union on 13 July 1886 for permission to take up employment in Charles's office, an unfair house, 'as he was unable to keep up with the times in College'. Although several employers complained bitterly about this practice of allowing union men to work in 'closed' houses, thereby putting the fair employers at a disadvantage, the committee took pity on Lawson and granted his request. However there is also evidence that Weldrick was flexible on timekeeping. The men in the trade in general were meant to be paid in the firms' time on Saturday mornings. At a quarterly delegate meeting of the DTPS on 30 October 1891 the College representative, Eyton Hayes, was asked to comment on the fact that the men at the University Press had to wait 'till a late hour every Saturday' for their pay. Hayes admitted that this was the case, but that the chapel had not pressed the matter 'as they were seldom in at work in the mornings a quarter or 20 minutes after 8 o'clock, and there was never any time deducted'.

The DTPS minutes provide some other interesting insights into the working conditions at the Printing House at this time. On 20 August 1889 a chapel dispute was brought before the committee for arbitration. It transpired that a comp, George Wade, suffering from a heavy cold,

5. Corrigan, *Printer and his world*, 84.
6. ibid. 144, 147.

had shut a window near where he was working. This was persistently reopened by a young man called Perrin. In frustration Wade eventually 'gave up' Perrin, that is complained of him to the chapel, an action for which he had to give 6*d*. surety. The chapel decided that Wade's complaint was frivolous, which was not acceptable to the complainant. However the union's executive overturned the chapel's conclusion. This decision soured Wade's relationship with his chapel. On 18 March 1890 it disputed his right to claim benefit from the Society when yet again he was taken ill. Sometime in February he had been appointed head reader in place of the late Mr O'Reilly (a William J. O'Reilly is mentioned as a College delegate in the DTPS minutes for 30 July 1875), but had been taken ill shortly afterwards. On this occasion he had been so ill he had taken to his sick-bed and had not signed the Society's book on Tuesday to ensure sick payment. The chapel's argument that he was not therefore entitled to benefit was overruled by the executive. The minutes also reveal that Weldrick had visited him at home to assure him that his new post would be kept for him until he had recovered. In the event when he returned to work he found Mr Doyle in his position. This harsh treatment after his long service to the University Press no doubt won him sympathy with the union.

There was a system whereby the chapel of a bedridden member could, with the permission of the executive, sign on his behalf to keep his entitlements open. Such was the case with George Keyser of the University Press in April 1883. But perhaps Wade was too proud to ask given the friction that existed within the chapel. Failure to sign on had earlier led to the refusal of mortality allowances to the family of another DUP employee, George Kennedy. On 26 February 1881 the union's minutes tell of his sickness and the mistaken understanding that the College chapel had been returning him as 'N.E.', that is 'Not Entitled' to pay his union dues, a rather indirect way of stating that he was not working and therefore entitled to benefits. He died on 23 February and a vote of the trade was needed before his family could be given the mortality allowance.

These incidents underline the fact that the employers took little interest in the welfare of their employees and there were no statutory entitlements provided by the state. The DTPS was far in advance of other unions in providing illness, emigration, pension and mortality allowances to its members or their dependants. On 9 July 1881 the College chapel suggested that the union should subscribe to some city hospital so that members could be treated there and this was agreed by the trade; Mercer's Hospital was mentioned in this regard. The superannuation fund run by the Society had a limited number of places and competition was keen for them. George Hoyle, a member of the union for half a century, was recommended by the College chapel for a place on 24 July 1885, but a decision was not recorded. Failure to secure promotion to the fund meant that old journeymen had to eke out a living on whatever piece work they could find, or rely on their families for subsistence.

The case of Patrick Thornton will serve to illustrate the operation of the piece-rate system at the University Press and how the union's unemployment payments compensated. On 10 October 1893 it was recorded that Thornton had been idle in the last week of September because there was no work at the College. His wife died on the Friday so he had not made an unemployment claim on Saturday. On the following Monday he was told there would be no work that week either and so claimed unemployment on the following Saturday. The College chapel wanted a ruling as to whether he was entitled to it since he had not claimed on the first Saturday. The committee showed compassion and allowed the claim. Emigration allowances were provided by the union to encourage unemployed journeymen to seek work elsewhere. Although these were relatively substantial amounts the union probably gained in the long run by not having to pay out heavy unemployment benefits. Philip Gaynor was an example of a former DUP employee who was granted English emigration money; this was paid on 29 October 1881. 1895 and 1896 were years of large payments of emigration allowances following a slump in the trade. The *Printing World* for September 1894 reported that the trade in Dublin was at its lowest ebb, with 120 journeymen unemployed. This represented perhaps 20 per cent of the trade, if the figures of 430 book comps, 200 newspaper comps and 70 pressmen, given as the size of the trade in the DTPS minutes for 31 July 1891, still applied.

The heavy involvement of the union in the overall welfare of its members also meant that it took a close interest in their conduct. This is illustrated by the case of John McLoughlin which came before the executive on 21 April 1891. He was accused of being so drunk and disorderly at the National Press that the police had to be called. The committee underlined that such conduct cast odium on the Society and stated with more than a hint of frustration that it was extremely difficult to answer these well-grounded complaints of employers. It warned that members must 'observe that discipline and decency which should distinguish a body of intelligent artisans'. It asked the trade to vote on his expulsion. The return on 29 July must have added to its frustration because the majority were indulgent of McLoughlin's drinking habits and voted against his expulsion.

There are a few cases in this period where the DTPS did take sanctions against DUP employees for indisciplined behaviour. For example on 18 October 1888 the committee considered the case of George Doyle who had had a frame prepared for him by Weldrick, but he had not turned up for work. He was fined ten shillings. On another occasion in March 1902 Ponsonby and Weldrick wrote to the DTPS to complain about a machineman, M. Stephenson, who had walked out without notice. It transpired that his foreman, Mr McGrane, had told him the sheets he was printing 'would not do'. Incensed by the foreman's manner, he had undone the make-ready and walked off the job. The executive was not sympathetic and fined him £1.

The individual chapel was a vital link in this chain of trade discipline. However the College workforce had a poor reputation in this area if John Patrick Dunne is to be believed. When he joined the University Press in the closing years of the century he 'discovered that trade-unionism in that companionship was "more honoured in the breach than the observance". My revelation re piece-work conditions therein started the movement to abolish same.'[7] On the whole however the College chapel took the interests of the union very much to heart. On 25 April 1890 it proposed an amnesty for 'non-unionists' because the heavy fines that would normally have been imposed in these cases deterred them from joining. The chapel felt it was best to have them as members for the protection of the union's interests. Later on 27 January 1893 the chapel suggested the publication of an *Irish Typographical Circular* which would cater for all the typographical societies in the country and would create 'a bond of brotherhood among Irish printers'. (It would also do away with the necessity of subscribing to the *English Monthly Circular*.) Despite the submission of detailed estimates and despite the fact that the trade voted in favour of the publication, nothing seems to have come of this laudable venture.

The long litany of disputes, illnesses and unemployment among the College printers, mentioned in the DTPS records, was only one side of the coin, and there was of course the positive side as well. But like all good news it was seldom reported. College representatives were quick to leap to Weldrick's defence at DTPS meetings when they considered that he was being unfairly criticised. This would indicate a good working atmosphere at the Printing House. And there were social occasions for the employees as well. There are two references to annual outings by members of the DUP chapel. The August 1885 issue of the *Dublin University Review* mentions that the annual excursion of the 'printing staff' took place to the Glen of the Downs in County Wicklow on Saturday 25 July, while the July 1892 issue of the *Printing World* carries the following report: 'In connection with the Trinity tercentenary, the comps of College chapel had an outing on final day of celebration to Glendalough, to which the College authorities contributed a munificent donation.'

As already mentioned Andrew J. Corrigan's *A printer and his world* (London 1944) provides a first-hand account of the activity in a Dublin book and jobbing house in the last years of the nineteenth century. His description was of Corrigan & Wilsons, but at least some of it would have applied equally well to the University Press. He recounts the frustration

---

7. IPU: J.P. Dunne's memoirs, in Dublin Press Club scrapbooks.

the comps experienced in justifying different sizes of type in the same line before the point system was introduced. This was compounded by the fact that different foundries had different sets for the same named size. The absence of standardisation meant that it was impossible to lock up different founts and sizes in the same chase and lift them from the stone without the use of a lot of card and cut leads. In addition to achieve the necessary tightness the forme would have had to have been damped so that the card swelled and locked up the type.[8]

Apprentices were used as 'jackals' by the comps to hunt down scarce sorts from standing matter. Corrigan tells us that it was necessary for the boy to strike up a relationship with some journeyman who would act as his mentor because there was no learning programme set out by the manager or overseer. The demand for a premium with each boy at the start of his apprenticeship was dying out in the 1890s. A first-year apprentice in 1897 could expect to earn 2-6 to 5-0 per week; in his second year 3-0 to 6-0; in the next year, when he was 'generally extremely useful', 4-0 to 7-0; and so on progressing to his final year when he might get £1. Although the apprenticeship took seven years it was Corrigan's observation that 'any apprentice who was not as good as a journeyman by the end of this fourth year . . . would never make a good one'. Among the duties of the pressroom apprentice was to turn the 'old devil's handle' on the flywheel of the presses when the gas engine would not start.[9]

Despite Corrigan's description of the lack of training we know from a contemporary standard printing indenture that the master undertook to 'teach and instruct' the apprentice 'by the best ways and means that he can' the chosen branch of printing.[10] The boy for his part undertook to serve his master and to keep his secrets; not to fornicate or marry; not to gamble or frequent pubs and theatres; nor, without permission of the master, to engage in buying and selling. Such restrictive clauses did not deter applicants for apprenticeships, and the DTPS had a constant battle with the employers to keep the numbers down. On 10 March 1891, for example, Weldrick through the College chapel applied to be allowed two apprentices when there was only one vacancy; the registrar of the College, George F. Shaw, wanted a position for the son of a friend of his. The committee refused because 'the apprentice question would in the near future occupy attention'. Thoms was one of the major offenders in this area throughout the century. The union minutes for 30 September 1893 reveal that they had 73 comps, 16 pressmen and 32 apprentices. On 24 October because of the excessive number of boys there the DTPS set a limit of one apprentice for every five men permanently employed in any house.

---

8. Corrigan, *Printer and his world*, 130–34.

9. ibid. 85–91, 110–111.

10. Robert Adams's indenture with John Purdon, 15 Mar. 1893; text given in *Cló*, vol. 33 no. 2 (Feb. 1983) 6.

Information on the suppliers to the Press at this date are scanty. Ponsonby & Weldrick's private account book records promissory notes to two paper merchants, Cowan & Co. and Spicer Bros, in 1885. And in 1893 when the University Press was chosen from a rota of fair houses to do printing for the DTPS, Weldrick was careful to use local paper from the Swiftbrook mills for it. On 16 January 1894 E.L. Richardson of the College chapel was quick to point out to the union that the printer for that year, R.T. White, was not using Irish-made paper for the Society's work. A stock book for this period gives what must be a fairly comprehensive list of the binders employed: Galwey & Co., Caldwell & Co., Miss E. Langan, Birdsall & Co., Ada Yates & Sisters, Miss O'Hara, Irish Bookbindings Co., Mrs Jevens, and the Dublin Bookbinding and Machine Ruling Co.[11] This latter was a co-operative set up by the Bookbinders' Consolidated Union in March 1896 during an intractable dispute with Galwey & Co. over the employment of 'excessive' female labour.[12] The stock book reveals that in most cases only part of the edition was bound at a time, and that it was sent to the binders within a few days of the completion of printing. It was returned to the Printing House within about a week and then dispatched to the publisher. The bursar's voucher book for 7 June 1881 provides some scanty evidence of type acquisition but not the name of the supplier: 'To Arabic points and quadrats to perfect Arabic fount 8-6'. The fount was still deficient however as the account indicated: 'To altering 200 Arabic types to represent a character deficient in the fount supplied to the College 6-8'.[13]

The College continued to be one of the largest debtors of the Press. For example a summary account at 30 June 1884 shows that £564-7-8 was due for several books and miscellaneous jobbing in the previous year.[14] Weldrick was rather remiss, given that he had held the job of book-keeper to Peter Murphy, in presenting his bills to the College and it was often a year and more before accounts were settled. In one extreme instance on 31 March 1882 he presented a bill for £160-7-8 for Trinity's half-share for printing *Hermathena* going back to November 1876![15] Such slovenly book-keeping was eventually to lead to his dismissal as University printer, as will be seen.

Among the jobbing done for Trinity was the *University Intelligence*. The accounts for the second half of 1884 include charges for it, but those for 1885 do not, so it can be taken that it ceased in 1884 after over forty years in print. Exam papers continued to be one of the largest recurrent items of

11. MUN/DUP/11/1A *passim.*

12. C.J. Bundock, *The story of the National Union of Printing, Bookbinding and Paper Workers,* Oxford 1959, 56–7.

13. MUN/V/62/24/144A.

14 MUN/V/62/26/145[a].

15. MUN/V/62/24/339.

printing for the College. Weldrick's charges were similar to those of Murphy: English 5-0 per page; Latin and Continental languages, 6-0; Irish, 6-0; Greek, 8-0; Algebra, 8-6; Hebrew, 13-9.[16] The papers were produced in editions of from 25 to 200 copies and cost about £110–130 for each of the Michaelmas and Trinity terms and about £60 for the Hilary term. As ever the board was worried about the mounting costs of printing, as can be seen from an entry in the register for 30 September 1882: 'On 1st July a syndicate was appd. to control the expe. of the Printing Office consistg. of the bursar, the registrar and the junior bursar, and they were instructed to prepare a report to the board on this subject for the first meeting in Michaelmas term — and espy. to express their opinion whether exm. papers cd. not be more economically prepared than at present.' (The choice of the word 'syndicate' would indicate that someone had been looking at the Cambridge model for the control of the University Press.) In fact it was 17 March 1883 before the report was considered by the board. The syndicate came out in favour of the current mode of production and publication so the board turned its attention to the *Calendar,* and set up a subcommittee to see if economies could be effected there. No record of its recommendations survives, but one of them must have been to reduce the edition size because only 750 copies of the 1884 issue were printed where formerly 1,000 were produced. (An edition size of 1,000 had been restored in 1880 after a similar cost-cutting reduction in 1877.) Correspondingly the supplement was reduced from 400 to 250, which proved too drastic, and for 1885 it was increased to 350.

These concerns reflected the fears of the time that, with the DUP series well underway, the cost of printing would run away with itself. This was shown in a series of enquiries made at the time which sought comparative costs for printing a mathematical work in octavo format. Benjamin Williamson, professor of Natural Philosophy, wrote to J.A. Galbraith on 16 October 1882 to say that his works on calculus printed at the DUP had cost £4-7-6 per sheet to print in an edition of 1,000 copies; composition was £2-12-6 per sheet. On 13 October Ponsonby & Weldrick had submitted estimates for various edition sizes, that for 1,000 costing £3-6-2 per sheet (composition £1-18-0). W. Metcalfe & Son in Cambridge were also approached and on 25 October returned an estimate of about £4-14-6 per sheet (composition £2-13-0).[17] This exercise proved that the College was getting good value from the University Press, and quieted any further complaints about excessive charges for a while.

A picture of the production and costs of the annual *Calendar* can be had from the bursar's voucher books. That for the 1883 issue shows the following:[18]

16. MUN/V/62/23/135, 7 July 1881.
17. MUN/P/3/1211, 1030, 1211.
18. MUN/V/62/25/376, 377, 8, 4 Jan. 1883.

1,000 medium 12mo. 702p.

Composition:	69p. new matter at 3-3	£11- 4- 3
	633p. standing matter with alterations	36-15- 0
Presswork at 14-6 per sheet		21- 7- 9
Paper at 14-6 per ream		43-10- 0
Cover		1- 4- 0
Advertisements		10- 6
		114-11- 6
5% discount		5-14- 6
		108-17- 0

The charges for the supplements were as follows:

400 medium 12mo. 500p.

Composition:	title and contents	£1- 6- 0
	remaking up standing exam papers	
	$20\frac{1}{2}$ sheets at 24-0 per sheet	24-12- 0
Presswork at 9-0 per sheet		9- 9- 0
Covers		16- 6
Paper at 14-6 per ream		12-10- 2
		48-13- 8
5% discount		2- 8- 8
		46- 5- 0

Other bookwork commissioned by the College in this period included T.K. Abbott's *Elements of logic* (1883). By a board decision of 27 June 1884 this supplanted Richard Murray's *Logic* (1759) as a textbook on the undergraduate course and it remained in use up to the early 1950s.[19] An edition of 1,000 *Excerpta e statutis* (1882) was also printed for student consumption. When Weldrick presented his account for this on 5 March 1883 he included charges for stereotyping it at 1-1 per page and for boxes for preserving the plates.[20] Parts 4 and 5 of the *Astronomical observations* were also printed in 1882 and 1884 respectively, each in an edition of 300 copies. The tercentenary celebrations were commemorated in *Records of the tercentenary festival* (1894), a handsome quarto volume. The board voted £50 to Arthur Palmer on 26 January 1895 for editing it. Strangely the College's official volume brought out in 1892, the year of the tercentenary, to record the history of the College, entitled *The book of Trinity College Dublin 1591–1891*, was printed in Belfast by Marcus Ward & Co. (When the blocks used in this volume came on the market in 1899 the board initiated efforts on 21 October to acquire them. No outcome is recorded, but they must have been at least partially successful because a few of them were discovered in 1990 by Alan Norris in a corner

19. McDowell and Webb, *TCD 1592–1952*, 305.

20. MUN/V/62/25/154.

of some office; the illustration of the interior of the dining hall was used on a Christmas card printed by Trinity Closet Press in that year.) Another celebratory volume of 1892 was Charles H. Oldham's *Trinity College pictorial: . . . a ter-centenary souvenir*. Although this was not a College publication and was printed by Thoms, the DUP was upstaged by the Cambridge University Press which took a full-page advertisement in it.

After the completion of the library's *Printed catalogue* in 1887 the board decided on 26 March, on the recommendation of a committee appointed to look into the matter, to continue to employ Henry Dix Hutton to catalogue the current intake. This time the limitations of the printed form of catalogue were recognised and guard books with paste-in entries were opted for. The entries however continued to be printed at the University Press. On 30 September 1887 Weldrick charged for the first batch of these: 'Library catalogue . . . To printing and paper 25 copies of catalogue forms 1 to 25 at 20-0 per form per estimate £25 . . .' With extras for alterations and Greek the cost was £27-5-6.[21] By mid-1890 form 345 had been worked off and Weldrick was still charging £1 each.[22] However after the increase in journeymen's wages in 1891 Weldrick appealed to the board on 17 October for an increase. An extra 3-0 per forme was granted on 24 October. T.K. Abbott's *Catalogue of the manuscripts in the library of TCD* (1900) was another work printed in this period. Planning for this went back as far as 1885 when the board authorised Abbott to investigate the possible costs involved.

Abbott was also favoured by the board with a subsidy of half the printing cost of his translation of Kant's *Introduction to logic,* printed at the University Press in 1885.[23] For his *Celtic ornaments from the Book of Kells* (1895) it is not clear if Trinity paid any of the production costs, although the elaborate College arms on the titlepage indicates that it at least had its blessing. In 1885 the College paid the full cost of £44-1-0 for Prof. A.M. Selss's *Brief history of the German language*.[24] Selss was not so successful when he applied to the board on 21 October 1899 for a subvention towards the reprinting of two textbooks. The minutes record that it was 'against precedent' to give assistance to reprints. The College did support a range of other DUP printings in varying ways, for example paying the full cost of William Lee's *University sermons* (1886) and subsidising E.H. Bennett and D.J. Cunningham's *Sectional anatomy of congenital coecal hernia* (1888) by footing the bill of over £50 for the elaborate colour lithograph plates.[25]

21. MUN/V/62/29/618, f. 267.

22. MUN/V/62/32/393.

23. MUN/V/5/15, 5 Dec. 1885; MUN/V/62/30/481, 19 Nov. 1885.

24. MUN/V/62/27/590, 20 July 1885.

25. MUN/V/62/28/376, 22 Nov. 1885, 500 Lee *Sermons* £62-8-6; MUN/V/62/30/488, 26 June 1888, 500 Bennett and Cunningham *Sectional anatomy*, £50-15-6 for plates.

The College's books continued to be published in Dublin by Hodges, Foster & Figgis, which became Hodges, Figgis & Co. in 1884, and in London by Longman, Green & Co., on terms similar to what had previously applied. Hodges, Foster & Figgis was the subject of a complaint from a student, John Dickie, in 1881 who pointed out that they afforded only 16.6 per cent discount on prize books while the state Intermediate Board prizes were given at 20–25 per cent discount. He also drew attention to the fact that Mr Kinsella of Anglesea Street even gave the general public 20–22 per cent and Mr Mullan in Belfast afforded as much as 25 per cent.[26]

The overall impression from the surviving stock books of the Press is that school and college textbooks were printed in editions of from 1,000 upwards and that other books were produced in editions of below 1,000 in multiples of 250.[27] Of the non-TCD customers of the DUP it will be found that institutions continued to provide important commissions. Such was the case with the RIA's *Transactions* and the Academy also gave its prestigious Todd Lecture Series to the Press. These were printed in six extensive volumes between 1887 and 1895. Another printing for the Academy was J.P. Mahaffy's *The Flinders Petrie papyri* (1891). Besides its *Proceedings* the RDS also provided such bookwork as *The Kerry and Dexter herd book* (1890) and the *General catalogue of the library to 1900* (2 vols, 1896, 1902). The Irish Texts Society, recently founded in London for the purpose of publishing texts in the Irish language, provided such commissions as Geoffrey Keating's *History of Ireland* edited by David Comyn (1902), one of the first of many books printed at the University Press for this society.

As in the period of Peter Murphy's tenure Ponsonby had a steady flow of law books printed by Weldrick, as well as a stream of textbooks. Among the most substantial in the former category were: G.W. Abraham's *Law and practice of lunacy in Ireland* (1886, 752p.); D.H. Madden's *Law and practice of the High Court of Justice in Ireland* 3rd ed. (1889, 741p.); W.G. Huband's *Practical treatise on the law relating to the Grand Jury . . . in Ireland* (1896, 1176p.; this was also issued with the London imprint of Stevens & Sons); T. DeMoleyns's *Landowner's and agent's practical guide* (1899, 1290p.); G.T.B. Vanston's *Law relating to local government in Ireland*, vol. 1 (1899, 674p.) and his *Law relating to municipal towns* (1900, 540p.). (Just as many printers today have cause to be thankful for the ever-changing complexity of computer manuals, so too did their predecessors celebrate the prolixity of lawyers.) In the category of textbooks Ponsonby provided such commissions as Mary O. Kennedy's *History of France 1789–1815* (1901), R.F.T. Crook's *Selections from the Orations of Cicero and the works of Vergil* (1902), and Crook's edition of Livy's *Ab urbe condita* (1902). W.E. Ellis's *Irish educational*

26. MUN/P/3/329, letter to T.T. Gray, 4 Nov. 1881.
27. MUN/DUP/11/1, 1A *passim*.

directory (1885), A. Vicars' *Index to the prerogative wills of Ireland 1536–1810* (1897) and A.G. More's *Contributions towards a Cybele Hibernica* edited by N. Colgan and R.W. Scully (1898) will give a flavour of the other commissions provided through Ponsonby.

The University publisher, Hodges, Figgis & Co., used an extensive range of Dublin printers, not to mention the occasional Belfast firm, for its own publications, among them the DUP. Examples were A.G. More's *Life and letters* edited by C.B. Moffet (1898) and W. Wood-Martin's *Lake dwellings of Ireland* (1887). (Fittingly this latter was reprinted photolithographically by the DUP for the Beaver Row Press in 1983.) Surprisingly M.H. Gill & Son, although it had its own printing plant, also provided some commissions to the DUP, indicating perhaps that there was no ill feeling towards the Press even if M.H. Gill seems to have left the College under a cloud. Viola Walda's novel, *Miss Peggy O'Dillon, or The Irish critic* (1889), is one such example. Interestingly the colophon reads 'Printed by Ponsonby & Weldrick, Dublin' without the usual mention of the University Press; perhaps the College would not have appreciated having its press associated with the production of a mere novel — a similar attitude to fiction in the College library existed for most of the century. Gills also provided some works connected with the Royal University of Ireland, among them F.E. Hogan, J. Hogan and J.C MacErlean's *Luibhleabhrán: Irish and Scottish Gaelic names of herbs, plants, trees etc.* (1900 — Petrie type was used extensively in this work) and John Casey's *Treatise on elementary trigonometry* (1901, a textbook for the RUI).

Weldrick seems to have done extensive business with the London publishers, especially when the works of Irish authors were involved. 1887 saw the printing of C.H. Keene's edition of the *Eclogues of Calpurnius Siculus* for George Bell & Sons. Macmillan & Co. commissioned the third edition of Horace's *Satires* edited by Arthur Palmer in 1888 as also J.P. Mahaffy and J.B. Bury's edition of the *Hippolytus* in 1899. Macmillans were later to write to the Press in July 1925 seeking the plates for this latter work or £15 compensation; Ponsonby & Gibbs denied liability.[28] A third edition of George Salmon's *Historical introduction to the study of the books of the New Testament* was printed for John Murray in 1888. Longman, Green & Co. also provided some work, as for example T.K. Abbott's *Essays chiefly on the original texts of the Old and New Testaments* (1891) and P. Alexander's *Treatise on thermodynamics* (1892). C.H. Keene's *Sketches of the Greek dramatic poets* was printed for Blackie & Son in 1898 and the form of the imprint on the verso of the titlepage is worthy of note. 1898 saw the introduction of a device for the Press having the name 'Dublin University Press' in a scroll beneath the College's arms (see plate 30). Ponsonby and Murphy used this device at the head of their estimate sheets in the 1870s (see for example MUN/P/3/1030) but this is the first time I have noted it

28. MUN/DUP/9/2/49.

30. The earliest noted use of this device in a book (from C.H. Keene's *Sketches of the Greek dramatic poets*, 1898), with a similar block still in the possession of the DUP.

in an imprint. Weldrick's successor, J.T. Gibbs continued to use this style of imprint into the 1940s. Adam and Charles Black was another London publisher who used the services of the DUP, as for example to print J.K. Ingram's *Human nature and morals according to Auguste Comte* (1901).

Weldrick also did some printing for private individuals. T.G. Rylands's *The geography of Ptolemy elucidated* (1893) and Margaret Stokes's *Notes on the Cross of Cong* (1895) are examples in this category. This latter work, printed for private circulation, has two colour lithographed plates done by Werner & Winter in Frankfurt. It also contains a wood-engraved tailpiece from another era, which made another appearance in the same year in T.K. Abbott's *Celtic ornaments from the Book of Kells*, the block of which survives in Trinity Closet Press (see plate 31). Another commission from a private individual was from P.W. Joyce in 1895 for an edition of 10,000 of his *Concise history of Ireland.* Three thousand titlepages with 'fifth edition' were printed and the remaining copies were left without titles. In September 1897 titleleaves with 'sixth edition' were provided for 1,000 copies.[29] The implications of such practices for future bibliographers trying to disentangle true editions of this work are daunting.

Ponsonby & Weldrick's private ledger provides a perspective on the financial health of the business. Net profits as a percentage of sales can be seen from the following table (the financial year ran from the beginning of October, and the figures quoted have been rounded):

Year	Sales	Net Profit	%
1881–1883	£15,460	2,975	19.2
	(5,153 p.a.)	(992 p.a.)	
1884	5,770	1,081	18.7
1885	6,391	983	15.4
1886	7,811	1,393	17.8
1887	6,098	268	4.4
1888	6,182	888	14.4
1889	7,006	213	3.0
1890–1899	73,203	10,498	14.3
	(7,320 p.a.)	(1,050 p.a.)	
1900	6,842	1,068	15.6
1901–1903	17,621	2,864	16.3
(28 mths)	(7,552 p.a.)	(1,229 p.a.)	

It is not clear why there was such a sudden slump in profits in 1887 and 1889. It may have had something to do with bad debts as £200 was set aside for these in the accounts for 1889, the first such provision. It is evident from the ratio of wages to sales that Weldrick used a formula of

29. MUN/DUP/11/1A/111, 31 Dec. 1895, 6 Sept. 1897

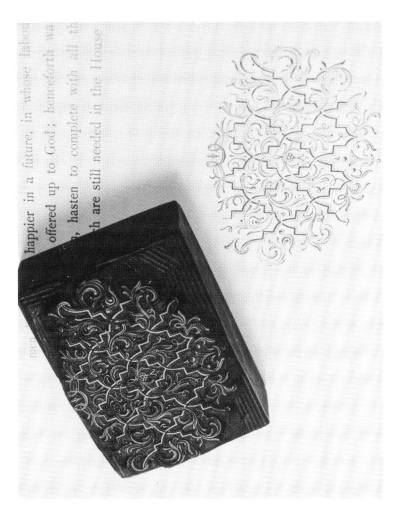

31. A very late use of a wood-engraved tailpiece (from Margaret Stokes' *Notes on the Cross of Cong*, 1895), with the original block now in the possession of Trinity Closet Press.

a 100 per cent mark-up on wages when estimating for works. The ratio of debtors to creditors was usually kept at an acceptable level of 2 or 3 to 1, although it did plummet to a dangerous 0.2:1 in 1885 and rose to a worrying 9.6:1 or thereabouts at the end of the century.

As we have seen Weldrick was somewhat remiss in presenting his bills promptly to the College. When in 1896 he sent in sixteen bills totalling £106-7-11 for work done on the DUP series going back to 1882 he was admonished in the board minutes of 8 February in these terms: '[resolved] that the University Printers be informed that the board view with extreme disapprobation this instance of gross carelessness in the management of the Printing Office accounts'. He was instructed henceforth to submit his bills quarterly as no arrears would be paid. It was the start of his downfall. His accounts with the College were even more seriously in arrears than his February bills indicated. On 27 June the board instructed the bursar not to pay any printing bill for which Weldrick could not produce vouchers. Some serious background negotiations must have been going on, which were not documented, because the board offered him £2,000 at the same time 'in satisfaction of all demands against the College up to the end of 1895'.

Weldrick presumably accepted this compromise as he remained in office. However three years later, on 24 June, the board had to consider a letter of complaint about the practices in the Printing House: 'A letter from the Professor of Astronomy was read, complaining of the great delays in the University Printing Office, also informing the board that the Royal Dublin Society has under consideration a proposal "that tenders for printing their scientific publications be invited". The board appointed a committee, consisting of the bursar, Dr. Williamson, Dr. Mahaffy and Dr. Bernard, to consider and report on the whole matter.' This was a kick for touch because nothing was reported by 21 October when the board had to consider another letter from the Astronomer Royal, drawing its attention 'to the dilatoriness of the printing in the University Press'. It was decided to reconvene the committee and to co-opt C.J. Joly, the complainant, on to it. Their findings must have been unfavourable because on 23 June 1900 the board directed the registrar 'to inform Mr. Weldrick . . . that they would determine his tenancy the 1st May 1901, pending new arrangements'. Work then began in earnest to determine what the best arrangement for managing the Printing House would be.

12
The Twentieth Century:
Ponsonby and Gibbs: 1902–1944

1902–1913

In preparation for Weldrick's departure the committee appointed in 1899 was reactivated with the brief of inquiring 'into the best manner of carrying on the College printing and of maintaining the Printing House', and its report was presented on 15 December 1900.[1] The nine-page typescript is worth considering in some detail. The committee consisted of Benjamin Williamson, an aging scientist; Thomas T. Gray, a fair-minded and conservative fellow; John P. Mahaffy, indefatiguable author and conversationalist, and future provost; John Henry Bernard, successor to Mahaffy in the provostship; Charles Jasper Joly, the Royal Astronomer whose complaints in 1899 led to the foundation of the committee; and Stanley Lane-Poole, professor of Arabic, Persian and Hindustani, who acted as secretary.

The report identified Weldrick's increasing age as the main cause for the decline in the Press's fortunes in the previous ten years. (He cannot have been too old however at this date as he did not die until January 1924.[2] Jimmy Stewart, now retired from the Press but a fund of information about its history in this century, told me that when he joined the Press in the 1930s he heard that the reason Weldrick had been let go was because he was a Roman Catholic. However this was an unlikely reason, given that Gill was a Catholic and Murphy probably so.) Most of the type and all the machinery belonged to Weldrick and he was prepared to accept a value of £5,000 put on these; the College only owned founts of type valued at £677. After consulting the secretaries of the OUP and the CUP the report concluded 'that a Committee of the College with the assistance of a secretary and a skilled manager could profitably undertake the business'. The problem was to find a suitable manager. It was deemed inadvisable to import an English one because he would not

---

1. MUN/P/1/2583.
2. IPU: DTPS EC mins, 15 Jan. 1924, vote of sympathy to his family.

know how to deal with Irish workmen and their unions. And anyone qualified for the job in Ireland was already a proprietor. The report cautioned that should any such proprietor be willing to amalgamate his business with that in the Printing House it would be essential that both be compatible.

The committee of course had found just such a proprietor — John Talbot Gibbs, manager of the long-established firm of C.W. Gibbs & Son (formerly Porteous & Gibbs) in Wicklow Street, where his lease was due to expire in May 1902. He did a lot of work for the Church of Ireland and the Representative Church Body, and the Printing House was 'peculiarly fitted' to this type of work. Gibbs's plant was valued at £1,950, and with his goodwill Trinity could have the lot for £5,000. He was willing to manage the combined businesses for a salary of £150 per annum, plus 20 per cent of the net profits. Were Gibbs to be appointed the report recommended that Weldrick be retained as assistant manager at a salary of £100, to liaise with members of the College, and that a secretary be appointed at a further £100 or 10 per cent of the net profits. The report stressed the need for a competent secretary to act as intermediary between the committee of management and the manager of the Press, and to provide 'fit representation of the College in correspondence with the learned men and societies' who had their printing done at the Printing House.

The committee had done its calculations well. According to its information the average net profit of the Press over the past five years had been £940 — most of it 'sure and permanent' because it was done for the University and other institutions 'not likely to transfer their business'; however to be on the safe side £850 per annum was allowed. To this could be added Gibbs's average of £572, providing over £1,400 net profit per year. Having deducted all the salaries and commission mentioned, and allowed £100 for the rent no longer to be paid, a projected net profit of £756 still remained, which on the College's outlay of £10,000 represented a return of 7.5 per cent. One other cost implication was also identified: 'the present inadequate accommodation' would need to be enlarged to cope with the combined plants and the increased business.

The chain of command recommended was to be very much along Oxbridge lines. The committee of the University Press was 'to have absolute control over the business'. It was to consist of five members, one to be from the College board, and was to be appointed annually by the board from the members of the university senate. It was to meet weekly in term and occasionally during vacation and was to report annually to the board. It was further recommended that the College solicitor draw up the contract with Gibbs to ensure the permanency of the arrangement and 'that all details as to the improved management of the Printing House and the method of publishing its works, be kept unreservedly to the Committee of the Press'.

The board had reservations about the scheme and on 17 December the provost directed the committee to examine if there was space for the proposed extension and what it would cost, and also to consider that since 'the present tariff for printing at the press was higher than [Gibbs's] . . . what reduction in the profits of our office wd. be caused by reducing the present tariff of our press to that of the other house'. The register of the board records that the committee replied on 12 January 1901, but gives no details. The board had initiated other negotiations with a Belfast firm through Anthony Traill, an Antrim man soon to succeed George Salmon in the provostship, and postponed a decision pending the outcome. Apparently they were unsuccessful as no further details are recorded. The Printing House committee was irritated by the delay and wrote to the board, which replied on 9 February that it would favour a more economical solution. The committee had then to go away and revise its recommendations. Three schemes that it came up with were considered at a meeting with the board on 14 March, as a register entry two days later notes, but again unfortunately no details were given. The board had sought legal advice as to its right to run the Printing House as a commercial concern, and pending the clarification of this and other matters it was decided to extend Weldrick's lease until 1 November.

One of the schemes proposed by the committee was to treat with Gibbs on different terms, but the preferred option was an offer from the General Advertiser and Wood Printing Company and with which Traill was acting as intermediary.[3] The bursar was given authority on 18 June to have the contract drawn up, and details were submitted to the board on 29 June. The rent was to be doubled to £200, but a reduction to £150 was to be allowed for the first five years. The College was to lend the General Advertiser Company £1,500 at 4 per cent to be repaid in five years, and was to build an agreed extension, provided it did not cost more than £500. The go-ahead was given to have the College solicitor draw up the definitive contract and signed. However the final negotiations became bogged down during July and August, as a cache of letters between the parties' solicitors in the College's muniments testify.[4] On 26 August Trinity's solicitor was insisting, among other things, that the proposed lessee make arrangements to purchase Weldrick's plant and that he be retained as manager or sub-manager. It would appear that the board wanted to implement these recommendations of the Printing House committee's report without having to pay for them. The General Advertiser Company baulked at these expensive propositions and attempted several times to interview Weldrick over the matter, but only succeeded in being referred to his solicitor, who proved equally elusive. In desperation it had its own solicitor write to the College's on 15 October, stating that it had

3. MUN/V/5/17, board register 18, 25 May 1901.
4. MUN/P/1/2588a.

met every condition except those referring to Weldrick; it was even ready to forgo the advance of £1,500. It requested that these propositions be put before the board. It was too late however; the board had already decided on 12 October to break off negotiations, 'not being satisfied with the solvency of the Company as tenants'. The bursar was given authority 'to treat with Mr. Ponsonby & Mr. Gibbs, who have proposed a new arrangement by which Mr. Gibbs shall take the place of Mr Weldrick'. Traill dissented from this decision as he did on 26 October when the bursar reported that he had had further correspondence with the company, which was offering to deposit £2,000 in cash if their offer as tenants was accepted; the board declined.

It was now so late that Weldrick must have been afforded an extension on his lease which terminated at the end of October, probably on a month-to-month basis. As was the case with the General Advertiser, the negotiations with Ponsonby, Weldrick and Gibbs were protracted and it was not until 31 May 1902 that the register records that agreement had been reached based on the conditions stipulated on 29 June of the previous year. A further three months was to elapse before Ponsonby and Gibbs were afforded their twenty-one year lease, starting from 1 October.[5] No copy of this lease has come to light, but the provisions were probably similar to those afforded in the lease of 1924 (see p. 282; essentially the lessees were charged rent of £300 per annum; their major obligation to the College was that they give priority to its printing needs over their other customers). The Printing House committee must have been disappointed at the outcome; yet again the College had failed to come to terms with its responsibility and potential as a publisher and printer, and had farmed it out to a paying tenant.

While these negotiations were in train the College was having the promised extension built. Several options for this were considered and some surviving plans show combinations of single and two-storey additions to the 1840 extension.[6] Estimates for these must have been beyond the £500 limit set by the board because what was built was a single-storey annex to the nineteenth-century building (see plate 32). Because it was constructed at an angle bringing it close to the rear of no. 35 New Square the board was worried about possible noise and on 18 October 'desired the Bursar to repeat to Mr. Gibbs . . . that the new annex was for compositors only & not for machinery'. Much of the church business that Gibbs brought with him was set here so that in time this annex was dubbed the 'Parochial Hall'. At this date very little of the College had been wired for electricity — indeed electric lighting was still being installed in the buildings of the Front and Library Squares in the 1920s — and although a

5. MUN/V/5/17, board register 8 Nov. 1902.
6. MUN/MC/86, 'Plans, elevations and sections shewing the proposed new additions to University Press', signed W. Golding (?).

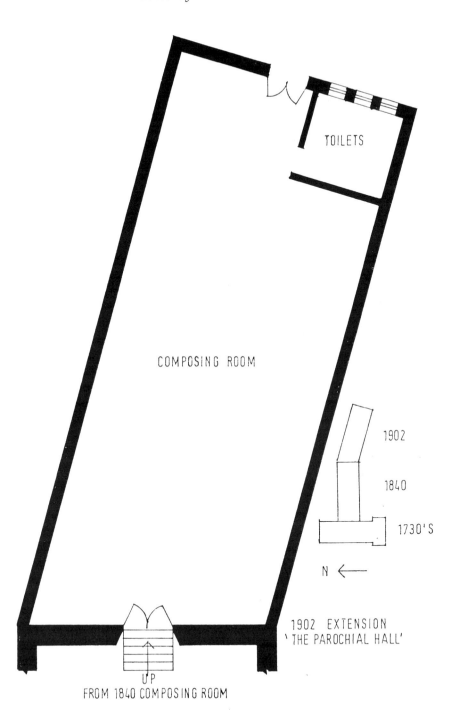

TOILETS

COMPOSING ROOM

1902

1840

1730'S

N ←

1902 EXTENSION
'THE PAROCHIAL HALL'

UP

FROM 1840 COMPOSING ROOM

32. Plan of the 1902 extension.

cable was laid close to the Printing House about the end of 1903, the Press relied on gas for power and light.[7]

Under the partnership agreement between William Ponsonby and Gibbs dated 7 October 1902 each was to have a 50 per cent share in the business. Ponsonby was a sleeping partner, as he had been with Weldrick and with Murphy before that, while Gibbs was to manage the Printing House at an annual salary of £100.[8] Gibbs (see plate 33c) was a son of Charles Warren Gibbs, at this date the oldest surviving master printer in Dublin. The father served his apprenticeship to William Porteous, later becoming a partner and eventually taking over the business. He retired about 1900 in favour of his son and died on 21 September 1908 aged 87. J.T. Gibbs had served two years of his apprenticeship under Weldrick at the University Press.[9] According to Jimmy Stewart, who worked at the Press from 1931, Gibbs was a very clever compositor and reader.

There are no exact figures for the size of the staff at the takeover in 1902, but a vote at a special delegate meeting of the DTPS on 14 November 1902 would indicate a chapel of thirty-one members. To this can be added Gibbs himself, some labourers to feed the presses and the apprentices excluded from chapel, bringing the total to perhaps forty. There was some staff shedding caused by the amalgamation. Apparently before Weldrick left, as a precautionary measure, he gave a fortnight's notice to the whole staff. This expired and still Gibbs had not taken over so the men continued on working for a further two weeks. When Gibbs did arrive he re-engaged the men, but early in November he found it necessary to let two young comps, John Chapman and Joseph Pasley, Junior, go because of slackness of business. He refused however to allow them two weeks' notice because he did not consider that they had been six weeks in his employ. The chapel disputed this and referred it to the DTPS on 4 November; the executive committee ruled that the men had never left the employment of the Press and so according to the rules were entitled to the regulation notice. Gibbs was very fair in this, and other, disputes and had indicated his willingness to abide by any decision arrived at by the Society. In another case brought to the attention of the DTPS on 5 May 1903 Gibbs had let a machine-room apprentice called Connolly go because after the amalgamation he had more than the allowed proportion of boys to journeymen. The Society made an exception in this case and agreed that the boy could finish his time.

A list of Christmas boxes given in 1903 puts names on many of the staff: Barnes £2; White £2; Corr £1; Sergison £1; T. O'R. £1; M. McG. 10-0;

7. MUN/V/5/18, board register 12 Dec. 1903 (electric cable at rear of north range of New Square); 27 Jan. 1904 (gas fittings in new Compositors' Room to be paid for by the College); MUN/DUP/1/2/51 ff., 3 Sept. 1904 (gas engine purchased).

8. MUN/DUP/1/2/1, 21, 31.

9. Philip White, 'The Printing trade in Dublin' in *Irish Printer*, (Aug. 1908), 7; (Oct. 1908), 12.

G. Smith 10-0; Conway 10-0; Pidgeon 10-0; W. McG[ouran] 5-0; W. O'Brien 5-0; Benson 5-0; Kit 5-0; Bayley 5-0; G. Smith 10-0; Frank 5-0; Connolly 2-6; Hempton 2-6; Maxwell 2-6; another (illegible) 2-6; 3 messengers 7-6.[10] Philip White is the best-known figure in this list (see plate 33b). He wrote the very interesting series of articles entitled 'The printing trade in Dublin' for the *Irish Printer* during the period 1908–1912, drawing on his own long experience and on the records of the DTPS which he was allowed to borrow for the purpose. (The secretary had unfortunately to write to him for their return on 16 March 1914 — how many other significant trade records get lost in this way?) He was born in Dublin in the early 1840s and served his apprenticeship as compositor to John Porteous in Moore Street, starting in 1858. After a succession of jobs he joined Porteous and Gibbs in 1870 as foreman in the caseroom, and transferred with Gibbs to the University Press in 1902. Some accounts state that he then became foreman in the caseroom at the Printing House, but the DTPS records indicate otherwise. On 23 December 1902 he sought and was granted readmission to the Society, saying that he had ceased to be a member in 1878 when he became a foreman, which would suggest he was now no longer an overseer. In fact the story of his secession from the Society is more involved than that. He had been an active member of the DTPS, and was president of council several times during the 1870s; he was also a founder member of the Dublin Typographical Benevolent Fund established in 1869. He was very much against the strike in 1878 and on 24 September was called before the committee to answer the charge that he was the 'Zoz' who had written and distributed scurrilous printed circulars castigating the officers of the Society. This he denied. When he was challenged that he had not paid any levies after the third month of imposition he insisted the strike was unconstitutional. His resignation from the Society followed shortly afterwards, on 19 November, because he refused to pay arrears on the levy. A staunch member of the Church of Ireland, he was active in several of the church's committees and bodies. He died early in 1926.[11]

Richard Barnes then must have been the incumbent caseroom overseer at the Press, and remained so at least until 1918 when he was still employed there; perhaps White was deputy overseer. No other person on the Christmas box list had such a public profile as White. John Corr was a senior member of the staff — he was trusted with petty cash — and later became manager as Gibbs withdrew more and more into his proof-reading. Unusually for a manager he was not a trained printer, having worked as a boy in the builders' providers, Brooks Thomas. James 'Jem' Sergison had been employed at the Press since the 1870s and at this date was probably the wareroom-keeper, as he was in 1931 when Jimmy

10. MUN/DUP/2/1, on sheet loosely inserted at end.
11. 'A tribute to a well-known Dublin printer' in *Irish Printer* (June 1914) 4, 6; obituary (Feb. 1926) 12.

Stewart, my informant about him, joined the firm. Later the young Fred Maybury found him to be 'a real character'; he had had some connection with the circus and was forever doing tricks, such as taking coals out of the stove with his bare fingers to light his pipe. His son George was his helper. Patrick Pidgeon was a pressman who became machine-room overseer in September 1914. Shortly afterwards his brother Sylvester, another printer, was shot dead by the military in a notorious incident on Bachelor's Walk; there is a printed portrait of him in the Dublin Press Club scrapbooks in the Irish Print Union. Patrick himself died in March 1918.[12] William McGouran had quite a reputation, not as a printer but as a choirmaster. He conducted the choir at the DTPS centenary banquet in 1909, as recorded in the February 1912 issue of the *Irish Printer*. The DTPS committee minutes for 8 July 1935 noted his recent death.

There were odd mentions of other members of the DUP chapel scattered throughout the DTPS minutes and the *Irish Printer*, but only in exceptional cases was any flesh put on the bones. One such case was Eyton Heath Hayes (see plate 33e). The *Irish Printer* for January 1912 tells us that he served his apprenticeship under M.H. Gill in the 1870s and had been at the Press except for a few years ever since. He was an active member of the DTPS and served as an officer on several occasions. Hayes was the University Press's representative at a special delegate meeting of the Society held on 4 December 1903. In times of financial crisis, such as during strikes or recessions when payments to unemployed members were high, the DTPS used to impose levies, which according to its rules were to be deemed loans, to be repaid in more secure times. 1903 was such a period of repayment, but the committee was proposing to suspend it because it was rumoured that the employers would soon be seeking an increase in hours or a reduction in wages, and all the money the Society had might be needed to resist this. (For the record the rumours proved groundless.) Hayes was sent with a resolution of his chapel opposing the committee's proposition. It caused quite a flurry when the resolution was carried and the committee resigned on the spot; (they were later persuaded to withdraw their decision). Thomas Murphy, the delegate from the *Freeman's Journal*, stood up and accused a prominent member of the College chapel of wanting to cripple the Society, so that it would be forced to amalgamate with the English Typographical Society, and that the anonymous member had been promised he would be made secretary of the resulting branch. Who the accused member was is not recorded, but it may well have been Hayes himself or perhaps Philip White who, as we have seen, had no great love for the DTPS after 1878. The matter did not end there. On 15 December the executive committee considered a request from the College chapel for the exact wording of Murphy's accusations as recorded in the minutes of the previous meeting. As some further action was obviously

12. IPU: DTPS EC mins 8, 24, 29 Sept. 1914; 12 Mar. 1918.

being contemplated by the accused, perhaps even recourse to the courts, the committee wisely declined to comply and the matter blew over.

Another person we have some handle on was Charles A. Sharpe, mostly recorded in Philip White's obituary of him in the *Irish Printer* for January 1913 (see plate 33d). He served his apprenticeship with Porteous and Gibbs starting on 1 May 1875. Sharpe spent most of his working life in that firm, except for two short periods in Thoms and Falconers, until he moved over to the University Press in 1902, where he was storekeeper in the composing room. As storekeeper he would have kept track of the thousands of pages of standing matter and stereoplates that were stored all over the building. He was an active member of the DTPS — he served as secretary to the subcommittee set up in 1910 to revise the rules relating to compositors — and was a frequent contributor to the *Irish Printer*. He died on 19 December 1912.

There are no details of the plant and machinery at the time of the amalgamation. Judging from other periods it is likely that the presses were not state-of-the-art models; the Press never bought the most up-to-date machines and as a consequence seldom had confrontations with the unions over new technology. The type was still being hand-set although mechanical setters had been installed in Dublin printing houses since the 1880s; the DTPS agreed rules for their operation on 21 December 1886. Something is known of the range of faces available about this date. Philip White in 1908 recorded Arabic, Coptic, Estrangelo, Ethiopic, German, Gothic, Greek, Hebrew, Hindustani, Irish, Persian, Samaritan, Sanskrit, Syriac, Doomsday and Music. Among the romans was a complete set of Miller and Richards's Old Style, bought by Porteous and Gibbs *circa* 1870, and in 1909 still in good shape and being used.[13] The value of the Press's plant and machinery on 1 October 1902 was set somewhat higher than that given by the Printing House committee in 1900 — £6,600 as against £5,000. That from Wicklow Street is recorded at the same figure of £1,950.[14] There was little investment in new plant in the first decade of the century. A second-hand double demy press was purchased for £88-14-6 in 1907, while two years later a new press was bought for £398. In 1910 '2 old printers [!] & 1 old rolling machine' were disposed of for £78.[15] Gibbs of course bought odd amounts of type in this period, but the College also made purchases for its own use. The board sanctioned the purchase of founts of hebrew for £19-16-0 and of arabic for £20-18-0 on 4 July and 13 October 1908.

Fortunately an account book survives which gives the annual accounts for the business during Gibbs's tenure.[16] The following picture of the performance in the period prior to the War emerges:

13. Philip White, 'The printing trade in Dublin' in *Irish Printer* (Aug. 1908) 7; (Dec. 1909) 8.

14. MUN/DUP/1/2/51 ff.

15. MUN/DUP/1/2/51 ff., 31 Aug. 1907, 31 Aug. 1909, 31 Aug. 1910.

16. MUN/DUP/1/2.

(a) W. McMullen

(b) P. White

(c) J. T. Gibbs

(d) C. A. Sharpe

(e) E. H. Hayes

33. Portraits of DUP members from the *Irish Printer*.

	Sales in £	Net Profits in £	%
1903	8,255	880	10.7
1904	7,880	1,066	13.5
1905	8,685	712	8.2
1906	8,548	588	6.9
1907	8,431	744	8.8
1908	8,864	796	9.0
1909	8,475	548	6.5
1910	8,560	674	7.9
1911	8,490	602	7.1
1912	8,648	574	6.6
1913	10,218	674	6.6

The ratio of current debtors to creditors was kept healthy while the turn-over ratio of sales to stock varied from a vigorous 7:1 in 1906 to a sluggish 3:1 in 1911 and 1912. The downward slide in profits was a reflection of the depressed state of the trade in general. An editorial in the January 1906 issue of the *Irish Printer* characterised the previous year as 'probably one of the worst . . . that most printers can remember' and the large number of unemployed men was a recurrent concern throughout the decade. The partners at the Press however were evidently satisfied with its perfor-mance and Gibbs's salary was increased to £150 in 1904, to £250 in 1909, and to £300 two years later.

Interestingly while the profits dipped the numbers employed increased; perhaps it was a case of running to stay still. At a meeting of the DTPS executive committee on 7 May 1907 forty-five votes from the College chapel were registered. And there is evidence in 1913 that there were about sixty members in the chapel. On 6 May the DTPS committee considered a request from Ponsonby and Gibbs to be allowed a sixth apprentice as under rules then being considered a staff of sixty to eighty men would justify the extra boy; other evidence confirms the figure as nearer sixty men. This is the biggest staff I have noted at the Press in the twentieth century. George Hogan, caseroom overseer during the 1940s and 1950s, told Peter Allman that there were 100 compositors working in the Printing House at the turn of the century, but none of the records substantiate this. Annual wages ran from a low of £4,331 in the financial year 1904–05 to a high of £5,154 for 1910–11. It would be dangerous to extrapolate figures for the size of the workforce from these figures, even though it is known that the basic wage was £1-15-0 per week, because there are too many unknown variables involved — overtime, merit money, labourers who got less than the journeymen, apprentices, and seasonal employees.

That basic wage of £1-15-0 for a fifty-two hour week had been static since 1891. On 13 October 1908 the DTPS committee drew up proposals for an increase to £1-17-6 for 50 hours. There was a meeting to no avail with the employers, but because of the perilous state of the trade the Society decided not to force the issue. The only concession in the next four years was a reduction of one hour in the working week, which is recorded in the committee minutes on 3 December 1912. At this date no paid holidays were afforded in the general trade — there were plenty of 'unpaid holidays' when things were slack — but Ponsonby and Gibbs were one of the few who paid staff for bank holidays. The June 1907 issue of the *Irish Printer* suggested that other firms should follow suit, a suggestion that was ignored until 1919 when it was conceded to the whole trade.

There is some scattered evidence of what working conditions were like at the Press in the decade before the Great War, especially in the caseroom. Because of the number of exam papers printed, work was very seasonal, and during the peaks many piece hands were employed setting them. The DTPS's drive to do away with piece work and have everybody on the establishment rate had only started in earnest about 1900; the Society's rules on the matter had become so complex that the committee wasted a considerable amount of time arbitrating over their interpretation. As we have seen, John Patrick Dunne, a very active trade unionist who worked at the Press at this time, claimed that his 'revelation re piece-work conditions therein started the movement to abolish same'.[17] What the abuses were he does not state, but complaints from the University Press piece workers continued well into the 1920s. For example William O'Brien protested to the DTPS on 11 December 1906 that he could not afford his dues because he was 'very poorly employed as a piece hand in the College'. Or again the complaint of a delegation on 7 June 1911 about the 'enormous expense of time to piece hands' in finding out-of-the-ordinary sorts such as accented letters when setting exam papers; at the same time they were not allowed the 'fat' of standing heads.

Life for the comp on the 'stab was not much easier. Joe Pasley, who had either been re-employed or had not been let go in 1902, told Sean Galavan in the 1950s that comps' fingers would sometimes bleed under pressure of setting. Pasley is one of the few employees who started their careers in the nineteenth century and is remembered by present-day staff. He was born on 6 July 1881 and served his apprenticeship at the Press, where his father, also Joseph, was working, and spent most, if not all of his working life there, retiring on 30 October 1959. He remained a bachelor and used to wear old-style clothes. He also wore a paper hat, common in printing houses in the nineteenth century, and in the turn-up had a cache of scarce sorts; his waistcoat pocket acted as another whang. He used to set Greek and the other exotics and was noted for his delight in quoting Shakespeare. For some unknown reason he was always referred to as

17. IPU: Dublin Press Club scrapbooks.

'The Noted'. (There were others who were also nicknamed, mostly obscurely: Jem Sergison was known as 'The Crier'; William Connolly as 'The Conger' — apparently he had been bitten by a conger eel; John Connolly, his son, as 'The Gawk'; and Fred Mortimer as 'The Guck'. The wonder is that none of the names related to printing practices.)

Comps in general were esteemed for the learning they were perceived to have, as an anonymous article on 'The compositor of fifty years ago' in a 1962 issue of the DTPS house magazine tells us.[18] The author provides a vignette of his subject that no doubt was also true for the comp at the Press. In cold weather the comps used to put their composing sticks on the stove to heat them up at the start of the day. The heat necessary in the caseroom to keep fingers dextrous would dry out the air and caused sore throats. As an antidote many of the comps used to chew tobacco or take snuff. From picking type their right forefingers and thumbs became noticeably flatter than their left, and the tips of these fingers turned 'a shiny black, just as though they had been smeared with blacklead and polished'. And of course some unfortunate comps, although the author in question does not mention it, suffered lead poisoning from handling the type, which could cause insanity or even death. There was no relief for such sufferers until the *Workers' Compensation Act* of 1909, and the DTPS prosecuted several cases on behalf of its members under this legislation.

Art. XXXIII sect. 2 of the DTPS rules at this date required that readers be trained compositors or at least members of the Society. This led to some conflicts at the Press. On 6 and 13 February 1906 the committee minutes recorded that a non-union reader called Hubert Briscoe had been employed at the DUP, having spent over thirty years in *The Irish Times*, which had not been a 'fair' house. The chapel had complained to Gibbs who had agreed — another example of his fairness — that he would not allow him to stay unless he became a member of the Society. Briscoe was admitted on a stiff fine of £5. In another incident the father of the chapel was summoned before the committee on 8 June 1909 to explain why a fifth-year apprentice was reading and revising proofs. A full explanation from the firm was recorded on 20 July. Apparently he had only been doing it for the past few months, and then mostly for works in Irish, a language in which he had some facility. As it was difficult to get Irish readers, and as he was paid extra for it, the firm asked for an exception to be made in this case. Given the special circumstances the DTPS agreed. (Finding Irish readers was a perennial problem in the trade. On 8 September 1931 Cahills complained to the Society about the difficulty and stated that a 'vast amount' of such work was going out unread to authors. The firm's petition was prompted by the Stationery Office's indication that it was going to double its Irish

18. *Míosachán na gClodoirí*, 4/3 (Nov. – Dec. 1962) 9–12.

language publications.) This problem of finding specialist readers prompted the Employers' Association to suggest at a meeting with the DTPS on 16 May 1912 that in exceptional cases, 'i.e. where classical and scientific work is produced', that non-printer readers be allowed. From the wording of this there can be little doubt that it was suggested by the University Press. To no avail however; it was rejected by the Society on 28 July.

Machinemen have always suffered in comparison to compositors, and the complexity of the latter's job has ensured that much of the deliberations of the DTPS's committee was given over to their concerns. As a consequence the committee's minutes do not provide any insight into the workings of the machine-room at the University Press, except in an oblique way. It was normal for the presses to be fed by lowly paid women, but because of the College rule that women had to be off the campus by 6 p.m. men feeders at higher wages were employed at the Press. One can imagine the attitude of the trade to this practice from the following colourful entry for 26 September 1905: 'Mr Warren (Kilmainham) attended — he was a little erratic in his manner — he wanted to employ <u>men</u> as feeders at machine, and he would pay them 12/- per week. The suggestion was ridiculous, and the Sec. to reply accordingly.' One other insight was afforded to me by Des Ryan, who started his apprenticeship at the Press in 1948. He was told that the old pressmen used to have containers of Guinness in the machine-room for occasional refreshment — a vestige from the strenuous period of the hand press? — and would use the sticky ullage on the backs of formes to keep any loose type in place. (It was certainly a better solution than the damaging practice of driving a bodkin point between the letters to make the distorted metal take up the slack.)

DTPS records give some details of the apprentices and their mode of appointment at the Press in the period prior to the War. One such case was that of John Waller. He started as a reader's boy in 1904 and on 8 January 1907 his father, William, also employed at the DUP, sought permission from the Society to allow him to start as an apprentice even though Ponsonby and Gibbs had its full complement. This apparently was refused, so when a vacancy was in the offing the father applied on 5 November for a remission of two years off the length of the apprenticeship, given the unusually long time he had spent as copyholder. Even though Gibbs was agreeable to this permission was again refused because it might have set a precedent. Undeterred the son's indenture was drawn up and signed on 25 March 1908 (see plate 34). On 8 March 1910 the father was back before the committee seeking a reduction on behalf of his son and this time it was unanimously agreed to allow him two years. There is no indication as to the reason for this volte-face. On 16 April 1912 John Waller read the apprentice declaration at the end of his time. Early in the War he enlisted in the medical corps.

This Indenture.

Made the 25th day of *March* 1908,

BETWEEN *Ponsonby and Gibbs* of *University Press, Dublin* hereinafter called "The said Masters" of the 1st part, *John William Waller*, son of *William Waller*, hereinafter called "The said Apprentice," of the second part, *and William Waller*, of "The said Apprentice, hereinafter called "The said Parent" of the 3rd part, and the Governors of Love's Charity and Gardiner's Charity, Dublin, hereinafter called "The said Governors" of the 4th part. **Whereas** "The said Apprentice" lately applied to "The said Governors" to advance the sum of £ 10/-/- as an Apprentice fee to "The said Master" for the purpose of apprenticing "The said Apprentice" to "The said Master" to learn the trade of *Compositor*, which "The said Governors" agreed to do on the terms that "The said Master" should enter into the covenants and agreements with them and "The said Parent" hereinafter contained.

Now this Indenture Witnesseth that in consideration of the sum £ 10/-/- now paid by "The said Governors" to "The said Master" the receipt whereof he doth hereby acknowledge, and in consideration also of the service of "The said Apprentice" to be done or performed to, or for "The said Master," and of the covenants and agreements hereinafter entered into by "The said Apprentice" and "The said Parent." He "The said Master," at the request of "The said Governors" and with the consent (hereby testified) of "The said Parent," and "The said Apprentice" doth hereby covenant and agree with "The said Governors" and also with "The said Parent" and "The said Apprentice" in manner following, that is to say—that he "The said Master" will take and receive "The said Apprentice" as his Apprentice from the day of the date of these presents for the term of *seven* years, and also will during the said term to the best of his power, knowledge, and ability, instruct "The said Apprentice" in the trade or business of *Compositor*, and in all things incident or relating thereto, in such manner as he "The said Master "doth now or shall hereafter during the said term use or practice the same, and will pay to " The said Apprentice" during the said term, or until the sooner determination of the said Apprenticeship the respective sums following :—

First year, 5-16 per week
Second " 6/6 "
Third " 7/6 "
Fourth " 8/6 "
Fifth " 19/6 "
Sixth " 19/6 "
Seventh " half his earnings, or else

And in consideration of the covenants and agreements hereinbefore contained on the part of " The said Master," " The said Governors" do hereby place and bind " The said Apprentice," and " The said Apprentice" with the consent of " The said Governors" and of " The said Parent " doth hereby place and bind himself with and to " The said Master" during the term aforesaid, during all which time " The said Apprentice" shall faithfully, honestly, and diligently serve him, " The said Master," and perform and obey all his lawful and reasonable commands and requirements, and shall not do any damage or injury to " The said Master," or knowingly suffer the same to be done without acquainting him therewith, but shall in all things conduct and acquit himself as an honest and faithful apprentice ought to do, and for the consideration aforesaid "The said Parent " doth hereby covenant and agree with "The said Master" that "The said Apprentice" shall faithfully, honestly, and diligently serve "The said Master" as his Apprentice during the said term. And it is hereby agreed that upon the expiration of the said Apprenticeship, and the discharge by "The said Parent" and "The said Apprentice" of all their obligations to "The said Master" hereunder this present Indenture shall be delivered by "The said Master" to "The said Apprentice."

In Witness

John William Waller
William

Witness to the

34. John Waller's indentures 1908, now in the possession of the DUP.

DTPS apprentice registers in the IPU provide an indication as to who the apprentices were in the period prior to the War:

William Carroll	case	registered 4 April 1909
Francis Wheelock	case	registered 4 April 1909
William Pidgeon	case	registered 14 July 1911
John Connolly	case	registered 4 April 1912
John Collins	case	registered 8 January 1913
John Mahon	machine	registered 5 November 1910

It is significant that there were five in the caseroom to one in the machine-room, which may indicate the proportions among the journeymen. The register also records that the first and last two joined the army; in fact all but Pidgeon joined as will be seen below.

Most matters of discipline within the firm were settled between management and chapel, but for more serious cases the DTPS was involved. The union took a close interest in the working conduct of its members and did not hesitate to take sanctions, either monetary or through loss of benefits, against transgressors. In this it was more akin to a professional organisation than a traditional trade union. This is illustrated by the case of R. Patterson, a machineman, who was summoned before the committee on 16 October 1906 to explain why he had left his work without giving any notice. His reply proving unsatisfactory, he was fined £1 and told that 'such conduct caused employers to import men from England and Scotland'. Other cases of his 'breaking down' — not in the mental sense, but meaning a disruption of production — are recorded and fines imposed. Given the tradition of hard drinking in the trade, one wonders if this was the root of his recurrent problem. It certainly figured in the case of another DUP employee, Andrew Jack, whose case of 'breaking down' was investigated on 16 November 1909. Later in June 1912 he was fired from Thoms for being drunk.

There was also a social side to the lives of the Press's workforce. The *Irish Printer* reported several gatherings at this time to wish parting members farewell, including one on 21 March 1910 when E.L. Richardson was leaving 'to take up an important position under the Labour Exchange Act [superintendent of the Dublin Labour Exchange]'. Following the fundamental principle of all low circulation newspapers and periodicals — of printing names, since everyone likes to see his name in print — the report usefully noted that music and song were provided by J. Pasley, M.J. Fitzpatrick, P. McGrath, J.F. O'Reilly (violin solo), W. Moore Jun., B. Boyce, E. Hayes, W. Connolly, Charles A. Sharpe, W. McGrath (violin solo), G. Hogan, R. Pasley, H. Bent, W. Walsh, F. Harvey and Mr. Mulvey 'in his usual style, presided at the piano'; the father of the chapel (often abbreviated to FOC) J.J. Currey presided. Another item in the August 1912 issue noted the 'first' carriage excursion of the College chapel (which was inaccurate, as we have seen, since other outings were recorded as early as 1885). It took place on a Saturday afternoon and wandered through the Dublin and Wicklow hills, taking in Stepaside, the Scalp, Enniskerry and Bray; Jack Thomas and Andy Mulvey provided the music.

This latter excursion caused a bitter feud within the chapel which lasted over half a year, the progress of which can be followed through the pages of the DTPS executive committee minutes. On the evening of the trip, 27 August, the FOC reported that H. Conway, B. Conway, M.J. Ennis, W. McGouran and W.J. O'Brien had refused to pay chapel dues. It was revealed on 10 September that they were withholding the money because they did not approve of the purpose to which it had been put. The secretary reminded them that it was compulsory to pay dues even though they might disagree with any resolution adopted for its use. The following week the FOC was told to revise the chapel rules to cover this case, indicating that these were written down if not printed. It was revealed on 21 January 1913 that the money had been voted for the excursion to Bray, and as a gesture of conciliation the committee suggested that the five complainants be refunded their proportion of the £1 that had been voted for it. This worked out at 4*d*. per person confirming that there were sixty in the chapel. That was not the end of the matter. On 18 February the clerk of the chapel had to be told that he could not refuse to take the 'head money' of the five men involved; he had obviously taken retaliatory action against them for their protest. The whole affair then boiled up to such a heat that on 11 March the committee suggested that a special College chapel meeting be called in the Society's premises, 35 Lower Gardiner Street. This must have defused the matter as no mention of it occurred thereafter.

An earlier incident along similar lines was less acrimonious, but serves to show why some of the men protested against these social occasions. On 10 May 1904 the chapel officers attended the sitting of the DTPS committee to explain why four members of the chapel had refused to pay an extra penny per week for a monthly social gathering 'in our Chapel meetings'. Weekly chapel meetings usually took place in the Printing House, so there can be little doubt that the monthly social gatherings were to take place in a pub; there had been a recent case where a member of Falconers' chapel had refused to pay dues because he maintained that all it was used for was drinking. The committee upheld the men's decision to withhold dues, deeming that the extra penny was not for legitimate chapel purposes. On 14 June the names of two of the men were given as Henry Richardson and James Waller, and from this entry it can also be deduced that the weekly chapel dues was one penny.

Turning our attention from the personnel to the building we find that Gibbs was quick to appeal for a reduction of the £200 rent — no doubt he had foreseen the coming recession — but this was refused by the board on 5 November 1904. Little was done to the building during the first years of Gibbs's tenure, beyond having the portico holystoned as reported in the *Irish Printer* in December 1908. Some major work had to be done in the period following March 1910, as the TCD board register notes, 'to bring it into complete conformity with the Factory Acts'. This entailed putting central heating into the 'Parochial Hall' at a cost of £60, the College paying half, installing additional toilets on the upper floor, and in 1913 a radical reorganisation of the heating plant which involved building a new boilerhouse measuring twelve by seven feet on the south side of the Printing House, costing over £150, the College again agreeing to pay half.[19]

There is some evidence as to who the Press's suppliers were in the period in question. J. McDonnell & Co. (Swiftbrook Mill) was the only local maker of paper among a 1903 list which also documented supplies from A. Pirie & Sons, C. Reed & Co., Grosvenor Chator & Co., J. Wrigley & Son and A. Armstrong & Co. Having to import so much paper led to difficulties in procuring supplies during transport strikes. Batches would sometimes arrive damaged and would cause great inconvenience while it was returned and new supplies dispatched. Large publishers might of course supply their own paper, as the APCK did in 1908 for its bourgeois hymnals.[20] There were several firms in Dublin at this period supplying blocks and illustration services, and no doubt the Press used them, but the only evidence that has survived shows an unusual source. The collotype portrait for T.K. Abbott's translation of Kant's *Critique of pure reason*, printed at the Press in 1909, was supplied by the OUP.[21] Several binders were used by the DUP: Galwey & Co., Hely & Co., Caldwell & Co. and Mrs. M.A. O'Hara at 30 Lower Abbey Street.[22] The College had had reservations about Galwey & Co. in 1902; the board register for 6 December records that the firm 'had been fined for overworking their female employees', but nothing seems to have come of it.

And so to a consideration of the output of the Printing House in the years prior to the War. The Press was given a drubbing in the June 1906 issue of the *Irish Printer* for the fourth issue of the *Arts and Crafts Society of Ireland Journal*. The 'colour' of the text was adjudged to be 'very variable' and the advertisements to be 'beasts' — 'Who passed these

19. MUN/V/5/20, board register 5, 19 Mar., 16 Apr. 1910; 3 June 1911; 1 Feb., 19 Dec. 1913; a separate lease for the boiler house was signed on 17 Feb. 1914 (MUN/D/3532a).

20. MUN/DUP/1/3/522, 1903; MUN/DUP/9/1, 1913 *passim*; MUN/DUP/9/1/395, 16 Feb. 1916, referring to 1908 APCK supply.

21. MUN/DUP/11/2/242, 13 Feb. 1909.

22. MUN/DUP/11/2/10, 15, 16, 109.

proofs! To what depths has our craft fallen!' This critique may have been biased however, coloured perhaps by an article by T.W. Rolleston in an earlier issue of the *Journal* urging printers to avoid a sterile 'trade finish'. The DUP was treated more favourably two years later. It was described in the British Association's *Handbook to the city of Dublin* (Dublin 1908, p. 420), a book printed at the Press, as specialising in work 'requiring high technical skill', reiterating a reputation that was long established. What was not mentioned was the Press's reputation for security printing, especially of exam papers. It was one of the things the board of the College was adamant about when negotiating with the General Advertiser Company in 1901; the lease was to be terminated if exam papers were divulged. An attempt was made to breach that security in 1906, but was successfully resisted. The board register on 30 June records that Reginald Adams was to be rusticated for a year for attempting to gain access to an Engineering School exam paper. Gibbs was given £2 'to reward the boys in his employment for disclosing the attempt to bribe them'. During the years 1906 to 1909 there must have been some uneasiness on Gibbs's part that some member of the staff was untrustworthy, as recurrent small amounts were recorded as 'unaccounted for' among the sundry expenses.[23] However no further details were documented.

The surviving account books of the DUP provide almost no breakdown of the prices charged at this date. What can be worked out is that since comps were paid at least £1-15-0 for a 52-hour week then labour cost at least 8*d*. per hour. In a contemporary article on estimating it was suggested that direct labour costs be doubled to allow for overheads and profit,[24] so a charge of 1-4 per hour for composition at the Press might be expected. An analysis of the sales to wages in the trading accounts shows that Gibbs added something more like 75 per cent, giving a charge of 1-2 per hour for composition. In fact this may be an underestimate in certain circumstances. On 14 October 1912 Gibbs replied to a customer complaint about the high cost of exam papers; he stated that the Press made a heavy loss on maths papers because they necessitated 'the employment of special compositors, paid by time at a high rate of wages'.[25] So the Press's specialist skills could only be had at an understandable premium.

Philip White, in his August 1908 article in the *Irish Printer*, states that the DUP 'had been mainly employed in the production of bookwork' prior to the 1902 amalgamation, but that the partnership 'had the effect of largely increasing the amount of general printing work done there'. This was the start of the trend towards jobbing that was to eclipse the production of bookwork at the Press in its last decades in the Printing House. From a variety of sources I have identified seventy books printed by

23. MUN/DUP/1/3/421 ff.

24. R. Worthington, 'Case room costs' in *Irish Printer* (Aug. 1908) 8–10.

25. MUN/DUP/9/1/103, to W.G. Griffith.

Ponsonby and Gibbs in the period 1902–1913. As it does not represent a systematic search it would be unwise to draw too many conclusions from the sample, but some patterns do emerge. 77 per cent were published in Dublin and 23 per cent in London. Hodges, Figgis & Co. was the largest Dublin publisher (24.3 per cent) and was the College's local publisher. Longman, Green & Co. in London accounted for 14.3 per cent of the output, no doubt accounted for by the fact that it was Trinity's London publisher. TCD was involved in the publication of only 14.3% of the books (I have not included the annual calendars or *Hermathena*), while the DUP itself only acted as publisher in 4 per cent of the cases. Academic/scholarly/legal books accounted for 57.2 per cent of the output; textbooks and literature 12.9 per cent each; religion 10 per cent; and popular/leisure 7 per cent.

I have made the following selection for closer scrutiny largely on grounds of typographic or publishing interest. An example of separate issues is to be had in P.W. Joyce's *Irish local names explained*, printed in December 1902 in an edition of 2,000 copies, half issued with the imprint and binding of the National Board of Education, and half with the imprint and binding of M.H. Gill & Son.[26] Tadhg Gaelach Ó Súilleabháin's *Amhráin*, edited by an tAth. Pádraig Ó Duinnín, was printed for Connradh na Gaelhilge in 1903. The text was set in the variant of the 'Newman' irish typeface that was acquired by the Press *circa* 1875. Most of the printing done for the London publishers had some Trinity connection, but one book that must have been awarded to the DUP solely for its reputation for technical bookwork was W.E. Lilly's *Design of plate girders*, produced for Chapman & Hall in 1904. An example of a work totally out of the norm of productions at the Press was *'Little Mary's' up-to-date dishes easily cooked*, published by Hodges, Figgis & Co. in 1905.

1905 also saw the publication of T.K. Abbott's *Catalogue of fifteenth-century books in the library of TCD*. Besides being a work of very complicated setting, it is also notable for the inclusion of three colour plates of initials from the edition of Plutarch printed by Jenson in 1478. The Press printed several works for the Dublin publisher Maunsel & Co., among them Mary A. Hutton's English translation of *The Táin: an Irish epic* in 1907. It is a small quarto of nearly 500 pages, and its typography and uncut edges give it a distinct arts and crafts look, very unlike the Press's normal sober, academic output. The edition size was 1,750 although only 500 copies of the title sheet were printed; Maunsels were obviously allowing for later 'editions' if they found they had a bestseller on their hands.[27]

Throughout 1906 the Press paid for carriage of type transported from Dellagana in London on behalf of P.W. Joyce. This may well have

26. MUN/DUP/11/2/215, 31 Dec. 1902.
27. MUN/DUP/11/2/236, 6 Nov. 1907.

been his ever-popular *Handbook of school management*, sent to England to have plates made. The DUP printed the twenty-first edition (27,000th) for Longman, Green & Co. in 1907; unusually the colophon states that it was printed by Ponsonby and Gibbs, with no mention of the University Press. I have noted three books printed for private circulation in this period, of which Denis R. Pack-Beresford's *Memoir of Maj.-Gen. Sir Denis Pack* (1908) is an example. The same year saw the production of one of the most elaborately illustrated books: Stanford F.H. Robinson's *Celtic illuminative art in the gospel books of Durrow, Lindisfarne and Kells*. It is a large quarto and has fifty-one plates, some in colour. The author was well satisfied with the book and thanks Gibbs in the acknowledgments 'for his careful supervision'.

The Press was noted for its ability to set music and may well have been the only printer in Dublin with cases in any quantity. They were put to extensive use in 1909 for P.W. Joyce's *Old Irish folk music and songs*, a large volume of over 400 pages. In the same year was begun the monumental five-volume *Records of eighteenth-century domestic architecture and decoration in Dublin* for the Georgian Society, which was completed in 1915. The volumes are generous quartos and are profusely illustrated. A block derived from one of the eighteenth-century vignettes of the Printing House portico is used appropriately as a titlepage device. 1910 saw the printing of an unusual item: 125 copies of sections of James O'Dea's *New explicit algebra*, produced to complete sheets of an old edition.[28] This is something that printers have done from the beginning, much to the perplexity of bibliographers, but this is a very late example; the rising cost of labour soon made such short runs uneconomic.

The partnership with Ponsonby provided a steady flow of law books for the Press, and as is the way with the law these were often weighty tomes. R.E. Osborne's *The jurisdiction and practice of the county courts in Ireland* (2nd ed.), weighing in at 824 pages, is an example from 1910. Only two new works in the Dublin University Press series were printed in this period: E.T. Whittaker's *A history of the theories of aether and electricity* (1910) and the *Argonautica* of Appollonius Rhodius (1912).

Since the early nineteenth century the DUP's privilege to print liturgical works had provided some handsome commissions. A vestige of this privilege was evident in 1911 when it printed the *Church hymnal* for the APCK. It ran to nearly 600 pages and on the titlepage stated, 'One million and 778th thousand', so it can be seen how lucrative even a fraction of this contract could be. The work was intended for distribution throughout Britain and Ireland, and Henry Frowde at the OUP warehouse was given as the London distributor.

---

28. MUN/DUP/11/2/250, 2 May 1910.

Shared printing is not a practice that one associates with this period, but the Press offers a few examples. For the edition of 1,000 of James O'Connor's *Irish justice of the peace* the Press's records stated: 'Printed at this office only. Title to 2Z also sigs. 3R, 3S, 3T, 3U and cancels'.[29] The works of P.W. Joyce provide some other cases. Another practice common in earlier times but rare in this era was the production of fine paper states. One of the few examples of this at the Press was George Coffey's *Bronze age in Ireland* (1913), 900 copies being printed on ordinary paper and 100 on thick paper.[30]

Although the College was associated in only 14.3 per cent of the Press's output in the sample, it did help with publications of other firms if they had some Trinity connection or were deemed to be of scholarly importance. On 13 November 1906 the board register recorded a grant of £50 towards a facsimile of part of the manuscript of Bedell's Irish Bible in Cambridge University Library. Or again on 30 April 1904 £25 was given to Dr P. Gerrard towards his book on beriberi. When this work was produced the register recorded on 5 November that the board wanted cancel titles printed saying the work was 'aided', not 'published', by it. The members of the board obviously had a very strict demarcation in their minds as to what was a College publication and what was not, although it is difficult to fathom what it was. The board did refuse to aid some seemingly worthy publications, as was the case on 19 October 1912 when Mario Esposito's application for £100 to help print a catalogue of medieval manuscripts in Trinity's library was turned down. Perhaps the board had had enough of expensive library catalogues, but without its encouragement the work was never produced.

In a few cases of works published at the expense of the College the printing contract was not awarded to the DUP. On 11 March 1905 the register noted that the copyright of George Salmon's *Analytical geometry of three dimensions* had been assigned to the College and that a new edition was to be prepared by Robert Russell. The work was delayed considerably and by 1911 a new editor, R.A.P. Rogers, had been appointed. On 4 February in that year he was instructed by the board to have the work 'printed in Aberdeen' i.e. at Aberdeen University Press. AUP had a good reputation throughout these islands for technical printing, but the fact that it also had a women's caseroom must have given it the edge in quotations. And the fact that Longman was the publisher chosen may also have had a bearing on the choice of printer. Nevertheless it must have been a bitter pill for Gibbs to swallow and may indicate a temporary souring of his relationship with the College. It was, however, a pill that had to be swallowed. Comparison of the annual

29. MUN/DUP/11/2/136, 2 Oct. 1911.
30. MUN/DUP/11/2/267, 8 Dec. 1913.

sales figures with the bursar's annual accounts show that Trinity provided perhaps 20–25 per cent of the Press's turnover at this period, making it one of its biggest customers, if not the biggest.[31] And besides the College was the landlord.

1914–1923

Business at the Press dipped to an understandable low during the War and rose to an artificial high during post-war inflation, and the figures show that Gibbs milked the situation (the figures are taken from the annual accounts mentioned on page 255):

	Sales in £	Net Profits in £	%
1914	8,528	692	8.1
1915	7,217	37	0.5
1916	7,806	587	7.5
1917	6,675	39	0.6
1918	7,129	1,124	15.8
1919	9,395	1,148	12.2
1920	12,370	3,086	24.9
1921	14,513	3,459	23.8
1922	12,402	368	3.0
1923	10,852	1,560	14.4

(The profits for 1922 were artificially low because of the imposition of an 'excess profits duty' of £1,403; Gibbs was awarded a bonus of £100 in the same year in an obvious attempt to minimise it. When both these items are added to the net profit the percentage to sales is 15.1 per cent.) The partnership was understandably pleased with the performance and Gibbs was awarded a 66.6 per cent increase in his annual salary, from £300 to £500. As in the former period Gibbs kept his current creditors low — he must have been a prompt payer — and his current debtors high, too high it could be argued because a ratio of 1:10 or even 1:20 is not healthy in accountancy terms. Few bad debts were recorded, however, the student clubs being the most notorious defaulters. The liquidity ratio of sales to stock dipped understandably to 3:1 in 1918, but rose to a respectable 6:1 in the early 1920s.

The effects of the War are clearly evident in these figures. Needless to say it caused considerable disruption among the staff. According to ratios agreed with the DTPS early in 1916 the above list of six apprentices would indicate that between thirty and thirty-five journeymen worked for the firm in the war years. From the whole staff of perhaps

---

31. MUN/V/58, bursar's annual accounts; MUN/DUP/1/2/171ff, DUP annual accounts.

45–50, six men and five boys, representing 20–25 per cent of the work-force, enlisted:[32]

Carroll, Owen William: enlisted June 1915.

Collins, John: apprentice comp, enlisted November 1915, killed in France 21 November 1917. Born St Finbar's, Cork.

Connolly, John Joseph: apprentice comp, enlisted April 1916, wounded July 1917.

Creely, Joseph: enlisted May 1915, wounded five times, prisoner of war 1918.

Currey, John James: enlisted November 1915, killed in France 23 or 26 September 1918 in his forty-second year, leaving a wife and four children; buried Thurlington cemetery. Born Canal House, Dublin.

Mahon, John Sylvester: apprentice machine, enlisted September 1914, frost-bite 1915.

Nolan, James: enlisted 1915.

Perrin, John Fawcett: enlisted 1917.

Torkington, Richard: enlisted 1915.

Waller, John William: comp, enlisted May 1915.

Wheelock, Francis: apprentice comp, enlisted May 1915, 'mentioned in despatches'.

Gibbs was generous in his treatment of those who enlisted. He gave half-wages to unmarried men or boys, and made special arrangements for those married because the state was already paying a separation allowance for them. These details are known because of a dispute that arose in relation to John Waller. On 1 January 1916 Gibbs wrote to the secretary of the Department of Recruiting for Ireland explaining the conditions that obtained for volunteers from the DUP and stating that since Waller had got married shortly after enlistment his wife was not entitled to the wages. However without admitting liability he offered Mrs Waller ten shillings per week.[33] These war allowances cost the firm £20 in 1915, £79 in 1916, £93 in both the following years and £71 in 1919 — a total of £356. Gibbs was also generous to those involved in war work. The *Irish Printer* for August 1915 informs us that he had promised to keep Eyton H. Hayes's position open for him while he was engaged in a munition's factory in Sheffield. The DTPS was less accommodating. On 6 July 1915 the firm applied for permission to replace the apprentices who had joined the army, but was refused. The fact that some of the 'stab hands had been let go through slackness of business may have had something to do with it.

32. University of Dublin, Trinity College, *War list February 1922*, Dublin 1922, 255, 'employés of the Trinity College Printing-House'. Further details on those killed have been added from *Ireland's memorial records 1914–1918*, Dublin 1923, and an obituary of J.J. Currey by Philip White in *Irish Printer* (Aug. – Sept. 1918) 6.

33. MUN/DUP/9/1/376; see also letters to Waller 30 Dec. 1915 and 4 Jan. 1916.

Another area where the Press was hard hit by the War was in supplies, especially of paper which was mostly imported. It was not just a case of shortage of raw materials; enemy action also played a hand. In December 1917 fifteen bales of paper dispatched by J. Wrigley & Son in Bury for the Press were lost when the steamer *Hare* was torpedoed and sunk in the Irish Channel. To compound matters there were periodic strikes in the volatile labour market. On 31 March 1916 Gibbs wrote to Wrighleys to say the DUP had been experiencing difficulties in having orders released from the Dublin docks and that it would supply its own carters. So problematic did supplies become that from 1916 onwards Gibbs would quote alternative types and weights in orders to paper merchants. And of course the cost shot up dramatically. Writing to a customer on 10 January 1917 Gibbs explained that paper 'now costs us almost exactly 130 per cent more than we paid for it last year'. So volatile did the situation become that from April 1917 onwards Gibbs included a proviso about fluctuating prices of supplies in all quotes, adding that estimates were only valid if accepted within seven days.[34]

On top of all that there was the disruption caused by the Easter Rebellion in 1916. John Joly provided a vivid picture of Trinity's role in the events.[35] To him it was inexplicable that the College was not taken over by the rebels, for it contained the military stores of the Officer Training Corps and 'the grounds and buildings . . . filled the function of a loyal nucleus, dividing the forces of the Rebels and keeping open to the troops some of the principal thoroughfares of the City'. With the consent of the provost the military made it their headquarters, billeting 4,000 troops there. Needless to say they caused a considerable amount of damage and when a motion was put before the board on 3 June to seek compensation from the military authorities for this, it was a case of divided loyalties — the votes for and against were equal. The Printing House was at the centre of the action. The Brunswick Street gate at the end of Printing House Lane was the main entrance and exit for troops going to the east and north sides of the city. Joly tells us that two 18-pound field guns were brought out through this gate 'and anchored to the pavement by lifting the setts. They were trained on Kelly's shop [a rebel stronghold on Carlisle Bridge] . . . the shells traversing the length of D'Olier Street'. McKenzie's hardware store, from which the Press bought its soaps and brushes, overlooked the Printing House, and was commandeered by the troops to prevent it providing a sniping position to the enemy. Through all this the Printing House came unscathed. Other printing houses were not so lucky: Easons, Maunsels, and Sealy, Bryers and Walker were all gutted. The only material damage that the Press suffered was not on

34. MUN/DUP/9/1/535, 413, 467, 22 Dec. 1917, 31 Mar. 1916, 10 Jan. 1917.
35. 'In Trinity College during the Sinn Fein Rebellion' in John Joly, *Reminiscences & anticipations*, London 1920, 218–64.

campus at all. £50 worth of pamphlets out for binding in Mrs M.A. O'Hara's at 30 Lower Abbey Street was destroyed when that building was burnt.[36] Business was resumed at the Printing House on 4 May, less than two weeks after the Rebellion began.

Another variable in the volatile situation was the drive for better wages and conditions unleashed by the effects of the War and which reverberated down to 1922. Having been stable at £1-15-0 for over twenty years the DTPS initiated an assault on the basic wage in February 1914, seeking an extra five shillings and a reduction of three hours in the fifty-one-hour week. For comparison in its printed memorandum to the 'Dublin Printing Employers' it gave the comparative rates in other cities: London £1-19-0; Glasgow £1-18-0; Leeds £1-17-0; and even Cork paid more than Dublin at £1-16-0. A strike was threatened in April, but before the notice elapsed a compromise offer of 2-6 per week was accepted; piece hands got an extra 3*d*. per 1,000 ens and were allowed three hours clearing-up time per week. A further 2-6 on the 'stab rate and half a penny per 1,000 ens on the piece-work rate were achieved late in 1915, but only after a four-week strike. Strikes followed annually thereafter. One in 1917, this time of six weeks' duration, brought an increase of 7-6 (18.8 per cent). In 1918 a strike resulted in a 12-6 (26.3 per cent) increase, but only after a bitter eleven-week dispute which so depleted the funds of the DTPS that it was forced to arrange a loan of £1,250 from the English Typographical Association. The piece rate was now 1-2 per 1,000. An equally damaging strike occurred in 1919 when an extra 15-0 (25 per cent) was achieved, together with payment for bank holidays and one week's annual leave; this time the Society funded it with a loan of £550 from the Transport Union. Obviously sickened by disputes an increment of 17-6 (23.3 per cent) and a three-hour reduction in the working week to forty-eight hours was granted without a confrontation in 1920. The establishment rate was now £4-12-6 or over 260 per cent more than it had been at the start of the War.[37]

The workers were in fact pricing themselves out of the market. When asked in 1919 to quote for printing sixty copies of an eight-page report, Gibbs got an estimate from the Smith Premier Typewriting Company for having it typed. The comparative figures were: printed £2-3-6; typed £1-19-0. Gibbs included both quotes in his estimate, no doubt having added something like 10 per cent commission to the cost of the typing.[38]

36. MUN/DUP/9/1/421, 8 May 1916, claim lodged with the Dublin Fire and Property Losses Association; see also MUN/DUP/1/2/96.

37. 'Wage movements from 1913–1970' in *Míosachán na gClodoiri*, 29/6 (Aug. – Sept. 1979) 13. IPU: DTPS EC mins, printed notice to employers dated 20 Feb. 1914 (inserted at end July 1914); 23 Apr., 17 June 1914; printed memorandum of agreement with employers dated 4 Jan. 1916 (inserted after 1 Feb. 1916); 22 Oct., 12 Nov. 1918; 20 May 1919; 28 Oct. 1919.

38. MUN/DUP/9/1/622, 623, 5 Feb. 1919, letters to Smith Premier Typewriting Co, and to E.B. Armstrong re report of the Irish Hospital Registrars' Association.

However the 1920s in Ireland was a period of retrenchment and early in 1922 the Master Printers' Association sought a reduction in wages. This was strongly resisted for over eight months, but on 3 October a special delegate meeting of the DTPS gave the committee power, 'in order to avert a strike and to conserve funds', to negotiate a more reasonable reduction than the 15-0 being sought by the employers. On 21 November it was accepted that wages ranging from £4-12-6 to £3-5-0 be reduced by amounts from 8-6 to 4-0 (9.2 to 6.2 per cent).[39]

There is not much evidence as to the disruption these disputes caused at the University Press, but it is likely to have been considerable. On 9 September 1919, with the nine-week strike just over, Gibbs wrote to a customer apologising for the delay in sending proofs; 'owing to labour troubles we were not able to do so sooner'.[40] Some firms were not closed by the strikes because their owners were not members of the Master Printers' Association and so could pay increases independently. However Gibbs was a member at least until 1919; payment of his dues was recorded in surviving account books.[41]

The knock-on effect of inflation in the price of supplies and in wages was a rapid increase in charges for printing. This is best shown in the prices charged for exam papers. An increase of 5 per cent was allowed for these by the College in 1916, another 10 per cent in February 1918, followed by a further 20 per cent in October, and 7.5 per cent in 1919.[42] Writing to one customer on 17 June 1920 Gibbs gave the comparative cost of printing a work then and in pre-war times: 100 large post octavo, long primer, 7.5 sheets 124 pages, including binding: 1919, £59-5-6; pre-war, £44-6-6.[43] That represents an increase of 33.7 per cent, modest enough when viewed in relation to the soaring costs of labour and supplies. What is clear from the trading accounts is that Gibbs, in his second decade at the Press, was using a different formula for estimating to that which he had used in his first. Where formerly he had added 75 per cent to the labour costs to calculate his selling price he was now adding over 100 per cent, sometimes as high as 130 per cent which was the case in 1916, 1918 and 1919.[44]

Some insights into the conditions on the factory floor in this period are to be had from a variety of sources, especially the minutes of the executive committee of the DTPS. The question of piece work loomed large as the Press was one of the few firms allowed to continue the practice by the Society; Corrigan and Wilson was another, while Thoms were

---

39. IPU: DTPS EC mins, 31 Jan., 3, 24 Oct., 21 Nov. 1922.

40. MUN/DUP/9/1/655, letter to Miss N. Disney.

41. MUN/DUP/1/3/481, 497.

42. MUN/DUP/9/1/553, 597, 633, 16 Feb., 14 Oct. 1918, 21 Mar. 1919.

43. MUN/DUP/9/1/704, letter to F.D. Darley.

44. MUN/DUP/1/2/171 ff.

refused permission in 1914 to hire men on piece rates. In July 1917 the DTPS forbade piece hands working in the College to continue, stating that the practice was not recognised by the Society. This elicited a letter from Gibbs quoting an agreement of 4 January 1916 on its recognition.[45] An accommodation was reached on 10 July only for the dispute to flare up within a few days. It is clear however that piece hands continued to work at the Press, as indicated by an application to the Society on 20 November for permission to increase the complement from six to eight men. Given the bad blood between the parties it will be no surprise to learn that it was refused.

Two of the piece hands, Thomas Cummins and [Henry?] Richardson, attended the committee meeting on 23 March 1920 to report a threatened reduction in the 15 per cent increase recently granted to them at the University Press. Cummins reported the following week that only 10 per cent was now being afforded. The secretary was delegated to deal with the matter, but although Cummins attended and wrote letters on several other occasions no outcome was recorded. The committee was obviously fed up with this vestige of the nineteenth century. Cummins wrote again in January 1923 with regard to piece-work conditions in the College to little effect, but when A. Richardson applied on 19 February 1924 for permission to resume piece work at the Press he was refused. Piece work in the trade was effectively dead by the end of the 1920s and the minutes of the special delegate meeting held on 24 January 1930 record its abolition. This change was reflected in the account books of the Press. As late as April 1927 there were estimates charged for by the page, suggesting piece work, while in the 1930s all charges are worked out by the hour, the unit applicable to 'stab wages.[46]

The spiralling costs in the period under scrutiny played havoc with estimating, as we have seen. This was especially true for academic bookwork where a volume might be a decade and more in production, as was the case with T.K. Abbott's *Catalogue of Irish manuscripts in the library of TCD*, which was started in 1910 but not published until 1921. The Press did try to cope with this problem in some measure by charging for standing type. For example Gibbs informed the College in 1917 that the annual rent on the 214 pages of the *Statutes* would be £4-3-0.[47] But my impression is that such charges were not imposed in any systematic way.

Some other vignettes of the work at the Press at this time are worth recording, as for example the unique case in 1915 when an estimate had to be withdrawn, fortunately before it had been accepted, because a charge for paper had been omitted. In November 1917 returns of proofs of music

---

45. MUN/DUP/9/1/509–510, 2 July 1917.

46. MUN/DUP/1/10/1 ff. 23 Apr. 1927, Representative Church Body report; MUN/DUP/4/1, 1930s *passim*.

47. MUN/DUP/9/1/465, 4 Jan. 1917.

and other exam papers from the CUP were noted; this was most likely because a comp skilled in setting music was not available because of war service. A case in 1914 provides an insight into the activity of proof-reading at the Press. Estimating for a chapter of German to be printed in black letter, Gibbs added: 'Our German (native) proof-reader says that the MS requires some corrections.' The only man with a European name working at the Press at this date was Emile Kolterman (from Alsace?), so he may well have been the reader in question. He retired shortly afterwards, but failed to get on to the DTPS's superannuation list because there was no vacancy. He must have been in dire circumstances because on 3 July 1917 he applied to the Society for some of his own mortality allowance, which naturally was refused! His relatives did not have long to wait however as he died the following January. From the machine-room comes evidence from 1916 as to the extra charge imposed for printing in red and black. For 5,000 copies of a proxy paper the cost was £4-11-0 per page printed in black, as against £5-11-0 printed in two colours, making it 22 per cent dearer; and it took twenty-four hours longer.[48]

Printing houses with all their large machines were dangerous places to work. There is evidence of two accidents at the University Press in the 1910s. On 4 January 1910 Philip White reported to the DTPS that John Currey had been injured, but as he was not being paid he could not afford his head money. The chapel undertook to pay this if he was restored to benefit with the Society; no decision was recorded. The case highlights the appalling social welfare provisions of the time. Chapel funds were sometimes used to help out sick members. The other case eight years later recorded some progress in this area. On 7 March 1918 Gibbs wrote to the London Assurance Co. reporting that the firm had paid £35-6-1 to Richard Barnes since his accident 'as required by law'. Compensation was being paid at the rate of £1-5-0 per week so the accident must have happened early in September 1917. He was not declared fully fit until June 1918.[49] He may well have retired at this point allowing Philip White's promotion to overseer.

From the firm's letter books we know that suppliers of paper during the 1910s included Armstrong & Co., Dickinson & Co., Wrigleys, Spalding & Hodge (who supplied paper from the Ballyclare Mills in Co. Antrim), J. McDonnell & Co., Spicer Bros, and G. Morgan. Process blocks were supplied locally by the Irish Photo Engraving Co.,[50] while Knight & Cottrell

48. MUN/DUP/9/1/349–350, 15 Sept. 1915 to Rev. W.J. Mayne; ibid./529, 8 Nov. 1917 to CUP; ibid./254, 26 Sept. 1914 to Hon. Ellen O'Brien; ibid./463, 26 Dec. 1916 to Hamilton & Craig.

49. MUN/DUP/9/1/562, 581, 7 Mar. to London Assurance Co., 13 June 1918 to R. Barnes.

50. This company was founded in 1917 by J.B. Aiken and only closed in 1982, having been for many years the oldest engraving company in Dublin (see note in *Irish Printer* (May 1982) 9).

provided brass blocks for stamping bindings. The Press also used Emery Walker Ltd in London for orders for special half-tone blocks from 1915 onwards. For example Gibbs enquired in 1916 for blocks for printing colour photos. There is no record that the work was printed, but this is one of the few pieces of evidence I have found at this date that the Press undertook full colour work. There is however the possibility that Walker was to print the plates, as a letter in 1918 asked for a quotation for printing supplied blocks by 'your special double tone . . . process'.[51] The Press also seems to have turned to London for electrotyping. On 5 February 1918 Gibbs wrote to B. Dellagana & Co. seeking a quote for electros for 648 pages of a ruby hymnal. A week later he wrote to the APCK saying the charge would be £77-6-6 plus carriage of the standing type to and from London and war risk insurance. War was not the only risk in shipping to London. On 7 January 1921 Gibbs claimed £4-10-0 against the carriers John Wallis & Sons for damage to ten pages of type during transport to Dellaganas.

TCD's account with the Press at this period was mostly for jobbing, foremost of which were exam papers. A committee was set up by the board on 28 January 1922 to consider the question of publishing them, and it reported favourably on 16 March. Thereafter extra copies were to be printed, divided into groups and published in pamphlet form. The annual *Calendar* continued to be the College's largest recurrent bookwork commission. The biannual scholarly journal *Hermathena* also provided valuable business, although the board was constantly complaining of the expense. There is a reference in the board register for 13 January 1917 to its 'discontinuance', but it survived through the period of spiralling costs. When the cost of the issue for June 1920 reached £190 the board had to remind the editor E.H. Alton to seek estimates in future and to try to keep the costs down. As an economy measure the issue for the second half of the year was postponed until 1921. Alton did get an estimate for the succeeding issue from Karras Kröber & Neitschmann in Halle and on 5 March the board authorised him to have it printed in Germany if he thought fit. This was a strange decision so close to the end of the War and it is not known whether it was motivated by respect for the firm's reputation or by the price on the estimate. *Hermathena* however remained at the University Press and sets were proudly sent abroad by the College as reflections of Trinity's scholarship. The board register for 27 June 1923 recorded that a set presented to the Apostolic Library had elicited the Pope's thanks, conveyed in a letter to 'Marquis MacSwiney of Mashanaglass'.

The drift away from bookwork during these years is reflected in the fact that I have identified less than thirty books printed at the Press in the period 1914–1923. Even allowing for the general downturn in the trade this

---

51. MUN/DUP/9/1/390–391, 7 Feb. 1916 to Emery Walker Ltd, 8 Feb. to Miss Eve White West, the author who wanted colour reproductions; ibid./607, 28 Nov. 1918 to Emery Walker Ltd.

was a remarkable swing from the seventy identified for the period 1902–1913. The College was involved in the publication of a third of this output. T.K. Abbott and E.J. Gwynn's *Catalogue of the Irish manuscripts in the library of TCD* is one of the few for which there is any detail of its production history. As has been seen printing began in 1910, but production was interrupted by Abbott's death in December 1913. On 26 June 1915 the board appointed E.J. Gwynn to complete it at a fee of £60. Gibbs was paid £100 on account on 16 March of the following year and a further £284 was owing on 30 October 1920 when the board sanctioned the payment to him of £150. Gwynn submitted a copy of the finished work at the board meeting of 26 November 1921, when it was decided that the selling price was to be £1 and an extra £40 was voted to the compiler for his trouble. There was one further cost implication: on January 21 of the following year the board sanctioned the spending of £5 by Longman, Green & Co. to advertise the work, one of the very few examples there was for such publicity of single works.

There were no new publications in the Dublin University Press series during this period. T. Alexander and A.W. Thomas's *Elementary applied mechanics*, printed at the Press, was included in the shelves of the series in the library of the College and the College arms appear on the title, but there is no series title in the book and it was published in London by Macmillan & Co., not Longman as usual. Volumes of the two bestsellers in the series — Cicero's *Correspondence* and Brunside and Panton's *Theory of equations* — were reprinted. The board register for 25 October 1923 provided publication details for the latter. The College was to pay all the expenses for the 'new issue' — no doubt it was printed from plates — of 2,000 copies. These expenses were to be recouped from sales and subsequent profits shared between the two authors and Trinity, each getting one third.

Hodges, Figgis & Co. continued to be Trinity's Dublin publisher. Longman, Green & Co. served that function in London, for which they were allowed a commission of 10 per cent on sales, increased to 15 per cent by the board on 17 November 1917. Very occasionally the College used the DUP as its publisher, as was the case for W.G. Strickland's *Descriptive catalogue of pictures, busts and statues in TCD*, issued in 1916. The imprint reads: 'Printed and sold at the University Press by Ponsonby and Gibbs'. The board accepted Gibbs's estimate of £21-2-6 to print 500 copies on 13 May of that year, and on 1 July voted £30 to Strickland for preparing it. Why Trinity did not use its usual publishers is not known; perhaps it was felt that the bulk of the copies would be sold within the College itself. The Press did not consider itself as a publisher. In a quotation to a customer in December 1913 for printing a pamphlet Gibbs concluded: 'With reference to the publication of the above, we regret we cannot give you any information'; he referred her to E. Ponsonby Ltd in Grafton Street.[52] In fact the Press took on a considerable portion of the

52. MUN/DUP/9/1/192, 4 Dec. 1913 to Miss Kavanagh.

burden of publication for a number of institutions for whom it printed by undertaking the dispatch of their journals; examples were the Royal Society of Antiquaries of Ireland, the Kilkenny Archaeological Society, the Memorials of the Dead Society and Trinity's *Hermathena*.

Other institutions continued to provide valuable business, the RIA and RDS being foremost among them. The Press printed *The book of Armagh* for the Academy in 1913. This Irish manuscript was edited for publication by John Gwynn and was printed in an edition of 400 volumes. The complicated type facsimile text runs to over 500 pages and there are a further 290 of introductory material. It also did considerable work for the APCK; in a letter to 'H. Bible Esqr.' (an unusual accommodation name that was used in correspondence to this association) on 6 May 1914 Gibbs reported that there were 10,000 nonpareil hymnals in stock and that a further 40,000 would need 360 reams of paper.[53] Now that was an account worth having. The Protestant outlook of the Press did not prevent it from doing work for several Roman Catholic customers, although you can imagine a staunch Orange comp gritting his teeth while setting *Promises of the Sacred Heart to families*, commissioned by the superior of the Dominican Convent, Blackrock, in March 1917.[54] Among the other institutions it printed for was the DTPS, which in a shrewd move had its printing done in rotation by the 'fair' houses in the city; the DUP's turn came in 1912, as recorded in the committee's minutes on 2 January.

The partnership with Ponsonby continued to provide some substantial bookwork, including the only work I have found that was generated by the war situation. *Tactical notes* by H.J. Kinsman, printed in 1914, was dedicated to the Royal Dublin Fusiliers and was bound by Galwey & Co. in a yapp binding, suitable for pocketing by the officer in the field. School and college textbooks were again a feature of the output. An edition of George W. Parker's *Elements of optics* was issued in 1915 and the Press over the years also produced editions of his *Astronomy*, *Mechanics* and *Hydrostatics*. The board register for 25 October 1923 noted an offer of the rights in a large number of unbound sheets of these, estimated value £900, from the sons of the late author; it was declined. The account books of the Press also recorded a bad debt of £92 against the representatives of G.W. Parker in 1924, among the highest noted. This must subsequently have been cleared because the Press continued to dispatch parcels of the works for H.L. Parker throughout the 1930s and the printing of another edition of the *Astronomy* (1,000 from plates) was recorded on 19 January 1940.[55]

A prestige volume that was printed despite the scarcities of the War was T.U. Sadleir and P.L. Dickinson's *Georgian mansions in Ireland*, issued in 1915 in an edition of 700 copies. The text of this quarto volume runs to

53. MUN/DUP/9/1/233, 6 May 1914.

54. MUN/DUP/9/1/484, 8 Mar. 1917.

55. MUN/DUP/1/2/81; MUN/DUP/1/8/71.

over 100 pages and there are 80 half-tone plates, all on good quality loaded paper. Gibbs reported to Miss Eve White West in the following year that he was having great difficulty procuring stock of similar quality to print her colour photographs. Maunsel & Co. was a good patron of the Press and in February 1917 Gibbs quoted for composing and printing 1,000 copies of Patrick Pearse's *Works*. Again as with the Roman Catholic material it was a strange work for a Protestant Unionist house to tender for — from the opposite pole it would have been like the Fodhla Press printing the speeches of Edward Carson — but perhaps commerce knows no bounds. In the event the Press did not get the commission; the first two volumes were printed by George Roberts and the third by Maunsel itself. In 1918 the recently formed Bibliographical Society of Ireland decided to use the DUP to print its series of papers; it printed two, but then lost the contract. 1919 saw the production of some of the works that Gibbs brought with him to the Press — the *Constitution* and *Statutes* of the Church of Ireland.

Electricity must have been installed in the Printing House by mid-1917 because the purchase of an electric motor was recorded at the financial year ending 31 July. Electric lighting was put in three years later.[56] With this source of power Gibbs could contemplate the installation of more up-to-date machinery and especially of mechanical typesetters. Such modernisation was of course contingent on the renewal of the lease in 1923, but this renewal was by no means certain. The downturn in profits of the Press during the War led Gibbs to appeal for a reduction of £50 in the £200 annual rent, but this was refused by the board on 30 October 1915. He tried again in December 1917 and again the board refused an abatement. It did however make a 'special grant' of £40 to the firm and this grant was repeated on 7 December 1918 and on 29 November 1919. The simmering discontent among the board members with the performance of the Press, which was to boil up in the following years, was evident as early as 18 December 1920 when Gibbs was refused a further 'special grant'. The board minutes made it clear that renewal of the lease would not be automatic.

On 12 February 1921 the board appointed a committee 'to enquire into the possibility and desirability of the College undertaking the control and responsibility for the Printing Office when Mr Gibbs' lease expires in October 1923'. This brief was in effect the same as that given to the 1900 Printing House committee and its enquiries covered much the same grounds. The committee consisted of Provost Bernard (the only survivor from the 1900 enquiry), the bursar L.C. Purser, the registrar Robert Russell, Matthew Fry and E.H. Alton. It met for the first time on 25 February when all that was decided was to enquire whether the advice of a printing expert should be sought. The person contacted was Cecil

56. MUN/DUP/1/2/51 ff., 31 July 1917; ibid./56, 1920.

Harmsworth, brother of Lord Northcliffe. He wrote to the provost three days later recommending R.J. Mecredy as consultant, or perhaps a person from the OUP. He went on: 'It would be a mistake, I am sure, to regard the Press as a purely financial proposition', but he felt that by the quality of its work it could enhance the reputation of the university. He suggested that perhaps the Press should confine itself to printing exam papers and suchlike jobbing and for bookwork 'to aim at something of the highest quality, rather on the lines of the Dun Emer Press, (now called the Cuala Press)'. One can imagine what the reaction at the University Press, with nearly two centuries of history behind it, would have been to this comparison with a press run by women and not two decades old. (Harmsworth put his enthusiasm for the Cuala Press on the line in the following year by having *Holiday verses*, written by himself and his brother Desmond, privately printed there.)[57]

Despite having pursued advice so quickly the matter apparently was then let lie for the rest of the year. Early in 1922 Robert Russell, recently appointed bursar, challenged Gibbs over the spiralling costs of printing. On 12 January he replied, vigorously defending the charges and stating that they were based on 'rates fixed by the local Printers Employers' Association . . . in accordance with a scientific costing system'. He cited the enormous increases in the costs of production in recent years and stated that these had not been passed on in full. Despite these protestations he agreed to a 5 per cent reduction in the cost of the *Calendar* and some other minor adjustments. His letter is one of the most strongly worded in the surviving letter books and concludes: 'In the circumstances it seems to us unfair that the prices charged should be cut down still further by unreasonable pressure brought to bear on us by the Board.' Russell, noted for his cheese-paring, was not deterred by this plea — perhaps he had had some inside knowledge of the 'fat' in the profits of the Press — and harried Gibbs for further reductions over the next six months. This onslaught culminated in June when Gibbs offered an 11 per cent reduction in a wide range of College printing and promised that any substantial reduction in the men's wages would be passed on.[58]

While these negotiations were underway the Printing House committee had one of its infrequent meetings on 26 April and recommended to the board three days later, following from what Cecil Harmsworth had written over a year earlier, that before it made its decision on Gibbs's lease, the advice of an expert from one of the English university presses should be sought. This was agreed and the provost wrote to several people, including Henry J. White, Dean of Christ Church, Oxford, and Thomas B. Strong, Bishop of Ripon and one of the delegates of the OUP.

57. MUN/P/1/2923, file of correspondence concerning policy on DUP, 18 Feb. 1921 – 25 May 1922.
58. MUN/DUP/9/1/807, 815, 816, 834, 836, 848, letters to Russell, 12 Jan. – 30 June 1922.

The former passed on advice from R.W. Chapman of the Clarendon Press at OUP who made the rather obvious points that it was necessary for university presses to take in general work to fill in the blank spaces in the ebb and flow of university printing, and that the printing expert brought in would need to know the local labour and market conditions. Strong went to some greater trouble and replied in two letters in May. He described the evolution of the OUP and how after various partnerships with sundry printers and publishers the delegates eventually took on the management of the whole business about the middle of the nineteenth century, employing their own publisher (Frowde) and manager (Hart). He had consulted the current publisher Humphrey Milford, who agreed that the OUP's experiences were not of much relevance to the plight of the DUP. (This conclusion was based most probably on comparisons of scale — the OUP catalogue at this date ran to nearly 500 pages.) Two requisites however were identified: sufficient working capital and a good secretary to supervise the whole work of the Press. If the business was successful and expanded it could then be broken down into separate components as the OUP had been.[59] All of these points and more had been covered in the report of 1900 and there is no evidence that the 1920s committee collated the advice it had sought and presented a written report. The attention of the board was diverted elsewhere — these were the transitional years of the Anglo-Irish Treaty when Trinity was fighting for financial survival and there was no relish for schemes that involved heavy capital expenditure.

The board decided on 28 October 1922 to let Gibbs know that his lease was under review but to understand that there was 'no pledge on their part to renew [it]'; he was to be given a year's notice of any change in arrangements. Gibbs had already had wind of the matter and was actively gathering testimonials to defend his corner. These, and others he collected in the years following, he had printed on single leaves and used as advertisement hand-outs to potential customers.[60] One of 21 August 1922 from R. Lloyd Praeger, librarian of the National Library of Ireland, will give the flavour:

> Dear Mr. Gibbs,
> You have asked me to set down the opinion I have formed of the work of the Dublin University Press during the many years' experience that I have had of it in connexion with the work of the Royal Irish Academy and other enterprises. I can say with truth that your work is extremely good. The most difficult mathematics hold no terrors for you, and in simpler work your typesetting and printing are models of accuracy and clearness. In particular I should

59. See note 57.
60. MUN/P/1/2960 contains 4 dated 8 July 1922 to 3 Feb. 1923; I have seen a larger selection containing 13, dated 25 May 1900 to 7 Apr. 1928.

like to refer to your proof-reading, which goes far beyond mere correctness of typography; your critical care in matters of spelling, grammar, and sense has frequently saved authors from inaccuracies. In these and in other respects your standard is of the highest.

The board came to no conclusion as regards its management of the University Press so on 19 May 1923 it agreed to grant a year's lease to Ponsonby & Gibbs from 1 October on the existing terms. Even though there were doubts over his long-term tenure Gibbs could no longer postpone investment in up-to-date machinery. He had purchased an Intertype machine in April 1923, the first mechanical setter at the Press. (In this the University Press was a decade and more behind the rest of the Dublin trade; the minutes of the DTPS committee for 22 November 1910 recorded that 'almost every office in the city possesses up-to-date typesetting machinery'.) The Intertype was included among the £2,140 invested in machinery during the financial year 1922–23, while in the following year a further £1,763 of plant was bought.[61]

1924–1934

On 1 October 1924, with his existing lease expired, Gibbs wrote to the board asking for renewal of the lease 'for a considerable number of years'. After a long discussion the board decided to offer one of three years on the current terms or ten years at an increased rent of £300 per annum. A month later Ponsonby and Gibbs wrote back suggesting a lease of twenty or at least fifteen years at £250, but the board stood firm over its original offer. On 8 November the board minutes recorded that the firm accepted a ten-year lease at £300 from 1 October and on 10 December the College seal was put on it. By the provisions of the lease Ponsonby and Gibbs were to maintain the inside of the building, the College the outside. They were not allowed to carry on any business there other than printing and publishing. The College's printing was to be done 'with all reasonable speed' and the lessees had to 'give preference to all such orders over all their other printing business'. Provision was made for the imposition of a fine of up to £50 if exam papers were not on time or were divulged. Finally the lessees were given charge of type and other printing materials belonging to the College (a schedule of these referred to in the lease is not present) to be used free of charge for Trinity's printing; Ponsonby and Gibbs undertook to take care of them and hand them back in good order at the end of the lease.[62]

61. MUN/DUP/1/3/473, 12 Apr. 1923, insurance paid on Intertype machine; MUN/DUP/1/2/51 ff., 31 July 1923, 31 July 1924.
62. MUN/D/3538c.

Ireland in the post-Civil War years was in a state of recession and poverty characterised the initial years of the fledgling state. Editorials in the *Irish Printer* throughout the 1920s speak of the depression within the trade — 10 per cent of DTPS members were unemployed in 1927 — and there were constant reports of the damage being done by the huge imports of foreign printing. The new government decided to foster native industries by the imposition of tariffs on imports and this attitude was reflected in the typographic trade by the foundation of a 'Protection for Printing' movement. This trend, at least as regards bookwork, was castigated by George Russell in an editorial in the *Irish Statesman* for 11 December 1926. He argued that there was no reason why book printing, both for the internal and export markets, could not be built up in Dublin. Tariffs would only protect the indigenous market which was limited to schoolbooks and some political works. The main drawback he concluded was not economic but that the books published in Ireland were 'utterly without taste' in regard to typographic design. The next issue published several replies including one from W.G. Lyon of the Educational Company of Ireland defending the book trade, instancing 'some very pleasing books from the University Press' and mentioning also the Mellifont Press, Browne & Nolan, Thoms and Gills. But there is no doubt that the style of the general output reflected the depressed state of the country. Colm Ó Lochlainn's Three Candles Press was the only house turning out well-designed bookwork with regularity. The imposition of a 15 per cent import duty on printed matter in 1932 'resulted in an extraordinary boom in the printing trade' according to the June issue of the *Irish Printer* and this duty was increased to 75 per cent from 30 September 1933.

The poor economic climate in the 1920s did not affect the business of the Press adversely, largely because its fortunes were not tied to the business trade; work for scholarly institutions provided a good buffer against the recession. The following figures are taken from the annual accounts mentioned on p. 255 above:

	Sales in £	Net Profit in £	%
1924	10,099	2,456	24.3
1925	10,580	2,312	21.9
1926	9,641	1,439	14.9
1927	10,117	2,304	22.8
1928	9,230	1,450	15.7
1929	10,988	1,417	12.9
1930	9,886	1,408	14.2
1931	10,399	1,644	15.8
1932	10,158	2,172	21.4
1933	10,664	1,775	16.6
1934	9,940	1,799	18.1

Gibbs continued to keep his current creditors low and his current debtors high except in the years 1924–27 when the ratio dropped to about 1:2; perhaps this reflected the heavy purchase of machinery. (There is little evidence of what machines were bought, but a charge for three Funditor electric heaters on 14 August 1931 indicates that by that date there were three Intertypes.)[63] The liquidity ratio of sales to stock was often as high as 9:1 and only once dipped to a low of 4:1. The trading accounts reveal that Gibbs continued to operate an estimating system of a 100 per cent mark-up or more on wages.

Because of the large number of unemployed in the trade in 1924 the DTPS executive decreed that no excessive overtime was to be worked; its policy was to reduce overtime so that more men would be employed. The father of the College chapel was summoned before the committee on 16 December and fined £1 for permitting overtime at the DUP which had not been sanctioned by the executive. The Society's prohibition continued throughout the 1920s and the University Press had to apply on a week-to-week basis during the busy exam paper seasons for permission to operate overtime. On most occasions this was allowed, but on 7 May 1929 the DTPS said that no more would be permitted until another case hand was employed. Gibbs resisted this and had representations made through the Master Printers' Association, but in the end he had to capitulate and employed a comp named McGrath as the extra man.

From 1931 we have a first-hand account of the workings of the University Press. In that year Jimmy Stewart, then aged sixteen, started work in the wareroom and he remained with the firm until his retirement fifty years later. His crystal clear memory provides a valuable insight. The layout of the building was much the same as it had been in earlier periods. The basement of the 1734 building was used for storing paper. Here too was a wetting room — for some reason now impenetrable called 'Tullamore' — in which was a very old wooden trough measuring perhaps 5 by 3 feet and 1.5 feet deep; with it were large granite slabs and wooden boards. Quires of paper would have been drawn through the trough and several of them laid flat between the wooden boards. These piles were then weighted down with the stones overnight to allow them to become evenly damp, ready for the pressmen next morning. It was the practice in the general trade to use damped paper until the 1890s, even though it was not strictly necessary given the power of the iron press, because it masked the wear in used type.[64] The trough in the Printing House may well not have been used since the nineteenth century, but was only disposed of in the early 1940s.

The machine-room was in the basement of the 1840 extension. The red-bricked 'Parochial Hall' was, as stipulated in the lease, a caseroom.

63. MUN/DUP/5/1/64.
64. Gaskell, *New introduction* (1979) 125, 261.

Besides the compositors' frames it contained three large imposing stones. Here also was a large hydraulic press that was used to force out the impression made in letterpress printed sheets; there was another such press in the wareroom. On the ground-floor level were the caserooms. That in the eighteenth-century building housed the Intertypes ranged along the west-facing windows. Jimmy Stewart confirms there were three of these and his impression was that after the first the others were bought second-hand. The two rooms at the back of this section were lined from top to bottom with stores of type. The one on the east side was known as 'the reader's box' and was where Peter Maher did his proof-reading. The other was at one time a dining room for staff, but was later used by the reader. The caseroom in the nineteenth-century building was lined with compositors' frames, and down the middle were two huge steel-topped imposing stones.

The warerooms were on the top floors. The printed sheets were stored in the 1840 extension, organised in bays by author. Even though all work was sent out for binding this area was sometimes known as 'The Bindery'. At the back of the 1734 section was the 'Book Room', an area caged off where the bound books were stored. The large music cases were also stored on this level of the original building; Ross Mahon, Senior, and later Jack Maher were the comps who most frequently set from them.

Jimmy Stewart recalls the staff as numbering between 30 and 40: management 2; comps 12–14; Intertype 3; reader 1; machine-room 8-10; warehouse 3–4; apprentices 3–4. He remembers the imposing figure of Gibbs, who because of his beard looked like King George V, arriving at 10.30 or 11 o'clock in the morning and spending his whole day reading, even taking it home in the evening. He was renowned for his accuracy in proof-reading, especially of biblical passages, and saved many an author from embarrassment, as the testimonials he gathered document. He was conferred with an honorary M.A. by the College in 1942 in recognition of his abilities. Gibbs was known to all as 'The Governor', and even addressed as such, while his son was called 'Mr Charles'. Fred Maybury remembers the father as being very strict but also very fair, and his whole bearing and behaviour was reminiscent of a Victorian gentleman. He was also very penny-pinching, as was demonstrated in a letter he wrote in 1918 to a Belfast supplier when ordering envelopes; since there was no rush on the order they were to be sent with the goods of another firm because he did not want to pay carriage![65] His character was encapsulated in an incident related by Jimmy Stewart. Stewart was often sent on messages by the manager John Corr and given the tram fare of a few pence. Jimmy would save this by using his own bicycle. Once on such an errand he was stopped in College Park by Gibbs who enquired about the boy's mission. When told he was very solicitous that Stewart be careful on his

65. MUN/DUP/9/1/560, 4 Mar. 1918 to J. Dickinson & Co.

bicycle, but he also reminded him to be sure to return the tram fare to Corr! The manager knew well what Jimmy did with the tram fare and refused to take it back. Gibbs's meanness meant that he became increasingly reluctant to invest in new machinery and in later years let things run down, as will be seen.

Since Gibbs spent most of his time reading he left the day-to-day running of the Press to his manager. On a Friday the staff used to queue up for their wages when Gibbs would dispense the £1 notes and Corr the coins. The men were paid more than workers in other firms because of the complexity of the work and the security element in their employment. Because of the recession the basic journeyman's wage in the trade remained at £4-4-0 throughout the period 1922–1934. On top of this it was general trade practice to add a sum of 'merit money', negotiated by the individual with the foreman, which reflected his ability and length of service; this amount was kept confidential. At the Press 'merit money' added from 5-0 to 15-0 to the basic sum.

The only industrial trouble during this period was a trade strike in 1934 for more pay by the labourers who assisted the machinemen, all members of the Irish Transport and General Workers' Union. At the full adult rate they were seeking £3 per week, and £2 for the top of the juvenile scale. The strike started on 19 July and four days later the DTPS instructed its members not to do any of the strikers' work or handle any material normally handled by them. In commercial houses this meant moving formes around so when the printers refused to do this there was a lock-out in fourteen houses controlled by members of the DMPA and these included the University Press. A special meeting of the DTPS executive on 25 July, when informed that it had been reported in the newspapers that the men at the DUP had 'ceased work', sent a correction to the papers stating that it was in fact a lock-out. (Jimmy Stewart related to me exactly what happened. The transport union men used to bring up the metal for the Intertypes from the basement. This of course the operators refused to do, so when Gibbs arrived in at about eleven o'clock he found the Intertypes idle. Upon discovering the reason he went himself and fetched the metal, and when the men still refused to handle it he told them to clear out.) A compromise settlement was reached early in August and the commercial houses resumed on the 10th. In the newspapers the dispute became entangled with the question of editorial autonomy and the bitter debate was not resolved until 21 September.

The overseers of the caseroom and the machine-room, and the warehouse-keeper each had to all intents and purposes control over the hiring and firing of staff in their area. The non-working caseroom overseer was George Hogan, aged about sixty in 1930, who was nicknamed 'Nightie' because he was a nightmare to work under. Hogan had come with Gibbs from Wicklow Street where he had been a stone hand. He was let go in the late 1920s and moved to Cahills, but was recalled as overseer soon afterwards. One of the most skilled comps at the Press, Richard 'Dick' Lattimore, served his time under Hogan. Because Lattimore's widow Maude is still alive and has kindly provided me with some personal details of him, it is worth examining the background of a comp at the Press of this period. Dick was born to Thomas and Mary Lattimore on 31 August 1914. During the War his father enlisted in the Royal Army Medical Corps, and died at Salonica in November 1916, leaving his wife with four young children. The family lived in Ballsbridge, a comfortable suburb of the city, and Dick was educated in the local Protestant national school. As a child he lost a finger on each hand through infection — middle and little fingers which did not interfere with his becoming an expert compositor. Through the offices of her local clergyman his mother had him indentured to Ponsonby and Gibbs on 1 April 1931 to learn the art of 'compositing' (see plate 35). He was very proud and when asked as an apprentice to wheel the Press's cart he refused and was nearly dismissed. One of his other tasks was to light the pot-bellied stove in the caseroom, which he did reluctantly.

Lattimore became a brilliant comp, especially of the classics, learning a lot from Joe Pasley. Although he did not understand any of these languages he came to 'know' when the conjunction of certain letters looked wrong and his hunch often proved correct. His wife told me that he did understand French. He was very quiet and of a nervous disposition, but would on occasion boil over, as when he chased somebody with a wooden mallet. What the occasion was is not remembered, but the fact that he used to get intensely annoyed at the way others handled the type will indicate his temperament. He emigrated briefly to the USA in 1961, but when he decided to return to Ireland after six months his skills ensured his ready re-employment at the Press. He married Maude, a Catholic, in the following year and this caused some strife in the families. To their regret it was too late to have children. In later years Dick became a reader and in 1975, when the staff at the Press moved out of the Printing House, he reluctantly followed the firm to Sandymount. He stuck it out for a few years, but took voluntary redundancy on 20 March 1980. In a poignant note to the end of a career of skill and accuracy there is a 'typo' in the inscription on the silver tray presented to him — his name was spelled 'Latimore'. He died from lung cancer four years later. Peter Maher was another comp at the Press at this time and later became a very reliable reader. From 1915 onwards he taught typography on the various printing courses run in Dublin.[66] He continued to work at the Press until his retirement on 27 February 1956.

Since 1925 the DTPS had been refusing to accept the cards of other typographical societies 'in an effort to retain all the available work for our members'.[67] The imposition of tariffs on imported printed matter in the

66. IPU: DTPS EC mins, 30 July 1912; *Irish Printer* (Oct. 1931) 2; (Feb. 1936) 1.
67. IPU: DTPS EC mins, 24 Jan. 1930.

Made the *First* day of *April* 19*31*

BETWEEN *Messrs Ponsonby & Gibbs* of *Trinity College, Dublin* hereinafter called "The said Master" of the 1st part *Richard D. Lattimore* son of *Thomas* hereinafter called "The said Apprentice," of the second part *Harry Lattimore* of "The said Apprentice," hereinafter called "The said Parent" of the 3rd part, and the Governors of Love's Charity and Gardiner's Charity. Dublin, hereinafter called "The said Governors" of the 4th part. **Whereas** "The said Apprentice" lately applied to "The said Governors" to advance the sum of £ *15* ———— as an Apprentice fee to "The said Master" for the purpose of apprenticing "The said Apprentice" to "The said Master" to learn the trade of *Compositor* which "The said Governors" agreed to do on the terms that "The said Master" should enter into the covenants and agreements with them and "The said Parent" hereinafter contained.

Now this Indenture Witnesseth that in consideration of the sum £ *15* ———— now paid by "The said Governors" to "The said Master" the receipt whereof he doth hereby acknowledge, and in consideration also of the service of "The said Apprentice" to be done or performed to, or for "The said Master," and of the covenants and agreements hereinafter entered into by "The said Apprentice" and "The said Parent." He "The said Master," at the request of "The said Governors" and with the consent (hereby testified) of "The said Parent," and "The said Apprentice" doth hereby covenant and agree with "The said Governors" and also with "The said Parent" and "The said Apprentice" in manner following, that is to say—that he "The said Master" will take and receive "The said Apprentice" as his Apprentice from the day of the date of these presents for the term of *Seven* years, and also will during the said term to the best of his power, knowledge, and ability, instruct "The said Apprentice" in the trade or business of *a Compositor* and in all things incident or relating thereto, in such manner as he "The said Master" doth now or shall hereafter during the said term use or practice the same, and will pay to "The said Apprentice" during the said term, or until the sooner determination of the said **Apprenticeship** the respective sums following:—

And in consideration of the covenants and agreements hereinbefore contained on the part of "The said Master," "The said Governors" do hereby place and bind "The said Apprentice," and "The said Apprentice" with the consent of "The said Governors" and of "The said Parent" doth hereby place and bind himself with and to "The said Master" during the term aforesaid, during all which time "The said Apprentice" shall faithfully, honestly, and diligently serve him, "The said Master," and perform and obey all his lawful and reasonable commands and requirements, and shall not do any damage or injury to "The said Master," or knowingly suffer the same to be done without acquainting him therewith, but shall in all things conduct and acquit himself as an honest and faithful apprentice ought to do, and for the consideration aforesaid "The said Parent" doth hereby covenant and agree with "The said Master" that "The said Apprentice" shall faithfully, honestly, and diligently serve "The said Master" as his Apprentice during the said term. And it is hereby agreed that upon the expiration of the said Apprenticeship, and the discharge by "The said Parent" and "The said Apprentice" of all their obligations to "The said Master" hereunder this present Indenture shall be delivered by "The said Master" to "The said Apprentice."

In Witness

35. Richard 'Dick' Lattimore's indentures 1931, reproduced by kind permission of his widow Maude.

early 1930s created an 'avalanche of work', to quote the words of the DTPS committee minutes for 12 May 1931. There was a consequent shortage of typesetter operators. The order of 1925 was therefore rescinded, except inexplicably for those from the six counties of Northern Ireland. The minutes for 22 September record that cards as linotype operators were issued to Typographical Society members from Bradford, Wakefield, Burnley, Kendal, Darlington and Kent. The University Press did not need to take advantage of this increase in available labour; it had other strategies. The DTPS minutes for 31 October 1932 would suggest that hand comps used to use the machines during dinner hours to cope with the increased demand. On that date the FOC Edward Wilcox and Ross Mahon, Junior, were summoned to explain why Mahon, a comp, was operating the Intertype during the midday break. The explanation, not elaborated, was accepted. Ross's permission to do this was withdrawn by the committee on 30 May 1933 when it was discovered that he was operating the machine during the regular operator's absence, but was not being paid the operator rates. Permission was sought on 24 April of the following year to allow him to operate an Intertype 'in emergency'. This was agreed as he was to receive a permanent increase to the linotype rate.

The fact that comps had been operating the Intertypes during break times created difficulties for the apprentices who wanted to gain some experience on them. This may have been the only time they were made available to them as petitions to the DTPS on 21 October 1930 and 25 August 1933 would seem to indicate. It was an apprentice's right to be afforded training as an operator in his final year and the difficulties at the University Press may be the reason why the FOC was summoned before the executive committee on 26 October 1926 'in reference to the suitability of that office to properly train apprentices'.

The training of apprentices in the trade in general underwent some scrutiny during the early 1930s. A subcommittee of the DTPS executive was set up to consider the matter in relation to newspaper offices and even though its report of 11 September 1931 applies only to that section of the printing craft, its recommendations are worth recording because the training in commercial houses like the DUP would not have been much different. The report related only to caseroom apprentices. It recommended that in the first year the boy do six months copyholding and six months random work. In the second year he could set headings and do distribution. The following year stone work and corrections. In the fourth year the first six months on posters and the second six on general case work, display and jobbing; this would continue in his fifth and sixth years. During his last year he was to be given experience on the Lino and Monotype machines. In 1933 a conference between the DTPS, the Dublin Master Printers' Association and the Vocational Education Committee was held to make recommendations about the teaching of apprentices in the Bolton Street Technical School. Its report was recorded in the DTPS committee minutes on 24 October and accepted on 7 November. It allowed for twenty-four hours teaching per week for first- and second-year apprentices: twelve hours practical printing; five on design and history of printing; one on arithmetic; and three hours each for English and Irish.

The tenor of the DTPS's politics was always somewhat radical, tending towards Gaelic republicanism (35 Gardiner Street was the headquarters of the Dublin Brigade of the IRA during 1920–21 — there was always a cons- tant flow of members coming and going, which covered the assembly of the IRA men). However when the Gaelic League approached the Society in 1931 with the suggestion that 25 per cent of the apprenticeship vacan- cies be set aside for native speakers from the Gaeltacht it met with a polite refusal.[68] The Society wanted all apprentices to be the sons of members; a census of apprentices reported on 2 December 1930 revealed that only 50 out of 130 were members' sons. The University Press was the centre of a controversy over this in 1931. On 3 January the FOC Charlie Keogh was told that an upcoming vacancy there was to be for a member's son. This was challenged by Gibbs through the DMPA, but the Society reiterated on 10 March that the boy nominated by the firm was not acceptable. It also decreed on 23 March that if Gibbs's choice was placed in the caseroom he was not to be recognised by members. This apprentice was in fact placed and some staff at the DUP had to be summoned before the committee on 16 June to explain why they had recognised him. They pleaded ignorance, an unlikely explanation given the elaborate channels of communication within the Society. After a meeting with the DMPA the apprentice was allowed to stay on the understanding that the next vacancy was to be filled by a member's son. In the interim a conciliation meeting had been held with the employers' association on 9 April where it was agreed that mem- bers' sons would alternate with owners' choices. It was also agreed on a mode of examination whereby suitable candidates would be chosen for a panel from which apprentices could be drawn.

According to the DTPS *Constitution* of 1928 the following ratios of apprentices to men were permitted:

Case	Machine
1:2	1:2
2:6	2:5
3:9	3:7
4:16	4:12
5:24	5:16
6:30	6:20 and over
7:35	
8:50	
9:70 and over	

68. IPU: DTPS EC mins, 31 June 1931; *Irish Printer* (July 1931) 3.

The DTPS apprentice registers give the following names for the University Press in the early 1920s: John Cuthbertson, Ross Mahon and Edward Wilcox — all case; and Charles Keogh — machine. The only date given for registration, 2 April 1924, was that for Wilcox. There were certainly more apprentices at the Press, but their names were not recorded here. It is known from the DTPS committee minutes that James F. Coleman probably registered in 1926 and John Maher on 24 August 1928.[69] The recurrence of certain names — Pasley, Mahon, Maher, Connolly — among the apprentices over the years points to the loyalty of the staff.

At the end of each apprentice's time, on the day he received his first wages as a journeyman, there would be a traditional noisy 'knock-down' on the factory floor with everyone banging stones with mallets or clanging chases to signal his 'coming of age'. Afterwards another tradition took place — a 'lash-in' in the local pub, Cosmo House, at the corner of Hawkins' and Townsend Streets. There is little evidence of any other socialising by the staff. On 10 July 1928 the chapel was granted a room at the DTPS premises to hold a prize-draw which indicates a small undercurrent of activity, but there was no annual 'wayzgoose' as in other houses in the city. This may in part be attributable to Gibbs's parsimony. Even for the bicentenary of the DUP in 1934 he would not spend any money on celebrations. It was left to the College to host a lecture on the history of the Press by Dr T.P.C. Kirkpatrick,[70] and articles on it appeared in *The Irish Times* and *Trinity News*.

From the remaining account books of the Press the following picture of its suppliers emerges.[71] Wiggins, Teape & A. Pirie was the major source for paper. Charles Morgan was another although the quantities bought decreased throughout the 1930s. It is Jimmy Stewart's recollection that England and Germany were the main sources for the Press's purchases. Small quantities were bought from the local Swiftbrook mill, but it was much more expensive than the imports. Early in 1932 Gibbs wrote to Terence De Vere White, then secretary of the College Historical Society, in response to a request for a quotation for the Society's stationery on Irish-made paper. It proved to be two to three times more expensive than for imported paper.[72] The Press sold its waste-paper in 1932 to John Irwin at £1 per ton, and in 1933 to M. Duan & Co. at 7-6 per ton for what was obviously a different quality. Among works pulped at this period were Crawley's *Handbooks*, and R.F.S. Crook's and J. Rice's classical textbooks.

69. IPU: DTPS EC mins, 25 Oct. 1932, Coleman enrolled as apprentice member in the last six months of his time; 4 Sept. 1928, noting Maher's registration.

70. Reported in *Irish Printer* (Sept. 1934) 3; the lecture was almost wholly based on what Philip White had written.

71. Principally MUN/DUP/1/10, 12; ibid./4/1; ibid./5/1, *passim*.

72. MUN/DUP/9/2/397, 1 Feb. 1932.

Miller & Richard was the chief source of type throughout the 1920s, while in the early 1930s small quantities were supplied by H.W. Caslon & Co., Stephenson, Blake & Co., and locally by William Miller & Sons. The quantities of founder's type were of course diminishing as the Intertypes were put to use. This pattern was reflected in the estimates sent out at the time: those for the 1920s continue to refer to the type size by name — brevier, long primer etc. — while for the 1930s point sizes predominated. Fry's Metal Foundry in London supplied the Intertype metal which cost £1-6-0 per cwt in 1931. Fry also bought old metal from the Press, paying 9-0 to 19-0 per cwt for dross and £1-10-0 to £1-14-0 per cwt for old founder's type. The DUP was not large enough to justify having its own stereotyping plant and William Miller & Sons provided this service for it, as also electrotyping. Quoins were purchased from Millers and steel furniture from John Murlos & Co. Ink came from Shackell, Edwards & Co. and from Raines & Porter.

As was always the case in the history of the Press, in periods of pressure it sent out work to be typeset or printed. Robert T. White and Droughts were two firms used by the DUP in this period. On 16 April 1932 there is a charge from White for setting twenty-one galleys of matter on an Intertype.[73] No doubt pressure of exam papers forced this situation. Droughts provided any rule work that needed to be done. The Press had no rolling press so the local firm of Cherry & Smalldridge provided plates and intaglio printing for it, as well as the occasional lithography. The DUP used to charge its customers a 10 per cent handling fee on these services. Relief blocks came from the Irish Photo-Engraving Co., the Irish Artistic Engraving Co. and the Premier Engraving Co. From an account with the latter we have the only piece of evidence of what half-tones cost at this period; on 30 August 1932 it charged 11*d.* per square inch. This must have been considered expensive because the firm went to extensive trouble during the period 1925–26, when a second edition of George Coffey's *Celtic antiquities* was being contemplated, to track down the eighteen full-page plates used in the original edition printed by W. & G. Baird in Belfast in 1909.[74] There is evidence of only one binder in the period 1930–1935 — Caldwell & Son of South Frederick Street just south of the College. The *Irish Printer* for August 1932 records the death of the proprietor Robert Caldwell on 6 April, at the age of 74. He was an alumnus of Trinity which in the normal course of things no doubt had a bearing on his choice as binder by the Press.

---

73. MUN/DUP/5/1/112, 16 Apr. 1932; £12-18-0 was charged for setting and £6-11-8 for the metal.
74. MUN/DUP/9/2/68, 94, 255, 25 Nov. 1925 to Bairds, 22 Apr. 1926 to RIA, 27 Nov. 1928 to Hodges, Figgis & Co.

Estimate books for the period 1932–1942 have survived for the Press,[75] but it is impossible to establish any tables of charges from them because of the number of variables involved and the way the figures are quoted. Charges for composition are given by the sheet, the page or just a blanket amount; those for presswork are set out by the sheet, the forme or again a blanket sum. What can be seen from these and other account books is that charges remained remarkably stable during the period 1926–1943, mirroring the stability in labour costs. Throughout this time the DUP charged for Intertype composition at 7-6 to 8-0 per hour, hand composition at 3-3 to 4-0 and presswork at 5-0 to 5-3. Machine setting was dearer because the hourly charge had to reflect the cost of the expensive plant involved, but because it was much faster jobs set on it were actually cheaper. On 20 September 1924 Gibbs quoted Dr L.C. Purser for composing a 52-page pamphlet of Latin inscriptions. Machine set it would have cost £47-12-6; hand set it would have been 40 per cent dearer at £66-16-6.[76] The same estimate books give some insight into the operation of the presses. In January 1934 four hours was estimated for machining a job of 500 copies, or five hours for 1,000. This would indicate that the press ran at 500 copies per hour and that three hours were allowed for make-ready and removal. This latter allowance was confirmed by an estimate in July of the same year of four hours to print 1,000 copies and five hours for 2,000; the press in this case was obviously twice as fast.[77] No half-hours were allowed for in estimates — everything was in round hours. This policy must have been general to the trade and was reflected in the overtime payments to the men, which the DTPS insisted were to be calculated in round hours.

The estimate books reveal that for non-trade customers an additional 5 per cent was charged; this was increased to 11 per cent in 1939. Where the Press supplied paper for a job it was charged to the customer at 25 per cent above the price at which it had been bought. There is occasional evidence of charges for standing type. For example in 1932 Gilbert Waterhouse was charged 10 per cent of the composition costs of Van der Stel's *Journal* for keeping it standing after it had been printed off. Another account book provides the odd entry for charges for storage of works printed by the Press. The County Kildare Archaeological Society was debited with 8-4 for storage of its journals in May 1927.[78] The same account book has one of the most detailed breakdowns of the production charges for a book during this period and for this reason is worth setting out in full:

75. MUN/DUP/4/1–2.

76. MUN/DUP/9/1/963.

77. MUN/DUP/4/1/35, 55.

78. MUN/DUP/1/10/49.

23 April 1927 — 250 Representative Church Body *Report*, 182p.

$11\frac{5}{8}$ sheets at £5-18-6 per sheet [comp and printing]	£68-17- 6
35 pages of plain brevier at 4-6 per page	7-17- 6
76 and a half pages of plain tabular at 9-0	34- 8- 6
39 and a half pages tables brevier at 13-4	26- 6- 8
5 pages tables extra large at 17-2	4- 5-10
Half page nonpareil at 16-2	8- 1
1 page table at £1-4-3	1- 4- 3
1 page table at £1-12-4	1-12- 4
	145- 0- 8
Proofs	12- 3- 6
Alterations	30- 8- 0
Cancel made	42-11- 4
	230- 3- 6
Paper	5- 0- 6
Cover	1-10- 6
Binding	3- 0- 5
	239-14-11

Throughout the 1920s and 1930s, and certainly earlier although there is no documentary evidence, the Press set exotic type for other printers who did not have these faces in stock and rented it to them. Small amounts of Anglo-Saxon, Greek and music were recorded as having been composed for Thoms, Droughts and Cahills, while in 1931 Cahill commissioned 137 hours of music setting.[79] All these were hand set and the type would have been returned for dissing when printed off. The Press was not the only source used by the Dublin trade for such setting. On 25 June 1931 the DTPS executive considered the matter as to why the music for the forth-coming Eucharistic Congress hymn book, then being printed by the Juverna Press, had been set in England. The committee came to no reso-lution and the matter was left in abeyance. At this remove in time one can speculate that a sectarian motive was involved for not giving the work to the DUP and that the Society had not the courage to challenge it.

Some idea of the pattern of production at the Press can be had from a series of jobbing books that document about 20 per cent of the output in the period 1930–1965.[80] Although not comprehensive they do show the peaks and valleys of printing. Take 1931 for example: in January £148 worth of business was recorded; February £179; March £153; April £544; May £175; June £210; July £173; August £27; September £185; October £165; November £164; December £75. As formerly exam papers

79. MUN/DUP/1/6/405 ff., 1926 onwards; MUN/DUP/1/7/521 ff., 1931; MUN/DUP/1/8/519 ff.
80. MUN/DUP/3/1–9.

made up a large portion of Trinity's business. The complaints of previous years as to the cost of printing these are not in evidence, but on 7 February 1925 the board recorded its dissatisfaction with the 'disorderly arrangement' of the pamphlets of exam papers, and ordered Gibbs to recall them from the bookshops and to reissue them at his own expense. It was a constant battle to get examiners to return the proofs in good time, so much so that the board decreed on 26 November 1927, no doubt on foot of complaints from Gibbs, that two clear days were to be afforded to the Press to print them off and in the case of honor papers a much longer time. The DUP's reputation in this specialist area continued beyond the College and commissions were received from the Bank of Ireland, the civil service, the Dublin Port and Docks Board, the Great Southern Railways and the County Dublin Libraries' Committee among others.

The printing of the College *Calendar* seldom created any problems, but there were complaints from the board late in 1923 about its distribution. Entries for 1 December 1923 and 2 February 1924 would suggest that the payment of commission on complimentary copies was at the root of the trouble. Henceforth all copies of the *Calendar* and of the examination paper pamphlets were to be delivered to J.H. Shaw, assistant to the registrar, who would distribute them to the University booksellers and also sell them in his office. The College's discontent with the service provided by its booksellers led to the appointment of a committee of investigation on 9 February 1924. It considered the provision of stocks of undergraduate texts, proper publicity for the books printed at the expense of the College, and the returns on such books. The committee reported a week later that the booksellers took reasonable care in anticipating undergraduate demand and that the annual accounts on TCD-sponsored books were sufficient. As regards publicity for the latter the committee recommended that a member of staff interested in each publication be appointed by the board to liaise with the publisher to secure the best exposure. There is no indication that this recommendation was ever implemented.

The cost of printing *Hermathena* continued to rise during this period peaking at £305 in 1932. The edition size was 350 copies so the unit production cost was about 17-6; a retail copy of this issue sold by the Press was charged at 6-0.[81] The board continued to sanction the heavy subvention involved and without any of the complaints of former years. It did however cast around for other sources for this subvention. During the 1920s the board started to use the surplus from the Madden Fund to underwrite suitable publications. The fund was set up following a bequest from Samuel Molyneux Madden, who died in 1782, to provide a prize for unsuccessful candidates for fellowship; the surplus could be used for 'the direct advancement of education, study, or research' within

81. MUN/DUP/1/7/131–2, 445–6.

the College.[82] On 30 April 1926 the board granted £100 from this fund towards the cost of a supplementary volume to *Hermathena*, G.W. Mooney's *Index to the Pharsalia of Lucan*. Although there were no explicit complaints in the board minutes about the cost of printing the journal at the Press there must have been some underlying discontent because Alton, the editor, was given permission on 22 May to accept the estimate for printing this issue from the 'Emprimerie Sainte Catherine, Bruges'. It, and the second supplementary volume in the same year, Edward Gwynn's edition of the *Rule of Tallaght*, were printed there.

During the latter half of the 1920s the bursar Robert Russell continued to harry the Press for reductions in the costs for College printing. In 1928 he turned his attention to the production of entries for the library's Accessions' Catalogue. This catalogue, which was closed in 1964, consists of hundreds of guard books in which individual entries were pasted in alphabetical order. Certain secondary entries were necessary, as for joint authors, and a subject file was also maintained, but it is a wonder that it was considered necessary to print them when three or four duplicates of each entry were the most that were needed. None the less the Printing House was supplying twenty-five copies of each sheet of entries at a cost of £2-19-0 per sheet. On 10 April 1928, following representations from the librarian, Alfred de Burgh, and from the bursar, Gibbs quoted 18-0 per galley for the catalogue, each galley containing half the number of entries of a sheet. In March of the following year he reduced this figure to 10-6 per galley, almost a third of the price of a year previously.[83] This commission did not stay long thereafter with the Press. Cyril Bedford has told me that it is his recollection that when he joined the library's staff in 1942 these catalogue entries were set in the library itself from a small fount of type and printed off on a tiny rotary hand-press. Later still the entries were produced on a typewriter and duplicated by stencil.

1926 saw the printing of an edition of the *Consolidated statutes* of the College and the University. The foundation of the Free State in 1922 was the impetus for this and a committee sat over several years redrafting them. On 3 May 1924 it was reported to the board that Ponsonby & Gibbs's charges so far, including those for standing type, had been £283-12-4, of which £150 had been paid on 6 November 1922. Final approval for the text was given on 20 April 1926 and they came into effect on 1 July. The volume contains 191 pages and 1,000 copies were printed at a cost of £560-17-7.[84]

The College had an edition of William O'Donnell's Irish translation of the New Testament, edited by J.E.H. Murphy, printed in 1928,

82. Regulation III (b) as set out in the College calendars.

83. MUN/DUP/9/2/59, 212, 218, 272, 11 Nov. 1925, 28 Feb., 10 Apr. 1928, 21 Mar. 1929.

84. MUN/DUP/1/4/150, 30 June 1926.

'cló-bhuailte le Cló Choláiste na Trínóide', one of the rare occurrences when the Press's imprint appeared in Irish. It was a substantial volume running to 479 pages. This work was first sanctioned by the board on 28 June 1902 when Robert Atkinson was named as editor, but on 23 May following Murphy was appointed in his stead.

Four volumes of the Dublin University Press series were printed in the period under consideration, two original and two reprints. Towards the end of 1930 George W. Mooney's edition of Suetonius' *De vita Caesarum* was issued in an edition of 500 copies, for which Gibbs charged £548-6-0 including the binding of 150 copies.[85] It was a late decision to include this in the series — the board gave its sanction on 11 October and provided £200 from the Madden Fund towards its cost a week later — and as a consequence there is no series title in the text. It was however bound uniformly with the rest of the series.

The Madden Fund also provided the money to print Simon Van der Stel's *Journal of his expedition to Namaqualand 1685–86* edited by Gilbert Waterhouse. The manuscript of this disappeared from the archives of the Dutch East India Company in 1691–92 and was rediscovered by Waterhouse in 1922 among the Fagel archives in the College library. Gibbs charged £250 for the edition of 500 on 23 May 1932 and a further £22 for alterations.[86] The editor evidently expected this to be a good seller and as has been seen the text was kept standing. In fact it was a slow seller, as Jimmy Stewart recalls, because it was poorly advertised and was not jointly published in Holland, its main potential market. Copies did begin to sell when they were marketed to the Dutch troops stationed in Britain during the Second World War. Waterhouse was evidently dissatisfied with the text and wanted to have it reprinted, but the board refused on 13 January 1934 to grant £30 for the correction and proofing of the standing type. A supplementary pamphlet was printed nearly two decades later, in 1953, giving the addenda and corrigenda.

The reprints in the series included inevitably Burnside and Panton's *Theory of equations*. In November 1927 Gibbs charged £74-8-6 for printing 2,000 copies of the ninth edition of volume one from plates. Interestingly when it came to reprinting the seventh edition of volume two in the following year the commission was given to Aberdeen University Press. The fact that Russell, together with Matthew Fry, had been appointed by the board as the panel to decide on the publication may explain the decision to send it abroad. Gibbs suffered the indignity of having to crate the stereotype plates and dispatch them to Scotland.[87]

85. MUN/DUP/1/7/135, 30 Nov. 1930.

86. MUN/DUP/1/4/185–7, 11, 23 May, 21 June 1932.

87. MUN/DUP/1/4/172 ff., 13 Nov. 1927; MUN/V/5/23, board register 19 Mar. 1927; MUN/DUP/1/6/405 ff., 7 May 1928.

Such College publications were used for exchanges with learned institutions abroad; the board register during 1931–32 notes such arrangements with bodies in Chile and Finland. It was important therefore for the prestige of Trinity to have a respectable selection of works. Given the slender number of its own publications the board achieved this by granting money towards College-related works issued by other bodies. An example of this would be the grants made to the RIA towards an edition of the mathematical works of William Rowan Hamilton — £100 from the Madden Fund was sanctioned on 8 June 1929 and a further £100 on 1 May 1935. It was first suggested to the board by one of the editors, J.L. Synge, on 19 March 1927 that this work be published by the College. He was instructed to seek estimates from the OUP, CUP and Clark of Edinburgh, but when these were considered on 7 May they were felt to be too high to proceed. Another example was the £50 granted on 8 March 1933 to Jessop and Luce towards the cost of printing their bibliography of the works of George Berkeley.

After the College itself the RIA provided the largest amount of business, both recurrent and single commissions. Its *Proceedings* were printed off in editions of 600–700 copies, bringing in a monthly income of up to £100 when several had been produced in that period. Another recurrent work was T.F. O'Rahilly's *Catalogue of Irish manuscripts*, issued in XXVI fascicules between 1926 and 1942, each costing well over £100.[88] Among the single bookwork orders was R.I. Best and O. Bergin's edition of *Lebor na huidre* issued in 1929. It ran to 340 pages with the Irish text set in roman type; 500 ordinary and 20 thick paper copies were printed at a cost of over £1,000.[89] One of the Academy's commissions resulted in a bad debt in this period. On 22 July 1924 Gibbs wrote to R. Macalister of the RIA to say that composing had begun on an unspecified work by C.J. Joly in 1909 and that some sheets had been printed off, but that others remained in standing type. He sought a reply within a fortnight as to whether the work was to proceed; otherwise he would have the type broken up. This provides another example of the huge amount of capital the University Press had tied up in standing matter, an investment that few commercial houses would have had. The Academy apparently decided not to have the work printed and on 21 December 1927 paid £50 of the £72-17-6 owed on it; the remainder was written off, no doubt amicably, as a bad debt.[90]

Another recurrent contract was provided by the Incorporated Council of Law Reporting whose monthly *Law reports* brought in £70–£80 a time. The return on this had to be reduced in 1927 after representations from

88. MUN/DUP/1/6/185, MUN/DUP/1/7/185–6, MUN/DUP/1/185–6,
      MUN/DUP/4/2, 1942; for original estimate of £8-13-6 per sheet see
      MUN/DUP/9/2/46, 8 July 1925.

89. MUN/DUP/1/6/173, MUN/DUP1/7/173.

90. MUN/DUP/9/1/955, MUN/DUP/1/6/51.

the Council and Gibbs conceded 15-0 per octavo sheet.[91] The APCK also provided recurrent business in the form of a series of twenty-five 'Penny pamphlets for Irish churchmen' issued in 1928.

A few books were issued under the University Press's own imprint, such as T.P.C. Kirkpatrick's *History of Doctor Steevens' Hospital Dublin* (1924) and C.H.P. Price's *Thoughts on things eternal* (1927), yet Gibbs continued to avoid becoming too involved in publication. In a letter of 25 July 1931 to A.A. Luce, quoting for the printing of two sermons by George Berkeley, Gibbs added: 'I could not undertake the <u>publication</u>, which would be better done through some well known publishing firm.' He went on to suggest the OUP.[92]

George Gavan Duffy's *Digest of criminal and quasi-criminal law* printed in 1925 provides interesting insights into the operation of the Press on several fronts. From information supplied by the author Gibbs estimated in October 1924 that the work would need 270 octavo pages, which he stated would take four weeks to set and proof, and a further four to print and bind. This was the estimate for an edition of 500 copies. In the event it was decided to print 700 copies on ordinary paper and a further 200 on thin paper because at 564 pages plus a long index the book proved more bulky than anticipated. The final proofs were ready on 10 April 1925; at the same time Gibbs quoted an approximate price of £650, to include alterations. When the author got the final bill which included £107 for alterations — he had obviously changed the manuscript heavily at proof stage — he challenged Gibbs over the charge in a letter of 14 February 1926, quoting some advice he had had. Gibbs replied rather testily on the 17th, explaining the costs per hour charged by the Press and finishing: 'It is not likely that your adviser was in a position to give even an approximate estimate of the total time required to make the alterations.' Gavan Duffy may well not have been satisfied with this as a bad debt of £20 was registered against him for 1927.[93]

One of the few works of literature printed during this period was issued in 1932. On 25 February Oliver St John Gogarty was charged £1 for printing 100 copies of his poem, 'Leda and the swan'.[94] This poem appeared in the *Atlantic Monthly* of March 1932, and the colophon of the DUP printing assigned the copyright to that magazine. In January 1934 Gibbs estimated for printing editions of 500 and 1,000 of R.L. Praeger's *Botanist in Ireland*. For each sheet of the smaller edition he quoted £7 for composition, £1-1-0 for presswork and 6-0 for paper, a total of £8-7-0 per

91. MUN/DUP/1/7/107 ff.; MUN/DUP/9/2/153, 31 Mar. 1927, to Dr A.D. Bolton.

92. MUN/DUP/9/2/369; these sermons may be Jessop and Luce, no. 680, printed in J. Wild's *George Berkeley* (Cambridge, Mass. 1936).

93. MUN/DUP/9/1/968, 971, 10, 15 Oct. 1924; MUN/DUP/9/2/27, 83, 10 Apr. 1925, 17 Feb. 1926; MUN/DUP/1/2/81, 1927.

94. MUN/DUP/1/7/521 ff.

sheet. For the edition double that size the cost was only £8-18-6 per sheet: composition was the same, presswork took only an extra hour, adding 5-3, and the paper cost was double. Praeger was tempted by these figures and opted for the larger edition.[95] It is interesting to note the minor element that paper now constituted in the cost of printing, a reversal from the days of the common press and cheap labour when it made up over 50 per cent of the cost.

Gibbs's partner in the business, trading as 'Edward Ponsonby, bookseller and publisher of 116 Grafton Street', had been made a private limited company in 1910 under the name E. Ponsonby Ltd, the first directors being William and Cyril Ponsonby, and Andrew Frew. The senior partner in the firm, William Ponsonby, described as 'Dublin's oldest bookseller' in the *Irish Printer* in 1910, died in 1912 at the age of 93.[96] The Printing House continued to be the warehouse for the firm's stock — including Vanston's *Local government, Municipal government* and *Public health*, and Nolan's *Law of poor rate in Ireland* — and the University Press sold them on its behalf, taking 10 per cent commission. Major customers were John Falconer, Frederick Price, Easons and Thoms.[97] Gibbs continued to provide this service even after he bought out Ponsonby's share of the printing business in August 1931. He paid £7,350 for the share and £2,335 for the goodwill.[98]

1935–1944

On 12 January 1935 the board approved the renewal of the Printing House lease for five years from 1 October 1934 on the existing conditions. Gibbs continued to trade under the name Ponsonby and Gibbs so the lease was in the firm's name. However when the next lease, on the same terms, was sanctioned on 5 July 1939 the board insisted that it was 'to be personal to Mr John Talbot Gibbs and not transferable to heirs and assignees'. The College was conscious that Gibbs was coming to the end of his working life and was obviously afraid of having no veto over some undesirable tenant, a fear that was to resurface at the end of the next tenant's tenure.

There is no evidence of major work being carried out on the building, beyond having it rewired early in 1939. Gibbs had obviously neglected his maintenance obligations under the lease and in a fit of activity as the renewal loomed had sixty-seven broken windows replaced. Evidence of investment in machinery is equally scant, except for oblique references to repairs on Summit, Meihle and Falcon presses during the 1930s.[99]

95. MUN/DUP/4/1/35, 2 Jan. 1934; MUN/DUP/1/7/441, 22 Nov. 1934.

96. *Irish Printer* (Aug. 1910) 14; (Nov. 1912) 9.

97. MUN/DUP/1/7/113–14, 521; MUN/DUP/1/8/251–6.

98. MUN/DUP/1/2/7, 1 Aug. 1931, 12 Mar. 1932.

99. MUN/DUP/5/1/540, 546, 18 Feb., 28 Mar. 1939, work done by J. Richardson; MUN/DUP/5/1/172, 408, 28 Jan. 1933, Nov. 1936.

This lack of investment did not reflect the state of the trade in general, which throughout the 1930s because of the tariffs on imports was buoyant. Employment in the industry increased from 4,353 to 4,966 in the period 1931–1935, and wages from £622,000 to £722,000.[100] This of course led to a shortage of skilled workers and cards from other typographical societies were readily accepted by the DTPS. When the market was saturated the Society withdrew the recognition on 23 September 1935. As a long-term solution it agreed on 27 May 1935 to allow an emergency batch of sixteen apprentices, twelve case and four machine, to join the trade. There is no evidence that the DUP took advantage of this release or indeed that it needed to; it did not benefit noticeably from the boom. The confidence within the trade was manifest in the production of *Progress in Irish printing* (Dublin 1936), a fairly lavish monograph containing articles on the history of the craft in Ireland, and sponsored by trade advertisements at the beginning and end. There was one perennial criticism in it however: George Russell's observations of 1926 were re-echoed in the foreword by F.R. Higgins. He castigated the printers for the low standard of most bookwork, styling their output as 'the imprint of the cloven hoof', and advocated the employment of 'typographical artists' as the solution.

Had the trade remained buoyant there was the likelihood that typographic standards would have improved. However the ending in 1938 of the 'economic war' that was spawned by the imposition of tariffs and the beginning of the Second World War threw the trade into disarray. In February 1939 the *Irish Printer* reported that unemployment in the trade was six times that of previous years. The University Press was not immune from the fall-out. On 15 April 1940 an application to the DTPS from a final-year apprentice, Victor Smith, to be allowed to practise on the Intertypes during dinner hour was refused, 'owing to the number of unemployed men available'. (This would suggest that copy used for practice was an actual job being printed at the Press.) And as ever in times of recession overtime could only be worked with the permission of the Society. This was particularly hard on the DUP because of the specialist composing skills required. The FOC, William Abbott, made application on 5 May 1941 for permission to work overtime on exam papers, citing this difficulty of finding men skilled in setting the different languages. He was instructed to put a notice in the 'Unemployed Room' seeking comps to set Irish, but that if there were not enough replies, then overtime could be worked.

So acute did the labour situation become that a 'rotational employment scheme' was suggested by the unemployed chapel of the DTPS in 1940. The idea was to even out employment among the

---

100. Official government figures quoted in *Irish Printer* (Feb. 1937) 13.

members of the trade; those employed would work fewer hours, and were paid accordingly, and the hours vacated were to be given to the unemployed. A start was made with the scheme, but it was recorded as operating unsatisfactorily on 22 July 1940. Such rotation would not have suited the specialist nature of the DUP business and so the Press apparently remained aloof from the scheme. Accordingly on 21 July 1941 a delegation from the DTPS was sanctioned to visit Gibbs to make representations on the matter. Unfortunately no report of the meeting was recorded.

Despite the boom in trade in the 1930s there was no great pressure from the DTPS for better conditions of employment. (The true nature of the Society was at last recognised on 12 March 1934 when it decided to register as a trade union.) Through negotiations with the DMPA an extra 5-0 was granted in January 1935, bringing the basic wage to £4-9-0 (£4-14-0 for typesetter operators), and a further 5-0 in 1940. The master printers also conceded *pro rata* increases early in 1937 to the unskilled workers in the trade, who were represented by the ITGWU. A forty-five hour week was successfully negotiated in the same year.[101] These changes had a cumulative effect on the prices charged by the Press, but they did not go unchallenged by the bursar, still at this date the prickly Robert Russell. In a letter to him on 8 December 1937 Gibbs defended his intention to raise the charges for exam papers (from other sources we know it was by 5 per cent), stating that they were 'quite reasonable in view of the increased cost of production due to the introduction in October of the forty-five hour week'. The College took what must have been retaliatory action by charging the Press £5 for a one-third page advertisement in the next *Register of electors*, and also deducting £3-15-0 from the payment due for the printing because of some mistakes in other advertisements. All this is known from a letter Gibbs wrote on 15 January 1938 complaining about this action; he stated that a half-page advertisement in the 1933 *Register* cost only £3 and that the deduction 'seems excessive'.[102] The only other increase in wages in the period under consideration was 16-0 (17 per cent) granted as an 'emergency bonus' during 1942–45 and which brought the basic wage to £5-10-0.

From a surviving record book we are afforded a picture of the operation of the caseroom during 1940–44.[103] It recorded the time spent per day composing various jobs, breaking it down into hand composing, machine setting or that done by the apprentices; also the time spent on alterations. Most jobbing was hand-set while bookwork was normally done on the machines. Mathematical bookwork was an exception to this pattern as the Intertypes could not cope with the formulae, and so items

101. *Irish Printer* (Feb. 1935) 1; (Feb. 1937) 20; (Oct. 1937) 4; see also note 37.

102. MUN/DUP/9/2/653, 656.

103. MUN/DUP/8/6, 13 Sept. 1940 – 5 May 1944.

like Shrodinger's paper for the RIA *Proceedings* in 1941 involved a lot of hand-setting. As many as twenty jobs were being set in any week and up to ten in any one day. The volume also provides a total of hours worked for each week and these varied widely. For example in the week ending 21 February 1941 61 hours were spent setting, a further 16 on alterations and none by the boys — a total of 77 hours or the equivalent of less than two full comps. With perhaps a dozen comps in the caseroom no wonder they used to stand round the pot-bellied stove in winter waiting for copy to be given out. During the exam season in the week ending 16 May 1941 257.5 hours were spent setting, 19 on alterations and 46 hours were put in by the apprentices — a total of 324.5 hours or work for just over 7 comps working flat out.

During the slack times of the war years the men in the caseroom used to play 'jeffers' and 'push-halfpenny' on the stones. 'Jeffers' was a common game in the trade. It was a form of dice where seven em quads were thrown and the winner was the player who had the most nicks facing up. 'Push-halfpenny' was like table-top football, with a halfpenny coin acting as the ball, lengths of furniture as the means of striking and quads used for the goal-mouths. The smooth surface of the stone provided the ideal pitch.

The DTPS apprentice registers give the following names and starting dates for the DUP during this period:

Victor Smith	case	[1933?]
Thomas Murren	machine	6 April 1935: 'left trade'
Duke Barnett	case	24 August 1935
Edward Smith	machine	18 September 1939
Samuel Styles	case	October 1940
Frederick Maybury	case	July 1943

Fred Maybury told me that he was the last indentured apprentice at the Press, if not in the whole printing trade in Dublin.

Murren was at the centre of an incident in 1938 which led on 22 August to the entire chapel of the University Press attending a meeting of the DTPS executive. The apprentice had been sent home and threatened with dismissal by the machine-room overseer, J. Byrne, for hitting Peter Redmond, a labourer at the Press. Members of the chapel testified that Redmond had been taunting the boy for a long time and had written 'scab' on his machine, which was the direct cause of the incident. It transpired that the labourer had also been insulting to other members of the staff, so much so that a letter of complaint had been written to his union. The executive decided to write to the DMPA about the matter — one wonders why not directly to Gibbs — to have Redmond checked. The DTPS executive minutes for 29 August record that after a meeting with the DMPA Gibbs insisted that Redmond apologise to the father of the chapel; 'it was hoped that harmony would now prevail'. It is not clear if Murren was actually dismissed and that this incident was the cause of his leaving the trade.

As well as Wiggins, Teape & A. Pirie the major suppliers of paper during the 1930s and early 1940s were Spicers Ltd and Spalding & Hodge; Baddeley Bros Ltd supplied card from 1938 onwards. The effects of the War on the supply of paper were as they had been during that of 1914–18 — scarcity, reduced quality and increased cost. The bursar antici-pated this by buying in over a ton of paper for the *Calendar* in September 1940. However in 1942 when the Minister of Supplies asked for a return of paper used in the *Calendar* and *Hermathena* the board decided on 13 May not to publish a full *Calendar* for 1942–43 (or for 1943–44; a full issue was restored in 1944–45) and to reduce the length of *Hermathena* by a half. From 1941 onwards Gibbs was charging extra to cover the increased cost of paper while Allied Paper Merchants (formerly Charles Morgan & Co.) was recorded as supplying 'Emergency' paper in April 1942.

The Press bought very little founder's type during these years as the setting became more and more concentrated on the Intertypes. There were constant purchases of matrices for these, DeVinne being the fav-oured display face and Old Style the text face. There were also orders for matrices for 8 and 10 pt greek, 4.5 pt gaelic and 10 pt fractions. The greek mats were for signs in mathematical setting and not as supplements to an existing greek magazine. Although the Intertype was easier to handle relative to the Monotype — which may have been the initial reason for its choice at the Press — the keyboard was not large enough to take the range of sorts needed for complicated setting. As a consequence the Press did not have the facility for the machine setting of Greek until it acquired a Monotype in the 1950s (and even then it took over a decade to acquire a greek die-case). Fry's Metal Foundry continued to be the supplier of the metal for the typesetters and also bought back the dross and old founder's type, now paying up to £1-8-6 per cwt for the former and £2-1-0 for the latter.

William Miller & Son did stereotyping for the Press, as for example in February 1942 when it charged 2-0 per page to provide plates of H.H. Dixon's *Practical plant biology*. This was for the second edition of this work, all the copies of the first edition having been destroyed in a bombing raid on London.[104] On 17 June 1935 the DTPS granted an application from the APCK for permission to print prayer books from imported plates; this printing may well have been done by the DUP. The union seldom greeted such requests so favourably. When the Fodhla Press sought such permission on 31 May 1932 it was told that the work

104. MUN/DUP/4/1/311, 11 Feb. 1942; MUN/V/5/25, board register 1 Oct. 1941, giving £150 from the Madden Fund to reprint it; MUN/DUP/1/9/353, Jan. 1943, charge of £232 for printing 750 copies.

had to be set and proofed by the Fodhla workers, and that then the plates could be used. A superfluous concession, but the Society was adamant that this was to be the procedure in all similar cases.

In April 1935 the *Irish Printer* reported that the Glenside Printing Ink Company had been founded recently, with a guaranteed loan of £4,000 from the government, in order to provide a domestic source of supplies to replace imports. The account books of the University Press show that it did just that; from 1936 onwards it ousted all foreign suppliers. In the same year the Educational Company of Ireland took over from Caldwell as the major binder used by the Press. It also did some ruling, not always efficiently. On 9 July 1936 250 sheets of paper 'destroyed in ruling' were charged against the Company. The Riverside Bindery was another firm occasionally employed, as for example for binding 100 copies of E.H. Dowling's *Instructive arithmetic* in 1939. (The Press's stock-book also shows that nearly half the edition of 8,500 of this work was 'ordered to be used for wrapping 18/7/44'). S.J. Bigger also did ruling work for the DUP at this date. There is not much evidence of work having to be farmed out in busy periods beyond a single reference to the Temple Press being paid £12-7-3 for jobbing work in March 1935.

The Press was sorely hit by the decision of the College's board to issue abridged calendars in 1942 and 1943. The exam papers however continued to provide the 'bread and butter'. As has been mentioned these were increased early in 1938 by 5 per cent after the introduction of the forty-five hour week in 1937, and a further increase of 13 per cent had to be imposed in 1943. The following table shows the prices charged per page for composition:[105]

	1937	1938	1943
English	7-10	8- 3	9- 4
French, German, Latin, Spanish,			
Italian, Dutch	12- 0	12- 7	14- 2
Greek, Irish, Welsh, Saxon	15-11	16- 8	18-10
Mathematics	17- 0	17-10	20- 1
Mixed	12- 5	13- 0	14- 7
Tabular	15-11	16- 8	18-10
Music	30- 3	31- 9	35- 9

The 1943 scale was abandoned almost immediately and surcharges of varying percentages imposed with the College's agreement. There is also evidence in 1942 that Arabic was charged at 31-9 and Assyrian at 16-8 per page.[106]

105. MUN/DUP/8/2 *passim.*
106. MUN/DUP/4/2, 1942.

The rush created by the exam season led to some acrimony over leave in 1937. On 14 May the FOC reported to the DTPS that an Intertype operator, E. Wilcox, was being refused permission to take two days off to compete in the International Ambulance Contest as a member of the St John's Ambulance Association. No outcome was recorded and one can only guess that the union understood the firm's viewpoint. There was some slippage in quality and security control on exam paper production in this period. In April 1935 Gibbs had to apologise to the Civil Service Commission for spoiled copies sent recently and to assure it that a responsible person would check them in future before dispatch. When a leak of the National University of Ireland matriculation papers occurred in 1937 Gibbs was quick to reply to the acting registrar stating it 'was not occasioned by any mistake or carelessness at the University Press'. He went on to describe the precautions taken which are worth quoting in full: 'Every necessary precaution is taken here against any possible "leakage" — the printed sheets being transferred direct from the machine-room to the warehouse keeper's room (no waste or spoiled sheets being kept), where they are carefully counted and packed by thoroughly trustworthy men — for many years in our employment — who know the very particular and confidential nature of the work.' None the less the system did very occasionally break down; a man was sacked in 1939 for taking a paper.[107]

The Madden Fund was pressed into service by the board of the College on 26 November 1941 to pay henceforth for the cost of *Hermathena*. The costs were not inconsiderable. When W.A. Goligher had been appointed editor on 16 June 1937 he was instructed that the net cost for two issues was not to exceed £300 per year. At the same time, to boost the revenue, he was given permission to appoint an assistant at £50 per annum plus 10 per cent commission on the advertising space he sold. Goligher kept to his brief and in most years managed to keep within his budget.[108]

The period under consideration was a productive one, relative to those immediately preceding, for publications in the Dublin University Press series: 1936, Aulus Gellius *Noctium Atticarum liber I*, edited by Hazel M. Hornsby; 1939, Daniel, Becclesiensis, *Urbanus magnus*, edited by J.G. Smyly; 1941, R.W. Tate, *Orationes et epistolae Dublinenses (1914–40)*; and 1943, the latter's *Carmina Dublinensia*.

Dr Hornsby, who was on the staff in the library, had chosen Gellius for her doctoral thesis and this edition was the fruit of her research. A detailed estimate for its printing is extant and can be analysed as follows. Gibbs estimated that the manuscript, printed in crown octavo, would take 304 pages or 19 sheets (when printed it came in at 294 pages). The

107. MUN/DUP/9/2/548, 637, 6 Apr. 1935 to Sec. Civil Service Comm., 7 July 1937 to NUI; information from Jimmy Stewart.

108. MUN/DUP/8/2, 1938–50.

introduction in English was allowed at 16 hours per sheet to machine set, and this was charged for at the rate of 8-0 per hour. The Latin text, notes and index, also to be machine set, would take 22, 20 and 18 hours respectively per sheet to set. The Greek interspersed and the make-up were to be done by hand at a cost of 4-0 per hour. The total estimate for composition was £188-4-0. Presswork for the edition of 500 copies was charged at 15-9 per sheet for 19 sheets giving £14-19-3. The work would need 10 reams of paper, at a cost of 14-0 per ream (10-6 plus 33.3 per cent handling): total £7. Half the edition was to be bound, for which Caldwell quoted 11$\frac{1}{2}$d. per copy, which equals £12; to this Gibbs added 25 per cent handling, bringing the total for binding to £15. The grand total came to £225-3-0. From these figures, allowing £30 for the binding of the full edition, it can be worked out that the composition accounted for 78 per cent of the estimate; presswork 6 per cent; paper 3 per cent; and binding 13 per cent. The board approved of the publication on 27 November 1935 and gave Hornsby £225 from the Madden Fund to have it printed. Unusually it allowed her to retain all profits. In most cases the author was asked to return half the profits to the Fund, or to repay the grant from the profits. Gibbs charged £223-16-6 plus £14-18-0 for alterations for the work on 5 October 1936, a total of £238-14-6.[109]

The Madden Fund also paid for Tate's *Orationes*, the board voting £100 for it on 16 October 1940, raised to £170 on 27 November. The reason for the increase was the decision to print each oration on a separate page and not as continuous text. Gibbs provided an original estimate on 5 July 1940, quoting £52-4-0 for an 80-page book in an edition of 100 copies. The alteration in layout took an extra 146 pages and there were heavy alterations. The final cost for the edition, increased to 120, and including £10-10-0 for binding, was £204-6-5.[110]

The RIA *Proceedings* supplied some of the most challenging work undertaken by the Press — and it charged accordingly. For example 950 copies of an 86-page paper by R. Southern, 'The food and growth of brown trout from Lough Derg and the River Shannon' (XLII sect.B no.6), was charged at £134-14-4 on 9 January 1935; an immense amount of tabular matter accounts for the high charge. From another account book of 1942 we know that £9-15-6 was the cost for composition per 16 pages of plain text. This rose to £19-7-6 for mathematical papers.[111] Again these charges would seem to be very high when compared to the composition charges for the Gellius above. One wonders if there was a lot of 'fat' for the Press in these institutional accounts. An estimate provided to the Dublin Institute for Advanced Studies in 1942 may well indicate that there was. On 19 October Gibbs quoted £96-1-6 for printing 500 copies of

109. MUN/DUP/4/1/100, 14 Nov. 1935; MUN/DUP/1/8/485.

110. MUN/DUP/4/2, [1941]; MUN/DUP/1/9/283, 9 July, 23 Sept. 1941.

111. MUN/DUP/1/8/29 ff., 9 Jan. 1935; MUN/DUP/4/1/337, 1942.

a 36-page paper, 'Quantum electrodynamics', by Prof. P.A.M. Dirac. This was obviously queried and on 10 November he provided a new estimate of £79, which proved acceptable. However when the charge was posted on 11 November 1943 the cost was £86-11-6 including £5-19-0 for alterations,[112] a compromise price one might say.

The RDS *Proceedings* was another valuable recurrent account for the Press. In 1935 it charged 14-0 per page for setting the scientific section and 10-6 for the economic section, plus a 5 per cent surcharge for a non-trade customer. By 1942 these prices had risen to 15-8 and 10-7, but the surcharge was now 11 per cent.[113] The value of a recurrent account, especially if standing matter was involved, is encapsulated in an estimate for the Clergy Daughters' School annual reports, given in 1940 to W.F. Pyle. It shows that Gibbs wrote the cost of standing matter off over a number of years and so could provide a lower estimate: 'In consideration of having some of the matter standing in type from previous years, we have made a reduction in the charge for composition of type. This is on the understanding that if our estimate is accepted now the work will be continued with us for a term of five years at least.'[114]

The Irish Texts Society provided some much needed bookwork in this period. 1938 saw the printing of part I of *Lebor Gabála Éreann*, the fifth and final part of which was not issued until 1956. The edition size was 750 and the first part cost £362, part II (1939) £306, part III (1940) £236, and part IV (1941) £402.[115] From the charges for the exam papers noted above it will be seen that the setting of Irish was considered as complicated as the setting of Greek. From figures for 1936 it is known that an operator took 14 hours to machine-set a demy octavo sheet of English and 24 hours to set the same of Irish. Charged at 8-0 per hour this worked out at £5-12-0 per sheet (7-0 per page) for English and £9-12-0 per sheet (12-0 per page) for Irish. In 1938 it took 64 hours to hand-set a demy octavo sheet of long primer irish, and 80 hours if it was brevier. Calculated at 4-0 per hour this works out at £12-16-0 and £16 per sheet, or 16-0 and £1 per page respectively.[116]

The shortages created by the War provided the opportunity for several clear-outs at the Press, mostly type and waste-paper, but among them the sale in 1942 of '3,000 secondhand school books' to the booksellers Fred Hanna Ltd for £15.[117] Why the Press had second-hand stock was not recorded; perhaps it was a euphemism for soiled or out-of-date stock.

112. MUN/DUP/4/1/345, 19 Oct., 10 Nov. 1942; MUN/DUP/1/9/303, 11 Nov. 1943.

113. MUN/DUP/4/1/99, 328–9, Nov. 1935, June 1942.

114. MUN/DUP/4/1/244, 29 Jan. 1940.

115. MUN/DUP/1/8/427, 25 Apr. 1938, 14 Mar. 1939, 4 Feb. 1940, 8 Mar. 1941.

116. MUN/DUP/4/1/119, 15 June 1936, Gordon Quin, *Stair Ercuil*; MUN/DUP/4/1/175, 3 Mar. 1938 for the *NUI Magazine*; this type may well be the Petrie irish face and hence the named rather than the point sizes.

117. MUN/DUP/1/11/221, 16 Nov. 1942.

Jimmy Stewart recalls that there was quite a market in second-hand books in Dublin because of the wartime scarcities. Easons even bought them in to keep trade going.

1925 had seen the establishment of another university press in Ireland — Cork University Press.[118] It was not an academic press in the older sense of having its own printing plant with specialist type stock and skills, as the DUP had. It was in the modern trend of being a publishing house, buying its printing in the commercial trade. And the DUP was one of the printers it used. For example in 1937 it had an edition of *Aratus* edited by W.H. Porter printed there.[119] University College Dublin, as we have seen, never successfully established its own university press although there is evidence that it resented being dependent on the DUP for technical printing. The March 1932 issue of the *Irish Printer* noted the following: 'At a meeting of Convocation of the National University a resolution was passed recommending the establishment at University College, Dublin, of a University Printing Press. The proposer stated they should be independent of the press of another university.' The board of TCD did not seem at all perturbed at these inroads into the small, specialist market that the DUP had carved for itself, perhaps because it made such poor use of the Press's potential. It did not even raise an objection when a company called 'Trinity Press Ltd' proposed to publish a *Dublin University year book*, as was recorded in its minutes for 1 October 1932.

The downturn in the fortunes of the Press is apparent from the following table taken from Gibbs's annual accounts:

	Sales in £	Net Profit /[Loss] in £	%
1935	10,620	1,861	17.5
1936	10,204	1,141	11.2
1937	10,355	1,305	12.6
1938	11,813	1,893	16.0
1939	10,695	1,218	11.4
1940	9,814	549	5.6
1941	9,119	[246]	[2.7]
1942	6,882	[1,593]	[23.1]
1943	7,857	[1,318]	[16.8]

The financial state of the firm remained buoyant until the start of the War. The liquidity ratio of sales to stock climbed to a healthy 9:1 in 1938

118. It was founded by Alfred O'Rahilly, who ran it almost singlehandedly until 1944, even providing finance. It published almost 100 titles in its first 25 years and continues to flourish, having recently established a separate post of University Press Publisher (see J.A. Gaughan, *Alfred O'Rahilly: I, Academic*, Dublin 1986, 82–4: *Irish Printer* (Aug.1991) 9, (Apr. 1992)).

119. MUN/DUP/1/8/187, 5, 6 Feb. 1937; 500 copies cost £232-4-3, and a reprint of 150 titlepages (for a variant issue?) was printed on 6 Feb.

and 1939, but slipped thereafter, dipping to 5:1 in 1942. That year represented the nadir of Gibbs's tenure at the Press. He was forced to borrow from the banks, something he had not done since before the previous war, and owed them £880 at the end of the financial year; this rose to £1,282 in the following year. Even the ratio of current debtors to current creditors, which Gibbs had always kept comfortably at 10:1 or more, was let slip, so that in 1942–43 it was about 2.5:1. With sales dipping and the same wages remaining to be paid his usual mark-up of 100 per cent on labour costs dropped to 40 per cent in 1942.

Gibbs did try and take remedial action. He wrote to the registrar on 23 October 1941 outlining the state of the Press, attributing the decline to the 'increased cost of skilled labour and a shrinking volume of business'. He also mentioned the heavy investment in materials 'purchased in anticipation of shortage of stocks of paper' and pleaded for a reduction in rent.[120] There is no record that the board facilitated him. Gibbs also cut back on staff wages, reducing them to £4,960 in 1943 from a high of £5,649 in 1938. The situation demanded more radical intervention if it was to be reversed. To compound it all he was injured in a fall on his way to lunch one day in 1943 and had to spend a considerable time convalescing. He was getting old and his son Charlie was not suited to take on the business. It was time for a radical change. On 15 November 1943 Gibbs, through his solicitors, informed the College that he had decided to dispose of the business as a going concern. He hoped that the 'principal if not the most' of the staff, including his son, would be retained. (He was loyal to his staff and had a reputation for keeping men on even when the work did not justify it.) He sought the board's opinion on the matter and on offering a ten-year lease. The registrar replied favourably on 24 November with the proviso that the board had to approve of the new tenant.[121] Gibbs then set about finding that person.

120. TCD Board Room files.

121. TCD Board Room files, 15 Nov. 1943, Alfred E. Walker & Son to registrar; 24 Nov. 1943, registrar to Walker & Son.

13
The Allmans: 1944–1976

There was some difficulty in finding a new tenant for the Printing House. Because he was ageing and in poor health Gibbs had left the Press in a poor state; no proper records were being kept and the business was making a loss. A contract that gave priority in printing to Trinity, the antiquity of the building and plant (not to mention of many of the men), and the collapse in profitability at the Press did not make it an attractive proposition to the trade. On top of that was the crippling recession due to the War. Cahills was one company which was approached but showed no interest. Thoms was another. It did an extensive survey of the business and plant, but in the end was willing to tender only for the goodwill. For a company that prided itself on keeping its plant up to date the prospect of taking on the antiquated Printing House was too daunting. The provost of the College, E.H. Alton, was insistent however that printing take place in Trinity.[1]

Early in 1944 the registrar of the College, Kenneth Bailey, approached the Rev. William Brown Allman, an uncle by marriage and also proprietor of the Brunswick Press, about the difficulty. The Rev. Allman had been running the Brunswick Press since 1929, when it had been inherited by his wife from her uncle, George Birney. Allman had retired early from the ministry following an accident which led to him losing a leg. He was a very determined man — in the words of his daughter Liala 'he didn't know the meaning of the word *can't*' — and although he had no training in the printing industry he undertook the business on his wife's behalf (see plate 36a). The same determination must have been a factor in his decision to take on the University Press, but there was also an incentive in the form of a loan of £7,500 for six months at 4.5 per cent per annum being offered by the College to help the tenant buy out Gibbs; there was

---

1. Much of the information in the following chapter is based on conversations with Liala Allman (1976, 1986, 1991), Peter Allman (1988, 1991), Jimmy Stewart (1988), Ned Behan (1989), Des Ryan (1990), John Breslin (1990), G.H.H. Giltrap (1990), Brian Allman (1991), Jim Lawler (1991), Seán Galavan (1991), Franz Winkelmann (1991), Maude Lattimore (1991), Douglas Williams (1991), Fred Maybury (1991), George Hetherington (1991).

(a) *Rev. W. B. Allman*

(b) *Liala Allman*

(c) *Peter Allman*

(d) *Brian Allman*

36. Portraits of the Allman family.

also a guarantee against losses up to £1,000 in the first year.[2] The agreement for sale was drafted on 20 April and included the following conditions: the price was to be the amount of the book debts on 5 May less 7.5 per cent, the value of unfinished work less 7.5 per cent, the value of the paper, and £7,100 cash; type owned by the College was to be retained for its use; certain employees (not stipulated but including Charlie Gibbs and John Corr) were to be retained; and Gibbs was to be indemnified against any claims as the purchaser wanted to retain the name 'Ponsonby & Gibbs'.[3] This agreement was signed by all three parties by 26 April, on which date Trinity made an *ex gratia* payment of £150 to Gibbs 'in part compensation for loss incurred during the period of negotiations for transfer of the University Press and in recognition of his services to the College'.[4] He died a few years later in a tragic accident, drowned while trying to save his daughter off Claremont Strand at Howth, Co. Dublin.

The lease afforded from 1 October 1944 was for ten years at an annual rent of £300, payable half yearly. Amazingly these conditions were to remain unchanged throughout the thirty years of the Allmans' tenure. There was also the stipulation that the College was to have priority in printing at the Press, and there was a clause which allowed it to check the records to see that it did. The lease also recorded a certain weight of greek type that belonged to the College and this had to be accounted for. When the lease came up for renewal in 1955 the Rev. Allman pointed out the absurdity of this clause — type cannot last forever — and insisted it be dropped.[5]

The College and Gibbs had neglected the building so it was a cold, dark and damp Printing House that Allman took over in 1944; one compositor said it had 'the smell of death' about it. And unfortunately it continued to be neglected by TCD throughout the Allmans' tenure — no doubt accounting for the low rent — so that later workmen's recollections of first impressions range from 'antedeluvian' to 'Dickensian'. Internally the Allmans changed it very little and the layout remained much as it was in Gibbs's time: paper store and machine-room in the basement; office and caseroom at ground level; and warehouse on the first floor. The basement continued to be subject to flooding, especially when there were high tides in the Liffey not far away, and duck boards were a permanent fixture on the floor. Under the weight of the tons of sheets and books in the

---

2. DUP/Brunswick Press files (seen April 1991): indenture between TCD and the Rev. W.B. Allman, 25 May 1944; MUN/V/5/26, board register 20 Apr. 1944.

3. TCD Board Room files, 'Agreement for sale of University Press, Trinity College, Dublin'.

4. TCD Board Room files, letter from registrar to Gibbs's solicitors, 26 Apr. 1944; MUN/V/5/26, board register 26 Apr. 1944.

5. Unfortunately I have been unable to trace copies of these leases and the details are based on Miss Allman's recollections; for the conditions in the 1965 lease see p. 344.

wareroom in the 1840 extension the floor used to belly and there were occasional fears that it would collapse. Central heating had been installed in the extensions, but not in the original building. There a big pot-bellied stove in the centre of the floor provided the heat in the Intertype room. It used to get red hot and during the slack periods in winter the men would gather round it, warming themselves until the next copy was handed out by the foreman. And it continued to be, as it always would, a most awkward building for printing, with heavy formes of type and reams of paper having to be hauled up and down stairs. The men however were not offput by the Dickensian conditions but rather intrigued by the antiquity; as Seán Galavan said to me it was like 'walking back in history'. Partly because of this attitude, and partly because of good industrial relations, there was a pleasant atmosphere in the firm.

A sixteen-page schedule attached to the 1944 loan indenture affords a comprehensive picture of the plant and machinery. In the machine-room were five printing presses, all hand-fed and driven by belts from overhead shafts turned by a single electric motor: a quad crown Summit Wharfedale (Wm Dawson & Sons); an SW4 Standard Wharfedale of the 'latest type' (no. 16989); a demy folio Falcon platen (Waite & Saville no. A7839); a double demy Wharfedale (Payne & Sons); and a double royal Wharfedale (Bremner Machine Co. no. 5469). Elsewhere in the building were three hand-presses used for proofing: a royal Columbian press (Clymer & Dixon); a double crown Columbian (Thomas Long); and a royal broadside Harrild Universal proof press. The Columbian press is of nineteenth century American origin, as is apparent from the large eagle which surmounts it, acting as a counterweight and giving it its popular name 'the Eagle Press'.[6] Of the two at the DUP the Clymer & Dixon model was the older, having been manufactured in London sometime in the period 1830–1845; it may well have been one of those acquired in the early 1840s. Des Ryan told me that this was sold to a German student in the mid-1960s. The model manufactured by Thomas Long in Edinburgh in the late 1850s was presented by the DUP to Trinity Closet Press in 1975 and remains in the Printing House (see plate 37).

In the composing room were three Intertype machines, nos 4556, 5084 and 5309, which between them had magazines for 8, 10 and 11pt Modern, and 6, 8 and 11pt Old Style typefaces. No. 4556 was also fitted with a side magazine of 10pt Modern, the capitals and figures of which had to be fed by hand. Not a very exciting range of text faces. The virtuosity at the Press came through the 1615 special matrices for 'Greek, mathematical signs, chemical and botanical [!] signs, old English, Spanish, French, Irish, accented letters, fractions, commercial signs, superior letters, etc.'. These, together with the vast range of founder's type and the skills to set them, gave the DUP its unrivalled position as premier printer of scientific and

6. James Moran, *Printing presses*, 64–6.

37. A drawing of one of the Columbian presses at the DUP, shown in the *Modern Irish Printer*, April 1970. The press is now at Trinity Closet Press.

mathematical works in Ireland. A Fryotype melting pot of three hundredweight capacity with six moulds serviced these Intertypes. A '"Challenge" portable router style C serial no. C1324 with small motor' was also mentioned as part of the machinery in the composing room. This was probably used for removing surplus metal from stereotype plates.

In the warehouse was a 32-inch Furnival hand clamp guillotine with power attachments. The only other substantial piece of machinery mentioned was a hydraulic press with platen measuring 41 by 28 inches. This apparently was an enormous affair and had been used to remove the indentation made in paper by letterpress printing. Stacks of perfected sheets up to five feet in height, sandwiched between pressing boards, were placed under the platen and huge pressure applied through a hand pump over a period of several days. This press was still in use in the late 1930s and was never moved from its position in the 'Parochial Hall'. It was broken up for scrap in 1975.

Stored throughout the building in every possible place were about thirty-four tons of founder's type: ten tons of it in over 1,200 cases; the rest standing matter. Three tons were listed as exotics (greek, hebrew, sanskrit, syriac, coptic, irish, arabic, music) or display faces (De Vinne, Flemish, Clarendon, Med. Egyptian, Ecclesiastical). On top of that there were four tons of Intertype standing metal. Thirty-one founts of poster type, probably mostly wooden, were also listed, in sizes from six to sixteen lines. Much of this type was obviously redundant and, regrettable as it is from a historical point of view, a lot of it was sold as scrap in periodic clear-outs during the 1940s, 1950s and early 1960s. For example the Non-Ferrous Metallurgical Company paid £223 for scrap founder's type in the period August to December 1954, while William Miller & Sons paid for substantial quantities of scrap metal and dross in late 1959 and early 1960.[7] The poster type lasted a bit longer: a surviving poster done in January 1964 for the Brunswick Press and printed in black and red, makes use of seven different founts of type.[8]

Twenty-nine compositor's frames were documented, as well as nearly 1,000 chases and over 280 galleys. Among the other compositors' equipment were three lead cutters, a stereotype planer and a mitring machine. There was also an intriguing entry for 'one type caster for casting single type'. Peter Allman remembers this and from his description there can be little doubt that it was an eighteenth-century hand mould. One wonders if it had been in the Printing House since the start. Its whereabouts today is unknown.

In appointing a retired Church of Ireland clergyman as university printer the College was reinforcing its own Protestant ethos and also that of the Press. Trinity perceived itself as one of the bastions against an

7. MUN/DUP/5/3/574 ff. and 561.
8. MUN/DUP/20.

increasingly illiberal, Roman Catholic society. 1937 saw the adoption of a Constitution that recognised 'the special position' of the Catholic Church and in the early 1940s Archbishop John Charles McQuaid imposed his notorious ban on Catholics attending Trinity. The University Press was known within the trade as a Protestant house, which did business largely within its own community, and in the main employed people of its own religion. The men of course were aware of each other's religious affiliations, but it was not generally devisive, more a cause for a joke, especially on 12 July. However a staff structure wherein all the compositors, the elite of the trade, tended to be Protestant and all the machinemen and labourers Catholic, did lead to ill feeling.

Some staff were let go at the takeover, perhaps ten or so. From a surviving wages book the following profile of the staff on 2 June 1944 can be constructed:[9]

Management:	Corr, Gibbs
Caseroom:	foreman: Hogan
	compositors: J. Maher, Mahon, Pasley, Mortimer
	Intertype operators: Abbott, Wilcox, Mooney
	reader: P. Maher
	apprentices: Styles, Maybury, E. Hogan
Machine-room:	foreman: Byrne
	machinemen: Keogh, O'Reilly
	apprentice: Smith
Warehouse:	keeper: Sergison
	helper: Stewart
Labourers:	Fletcher, Redmond, Hyland

The weekly wage bill for this staff of twenty-three was just over £90. Each full worker paid a contribution of 8*d.* towards health insurance and 9*d.* union dues; the firm also paid 10*d.* and 8*d.* respectively towards these funds. The basic weekly rate for a printer at this date was £5-10-0,[10] and all the men's wages ranged round this; Corr as works manager was paid £6-10-0. The warehouse men and labourers got sums in the region of £3 to £5.

The ratio of compositors to machinemen was much higher at the University Press than in the trade in general. This was because of the complexity of the work undertaken. The University Press men as a consequence used to consider themselves a cut above the general trade. There was also great pride in the connection with the College. Staff tended to stay for these reasons, and also because the overtime afforded was generous. Printing is not a trade that can be taken home, like carpentry or

9. MUN/DUP/6/1.
10. 'Wage movements from 1913 to 1970' in *Míosachán na gClodoiri*, 29/6 (Aug. – Sept. 1979) 13.

plumbing, to earn 'nixers', so overtime was a major attraction. During the exam paper 'season' from February to September the men would often work an extra three hours per night, and four on Saturday; this was paid at time and a half. In real pressure periods work was also done on Sundays. At times like this payments for overtime would nearly match that for basic pay. For example for the week ending 13 February 1948 the gross wages were £183 while overtime was £176. In fact so much overtime was being offered in 1952 that the DTPS ruled that two extra compositors were to be employed before overtime was allowed.[11] The working week in 1944 was forty-five hours, starting at 8 o'clock and ending at 5.30, with a fifteen-minute tea break at 10.15 and lunch from 1.15 to 1.45. On overtime a twenty-minute break was allowed. There was a reduction to a forty-two and a half hour week in October 1948. Two weeks' annual holidays were taken in the first fortnight in August.

The men entered the building through the side gate in Printing House Lane. This was shut at 8.05 and did not reopen until 8.15. Those let through then were docked a quarter of an hour's wages. The gate was immediately shut and those who missed the inflow at the quarter hour had to wait until it reopened on the half hour, thereby losing half an hour's money. This system was in existence in Gibbs's time; the Allmans introduced 'clocking in' as a way of monitoring the timekeeping. (There was a proposal at a chapel meeting in 1961 that this system be done away with, citing the hardship of having to stand around for fifteen minutes in severe weather. It was rejected as it was considered that the management were already very lenient to late-comers.) John Connolly, one of the older comps, had a ritual to signal the closing of each day. An hour before knocking-off time he would announce: 'Gentlemen, we're on the run.' All the comps would then do a mini 'knock-down' with whatever they had to hand. With a half hour to go it was 'Gentlemen, we're on the gallop', whereupon there would be cheers and a noisier 'knock-down'. Connolly and Joe Pasley, being among the oldest comps at the Press, were the first to be laid off in slack times; their output could not match the dexterity of the younger men. They would remain idle until the next period of pressure when they would be re-employed.

Gibbs carried on until October of 1944 when the Rev. Allman took over. Allman was not an active manager, leaving a lot to his works manager. He liked to come in for a few hours a day to see the activity, and it must be added, on occasion to strike fear into the men. The measured sound of his stick on the wooden factory floor sent everybody anxiously about their business. The apprentices got some revenge, in the cruel way of adolescents, by nicknaming him 'Woodener'.

The works manager, John Corr, died in August 1945 as the result of a road accident, so the manager at the Brunswick Press, Percy Williams,

11. IPU: DTPS EC minutes, 18 Aug. 1952.

used to divide his time between the two houses. Williams had been for many years works manager at M.H. Gill & Son before joining Brunswick, where he was elected a director in 1929. W.B. Allman also sent his son Claude down from the Brunswick Press to help out. Early in the 1950s he returned to the Brunswick, which his father transferred to him subsequently. He retired as managing director of the firm in 1968 and died in 1981. The father also insisted that his daughter Liala (see plate 36b), who had recently been demobbed from the British Army, return to work at the University Press in order to fill the gap left by Corr's tragic death. She was a graduate of the University, and had spent six years working in the Brunswick Press before joining the army in 1939, so she was not coming 'cold' to the printing trade when she joined the University Press in March 1946. She inherited this arm of her father's business and ran the Press from 1958 to 1975.

Today Liala Allman is a very erect and mobile octogenarian who speaks with enthusiasm about her tenure at the Press. She inherited much of her father's determination, and wanted things done in a hurry. This was counterbalanced by an inheritance of his financial conservatism. She never spent what she had not got and never took a bank overdraft or loan. This inhibited modernisation of the plant and was a cause of friction between herself and her nephew Peter (see plate 36c) when he came to work at the Press in the 1950s. Her financial conservatism had a beneficial spin-off however: she was always scrupulous in paying her bills on time — echoes of M.H. Gill — and as a consequence could get materials from suppliers during periods of shortage.

She is universally known as 'Miss Allman', primarily out of respect, but no doubt the difficulty of pronouncing and spelling her unusual Christian name had a bearing. Initially some of the staff found it difficult to accept her because she was a woman in a trade dominated by men. She was aware of this and would ease matters by getting some intermediary to convey her instructions. She also addressed the men in the direct manner of her father by calling out their surnames, and this was resented. Apparently there was even a chapel meeting where it was resolved that the men were to be addressed as 'Mr So-and-so' or by their forenames. In general however she had a good relationship with her staff, and is remembered for her kindnesses — perhaps an advance of money in straitened times — and for the personal interest she took in the men's families.

Her presence also caused problems for the College. Although women students were admitted to Trinity in 1904 they were barred from residence in College rooms until 1972; as old Prof. A.A. Luce said on the question, it was 'against Nature — and the Statutes'. In 1944 all women had to be out of the grounds by six o'clock in the evening. This was the reason why the three men labourers, whose primary tasks were to move heavy formes and metal around, also used to hand-feed the printing machines, work generally done by women at much lower wages. So Miss Allman had to get special dispensation to remain on in the Printing House after that hour. One of the conditions of this being granted was that, when the work was finished, she be escorted to the Front Gate by one of the men on the staff.

For several years after the Allmans took over they continued to trade as 'Ponsonby and Gibbs' so as not to lose the goodwill attached to the name; the imprint on the verso of the titlepage to the second edition of Robert W. Tate's *Carmina Dublinensia*, published in 1946, testifies to this. Provost Alton took a personal interest in the affairs of the Press — he used to speak of 'my Printing House' and would walk around the building suggesting repairs and then organised maintenance staff to do them — and it is Miss Allman's recollection that it was he who insisted that the name 'University Press' be registered. However a cache of records among the files in the College's boardroom safe reveal a more complicated story.[12]

Early in 1948 W.B. Allman decided to incorporate the University Press as a private limited company. This was done on 4 May 1948. A copy of the *Memorandum and articles of association of University Press Limited*, for secrecy no doubt printed by the Drogheda Independent Co., is among the boardroom records and gives the share capital as 12,000 £1 ordinary shares; Liala Allman and Percival Frank Williams were to have one share each. Unfortunately the College had only been informally told of this move and no official consent had been sought, so that when the board considered a belated application for permission on 9 June 1948 it was refused. Informal pressure to have this decision reversed must have been applied because in August opinion of counsel was sought by Trinity on the matter. In the brief prepared by the College solicitor it was stated that Allman sought permission to transfer the lease on the Printing House to the company (the College by this date must have accepted the fact of its existence). The brief went on to note that Allman had managed the Press 'most efficiently' and that it was now back in profit (£5,000 of the £7,500 loan had been paid off); consequently Trinity wanted to accommodate the tenant. However the College was worried that shares might get into the hands of unsuitable persons and that it would have no say in the matter.

E.C. Micks, the counsel consulted, gave his opinion on 6 September. He stated that the College had the right to refuse the transfer. The appointment of a College director who could veto any transfer of shares deemed unsuitable by TCD, and the incorporation of this in the articles of association — a safety measure suggested as a compromise by Allman

12. TCD Board Room files: *Memorandum and articles of association of DUP Ltd* (1948); letter 15 July 1948 from registrar to law agent mentioning letter from UCC about name 'UP Ltd.'; brief to counsel E.C. Micks, 27 Aug. 1948; opinion of counsel, 6 Sept. 1948. See also DUP/BP files, certificates of incorporation.

— had no legal standing as the company could change any of the articles by a simple vote at any time. Should the board allow the transfer of the lease it would have to take the risk that the 'College director' clause would be respected.

On 1 October the board decided to take that risk. The articles of association had therefore to be amended to include the clause about the College director. At the same time the opportunity was taken to change the name to Dublin University Press Limited. Apparently the President of University College Cork, A.J. O'Rahilly, worried about his own burgeoning university press, had written to the provost in July strongly objecting to the loose name 'University Press Limited'. W.B. Allman stated that the omission of 'Dublin' had simply been a mistake in drafting, but this was a *post factum* rationalisation. At this date and for many decades previously the business in the Printing House had been known as 'the University Press'. Even the normal style of imprint bears this out: 'Printed at the University Press by Ponsonby and Gibbs'. Both these changes were ratified at an extraordinary general meeting of the company on 27 October — the College director was to have one share — and on 6 December 1948 'Dublin University Press Limited' was registered. William Duncan was the first College director to be appointed.

Remarkably it had never occurred to anyone to register the name before, because there were candidates in the nineteenth century who could have snatched the name and with it the reputation. As we have seen John Henry Newman contemplated the setting up of a press attached to the Catholic University in Dublin in the 1850s, while in Belfast in the 1880s a 'University Book-printing House' was in operation. The registration in 1948 was just in time for a few years later a 'Universities Press' was established in Belfast. The foundation of the Irish University Press at Shannon in 1966 caused a later scare, and because it was felt to be trading on the DUP's reputation it was challenged, unsuccessfully, in the courts. This experience did however spur the board of the company on to register a separate company, reviving the original name 'University Press Ltd', in 1968. The board of the College had no say over what carried the DUP imprint, but the Press would not have printed anything repugnant to it, and this was never a point of contention between the Allmans and TCD.

When the Allmans took on the Press in 1944 they inherited a well-established *modus operandi*, which they continued to use, adjusting it as they found necessary. Jim Lawler, who was machine-room overseer in the 1960s, told me that the resulting fine-tuned system allowed greater production than that in any other firm where he had worked, which included Helys and Dollards. The following description of that system and of the staff structure is a composite derived from the reminiscences of several of the personnel who worked at the Press under the Allmans. The office staff consisted of the proprietor W.B. Allman; Miss Allman, who was in effect the manager; and a girl for secretarial and book-keeping duties. No traveller was employed; the College provided a large portion of the business, and also contacts to a wide range of customers. It was to the office that the customer came to get an estimate or to work out specifications. Because so much of the Press's printing was repeat work it was often easy to give a quick quotation based on the records of the previous printing. If it was work new to the Press then a much more elaborate process was involved.

The first thing done was to cast off the copy to see how much printed matter it would make. Copy was almost invariably in the form of typescripts; the only manuscripts remembered were exam papers in Irish which had to be handwritten because there was no typewriter that had the Irish character set. When there were manuscript interpolations in typewritten matter it sometimes led to bizarre settings. 'Londonderry' in one such addition to an article by Professor T.W. Moody was set by the compositor as 'Haberdashery'; the professor was highly amused. Typescripts presented were often difficult to calculate because of varying line spacing and length. For these averages would have been taken. If it was bookwork a few sample lines might have been set to get a more accurate estimate, and there might have been consultations with the foremen of the caseroom and of the machine-room over the setting and press times, and with the warehouse-keeper about the paper chosen. A good specialist estimator, as Brian Allman was (see plate 36d) when he came to the Press in 1966, could short-circuit these consultations. Tables published by the British Federation of Master Printers could also be used for estimating, but experience soon came to count more than rigid calculations. And for jobbing experience was the only criterion. The times estimated for composition and presswork were always calculated in round hourly figures. When the labour costs were calculated a certain percentage would be added to cover overheads and profit. This could be as high as a third, but was more likely to be around 25 per cent, or if the competition was keen it could be as low as 5 per cent.[13]

Commercial publishers would stipulate the paper, type and size of their work, but if advice was needed by a non-book trade customer the office provided this, perhaps bringing down samples from the book ware-room. If the contract was struck a large manilla envelope, known as the 'docket', was prepared for each job. On the outside were printed forms to be filled out giving such details as job number, customer, title of work, dates received in caseroom and machine-room, details of outwork (blocks, ruling, binding etc.). On the verso details of setting and machining were entered and below the costs calculated there was a box for adding the house's mark-up. The total figure arrived at provided a cross-check on the accuracy of the estimate given. Copies of the proofs and of the finished work were put in each docket which was then filed away

13. MUN/DUP/19 *passim.*

among the others — and there were thousands of them — to await a reprint or to be cleared out after a number of years.[14] The office kept work-books recording the status of each job as it went through the system — whether it was set, out on proof, printed, or dispatched.

After the office next in the chain of command was the works manager, who in 1944, as we have seen, was John Corr. The works manager was nearly always a fully trained printer and provided the detailed knowledge of the production processes on the factory floor. It was by closely observing Percy Williams and compiling a book on the jobs he handled that Miss Allman readied herself to take over from him.

When the copy arrived in the caseroom the foreman decided which compositor or Intertype operator should handle it, or indeed if it was a large job several men might be involved setting it. His decision was based on a knowledge of the skills of his men, and because of the recurrent nature of the Press's business certain comps became very familiar with certain types of jobs. The caseroom foreman acted as works manager at times when there was no one appointed to this position. He was 'non-working' — known in the trade as 'a waistcoat man' — in that he did no setting, although a fully trained compositor. His non-working position was considered to be a symbol of the status of the caseroom and jealously guarded. In 1959 there was a chapel complaint about Davy Deegan, then foreman, doing such work. Deegan referred it to the DTPS, adding that the men had threatened to walk out. The chapel through its officers stated that his doing such work 'was incompatible with the dignity attached to the position of Works Manager and was contrary to custom and usage'. Deegan countered that he was not infringing any of the Society's rules and that he was doing the work only because the College exam papers were behind schedule. The DTPS ruled that he could do such work in an emergency but that he should consult the chapel officers before doing so.[15] The foreman collected the time dockets filled out by the men; these served as a cross-check on the accuracy of the estimate for a job.

The compositors were the elite of the trade. Peter Allman remembers being told that they once had the privilege of dining at fellows' table in the College and were much put out when this was withdrawn. This story of course is apocryphal and was probably based on an account read in some history of the College of the offer made to the printer William Kearney in 1597 to induce him to remain in Trinity, an offer that included commons at fellows' table (see p. 2). Dining with the fellows was always considered to be a special privilege; as late as the 1940s even lecturers had to have the board's permission to join them. But that the story gained any currency is indicative of the compositors' self-image. The following story

14. There are examples of such dockets for 1946, 1962–4 and 1968 in MUN/DUP/19–21.

15. IPU: DTPS EC minutes, 7, 10 Sept. 1959.

underlines the point. Apparently one of the Press's comps was drinking in a pub one day and got into conversation with a coalman. Without disclosing his trade the comp, who was big and strong, boasted that he could do the coalie's work — all too apparent — but that the coalie could not do his. A bet was laid and out they went to the coalman's dray, where the comp was told to take a huge bag of slack across the street and up some steps. He staggered across the street with the bag on his shoulders and started to climb the steps. Halfway up he faltered, was overbalanced by the weight and fell heavily on his knee. The injury hospitalised him for several weeks. Thereafter he was known, though not to his face, as 'Sack o' slack'.

Each compositor had his own frame, a tradition that was going out in Dublin at this time; comps were now setting more and more from cases placed on the stone. At the DUP each man's frame was nominally considered inviolable. Down among the lesser used cases he would have his 'whang' of scarce sorts. Seán Galavan remembers as a fourth-year apprentice getting a kick in the backside from Ross Mahon when caught hunting in his cases. (Seán, who is now national organiser of the Irish Print Union, wondered what the repercussions of such treatment would be today; a strike or a court case no doubt, but, as he said with a smile, 'the 1950s were different'.) Fred Maybury recalls 'whanging' away scarce brevier quads in an old pair of boots he kept under his frame, but he must have been spotted in the act and they were all 'liberated'. Hand-setting was much in evidence at the Press at this date, as it continued to be, although to a diminishing degree, right into the 1970s. This was even true for bookwork; very little of this type of work was being hand-set in Dublin outside of the DUP during the 1950s. Bookwork was considered to be more skilled than jobbing. Even though there is a large degree of display work in the latter, the justification of lines and the fine judgment of spacing put bookwork on a higher plane.

Several of the comps specialised in setting the exotic faces — Greek, Hebrew, Arabic ('the barbed wire language') and music. Throughout the 1940s Dublin printers continued to come to the DUP for a few lines of Greek or music. Ross Mahon and John Connolly used to set the music in the wareroom of the 1734 building where there were three cases, each of which had hundreds of boxes. It was so complicated that Percy Williams decided in 1946 to have the music drawn instead and a block made from this. His son Douglas, a trained draughtsman, provided the first of many such drawings in June of that year.[16] Another solution was found when the skills in setting Hebrew waned; the passages needed for exam papers were photographed from textbooks — considerations of copyright were blithely banished — and a block made. In 1961 Des Ryan, the works manager, suggested that the same be done for Greek. Several of

16. MUN/DUP/5/2/331, 23 June 1946.

the old hands could still handle that language, but the skills were in decline; the Press's best Greek comp, Dick Lattimore, had just emigrated to the United States. However the compositors rebelled and had the chapel refer the matter to the DTPS for arbitration. The decision was in favour of the men — Greek must continue to be set by hand. Only in emergencies would a joint chapel-management application to have blocks made be considered by the DTPS, and 'even in that case the text would more than likely have to be set later'.[17] Fortunately the States did not prove to be to Dick Lattimore's taste and in the light of the union's decision his application to be re-employed at the Press was accepted with some relief. This incident also persuaded the management to buy a Monotype greek die-case shortly afterwards.

If matter was to be kept standing, after it was printed off the comp would drop it from the chase and tie up each page. These were then packaged in waste-paper and prominently labelled. Matter for distribution would also be dropped, some being tied and wrapped up, and some remained in galleys for later dissing. It might stay in that state for several months until pressure for sorts in that fount dictated distribution. Dissing took place with regularity in the first hour of work, or when things were slack. To keep track of all this matter the storekeeper — in the 1950s Chris 'Kit' Holden — had what was aptly known as 'The where-is-it book'.

Also under the caseroom foreman were the three Intertype operators, and from 1950 the Monotype operator and caster. These operators were rigidly segregated. On 10 March 1958 the chapel heard a complaint that an Intertype operator had made up his matter with Monotype matter on a galley. The offender pleaded that the management were complaining of the time spent on some jobs 'and were trying to get back some work lost to Dundalk [i.e. the Dundalgan Press]'. None the less the chapel ruled against the practice and apologies were tendered by the man involved. The Monotype caster was not a qualified printer but was a member of the union, while his assistant was not. On occasion under pressure of work and because of the shortage of skilled labour in the trade the Press would apply to the union to have an assistant promoted to caster and so obtain his union card. In 1969 an assistant at the DUP applied on his own behalf. The management said that although there was no full position for him at present it was willing to retain him at the full rate should he be issued with a card. This he was duly given, but with the condition that he stayed with the firm for three years. When he applied to the union less than a year later for permission to transfer to a higher paid job he was refused because it would have been a breach of faith with the DUP which had treated him so fairly.[18]

17. IPU: DTPS EC minutes, 13 Apr. 1961.
18. IPU: DTPS EC minutes, 29 Jan., 17 Nov. 1969. He did wriggle his way out of the Press a year later, leaving the trade to go into the record business (17 Nov. 1970).

Also attached to the caseroom was the reader and his copy holder. The reader had, according to union rules at this date, to be a fully trained compositor. Since a comp normally started his apprenticeship after primary school it has been argued that this rule was absurd; far better to hire a retired school teacher or at least somebody educated to Leaving Certificate standard. To counter this it should be remembered that the apprentice continued his general education during his training and that the reader's job involved more than just looking for textual mistakes; his brief also included spotting typographic errors — broken or turned letters, uneven spacing and faulty printing etc. — matters that only the keen eye of a trained printer would appreciate. Peter Maher was the reader at the Press when the Allmans took over and is acknowledged to have been one of the best they ever had; it is said that he cried anytime it was discovered that a mistake had eluded him. He retired in 1956.[19]

The reader was assisted by a copyholder or 'reader's boy' who read the copy out loud, word by word, or if it was Latin or Greek, letter by letter, while the reader checked the proof. This 'boy' might be a retired bank manager or garda, glad to do something in his spare time even though the pay was as low as a first-year apprentice's; or he might actually be a boy putting in a year or so of unpaid work in the hope of getting the next apprenticeship vacancy. The level of the job dictated the level of proofing. At the highest level, say for exam papers, a comp would correct his own proof. Another pull would be taken and this 'first proof' would be sent out with the manuscript to the relevant institution, sometimes, depending on the number of examiners involved, in as many as twelve copies. The corrected proofs, when returned, would be collated with that of the reader, the corrections made in the metal and a revise sent out. On its return the same process would be gone through and a second revise dispatched. Only after it was returned clean would the job be sent to press. So many proofs needed to be pulled at the DUP that there was a proofer employed full-time; Sammy O'Neill filled this post in the 1950s.

Nobody could read proofs unless the reader was present on the floor. Since there was normally only one reader this led to problems in times of sickness. This happened during a rush period in April 1958 when Peter Maher was just back from serious illness and Miss Allman was worried that he might not be fit for the extensive overtime that was taking place. The chapel insisted however that no one could read on overtime unless he was present. This even applied to reading being done in the office, as the chapel minutes for 21 January 1958 testified; Miss Allman agreed to discontinue the practice except in cases of extreme emergency. The union later recognised this 'custom', but insisted that it must not jeopardise the normal overtime for the reader.[20]

19. MUN/DUP/6/5, 27 Feb. 1956.

20. IPU: DTPS EC minutes, 29 June 1967.

Once the job was cleared 'for press' the docket was passed from the caseroom to the machine-room foreman. Being one rung down the ladder in the unwritten pecking order of the printing industry the overseer in this department was 'a working foreman'. He would judge which was the best machine on which to do the job and slot the work into the schedule. Each of the hand-fed machines had its own permanent minder and a labourer to feed the paper and help move heavy formes. There were occasional demarcation disputes, as when the Transport Workers' Union labourers complained that machinemen were pulling proofs on overtime without one of their members being present to assist with the lifting of the formes. This was rejected by the chapel and the DTPS later ruled that its members handled type as of right, while TWU members did so by invitation.[21]

The cylinder presses, such as the Wharfedales, were operated by full journeymen. The platen machines on the other hand were usually operated by men who may have served a few years' apprenticeship, or more likely by a labourer promoted to the position. Such was the case with Peter Redmond who was promoted from labourer to platen machine minder in 1947. Early in 1950 the DTPS took the very unusual step, because of the acute shortage of labour in the post-war printing industry, of allowing him to be elevated to cylinder minder.[22] When pressure of business warranted it the Press would occasionally seek permission from the union to allow a man to operate two machines. This was usually granted in these 'emergency' conditions. On one occasion when it was refused the chapel pleaded for it to be allowed as the operator earned extra money; the union capitulated and granted permission for three months as long as it did not interfere with the training of the apprentices on the machines in question.[23]

The proper paper, cut to size if necessary, was brought from the ware-room in the basement to the machine-room and the printed sheets of the job were delivered to the wareroom on the first floor. There the warehouse-keeper and his helper would collate the work, wrap it for storage, send it for binding, or dispatch it to the customer as necessary. As much of the business was within the College a cart was used for these deliveries, and even for dispatches to the RIA in Dawson Street. Miss Allman remembers it was painted maroon, and was in use right up until the Press left the campus in 1976. There was also a messenger boy's bicycle for further-flung customers. During the period in question the DUP never had a delivery van; for any large order one of the Allmans would take it in his or her car.

The final block in the staff structure under consideration was the apprentice. He was likely to start as a boy of fourteen having completed

21. IPU: DUP chapel minutes, 2 May 1958.
22. IPU: DTPS EC minutes, 8 Dec. 1947, 13, 27 Mar. 1950.
23. IPU: DTPS EC minutes, 17, 23 Nov. 1970.

his primary school education and who had sat and passed the apprenticeship examination in English, Irish and maths set by the Dublin Master Printers. The union allowed the house to have a decreasing ratio of apprentices to journeymen, and he had to be alternately a member's son or the house's choice. The house would choose between qualified candidates by interview. The period of apprenticeship was still seven years in the 1950s, but was reduced to five in the following decade.

The conditions of the apprenticeship were governed by the Printing Apprenticeship Authority (Dublin) under a joint agreement between the master printers and the DTPS. First-year apprentices were not allowed to do a lot. If he was in the caseroom he might be given leads to cut, sorts to fetch, furniture to wash, or be put to dissing, especially of pie; he might also act as copyholder for the reader, although the DTPS ruled against this practice on 10 September 1964. If in the machine-room he might be set preparing paste for the make-ready, or watching over a flat-bed job that the journeyman would have set up. In his initial year he had to attend the Printing School in Bolton Street Technical School for technical training for half of every day in the first six months of his apprenticeship. He also had to attend night classes there in English and Irish. Each boy had a log book of his work in the Tech. which was signed by his foreman each week and checked by the Authority. At the end of his second year he had to sit a state exam for a Junior Trade Certificate. That for the Senior Trade Certificate at the end of the fourth year or the London City and Guilds exam at the end of year five were optional, although many did sit them, relishing the competition with their peers at a time when there were less distractions for a youth than there are today.

An apprentice compositor would be put to setting the odd line, doing corrections or making up pages in galley during his second and third years. Each was expected to have his own setting stick, tweezers and type scale; the firm usually bought these and deducted the sum over time from his wages. Each had his own cases and would guard his sorts, leads and spaces as jealously as the journeyman guarded his whangs. There was no formal training given, but if the boy showed initiative some compositor might take him under his wing and he would get to do more rewarding work earlier. Des Ryan had such a relationship with John Connolly, as did Seán Galavan with Ross Mahon, during the 1950s. In the machine-room the apprentice would be given simple make-ready to do in his second year. By his third year he would have had enough training to be allowed operate one of the flat-beds, and from then on would be gaining experience so that in the last few months of his apprenticeship he would be allowed operate the best machine at the Press. As there was little colour work done machine apprentices at the DUP got a limited training.

In the caseroom serious composing began in the fifth year. At the Press the apprentice might be given some bookwork to set or Monotype maths to comp in the stick. This was the period when the apprentice could opt for some training on one of the setting machines; the firm was obliged to provide six months' training on either the Intertype or the Mono keyboard. In his seventh year he would be trusted to set full exam papers. Many apprentices left the DUP upon completion of their time, much to the frustration of management, realising that the nature of the Press had given them an in-depth training, but in a narrow, specialist range of material. (To avoid this limitation in the trade in general the Apprenticeship Authority arranged for the exchange of boys between firms in their final year.)

Occasionally during the 1940s and 1950s the Press would apply to the DTPS for permission to take on a supernumerary apprentice, citing shortage of skilled labour, the specialist nature of the output and the fact that apprentices, trained in these specialities, did not stay after serving their time. Usually the union was sympathetic, but on one occasion the chapel vetoed the request.[24] The union was also called upon to bring recalcitrant apprentices to book, as was documented in the case of a DUP member in August and September 1972. Just as the DTPS took the rights of its members very seriously, it considered their duties equally seriously, and accordingly the boy — described by the father of the chapel as 'incorrigible' — was called before the committee. It was decreed that if he wanted to continue his apprenticeship he would have to improve his behaviour, otherwise the Press could dismiss him. The chapel father was instructed to send monthly reports to the committee. The dressing down had the desired effect and the September report was favourable.

For any complaint at the Press the first recourse was at the chapel meeting. These took place regularly on the factory floor usually at break times, unless the management wanted something urgent settled, in which case it would happen in the firm's time. The chapel consisted of all the journeymen; overseers and apprentices were not included. It was presided over by the father, assisted by the clerk who took the minutes and collected the dues; occasionally when there was a large chapel a sub-father would also be appointed. The dues were used to pay for various expenses and to give the officers a nominal sum for their trouble; for example in 1962 a shilling per week was collected from each man so that the father could be afforded 5-0 and the clerk 7-6. Theirs were thankless tasks and it was a recurrent problem to fill the posts. Attendance was compulsory at chapel meetings and the father had to give permission to anyone who wanted to absent himself. However foremen, although members of the union, were considered to be part of management and could only attend by invitation. There were other rules governing the procedures within the chapel and it was suggested in January 1963 that these be codified, but nothing seems to have come of this and they continued to exist in the folk memory.

24. IPU: DUP chapel minutes, 1 Feb. 1956.

The complaint might be settled at the chapel meeting; if not the officers might have to bring it to the management. More intractable problems were referred to the DTPS; I have instanced several of these above. The rulings of the committee indicate how powerful the printing union was; many of its decisions, especially as regards personnel, would in other industries be considered usurpations of management's function. There are historical reasons as to why the print unions are so powerful. Printers were one of the first to organise themselves in combinations to set conditions of employment, and the complexity of their skills ensured that they were not easily replaced. To guard against any misuse of this power a very democratic structure has evolved at the Irish Print Union (formerly the DTPS and later the Irish Graphical Society). Members' interests can be represented at weekly council and committee meetings, and at special delegate meetings. The members elect all representatives and are frequently asked to vote on key issues. And there is a monthly newsletter to keep them abreast of all issues. The University Press is proof that the system of chapel and union can work; there was only one strike at the DUP during the Allmans' tenure in the College, and that at the very end.

Besides the 'lash-in' at the end of each apprentice's time there were other social occasions for the staff, often subsidised by the firm. Fred Maybury remembers an excursion to Wicklow, sports days and dances organised during the 1950s. It is Jimmy Stewart's impression however that such matters were more restrained under the Allmans than under Gibbs.

A perspective on the Press's network of suppliers during the first two decades of the Allman era is to be had from several account books in the DUP muniments.[25] Naturally paper constituted the largest purchases. Local mills that provided substantial quantities were Swiftbrook Paper Mills and Drimnagh Paper Mills; the latter's monthly accounts usually ranged between £100 and £200. Other mills and paper merchants which did large business with the Press were Wiggins, Teape & A. Pirie (which later became Pirie Armstrong Ltd); A. Armstrong & Co.; Spicers; Barrow Paper Mills; and Glenvalley Paper Co. There was a whole shoal of lesser suppliers. Capital Stationery Co. was a major source for the considerable amount of stationery used.

As regards type Intertype and Monotype were obviously the most frequent suppliers, although it is surprising how few magazine founts and die-cases were bought from them. Fry's Metal Foundries, Non-Ferrous Metallurgical Co. and Pass Printing Metals provided the raw material for these hot-metal machines. It is interesting to see how the war inflated the price: Fry's Intertype metal cost £1-10-0 per cwt in May 1939, £2-14-6 in January 1945 and £3-15-6 in May 1946. There was also need for occasional small quantities of founder's type, supplied locally by William

25. MUN/DUP/1/13; -/5/2, 3; -/17, 18 covering the period 1944–1961.

Miller & Sons, and from England by Yendall & Co. and by Stephenson, Blake & Co.

Ink came from the Glenside Printing Ink Co., Amalgamated Paints & Inks, Coates Bros, and Associated Printing Inks. The most frequent block makers used were Dublin Illustrating Co. and Irish Photo-engraving Co. The orders were small but frequent, so the accounts were cumulatively substantial. For example a total of £213 worth of business was done with the latter company in May–June 1954. Smaller accounts were also run up with half a dozen other local firms. On one occasion the Press even hired blocks: in February 1961 Bord Fáilte, the Irish tourist board, rented it four colour half-tone blocks of the Ardagh Chalice for five guineas. As we have seen above, Douglas Williams provided many drawings for these blocks from 1946 onwards, mostly music but also plans and on one occasion in October 1947 he drew a complicated crest for the University Philosophical Society. One of the comps, Derek Wearen, who was known for his artistic ability, occasionally provided designs during the 1960s. The only commercial graphic designer used during this period was the Noel Goulding Studio, which provided art work in 1960 for such commercial jobbing as menus and advertisements. Ruling when necessary was done by S.J. Bigger and embossing by Ardiff Diestamping Service.

There was no in-house bindery at the Press; it was only in 1970 that a folding machine was acquired. The Educational Company of Ireland led the field of binders to which work was sent. Capital Bindery, part of the Capital Stationery Co., was used in the period 1948–58, as was Cahill & Co. during the 1950s. Lesser accounts are documented with five other binders.

On occasion, due to pressure of work or the specialised nature of the job, the DUP, like other printers, would farm out printing to be done. For example in the period 1944–56 Thoms printed the TCD *Register of electors* for it. The Dargle Press in Bray, Co. Wicklow, used to print the Trinity Week programme. And of course the Brunswick Press did printing for the DUP, and vice versa, depending on the workload in these two prongs of the Rev. Allman's business. (Brunswick also supplied printing materials and binding with regularity.) The Press used to dispatch many of the periodicals it printed, and engaged Mayne's Typewriting Bureau to address the envelopes.

Some indication of the costs of these supplies relative to each other can be had from a half year's summary for July–December 1946 (to the nearest £):

Paper	Other purch.	Type	Repairs	Fuel	Gas/Elec.	Sundries	Total
£686	£666	£24	£9	£48	£87	£67	£1587

And an 'analysis of sundries' is to be had from figures given for the year July 1960–June 1961 (again to the nearest £): die stamping £99; ink £52;

drawings £73; setting £71; 'erecting new office' £67; house stationery £97. Given that the total is £459, and even allowing for inflation, this figure must include items disguised under 'other purchases' in 1946. Despite not being totally transparent both accounts serve to show the relative outlay on supplies at the Press.

Before I begin to consider the output at the DUP it would be as well to define the distinction between bookwork and jobbing. In the nineteenth century when compositors on the piece rate were paid at a different rate for these, it was important to have a precise definition. William Savage's *Dictionary of the art of printing* (1841) defines a job as 'any thing which printed does not exceed a sheet'; implicitly bookwork is anything that exceeds a sheet. A jobbing house had a wide variety of types in small quantities, while a bookwork house had a narrow range of text faces but in sufficient quantities to set large formes. As more and more printers were paid a flat weekly rate and with the advent of hot-metal setting, these distinctions became redundant. The only constraint might be that a book house would have to have presses large enough to take multi-page formes. Today although all printers use the terms none seems to have a precise definition. Jobbing is thought of as small commercial work and display work; bookwork is something with a longer continuous text.

The DUP in the period of consideration had a foot in both camps. It aimed to serve a narrow specialised niche, describing itself on its own headed stationery of the period as 'Specialists in printing foreign languages and scientific and mathematical works'. It was geared up to provide both jobbing and book printing for this academic market. The importance of bookwork declined over the decades, but this was counterbalanced by the rise in jobbing, especially in the area of exam papers. 'A scholarly jobbing house' is Miss Allman's own description of the Press in its last years in the College.

Because of the connection with the Brunswick Press, which was a general commercial jobbing house, the range of jobbing did expand at the Press in the 1940s. Where formerly it was extensively College related, now much more work was being done for businesses.[26] This did settle down after a few years, but there was always a steady trickle of commercial jobs. Evidence of examples from the 1960s include labels for Bush television cartons; 50,000 leaflets for R. & H. Main Ltd of London, advertising a cooker and printed in four colours; and typesetting for the record sleeve of Seán Ó Riada's *Mise Éire*.[27] It is evident from a surviving jobbing book that up to a dozen jobs were completed each day.[28]

Scholarly jobbing was however the bread and butter, and this increasingly meant exam papers. Trinity alone provided copy for 1,500–2,000 per

26. MUN/DUP/1/9 *passim.*

27. MUN/DUP/19, 20, Nov. 1962, 7 Apr. 1964.

28. MUN/DUP/8/1, 1937 – Sept. 1944.

year; for example in the 1946–47 academic year 1,447 were printed, while in 1956–57 the number had risen to 1,995.[29] These were printed in edition sizes of perhaps 700–800, fifty for the exam and the remainder to be bound into pamphlets for students preparing for exams in later years. When the Allmans took over in 1944 they introduced some order into the chaotic charging that had been taking place. A 20 per cent surcharge for 'increased cost of production' was added to the scale of charges for exam papers set in 1938. There was a post-war boom in the Irish printing industry and the rescinding of the Wages Standstill Order which had applied from 1941 to 1946 led to a rapid inflation in wages. These factors were reflected in the charges for printing at the Press. The exam papers for 1947 showed increases for composition in the order of 50–100 per cent over those for 1938. For example English was charged at 12-6 per page as against 8-3 in 1938; Greek and Irish at 28-6 against 16-8; 'Algebra' (used generically as meaning maths) 28-6 as opposed to 17-10; German at 25-0 after being 12-7.[30] The resulting revenue was substantial and all the better because it was recurrent; for example in the academic year 1952–53 College exam papers generated £1,293 worth of business.[31]

The Press's reputation in this area, going back to the nineteenth century, ensured a broad range of customers. In the period 1940–54 there were over thirty bodies having their exam papers printed at the DUP: the universities, state bodies, the Vocational Education Committee and such commercial firms as the Bank of Ireland and Guinnesses.[32] As many as 5,000 separate papers might be printed in a year. The Press's reputation was built on high security, accuracy and meeting the deadlines. Separate sections of the factory were partitioned off where only staff working on these jobs could go and a paper shredder was used to dispose of the make-ready and spoiled copies. Staff got an extra premium in their 'merit' money in recognition of the security element in their jobs. The men were acutely aware of the need for confidentiality. In one case in 1961 the chapel minutes recorded the discovery that the clerk had misappropriated its funds; the father regretted the disgrace in having to tell the management, but 'the "security" nature of [the] House must be understood'. In another case in the 1970s a machineman was set to work on a paper for an exam that he knew his son would be sitting. He declared this conflict of interest to Miss Allman, suggesting that he be taken off the job, but she had confidence in his integrity and he completed the work. I have described above the level of proofing that was done to ensure accuracy. Meeting the deadlines was sometimes hair-raising, with TCD exam papers being printed at 8 a.m. for a 9.30 exam! Such cases were rare and were usually due to an

29. MUN/DUP/8/3, 4.
30. MUN/DUP/8/2 *passim*.
31. MUN/DUP/1/5/461 ff.
32. MUN/DUP/8/5.

examiner returning proofs late. Miss Allman tried to have a day's leeway on the delivery date on the docket — something the men were not aware of — so that papers would be printed a day before that stipulated by the examiner. The system worked and no deadline was ever missed.

Exam papers dictated the pattern of production at the Press. This can be followed in the surviving wages books.[33] For example in 1954 wages in January to April were static. Then overtime started in May and continued to the end of June, catering for the summer exams. Work fell off in July, and the factory closed for holidays during the first half of August. To cope with the autumn papers overtime picked up in late August, reached a peak in September, and then tailed off in October. Overtime for the year was finished except for a brief spurt before Christmas. The same pattern was followed in 1955–57.

The Press aimed to do its bookwork in the valleys between the exam peaks. In the nature of academic books the runs were small and lengthy production times were involved, some held in proof for as long as ten years. Unfortunately the Press did not keep examples of all its bookwork, or records of it, so it is impossible to indicate its extent. However some evidence is available for some works, giving production details and costs. The College of course was a major customer, the annual calendar being the largest bookwork undertaken for it. Fortunately we have details of the first that was printed by the Allmans, that for 1944–45. The edition size was 1,050 copies and it contained 24 sheets:[34]

Composition:	hand: 515 hours @ 5-6 per hr	£141-12- 6
	machine: 126 hours @ 8-6	53-11- 0
	hand (apprentice): 205 @ 3-0	30-15- 0
		225-18- 6
Rent for standing type (20% on £225-18-6)		45- 3- 9
Proofing:	1 hr per sh. @ 5-6 on 24 sh.	6-12- 0
Presswork:	5 hrs per sh. @ 11-0 (£2-15-0)	
	24 sh. @ £2-15-0	66- 0- 0
		£343-14- 3

These figures represented significant increases on those charged by Gibbs. For example for the 1940–41 calendar the following obtained: composition (per hour): hand, 4-0; machine, 7-6; hand (apprentice), 2-0; presswork: £1-15-9 per sheet for an edition of 900 copies.[35]

When paper and binding charges were included the TCD calendar provided a handsome amount of recurrent business. The total cost of the 1944–45 issue was £426, and this had risen to £1,069 for the 1954–55

33. MUN/DUP/6/4.

34. MUN/DUP/4/3, late 1944.

35. MUN/DUP/4/2, 30 Sept. 1940.

edition of 1,400 copies.[36] Trinity was alarmed at the escalating cost and put the contract for the 1960–61 calendar out to tender; Helys won the order. The calendar had been described as 'the most difficult book to read in all the College courses'[37] so the change in printer was used as the opportunity to have it redesigned professionally. William Webb, an English designer, was engaged to sort it out, and advice was also sought from the Oxford University Press. Webb's brief also included redesigning *Hermathena* and the house stationery.

Hermathena was issued twice a year and cost about £150–200 per issue in the late 1940s.[38] The board of the College continued to subsidise it heavily, considering it as the flagship of scholarship for the University. On 28 January 1953 it ordered that a set of the journal, together with volumes from the DUP series, be dispatched to aid in the restocking of the Monte Casino library which had been destroyed in the War. There was also a domestic side to the production of *Hermathena*. The wife of the editor, Dr Edmund Furlong, would on occasion bake a cake to celebrate the publication of a special issue, as for example the launch of the Spring 1967 Swift number. *Trinity* was another recurrent bookwork order. This was an annual documenting the happenings in the College and was aimed at the alumni. As a consequence, although its pagination was small at fifty-two pages, its edition size was large at around 10,000. Charges for it depended on the number of illustrations included, but some figures for the 1950s will give an indication: 1950, £439; 1953, £681; 1955, £539.[39] It was published from 1949 to 1967.

TCD did of course provide other non-recurrent bookwork business, but this tended to be for pamphlets rather than challenging full-length books. What books it did commission from the Press were inward looking, not the stuff of a vital university press. In a list of fifteen 'Dublin University Press publications' given in the 1958–59 calendar no less that eleven relate to Trinity. It is also significant that the latest date of publication on this list was 1951. The Press published three histories of the College in a six-year period from 1946: Constantia Maxwell's in 1946 covering the period 1591–1892; Kenneth Bailey's in 1947 covering 1892–1945; and H.L. Murphy's in 1951 dealing with the period to 1702. The Press was not geared up for the problems of publication. For broader distribution — and what academic does not want to get the widest readership for his researches? — the College favoured Longmans in London as its publisher. This underlines yet again the fundamental failure of the DUP as a university press — it remained essentially a printing house and did not take on the role of a publishing house. A stock book for the period

36. MUN/DUP/1/5/167 ff., 341 ff.

37. 'House styles and the Irish printer' in *Modern Irish Printer*, 3/4 (Mar./Apr. 1962) 9.

38. MUN/DUP/8/2 *passim*.

39. MUN/DUP/1/5/277 ff., 589.

shows the complexity of publishing Maxwell's *History of TCD*; ten pages are taken up keeping track of the 1,000 copies printed. No wonder the Press did not want to get involved with this part of the book trade!

One of the few 'bestsellers' in the Dublin University Press series was Burnside and Panton's *Theory of equations* which in 1954 had reached its tenth edition. This work was on the academic curriculum in India so there was great demand for it there and in fact the board of the College gave permission on 18 March of that year to S. Chand & Co. in Delhi to reprint an abridged version there; Trinity was to get 5 per cent royalty on the sales. The Press continued to act as wholesale distributor for the DUP series, but the business was small.[40] Credit sales in 1947 were less than £30 when commission, unspecified, was deducted; there were also some retail sales, on which the Press took 10 per cent commission, but the amount was miniscule. Stock owned by J.T. Gibbs was also held at the Press and distributed on his behalf. The retail booksellers Easons and Hannas regularly purchased such law books by Vanston, and Nolan and DeMolyns. When Gibbs died in 1948 W.B. Allman bought this stock for £100.[41]

Bookwork undertaken for customers outside of Trinity was primarily for institutions, learned or religious; among them the RIA, RDS, the Institute for Advanced Studies, the Irish Texts Society and the Church of Ireland. The *Proceedings* of the RIA was, and continues to be, one of the most challenging works undertaken by the Press, involving complicated mathematical and scientific setting. 1956 saw the completion of the five-volume *Lebor Gabála Érenn* edited for the Irish Texts Society by R.A. Stewart Macalister; Ponsonby and Gibbs had issued the first volume almost twenty years earlier in 1938. One book totally out of the academic pattern of production at the Press was Austin Clarke's *Viscount of Blarney and other plays*, printed in an edition of 200 copies, for which £35 was charged in November 1944; a further 100 were printed in February 1945.[42] These were published under Clarke's own Bridge Press imprint, with Williams and Norgate acting as London agents; the DUP device was used as a colophon, the last time that I have noted its inclusion. Williams and Norgate also acted as agents for another book printed by the DUP: Arland Ussher's *Postscript to existentialism and other essays*, which was published in Dublin by another 'domestic' house, the Sandymount Press, in 1946. At about this date the Press did business with one of its furthest flung and most exotic customers — the Government Printing Department in Accra (Gold Coast) — when it printed *Selected judgements of the West African Court of Appeal for the year 1945*.

It is not possible to say what percentage the College provided of the Press's business during the Allman era because the account books have

40. MUN/DUP/1/5/173 ff.

41. MUN/DUP/1/9 *passim*; MUN/DUP/17, 2 July 1948.

42. MUN/DUP/1/9/441–2.

not survived. However the general impression expressed was that Trinity was the biggest customer. Some idea of the turnover with TCD can be had from an account book that has survived. It gives the term and September quarter totals for work done, excluding *Hermathena* and a few other works, but including the calendar and exam papers for the years 1936 to 1950. The following are a few samples for the start of the Allman era: 1944, £2,512; 1947, £3,685; 1950, £4,665.[43]

The size of the workforce in the 1940s and 1950s after the Allmans took over never went above thirty-four. After the consolidation of staff numbers in 1944, business had improved by early 1946 to such an extent that four new men were taken on in March and April, bringing the total to thirty in July of that year. Plate 38 shows twenty-three of the staff of 1948.[44] The huge post-war wage increases negotiated in the trade — 22.7 per cent in 1946 and 10 per cent the following year — brought the weekly wage bill up to around £150–190. Two more men were taken on by January 1950; in that year the wages averaged about £205. Further general increases of 11.1 and 9.7 per cent in 1951 and 1952 respectively pushed the weekly bill to around £240. The Press was not affected by the bitter seven-week strike that culminated in the 1952 increase. At the busiest times in 1954 the wages ran as high as £290. Staff reached a peak in 1954 when thirty are documented on the factory floor with perhaps a further four in the office. The men's basic rate was now £9-1-0 which with merit money pushed a few of the workers into the exalted ranks of the £10-a-week men. Apprentices earned from 20 per cent of a journeyman's wages in their first year to 65 per cent in their seventh. Although there were general increases of 9.4 per cent in 1955 and a further 5.1 per cent in 1957 the wages bill was dropping at the Press, indicating a downturn in business. This was reflected in a reduction to twenty-nine men on the factory floor, with perhaps three, now that the Rev. Allman was dead, in the office.[45]

---

43. MUN/DUP/8/2.

44. I am grateful to Jimmy Stewart for this photo and for the identifications. It is one of only a few taken at the Press. The occasion for this picture was the impending emigration of Jack Maher and Frank Mortimer to South Africa. The men are gathered round a field gun — the barrel is just visible on the left — which was parked in the 'Paddocks', the area between the Printing House and the backs of house nos 33–35 of New Square. Apparently there were two of these guns, captured from the Germans in the First World War and presented to the College — the board register on 21 December 1918 records the gift of one — and they had been placed on the lawns at the front of the College. Cyril Bedford of the library staff told me that he remembers the students drawing these out like chariots on the day of Commencements (the University's graduation ceremony), to have races round Front Square. Other points worth noting in this photo are the sods of turf drying on the roof of the shed behind — coal was scarce in post-war days; and the brick building at the rere which is the old Queen's Theatre.

45. Based on an analysis of MUN/DUP/6/1–5.

38. Photograph of most of the workforce in 1948.

Key to Plate 38:

1. Jimmy Stewart, warehouse;
2. Ross Vincent Mahon, compositor;
3. Tommy O'Connell, apprentice compositor;
4. Roddy Quinn, warehouse;
5. Eddie Hogan, apprentice compositor;
6. Peter Maher, compositor and reader;
7. Robert Fletcher, machine feeder;
8. Jack Wiggins, machine minder;
9. Jack Maher, compositor;
10. George Hogan, caseroom foreman;
11. Frank Mortimer, compositor;
12. John Connelly, compositor;
13. Tom Mooney, Intertype operator;
14. Joe Pasley, compositor;
15. Joe Byrne, machine-room foreman;
16. Billy Maxwell, compositor;
17. Fred Maybury, apprentice compositor;
18. Ned Wilcox, Intertype operator;
19. Billy Abbott, Intertype operator;
20. Ned Smith, apprentice machine minder;
21. Frank O'Reilly, hand-fed platen machine operator;
22. Jack Hyland, machine feeder;
23. Charlie Keogh, machine minder.

Not present:
George Sergison, warehouse overseer;
Dick Lattimore, compositor;
Peter Redmond, labourer.

A few years after the Allmans had settled in they set about a much-needed modernisation of the machinery. A Monotype keyboard and caster was acquired in the first half of 1950 at a cost of £2,239.[46] Small purchases of Monotype matrices had been made since February 1945, but these may have been of odd sorts needed for hand-setting, to be cast by other printers who had the equipment.[47] One of the major attractions of the Mono system for the DUP was its facility in setting maths. Hitherto this had to be hand-set because the Intertype machines, which produced each line as a metal slug, were not suitable. (One wonders, given this overwhelming drawback for a scholarly press, why the Intertypes were chosen in 1923.) Now much of this work could be set mechanically, with the compositor 'comping' the final matter in the stick. The introduction of the Patten four-line system a few years later reduced the amount of complicated handwork involved.[48]

The Intertypes were in constant need of attention; the Press's account books are littered with payments for spare parts and for servicing them. However this apparently was not exceptional; other printers had similar problems, and Monotypes were nearly as fickle. Certainly the DUP was not put off and upgraded its Intertypes during the 1950s. Miss Allman remembers one bought c.1960 having to be brought in through a window because the doors were not wide enough.

The 1950s also saw the introduction of the first printing presses with automatic feed. As always with machinery at the DUP this was a belated introduction, as such presses had been installed in Dublin printing houses since the early 1930s; rates for their operation were promulgated by the DTPS on 25 August 1931. About 1955 a small Heidelberg with a 13 by 10 inch platen was bought new; another was acquired in the early 1960s. Jim Lawler, foreman in the machine-room in the 1960s, remembers an American Centurian double crown machine, bought in the late 1950s from Helys, where he had used it, and a Furnival. An automatic SW4 Wharfedale was bought second-hand in London. It was huge — it could take sixteen page formes — and not very fast, which suited the DUP with its relatively small runs. Charlie Keogh, Jim Lawler's predecessor as machine-room overseer, could not adapt to the automatic machines, and he was one of the few to continue to use the old Wharfedales. Otherwise they remained idle. The small platen jobbers were kept in use, most often manned by the apprentices. In January 1948 the then considerable sum of £105 was invested in a Gestetner model 160T duplicating machine, but I have been informed that this was for office use and not for short print

46. MUN/DUP/5/3/1; it is entered 'as 1 July 1950', but was probably installed earlier.

47. MUN/DUP/1/13/125.

48. For a description of the development of the Patten system see Roy Gurney 'The printing of mathematics', in *The university as publisher*, ed. Eleanor Harman, Toronto 1961, 127–33.

runs.[49] All the machinery was kept in order by the manufacturers' agents or by general printers' engineers — Stewart & Curry, Stankley, Smith & Co., T. & C. Martin Ltd, and Patrick Bros. Ault & Wiborg supplied rollers for the presses.

The first type specimen book issued by the Press that I know of was printed, although not dated as such, in 1961. It is an eighteen-page pamphlet, simply entitled *Type faces*, and shows 125 text and display founts. The backbones were the Intertype and Monotype faces. For the former the following text faces were listed: 8, 10, 11 pt Baskerville; 6 pt Old Style; 10, 11 pt Caslon; 8, 10 pt Modern; 10 pt irish. Monotype text faces were: 11 pt Old Style; 6, 8, 10, 11 pt Clarendon; 6, 8, 10 pt Modern. Greek in 8, 10 and 12 pts, and hebrew and Mathematics in 10 pt were also shown, but it is not clear if these were hand or machine set. Petrie's irish face, described as 'Round Irish', was present in its three sizes. The remainder were a broad selection of display faces, ranging through Gill Sans, Grotesques, Edina, Minster, Egyptian, Missal, Recherche, Encorial, Runic, Ultra Bodoni, Black, Tudor, De Vinne and many more.

The board of the College agreed on 19 October 1955 to grant another ten-year lease under 'existing conditions'. W.B. Allman, as we have seen, died in 1958. Liala took on the DUP, while her brother Claude managed the Brunswick Press; each had a very small shareholding in the other's firm. At the DUP there was an immediate change for the better, and it was needed as profits had been flagging. A crucial decision that had to be made early on was the replacement for Davy Deegan, the works manager. To her credit Miss Allman chose not mature age but vital youth, for the successful candidate, Des Ryan, was in his late twenties. He had served his apprenticeship as a comp at the Press in the years 1948 to 1955. He then left and in the next five years before rejoining it he worked in a whole host of firms — Hely Thoms, Browne & Nolan, *The Independent* newspaper, the Sackville Press and Bailey Gibson among them — staying a few months and then moving on in his need for challenge and change. It is a wonder that anyone gave him a job with a restless career like that. He now laughs at the arrogance of youth which made him apply for a job that would put him in a position of authority over men twice his age and who had trained him as an apprentice. He joined the staff in November 1959 at a salary of £15 per week, plus a company car and a Christmas bonus of around £400.

He set about reorganising things with relish, which caused some friction among the older members of the staff, well set in their ways. Part of the reorganisation involved moving printing presses into the 'Parochial Hall' early in 1961 and there was a flurry of letters to the College a year later when it was realised that this was prohibited by the lease. However the board granted permission for the change, so long as no noise was caused, and this was incorporated in the next lease. Ryan's motto for

49. MUN/DUP/5/2/405.

success in business is 'Common Sense' and he saw no reason why long-established practices should not be scrutinised. As we have seen it was he who suggested that Greek no longer be hand-set, but printed from a block made from a textbook. Although he lost this one to the union, he did make the setting more efficient by purchasing a set of the Latin and Greek classics, so that the comps did not have to spend hours in the library transcribing passages missing from the tattered volumes that existed in the Printing House. The Press did little or no advertising so Des Ryan put some effort into the production of house calendars. He had Derek Wearen and also a firm of graphic designers called Verbiage, run by Bill Bolger and Bernard Share, design a series of very attractive wall calendars for the Press. For each they chose such themes as *From Shakespeare to Sheridan* (1965), *Irish universities in transition* (1968), and *The Irish alphabet* (1973, designed by Jarleth Hayes). In these the notions of history, scholarship, literature and printing are all combined through good design to give a very positive image of the Press. The motif of the Columbian press became a device for the DUP in the 1960s and 1970s and was used on its advertising and stationery (see plate 39).

Des Ryan brought in accountants to measure the efficiency of every aspect of the business, and generally made things hum, so that the minutes of the board of directors on 19 November 1962 could report that the year's results were good. At the same meeting it was decided that he be elected to the board. He was also appointed to the board of the Brunswick Press and also helped return that to profit. In February 1966 Brian Allman came to the DUP having served his time as a compositor at the Brunswick Press. He worked in the office and when Des Ryan resigned in 1966 to take up the job of works manager at the *Connaught Tribune* in Galway, he was appointed a director. Despite Ryan's departure profits remained buoyant for the rest of the decade.

The board of the DUP in 1962 consisted of Miss Allman in the chair, Claude and Peter Allman as directors, and Prof. T.W. Moody, who had taken over as the College director from William Duncan in October 1952. At various times during the 1960s and after, Norman or Howard Kilroy, or R.G. Walsh, representing the company's accountants, J.A. Kinnear & Co., acted as secretary.

The turn-around that happened in the early 1960s necessitated the employment of more staff. Unfortunately there was an acute shortage of skilled labour in the trade. Throughout 1960, 1961 and 1962 the Press advertised widely in the newspapers for Monotype and Intertype operators, compositors, machine feeders, a reader, and even a printer's representative (obviously the past policy as regards travellers was changed).[50] The text of the advertisement in the *Evening Mail* for 7–10 February 1962 will give a flavour of the calibre of person the Press wanted:

50. MUN/DUP/18 *passim*.

COMPOSITOR: are you the compositor we want? We are looking for a really first-class man, preferably in the middle-age group. He must be very well versed in all apects of his trade and possess initiative. We offer in return good working conditions and a secure position in a well established firm.

So bad was the shortage that in February 1961 the Press even appealed to the DTPS for relief. This was rather reluctantly afforded by giving a local card to a British Typographical Association man who had been seeking work in Dublin, on condition that he stay for a year.[51] That the workforce remained conservative was illustrated by an amusing incident that happened in 1960. The author and journalist, Bruce Arnold, then a student in the College, wrote an article on Modigliani for the March 10th issue of the undergraduate magazine, *TCD: a College miscellany*, and proposed to illustrate it with one of the artist's paintings of a nude. The printers were indignant and refused to handle it. Arnold tenaciously held his ground and in the end the men capitulated and printed the issue.

Printers' wages throughout the 1960s rose almost annually by 6 or 7 per cent, so that the weekly basic of £11-16-1 in 1961 had inflated to £19-6-5 in 1970. There is little evidence of what the wage bill at the Press was at this time except for an oblique reference for the financial year 1964–65 in a schedule of insurances which gives the annual figure as £16,290; this gives a weekly bill of £313.[52] This figure I suspect excludes the office staff, and suggests a factory workforce in the mid-twenties. The DUP's own files give the figures of twenty-eight men and no women as the workforce in 1970, which obviously does not include the office.[53] 1964 saw the reduction of the working week in the trade to forty hours, so that the men at the Press now worked from 8 a.m. to 1.15 p.m., and from 1.45 to 4.30 p.m. A third week's holidays was afforded in the following year, which the DUP management insisted be taken in the slack winter period. 1965 was also the year of a protracted ten-week general printers' strike, in which the Press, as in 1952, managed not to get embroiled.

1965 however was a year of disaster for the Press. About 1.30 a.m. on 24 February a fire started in the recently reorganised Monotype setting department, part of the caseroom of the 1840 building. Although it occurred in the small hours of the morning, fortunately it was spotted by a student from his rooms in the New Square buildings that overlook the Printing House. Miss Allman remembers being woken at three o'clock by a phone call from the Junior Dean, Dr R.B. McDowell, telling her of the fire; she could hear it crackling in the background. The Pearse Street fire

51. IPU: DTPS EC minutes 27 Feb. 1961.
52. DUP/BP files.
53. DUP/BP files: Application to the Industrial Development Authority for re-equipment grant, 8 Dec. 1970.

station is just across the road from the Printing House so there was no delay in tackling it. However major structural damage was caused to the building. Floors and supporting beams had to be replaced and the flames had spread to the 1734 section and penetrated the wareroom floor there. And of course there was smoke and water damage everywhere. The machinery suffered badly and rivers of molten metal flowed from incinerated typecases.

March was the start of the exam paper season so there were grave fears that some had perished in their entirety. Much to Miss Allman's relief all but a few were saved. Not saved however were the manuscripts of a work by Dr David Greene and the latest issue of the *British Numismatic Journal*. Des Ryan recalls that no other copies of these had been kept. David Greene apparently laughed when told and set about rewriting it from his notes. The *BNJ* articles also had to be rewritten. The trade rallied round to help the Press. At nine o'clock the next morning the managing director of Cahills, Gerry Agnew, came unsolicited to offer what assistance his firm could. On 15 March the DTPS sanctioned the transfer to Cahills of a Monotype operator and a caster from the DUP to do the Press's work there, and the firm provided these facilities free of charge. Despite the extensive damage the Printing House was back in full operation by early May. The Press was to suffer once more in this decade through fire. In 1969 a huge fire gutted McKenzie's hardware store behind the Printing House, which resulted in some water damage to the printing presses in the 'Parochial Hall'.

The fire in 1965 was the occasion for the replacement of some of the machinery. Three Monotype keyboards and a second caster were acquired at this time. Peter Allman recalls that one of these keyboards and the caster were acquired at the sale of M.H. Gill & Sons' printing plant in February 1966. Michael Gill told me that the decision was made to get out of printing because of the over-capacity in the Dublin trade at the time. There is something satisfying in contemplating this reconnection with the spirit of Michael Henry Gill. In 1968 the Centurian printing press was traded-in against a new Heidelberg KSBA cylinder press (medium size, no. 329266); it cost £3,240 and the £100 allowed on the Centurian was obviously only scrap value. Two other expensive pieces of machinery bought about this date were a 36.25 inch Como guillotine, model H2, that cost £2,430 in September 1969, and a Camco Crown folding machine, model U, purchased in February 1970 for £1,030.[54] Investment in an Elrod caster, which allowed the Press to produce its own titling type, rules and leads, was made in mid-1975 at a cost in the region of £5,000.

The lease on the Printing House came up for renewal on 1 October 1965. There is a copy of it in the treasurer's office in TCD and as it is the only lease for the Allman era that I have managed to trace it is worth treating in some detail. The lease, signed and sealed by Trinity and the DUP Ltd on

54. ibid.

17 June 1966, was for the Printing House and the adjoining boilerhouse. As we have seen the annual rent remained at £300, to be paid half-yearly; the lessees were also to pay the water rates. Trinity was to carry out structural repairs while the Press was responsible for routine repair and maintenance of the building and fixtures, internal decoration and glazing. However allowance was made for the age of the building. The premises were not to be used other than for printing and publishing. The portion built 'about' 1902 as a compositors' room, and the machinery installed there with the College's consent 'in or about' 1962 was to be used only for that purpose. However if the machinery there created noise the College could insist that it be removed. The Press had to execute all printing for TCD 'with all reasonable speed' and 'give preference to such orders over all their other printing business'. Should any exam paper or other document be not printed in time, when sufficient time had been given, or if any of these were divulged, the College could demand a fine of up to £50 from the Press. The other leases afforded to the Allmans were most likely identically worded. Given these conditions it is no wonder that other printers refused to take on the business in 1944.

One of the most interesting DUP publications during the 1960s was Prof. Emile Arnould's *La genèse du Barbier de Séville* issued in 1965. This was the first critical edition of the *Barbier* and has been described in the critical literature as 'a fundamental work of great importance'.[55] Arnould was one of the few Trinity academics to take an interest in the Press and have their works printed there. It was probably the largest book produced during the Allmans' tenure, running to over 500 quarto pages with nineteen plates. In fact it proved too much for the Press. Although it was set there, Des Ryan decided, because of exam paper pressure, to have it printed by Hely Thoms. It is exceptional in the output of the Press for another reason, in so far as it was a joint publication with Minard of Paris, the only such tie with a French publisher that I have encountered.

The Institute for Advanced Studies continued to be one of the major customers for bookwork throughout the 1960s. Calvert Watkins's *Indo-European origins of the Celtic verb*, issued in 1962, proved very difficult to set and many special Monotype sorts had to be commissioned for it. The Institute also commissioned an edition of the *Táin Bó Cúalgne* edited by Cecile O'Rahilly from the Press in 1967, which ran to over 400 pages.

An exceptional piece of jobbing printed during this period was the oration spoken at Trinity's conferral of the honorary degree of LL.D. on John F. Kennedy, President of the United States, on 28 June 1963 during his visit to Ireland. The oration was printed in Latin, English and Irish, and for the latter the formality of the Petrie Irish face was put to excellent use.

---

55. David C. Cabeen, ed., *A critical bibliography of French literature*, Syracuse (NY) 1947– (in progress) no. 3668.

Some idea of the charges at the Press at the start of the 1960s can be had from a detailed breakdown of the cost for producing the RIA *Proceedings* late in 1962. Hourly rates were: Monotype 28-0, Intertype 21-0, hand composition 16-0, proofing and machining 22-6, imposition 16-0.[56] These charges can be compared with those of 1944 given on p. 334, where it will be seen that Intertype was charged at 8-6, hand composition 5-6, and machining 11-0. These increases of from 100 to 200 per cent are not extraordinary when it is considered that the basic weekly wage in the trade rose from £5-10-10 to £12-10-10 in the same period.

The Irish printing trade in the 1970s was dominated by two topics: the advent of computer typesetting, and soaring costs. The former, allied with offset litho presses, was threatening the survival of hot-metal letterpress printing, while the latter, fuelled by the oil crises, had led to huge wage rises and many redundancies.[57] The basic weekly pay in the trade more than doubled in the five-year period from 1970: it was £22-6-5 in 1970 and £50.35 in December 1975.[58] The DUP was not immune from these trends. On 2 December 1971 the board minutes recorded a major decrease in the rate of gross profits. At that stage the Brunswick Press was planning to move from Pearse Street to larger premises about two miles away in Sandymount, and Peter Allman suggested that there would be 'obvious advantages' in the merging of both companies there. Such a merger he argued 'would help eliminate the peaks and valleys of production'. This was strongly resisted by Miss Allman who stated that 'the overall services of her company to the colleges was far greater than just a printing service', and she insisted that the DUP should remain in Trinity. However it is also evident from the same minutes that she was concerned about the future. On her instructions the secretary, R.G. Walsh, had discussed the College's future plans for the Printing House with Trinity's treasurer; he apparently had not been forthcoming. Neither was the College forthcoming in 1974, as the minutes for 27 February reveal, when the DUP wrote to it about the Press's intention to purchase expensive new machinery, most especially to deal with exam papers, asking what Trinity's plans were in this area.[59] Given the flux of these conditions it is understandable that there was not much investment in new machinery in these years.

The unsettled times were reflected in industrial relations at the Press. In March 1973 two officers of the DTPS were called in by the father of the

---

56. MUN/DUP/19, 4 Dec. 1962.

57. Frank Corr, 'Trade house battle for survival in era of change' in *Irish Printer*, 7/9 (Sept. 1975) 11–12.

58. 'Craft rate past 60 years' in *Cló*, 1/6 (Sept. 1984) 4.

59. In fact the College continued to have its exam papers printed by the Press until 1977 when they were done in-house. This trial proved a failure and they were returned to the DUP in 1978. However the College again took them in-house in 1979 with more success.

chapel because of a 'general breakdown in the relationship between management and staff'. The air was cleared after a discussion between the chapel officers, the union representatives and Liala and Brian Allman.[60] Problems flared up again later that year. The men were on protective notice because of an electricity strike, and there was also that perennial complaint about the Printing House — the lack of heat. The chapel reported at a DTPS Council meeting on 26 November that at 8 a.m. recently the temperature had been marginally above 50°F; '. . . are men expected to work in these conditions?'[61] No decision was reported, but early the following year the chapel took the decision not to work until the temperature was 62°F. When the case men refused to work for the first hour on 7 January, management said their wages would be docked. The position was considered by the DTPS on 9 January. The father said that because of the oil crisis there had been an agreement to reduce consumption by 25 per cent, but that management had taken advantage of the situation. The committee ruled that the heating must accord with the *Factory Act*, and that the men must not lose pay because of inability to work in cold conditions. It was a complaint that in more settled times would have been resolved within the firm. Sometimes the animosity was between the men and not between management and workers. Such was the case in September 1974 when one of the comps threw a bucket of water over the foreman. Fortunately the man had already given notice so the firm was spared having to dismiss him, but it did write a letter of complaint to the union.

There were thirty-three employed at the press in October 1975. From a notebook in the possession of John Breslin and from the memories of others the following profile can be constructed:

Management:	L. and B. Allman.
Caseroom:	compositors: E. Gargan, G. Cromwell, A. Brougham, J. Ryan, F. Ward, J. Joyce, B. Doyle, F. Crawford, B. Flood
	Intertype operators: J. O'Reilly, M. O'Brien
	Monotype keyboard: B. Lynch, K. McCormick, E. Behan
	Monotype caster: M. Sheehan
	apprentices: E. Finlay, D. Curtis, N. Wearen, P. Brennan, D. McCluskey
Machine-room:	J. Lawler, J. Stevenson, T. Halpin, E. Hanlon
Warehouse-keeper:	J. Stewart; helper: S. Stewart
Another five unidentified workers	

60. IPU: DTPS EC minutes, 2 Apr. 1973.

61. *Míosachán na gClodoiri*, 23/10 (Dec. 1973) 5. The same report of Council also noted that the DUP men were under protective notice because of an electricity strike.

A very stylish forty-page type specimen book designed by Verbiage, entitled *Signs & sorts*, was issued in 1975 (see plate 39). Its subtitle reads: 'A comprehensive catalogue of linguistic, mathematical and other specialised signs and sorts available at Dublin University Press Ltd.' The typefaces it displays were all machine set: Monotype Modern, Old Style, Baskerville, Times and Gill Sans; and Intertype Baskerville. All the specialised sorts for each face are illustrated in the first section. The second section shows the mathematical, irish and greek faces. And the last section shows all the faces of the first set as continuous text, taken appropriately from Tyrrell and Purser's *Correspondence of Cicero*, printed at the DUP in 1904. Gone were all the exotic hand-set faces.

Charges at the Press at this time were very low relative to the rest of the trade. For example Intertype setting was being charged at £1.20 per hour while at the Brunswick Press it was nearly double that. The output was increasingly dominated by scholarly jobbing, especially exam papers. There were a few books of note. 1971 saw the publication of T.W. Moody's *Irish historiography 1936–70*, printed for the Irish Committee of Historical Sciences, and James K. Walton's *The quarto copy for the first folio of Shakespeare*, which appeared under the DUP's own imprint. Anne Heiermeier's *Die indogermanisch orientierte ursprachliche Konzeption* was being printed at the Press throughout the 1970s, and an interesting folder among the DUP/Brunswick Press files gives a detailed insight into the production of a book at that stage in the Press's history.

The file opens with a letter dated 5 June 1969 from Prof. Heiermeier of Würzburg University saying that she admired the printing that the Press did for the RIA and wanted it to undertake some work for her. That was the first of a long correspondence that stretched over the next fourteen years, Prof. Heiermeier sending very badly typed letters and postcards in very poor but colourful English. The relationship that developed was reminiscent of *84 Charing Cross Road*, with the professor sending boxes of chocolates and being solicitous about the health of the Allmans. Sample proofs were sent in October 1969 — 'I am full of admiration for your printer' the author comments — and later in December special matrices for exotic sorts had to be ordered. Several times she indicated her intention of visiting Dublin, but was put off by the violence in Northern Ireland. Brian Allman had to write reassuring her that Dublin was not Belfast, and in the end she did come and visit the Printing House. By November 1975 the Press wanted to know how long the book was likely to be; 'we are very anxious to finish this book because of the amount of metal tied up'. No answer was recorded, but the professor was scrupulous about payment so the Press bore with her. Some worksheets in the file give an idea of the costs charged at this period. In October 1973 Monotype keyboarding and casting cost £1.66 per hour while, in a reversal of the pattern thus far, hand comping cost 11p. more. By February 1975 the cost of all these three processes had been inflated to £2.32 per

A comprehensive catalogue of
linguistic, mathematical
and other specialised signs
and sorts available at

DUBLIN UNIVERSITY PRESS LTD.
Trinity College Dublin 2
Telephone: 773072/779260

39. A type specimen book issued in 1975.

hour. A mark-up of 25 per cent was added to production costs to cover overheads and profits. (Although outside the scope of this history it is worth recording the rates charged in the latter half of the 1970s after the DUP had left the College: Monotype keyboard, £4.68; Monotype caster, £3.70; hand comp, £3.90 to £5.20; reading, £4.83 to £5.20; the mark-up was 18 per cent.) The book was eventually published in 1980, but the professor only survived another five years to enjoy her success.

The serious downturn in profits in the early 1970s was reversed by the middle of the decade and a good net profit was returned in the financial year 1974–75, due, as the board minutes of 22 January 1976 recorded, to Miss Allman's 'staunch efforts'. The accumulated surplus left the firm in a 'strong position', so why did the Press move off campus? Although as we have seen the question of merging with the Brunswick Press in Sandymount was considered as early as December 1971, when the decision was made it came all in a rush. Four main factors were involved: difficulties over renegotiating the lease; a labour dispute; the need to modernise the machinery; and the approaching retirement of Miss Allman.

The lease was due to expire on 30 September 1975 and on 15 July the Press's solicitor, W.L. Carroll, of T.P. Robinson & Co., met the College authorities.[62] He had been instructed to seek a twenty-one year lease, to which the Press was legally entitled. Trinity opposed this saying the property was needed for redevelopment; however it would offer a three-year lease at a reduced rent. This proved unacceptable to the DUP as such a short lease would not have allowed for long-term planning. At later negotiations the College indicated that if the Press insisted on a twenty-one-year lease, it would insist on an economic rent, which was set at £10,000 per annum. The DUP's own valuer had assessed the rent at £6,000 without review, so at a board meeting of the firm on 5 September it was agreed to pursue the long lease 'on an economic rental basis' or, if that failed, to seek compensation.

Trinity's board, besides wanting the building under its plans for rapid expansion in the 1970s, also expressed concern about the possibility that the Press might be taken over by some undesirable firm. The DUP had survived two relatively recent takeover bids, one by Hely Thoms in 1966. The College was apprehensive that the Press projected part of Trinity's image yet was not under its control. It also realised that the introduction of new technology would lead to problems with the union (which it did), and that it would be better if any disruptive disputes took place off campus.

While these negotiations were still underway one of the most serious industrial relations disputes in the history of the Press flared up.[63] Three

---

62. This relation of the negotiations over the lease is based on DUP/BP file 'Move to Sandymount', DUP board minutes and TCD board minutes.

63. This description is based on DUP/BP file 'September 1975 Dispute' and on IPU: Irish Graphical Society EC minutes.

of the four machinemen, who had been drinking, returned an hour and a quarter late from lunch on 10 September. Schedules for exam papers were very tight that day, some papers having to be machined that afternoon for examinations the following morning. In the circumstances the three men were given a fortnight's notice. The Irish Graphical Society was immediately informed of the situation, and all three men were called before the committee to explain themselves. They did not deny being late, but insisted that no conspiracy was involved; they had become engrossed in conversation and had lost track of the time. The committee felt that notice was too severe in their case and decided to send officers to see the DUP's management. This meeting took place on 23 September, without any resolution, and the men's notice expired on the 26th. The union then issued an order that no member was to accept a position in the DUP's machine-room pending further consideration by the committee. Given this blacking the Press had no option but to issue two weeks' protective notice to all the men.

Despite some intervening conciliation attempts the protective notice ran out at the end of work on Friday 10 October. A special executive committee meeting of the union was held on the following Sunday at which the secretary reported that Miss Allman had agreed to refer the dispute to a rights commissioner of the Labour Court, but that the men would be locked out until the dispute was settled. The committee then considered the question of picketing. It was obvious there was no way the gates of the College could be picketed without paralysing the whole of the campus, and the secretary pointed out that if the College obtained an injunction against such picketing it could cost the union £1,000. It was therefore agreed to post 'observers' without pickets. The DUP chapel had all been summoned to attend headquarters that day and it was now informed of the committee's decision. The decision to pay £14.50 weekly to each member 'in benefit' during the dispute led to a flurry of activity as members tried to pay off arrears in dues; four were deemed to be 'out of benefit'.

An article on the dispute entitled 'Press in jeopardy' appeared in *Trinity News*, one of the student magazines, on 14 October which, had it been taken up by the national media, would have been very damaging for the Press. It related the College's decision to increase the rent from a nominal to an economic rate, a rate that 'could force the Press out of business'. It stated that the College did business worth £35,000 per annum with the Press, but that for the past four years it had been transferring business to outside firms 'because of the inefficient process used' there. It also mentioned that legal action was almost certain over the lease. (One wonders what Machiavelli fed the editor this story?)

The rights commissioner, Con Murphy, spent that week considering the submissions of the various parties and made his recommendations on Monday 20 October. He said that printing at the DUP was 'too sensitive and exacting to be at the mercy of irresponsible behaviour from employees who are paid a premium [of £10 per week] to be exact and responsible'. All that management had submitted about the behaviour of the men had been valid and reasonable. It had transpired that the men had also been late on 8 and 9 September, but they had not been cautioned about these. Had they been, the commissioner would have upheld the dismissals 'without hesitation'. However he felt that for the one time they were challenged dismissal was too severe a consequence. He therefore recommended that the men be reinstated within a month, but that the intervening period remain unpaid; that the men be on final warning as regards lates for a year; and that any overtime earnings of the men in the first four weeks of employment go to an agreed charity.

Management was obviously perturbed by these recommendations. At the most fundamental level no consideration had been given as to who was to man the printing presses in the intervening month. However to its credit it accepted the judgment and the Press reopened on Wednesday 22 October.

The board of the company met on the following day to consider the aftermath of the dispute and Trinity's terms of compensation for the relinquishment of the Printing House. The latter included an offer of £22,500 compensation and an extension of the existing lease to 31 March 1976. It was unanimously resolved to accept these and 'to form an association' with the Brunswick Press in Sandymount. An 'Agreement to surrender' the Printing House was signed on 20 November.

Many in Trinity were saddened by the prospect of the Press leaving the Printing House after nearly 250 years there. The printers were devastated when they heard of the decision; no one wanted to leave the College. In fact three men took voluntary redundancy under the rationalisation that took place shortly after the staff moved to Sandymount in November. Miss Allman deeply regretted the move, but she realised that it was a watershed time in the history of the Press. In a dispassionate letter to Prof. T.W. Moody on 10 November she wrote that the DUP could not afford to pay an economic rent and retain profits to buy the expensive new machinery needed, 'unless prices were raised substantially'. Besides she admitted that the Printing House was 'not suitable for efficient production' and the College needed the building within a few years. It must have been a difficult letter to write, reflecting as it does the conclusion of thirty years of her working life, but there is a sense of relief that the reality had been faced.

During late October and early November Miss Allman wrote to all the senior College officers telling them of the circumstances of the move and also informing them that the DUP was willing to continue to provide the same priority service that it had given in Trinity. She also wrote to her customers outside of the College, among them John Briggs of the

Representative Church Body who replied thanking the Press for 'an efficient and gracious service' over the years.

In November with many of the staff already installed in Sandymount the task of moving the machinery was started. All the Monotype plant as well as an Intertype model C4 were dismantled and reassembled in the new premises; the other Intertypes were disposed of. A contemporary list of the printing machines records four Heidelbergs (KSBA and SBB cylinders, and two platens), an SW4 Wharfedale, and a Dawson (automatic Wharfedale). Only the Heidelberg presses made the move. While this machinery was being moved other clearance was being done including the melting down of old metal. An apprentice, Tommy Shields, sent down from the Brunswick Press to help, was working alone on overtime in the smelting room of the 1734 building. Because of the cold winter weather he neglected to open the window for ventilation and was overcome with the fumes and died. It was a tragedy that echoed the injury to the labourer in June 1734 when the Printing House was being built.

Late that year, when the building was clear of anything the Press wanted to move and before it started throwing out the dross, Miss Allman allowed Mary Pollard of the department of Early Printed Books in the library to rescue what she wanted of the remainder. As a recent recruit to the department I remember ferreting round with her in the gloom, among hundreds of cases of type and mounds of old bookstock and records; everywhere and everything was covered in layers of dust and fallen plaster. As has already been noted Miss Allman had donated the remaining Columbian to Trinity Closet Press; we were on the look-out for unusual type and other printing artifacts to enhance the stock of that private press, as well as taking any old records of the DUP and a representative selection of its bookstock and jobbing for the library collections.

In the cellars under the portico we found several frisket frames for hand presses, broken and rusting, that must have been there for over a hundred years; elsewhere we found old and modern chases and galleys, and copper plates for printing certificates. Among the furniture that we were allowed to keep were two very unusual cupboards that had been adapted to hold cases of type and which as we have seen may be survivors from the eighteenth century. We took eighty-three cases of founder's type ranging in size from nonpareil to four-line pica (6 to 48 pt) as well as other display caps, wooden type and ornament cases. Dr Don Cruickshank did a census of these and identified some interesting faces: a brevier fat gothic from Drugulin, Leipzig; some brevier greek that came from Porteous and Gibbs's office in Wicklow Street in 1902; long primer irish (Petrie's); pica, great primer and double pica greek labelled 'College' (these must be the nineteenth-century founts included in the 1945 lease); two-line brevier sanskrit; the rest were romans and italics or display faces. Stephenson Blake was the predominant founder noted, but others come from Reed & Sons, Millar & Richard, Besley & Co., Figgins (including some border cases), and Ludwig & Layer (ornaments). We came across no hebrew or music type, and the only mathematics was a case of long primer split fractions. Hundreds of cases of type remained after we had sorted through them; the metal was melted down and the wooden cases thrown out.

We removed fifty-nine volumes of records that now make up the bulk of the DUP muniments in the library, and hundreds of printed books, both the Press's output and some of the Leipzig classics that the comps set from, as well as boxes of jobbing. The earliest stock found was several copies of J. Kennedy Bailie's *Fasciculus inscriptionum Graecarum* printed by M.H. Gill in 1842. This printed material is now under the care of the department of Early Printed Books. Various departments within the College were allowed to choose books from the stock, but the remainder was disposed of as waste, including, through some misunderstanding, all the back issues of *Irish Historical Studies*.

The DUP vacated the Printing House on 5 March 1976, when the keys were handed to the buildings' officer, thus bringing to an end a tradition of printing in Trinity after nearly 250 years. The merger with the Brunswick Press took place on 1 January of that year although it was agreed that 'the separate identities of both Companies be maintained for the continuity of individual sales policies'.[64] At the first board meeting in Sandymount on 22 January 1976 Miss Allman resigned as managing director of the DUP and Peter Allman was appointed in her stead. She made over most of her shares to her nephews. She helped out with production until Christmas of that year, but has since then withdrawn totally from the affairs of the Press. It is as if her interest was coterminous with the Press's tenure in Trinity. Prof. Moody continued as the College's representative on the board of directors until 22 September 1977, when the treasurer Franz Winkelmann took on the mantle. In the 1980s the articles of association were altered, removing the College's right to nominate a director and although Trinity continues to do substantial business with the Press, this marked the severing of the last official ties between TCD and the DUP.

The amalgamation of the two workforces and the introduction of new technology at the Press in the late 1970s did lead to unsettled industrial relations, including a strike at the end of 1976. However the DUP weathered that and other storms, and continues to provide its specialised services in Sandymount, carrying on the tradition of the oldest printing house in Ireland.

64. DUP/BP files: 'Draft procedure notes on Dublin University Press Limited takeover of the majority shareholding in the Brunswick Press Limited'.

Select Bibliography

Printed sources (in the main only works that have been cited several times are included here; however all the sources that deal extensively with the DUP are listed):

Benson, Charles, 'Printers and booksellers in Dublin 1800–1850' in R. Myers and M. Harris eds, *Spreading the word: distribution networks of print 1550–1850*, Winchester 1990, 47–59.

Boyne, Patricia, *John O'Donovan (1806–1861): a biography*, Kilkenny 1987.

Carter, Harry, *A history of the Oxford University Press*, vol. 1, Oxford 1975.

Christian Examiner v.6 (1828) 423.

Coleman, Edward, 'TCD's Doric temple' in *Trinity News* (22 Feb. 1968) 5.

Corrigan, Andrew J., *A printer and his world*, London 1944.

Dix, E.R. McC., 'William Kearney: the second earliest known printer in Dublin' in *Proceedings of the Royal Irish Academy*, 28/C/18 (1910) 157–61.

Dublin University Commission: report of Her Majesty's commissioners appointed to inquire into the state, discipline and revenues of the University of Dublin and of Trinity College, Dublin 1853 (House of Commons Papers, 1852–2, XLV).

'DUP celebrates 250 years' in *Irish Printer* (July 1988) 6–7.

French, Francis-Jane, 'The Printing House' in *Trinity handbook* 5th ed. (1961) 14–16.

Gaskell, Philip, *A new introduction to bibliography*, Oxford 1979.

Kelliher, 'Plato's Dublin Dialogues' in *The Warden's meeting: a tribute to John Sparrow*, Oxford 1977, 32–5.

Kinane, Vincent, 'The Printing House: "A small Doric temple of stone"' in *Trinity Trust News*, v. 12, no. 1 (Nov. 1987) 9–10.

Lynam, E.W., *The Irish character in print 1571–1923* (1924), Shannon 1969.

McCarthy, Muriel, *All graduates and gentlemen: Marsh's Library*, Dublin 1980.

McDonnell, Joseph and Patrick Healy, *Gold-tooled bookbindings commissioned by Trinity College Dublin in the eighteenth century*, Leixlip 1987.

McDowell, R.B., and D.A. Webb, *Trinity College Dublin 1592–1952: an academic history*, Cambridge 1982.

McGuinne, Dermot, *Irish type design: a history of printing types in the Irish character*, Dublin 1992.

McKenzie, D.F., *The Cambridge University Press 1696–1712: a bibliographical study*, 2 vols, Cambridge 1966.

Maclehose, J., *The Glasgow University Press 1638–1931*, Glasgow 1931.

McParland, Edward, 'Trinity College Dublin II' in *Country Life*, v.159 (1976) 1242–5.

MacPhail, Ian, 'The Dublin University Press in the eighteenth century' in *Friends of the Library of Trinity College Dublin Annual Bulletin* (1956) 10–14.

Maxwell, Constantia, *A history of Trinity College Dublin 1591–1892*, Dublin 1946.

Moran, James, *Printing presses*, London 1973.

Mores, Edward Rowe, *A dissertation upon English typographical founders and founderies* (1778), ed. H. Carter and C. Ricks, Oxford 1961.

Moxon, James, *Meckanick exercises* (1683) ed. H. Davis and H. Carter, Oxford 1962.

Ó Seanóir, Stuart, and M. Pollard, '"A great deal of good verse": commencement entertainments in the 1680s' in *Hermathena*, no. 130–31 (1981) 7–36.

O'Sullivan, William, 'The University Press' in *Quarterly Bulletin of the Irish Georgian Society*, no. 4 (Oct. – Dec. 1958) 48–52.

Philip, I.G., *William Blackstone and the reform of the Oxford University Press in the eighteenth century*, Oxford 1957.

Pollard, Mary, *Dublin's trade in books 1550–1800*, Oxford 1989.

Pollard, Mary, 'The Provost's logic: an unrecorded first issue' in *Long Room* no. 1 (Spring 1970) 38–40.

A second letter to G- W- Esq. concerning the present condition of the College of Dublin, [Dublin] 1734.

Sir Tague O'Ragan's Address to the Fellows of T[rinity] Col., London [i.e. Dublin c.1750].

Strickland, Walter G., *Typefounding in Dublin*, Dublin 1922.

Stubbs, John William, *The history of the University of Dublin*, Dublin 1889.

Tipping, H.A., 'The Universities of Oxford and Cambridge: the old Clarendon Buildings, Oxford' in *Country Life*, 63/1637 (June 1928) 800–807.

'A tour through Trinity College, by Tim Tickle' in *Walker's Hibernian Magazine*, 2 (1793) 525.

Trimble, W.C., 'Correspondence' in *Irish Printer* (Oct. 1934) 16.

'Wage movements from 1913 to 1970' in *Míosachán na gClodoiri*, 29/6 (Aug. – Sept. 1979) 13.

Wall, Thomas, *The sign of Doctor Hay's head: being some account . . . of Catholic printers and publishers in Dublin*, Dublin 1958.

Walsh, Paul, and Colm Ó Lochlainn, *The Four Masters and their work*, Dublin 1944.

Wharton, Kay, 'Trinity's unique printing record' in *Irish Printer* (Sept. 1978) 35.

White, Philip, 'The printing trade in Dublin: the first book printed at the University Press, TCD' in *Irish Printer*, v.7, no. 11 (June 1912) 4–8.

White, Philip, 'The printing trade in Dublin: the University Press, Trinity College Dublin' in *Irish Printer*, v.3, no. 11 (June 1908) 8–10; v.3, no. 12 (July 1908) 8–9; v.4, no. 1 (Aug. 1908) 6–8.

Theses:

Kinane, Vincent, 'The Dublin University Press in the eighteenth century, with a descriptive bibliography of its known output', Fellowship of the Library Association of Ireland, 1981.

MacPhail, Ian, 'Bibliography of books printed at Trinity College Dublin, 1734–1875', Dip. Lib., University of London, 1956.

Phillips, J.W., 'A bibliographical inquiry into printing and bookselling in Dublin from 1670 to 1800', Ph.D., Trinity College Dublin, 1952.

Manuscripts:

The following are the main TCD manuscript series consulted:

Board Room files (transferred to the Library since consultation).

DUP stock book *c*.1910–1972, xeroxed in 1972 (copy in TCD Library at OLS Xerox 1 no. 1); present whereabouts of original not known.

MS 10308, correspondence of M.H. Gill.

MS 10309, papers of M.H. Gill and H.J. Gill.

MS 10310, typescript of J.J. O'Kelly's 'The house of Gill'.

MSS 10311–3, J.J. O'Kelly's notes for the 'House of Gill'.

MUN/D/3538c, lease for DUP 1924.

MUN/DUP, Dublin University Press account books and papers:

1/ Ledgers:
    1a. Ponsonby and Weldrick private ledger, 1880–1903.
    2. Ponsonby and Gibbs private ledger with annual accounts, 1902–22.
    3. Volume of accounts for receipts and expenditures by categories (e.g. sales, purchases, wages) 1902–1944.
    4. Accounts within Trinity for various official printing jobs, 1923–38.
    5. Continuation of 4, 1939–55.
    6. Accounts with Trinity societies and individuals and some outside bodies, 1925–29.
    7. Continuation of 6, 1929–34.
    8. Continuation of 7, 1935–41.
    9. Continuation of 8, 1941–45.
    10. Accounts with individuals and outside bodies, 1927–35.
    11. Continuation of 10, 1935–40.
    12. Creditors' ledger with individuals and outside bodies, 1930–43.
    13. Continuation of same series as 12, 1944–54, but the intervening volume is not extant.
    14. 'Accounts of the University Press Series', 1877–1914.
    15. Continuation of 14, 1914–28.
    16. Continuation of 15, 1928–38.
    17. 'Dublin University Press Series Booksellers' Accounts 1879 to 1888', but also includes other official Trinity publications.
    18. As 17, but all in account with Longman, Green & Co., London, 1889–1918.
    19. As 17 except all in account with Hodges, Figgis & Co., Dublin, 1889–1918.

2/ Cash books in chronological order:
    1. Oct. 1902 to Oct. 1909.
    2. Nov. 1909 to July 1918.
    3. July 1918 to Feb. 1929.
    4. Feb. 1929 to Apr. 1942.

3/ Job books in chronological order:
    1. June 1930 to Jan. 1938.
    2. Feb. 1938 to Aug. 1945.
    3. May 1935 to Nov. 1939.

4.   Dec. 1939 to Sept. 1944.
5.   Sept. 1944 to June 1948.
6.   July 1948 to Apr. 1951.
7.   May 1951 to June 1955.
8.   July 1955 to May 1959.
9.   June 1959 to Jan. 1965.

4/   Estimate and work books in chronological order:
1.   Oct. 1932 to Aug. 1943 (estimate book).
2.   Sept. 1940 to Dec. 1942 (work book).
3.   Oct. 1944 to Nov. 1945 (work book).

5/   Purchases invoice books:
1.   Sept. 1930 to Mar. 1939.
2.   Apr. 1939 to June 1950.
3.   July 1950 to June 1961.

6/   Wages books:
1.   June 1944 to Dec. 1948.
2.   Jan. 1949 to Feb 1951.
3.   Feb. 1951 to Mar. 1953.
4.   Mar. 1953 to Jan. 1958.
5.   Jan. 1958 to Sept. 1960.

7/   Petty cash books:
1.   Oct. 1931 to Oct. 1935.
2.   Nov. 1935 to May 1938.
3.   June 1938 to Feb. 1943.
4.   Mar. 1943 to Mar. 1946.
5.   Apr. 1946 to June 1948.
6.   July 1948 to Sept 1951.
7.   Oct. 1951 to June 1952.
8.   July 1952 to June 1956.
9.   July 1956 to June 1960.

8/   Miscellaneous account books:
1.   Jobbing work done Jan. 1937 to Sept. 1944.
2.   Term and academic year end accounts with Trinity, 1936 to 1950.
3.   Record of TCD exam papers printed 1937 to 1947.
4.   Continuation of 3, 1947 to 1957.
5.   Record of exam papers printed for outside bodies, 1940 to 1954.
6.   Record of time spent composing particular jobs, 1940 to 1944.
7.   Number not used.
8.   Postal expenses, 1945 to 1948.
9.   Monthly accounts of sums due to and by Ponsonby and Gibbs, with statements of unfinished work, Sept. 1910 to July 1935.
10.   Bank book of Ponsonby and Gibbs, June 1944 to June 1949.
11–12. Address book of subscribers to *Life and light*, the magazine of the University mission to Fukien and Chota Nagpur, 1930.

9/ Letter books:
    1.   Press copy book of letters from Ponsonby and Gibbs, mostly giving estimates, Nov. 1911 to Dec. 1924.
    2.   Continuation of 1, Dec. 1924 to late 1929.

10/ Warehouse dispatch books:
    1.   1895–99.
    2.   1899–1904.
    3.   1904–15.

11/ Delivery and stock books:
    1.   1870 to 1887.
    1A.   1882 to 1902.
    2.   1902 to 1915.
    3.   'Stock book warehouse', 1893–99.

12/ Dispatch books:
    1.   Apr. to July 1914.
    2.   Jan. to Nov. 1932.
    3.   Nov. 1932 to June 1933.
    4.   June 1933 to Mar. 1934.
    5.   Mar. to Oct. 1934.
    6.   Oct. 1934 to June 1935.
    7.   June 1935 to Feb. 1936.
    8.   Apr. 1940 to June 1941.
    9.   Oct. 1935 to April 1944 (another series).

13/ Receipts for illustration blocks returned to owners:
    1.   1905–15.
    2.   1915–30.
    3.   1934–44.

14/ Booksellers' orders (mostly E. Ponsonby Ltd):
    1.   1921–26.
    2.   1926.
    3.   1931–32.

15/ Receipts for registered letters:
    1.   1932–35.
    2.   1936–41.
    3.   1941–44.

16/ Copy order books 1937, 1941–42, 1945–46 (sometimes includes indication of when set, by whom and how long it took; also instructions for binding).

17/ Invoices and receipts, 1948–49, 1961.

18/ Invoices and receipts, 1960–62.

19/ Job dockets, 1946, 1962.

20/ Job dockets, 1963–64.

21/ Job dockets, 1968.

22/ Ledgers:
    1.   Accounts of Graisberry and Gill, 'College Printing Office', 1827–37.
    2.   Day book of DUP, Sept. 1851 to Apr. 1856.
    3.   'TCD Legers FGHI 1833–1862' (this volume actually covers 1857–70).

MUN/LIB/2/1, Library minute book 1785 onwards.
MUN/LIB/10–12, Library miscellaneous papers and accounts.
MUN/MC/86, 'Plans, elevations, and sections, shewing proposed new additions to University Press' c.1900.
MUN/P/1, general papers.
MUN/P/2, papers relating to buildings.
MUN/P/3, bursar's correspondence, 1880s.
MUN/P/4, bursar's receipted bills, 18th and 19th centuries; continued as bound volumes in series MUN/V/62.
MUN/V/5, Board registers.
MUN/V/57–58, bursar's annual accounts.
MUN/V/62, bursar's recipted bills in bound volumes.

Other manuscript material consulted:

Irish Print Union: Committee and Council minute books, 1827 onwards, of the Dublin Typographical Provident Society and its successors, the Irish Graphical Society and the IPU; DUP chapel minute book 1955–1979. (Microfilm copies of these are available in the department of Early Printed Books in Trinity's Library).
DUP/Brunswick Press files.

Index

Those works marked with an asterisk were printed at the DUP.